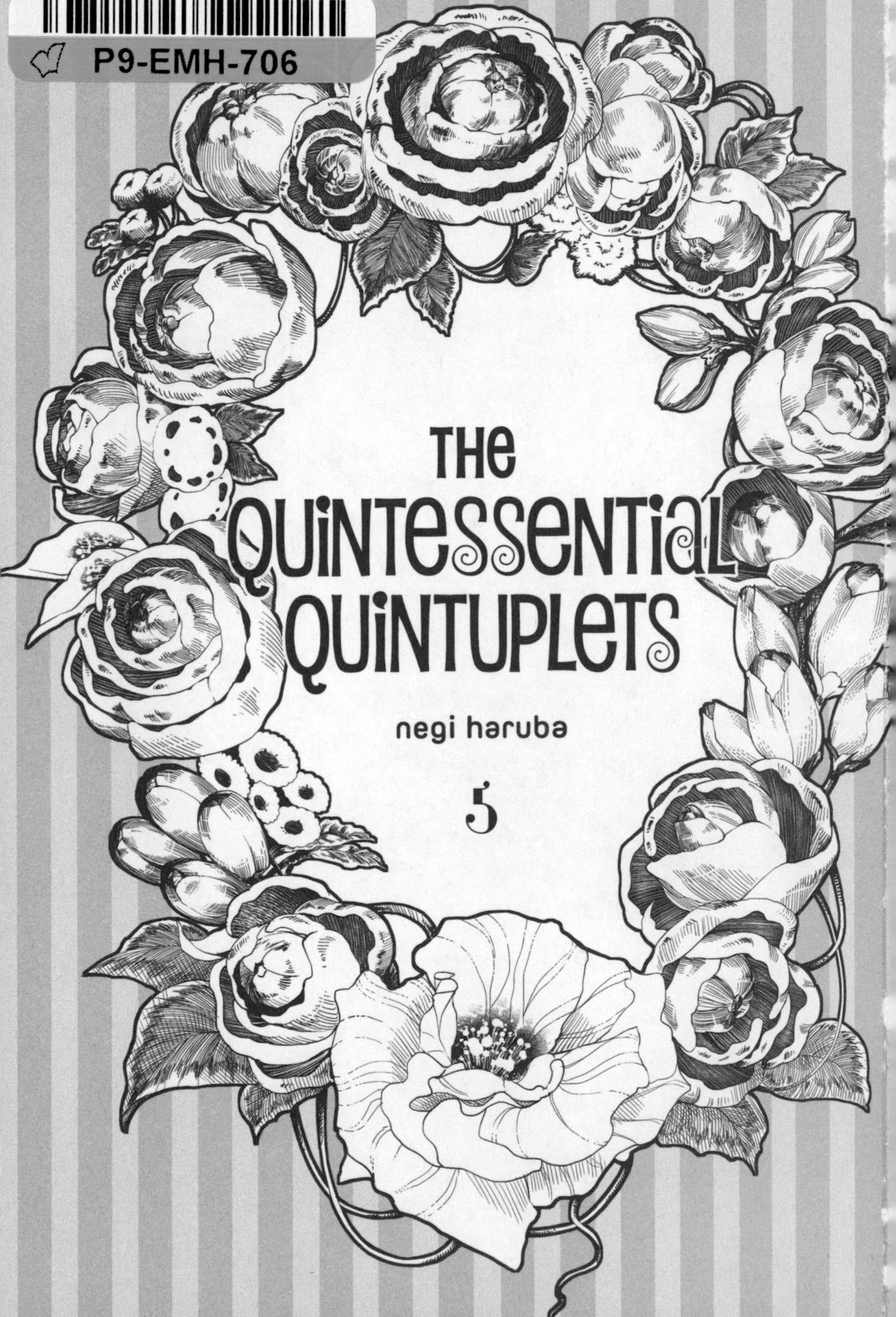

# THE QUINTESSENTIAL QUINTUPLETS

negi haruba

5

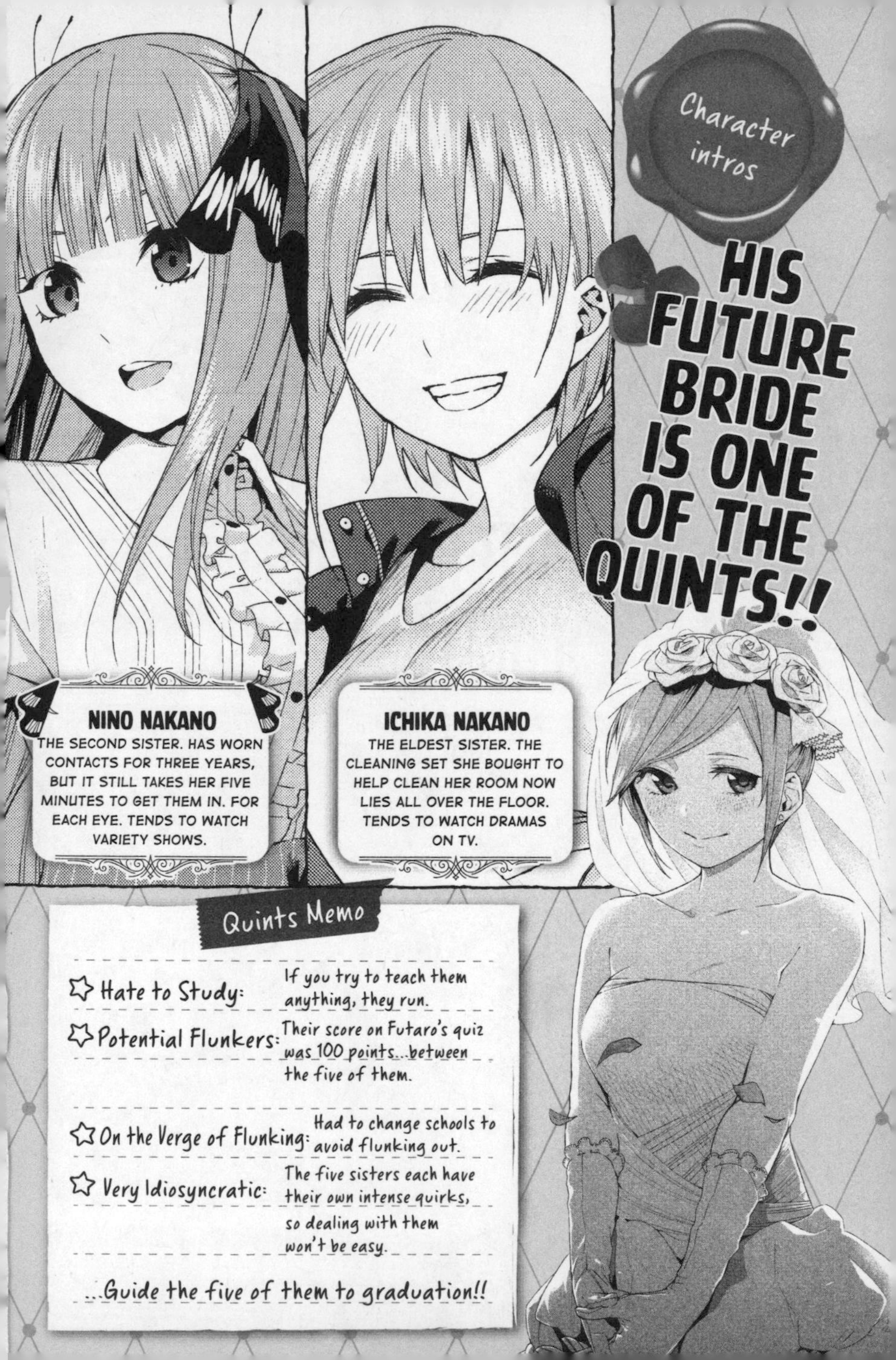
Character intros
HIS FUTURE BRIDE IS ONE OF THE QUINTS!!
ICHIKA NAKANO
THE ELDEST SISTER. THE CLEANING SET SHE BOUGHT TO HELP CLEAN HER ROOM NOW LIES ALL OVER THE FLOOR. TENDS TO WATCH DRAMAS ON TV.
NINO NAKANO
THE SECOND SISTER. HAS WORN CONTACTS FOR THREE YEARS, BUT IT STILL TAKES HER FIVE MINUTES TO GET THEM IN. FOR EACH EYE. TENDS TO WATCH VARIETY SHOWS.
Quints Memo
☆ Hate to Study: If you try to teach them anything, they run.
☆ Potential Flunkers: Their score on Futaro's quiz was 100 points...between the five of them.
☆ On the Verge of Flunking: Had to change schools to avoid flunking out.
☆ Very Idiosyncratic: The five sisters each have their own intense quirks, so dealing with them won't be easy.
...Guide the five of them to graduation!!

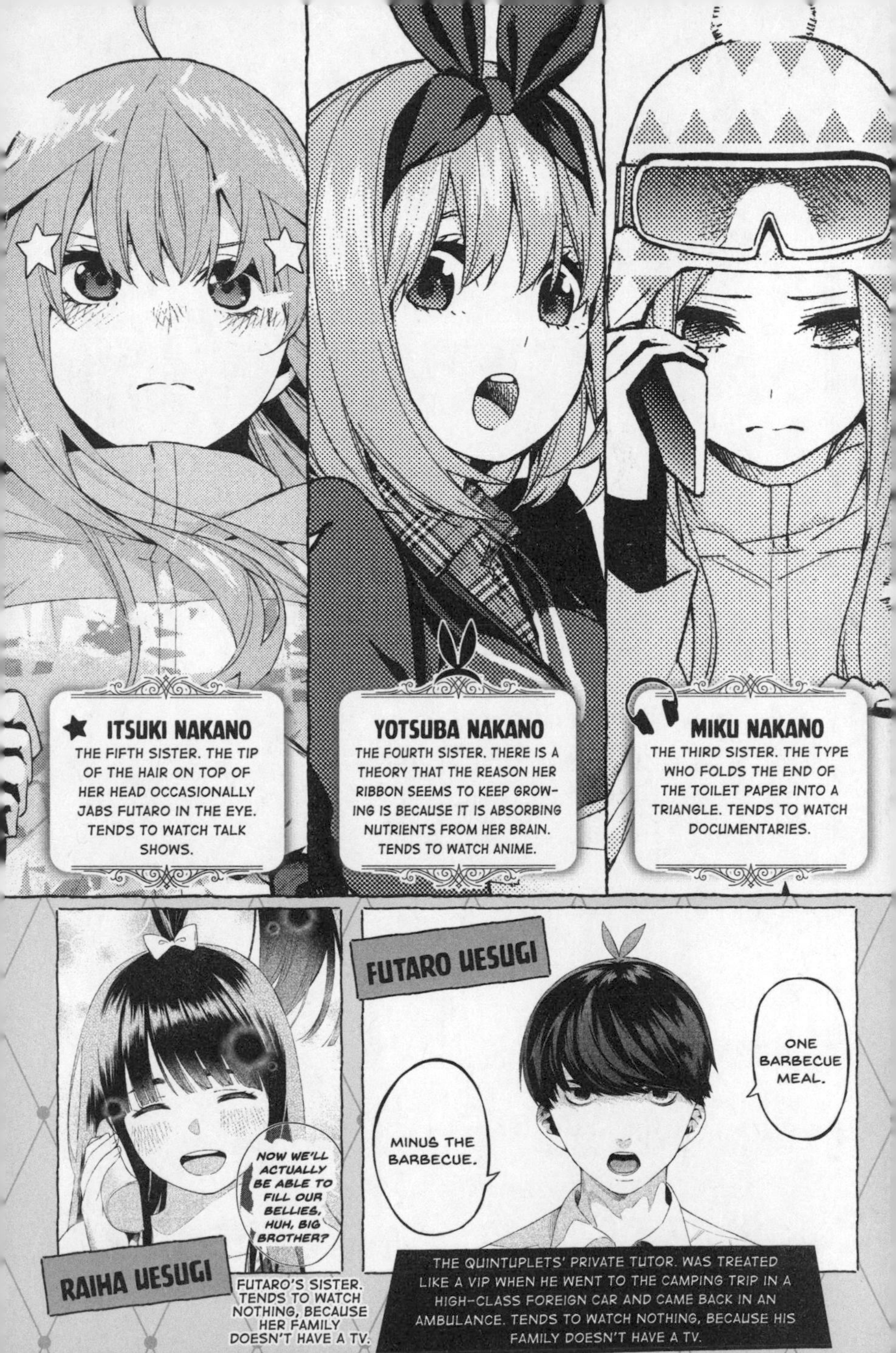
MIKU NAKANO
THE THIRD SISTER. THE TYPE WHO FOLDS THE END OF THE TOILET PAPER INTO A TRIANGLE. TENDS TO WATCH DOCUMENTARIES.
YOTSUBA NAKANO
THE FOURTH SISTER. THERE IS A THEORY THAT THE REASON HER RIBBON SEEMS TO KEEP GROWING IS BECAUSE IT IS ABSORBING NUTRIENTS FROM HER BRAIN. TENDS TO WATCH ANIME.
ITSUKI NAKANO
THE FIFTH SISTER. THE TIP OF THE HAIR ON TOP OF HER HEAD OCCASIONALLY JABS FUTARO IN THE EYE. TENDS TO WATCH TALK SHOWS.
FUTARO UESUGI
ONE BARBECUE MEAL.
MINUS THE BARBECUE.
THE QUINTUPLETS' PRIVATE TUTOR. WAS TREATED LIKE A VIP WHEN HE WENT TO THE CAMPING TRIP IN A HIGH-CLASS FOREIGN CAR AND CAME BACK IN AN AMBULANCE. TENDS TO WATCH NOTHING, BECAUSE HIS FAMILY DOESN'T HAVE A TV.
NOW WE'LL ACTUALLY BE ABLE TO FILL OUR BELLIES, HUH, BIG BROTHER?
RAIHA UESUGI
FUTARO'S SISTER. TENDS TO WATCH NOTHING, BECAUSE HER FAMILY DOESN'T HAVE A TV.

# CONTENTS

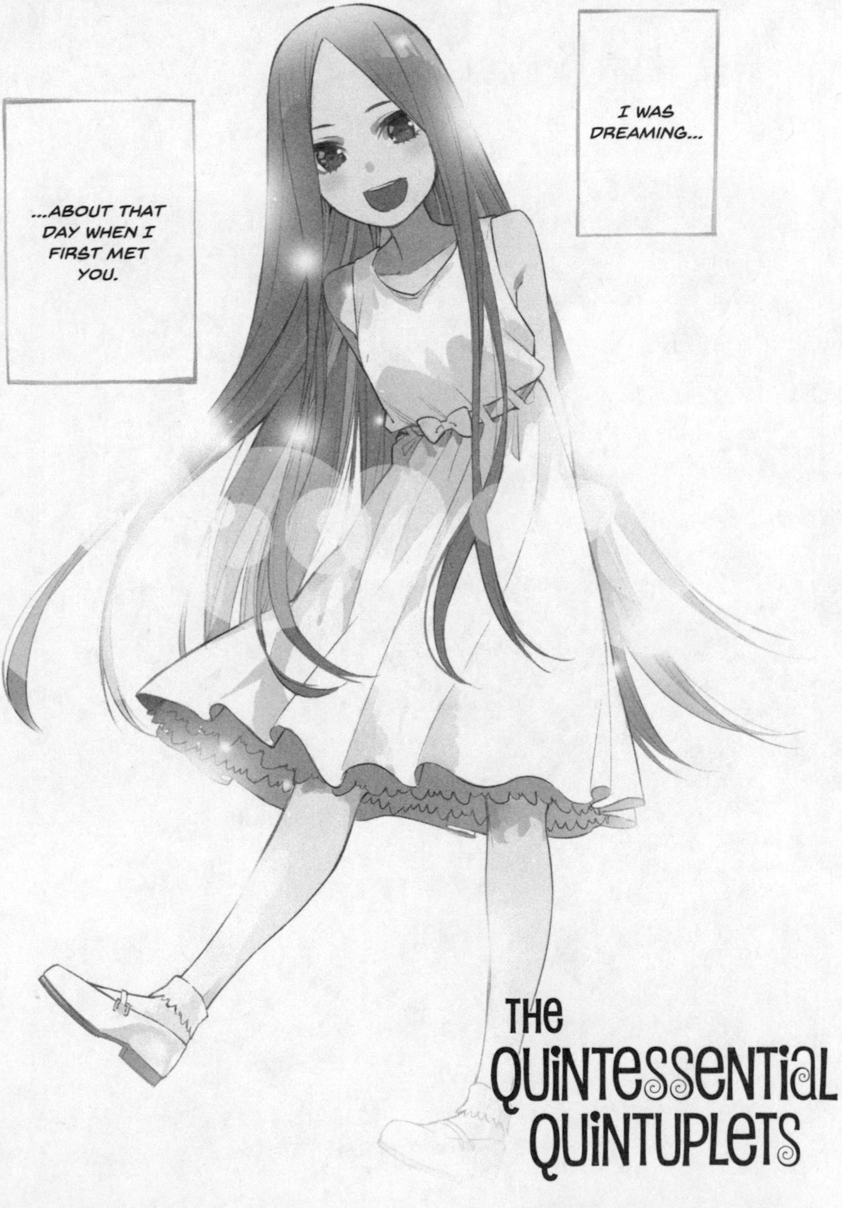
I WAS DREAMING...
...ABOUT THAT DAY WHEN I FIRST MET YOU.
THE QUINTESSENTIAL QUINTUPLETS

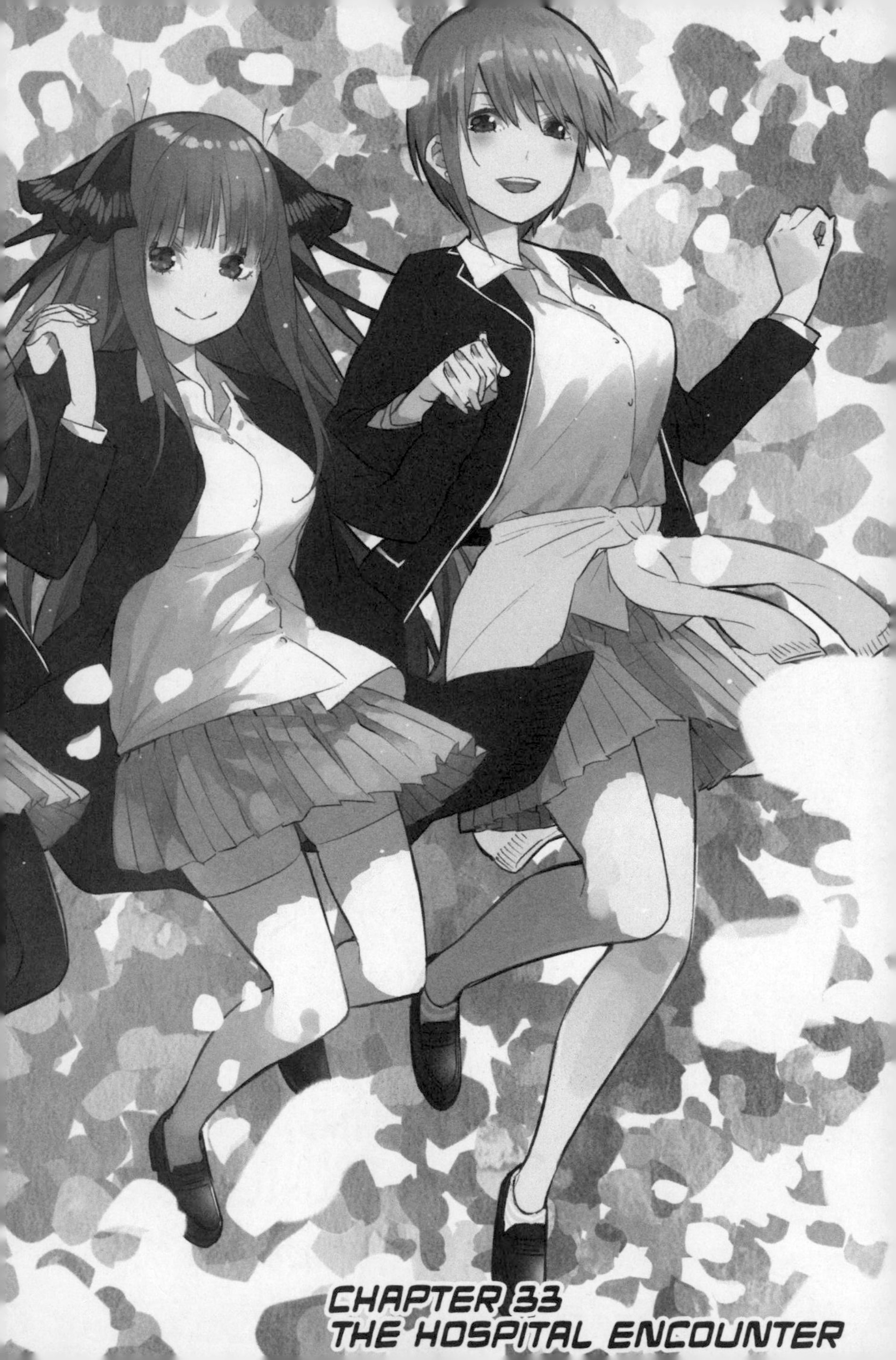

# CHAPTER 33
# THE HOSPITAL ENCOUNTER

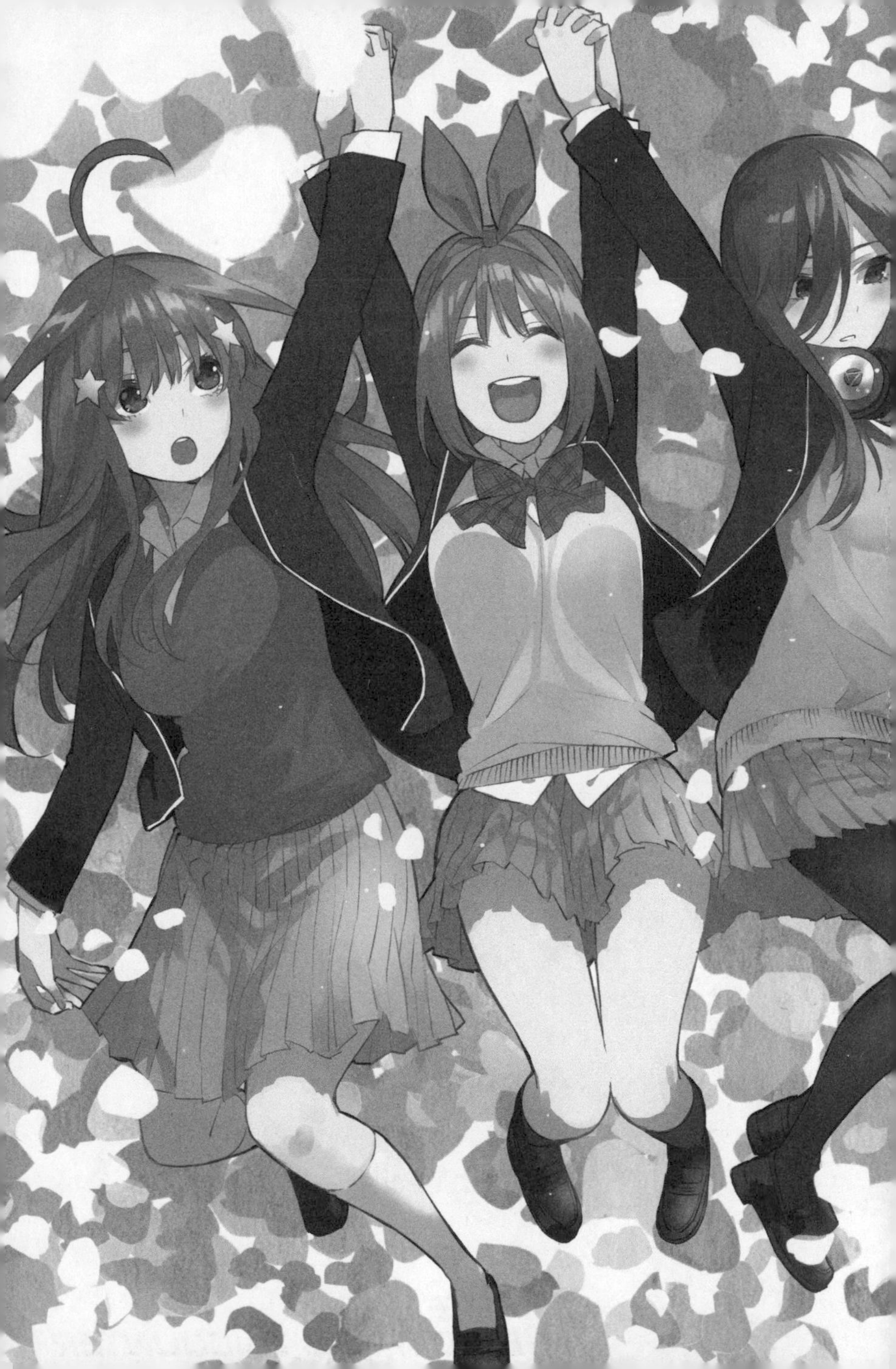

The Quintessential Quintuplets

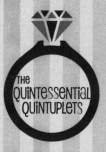

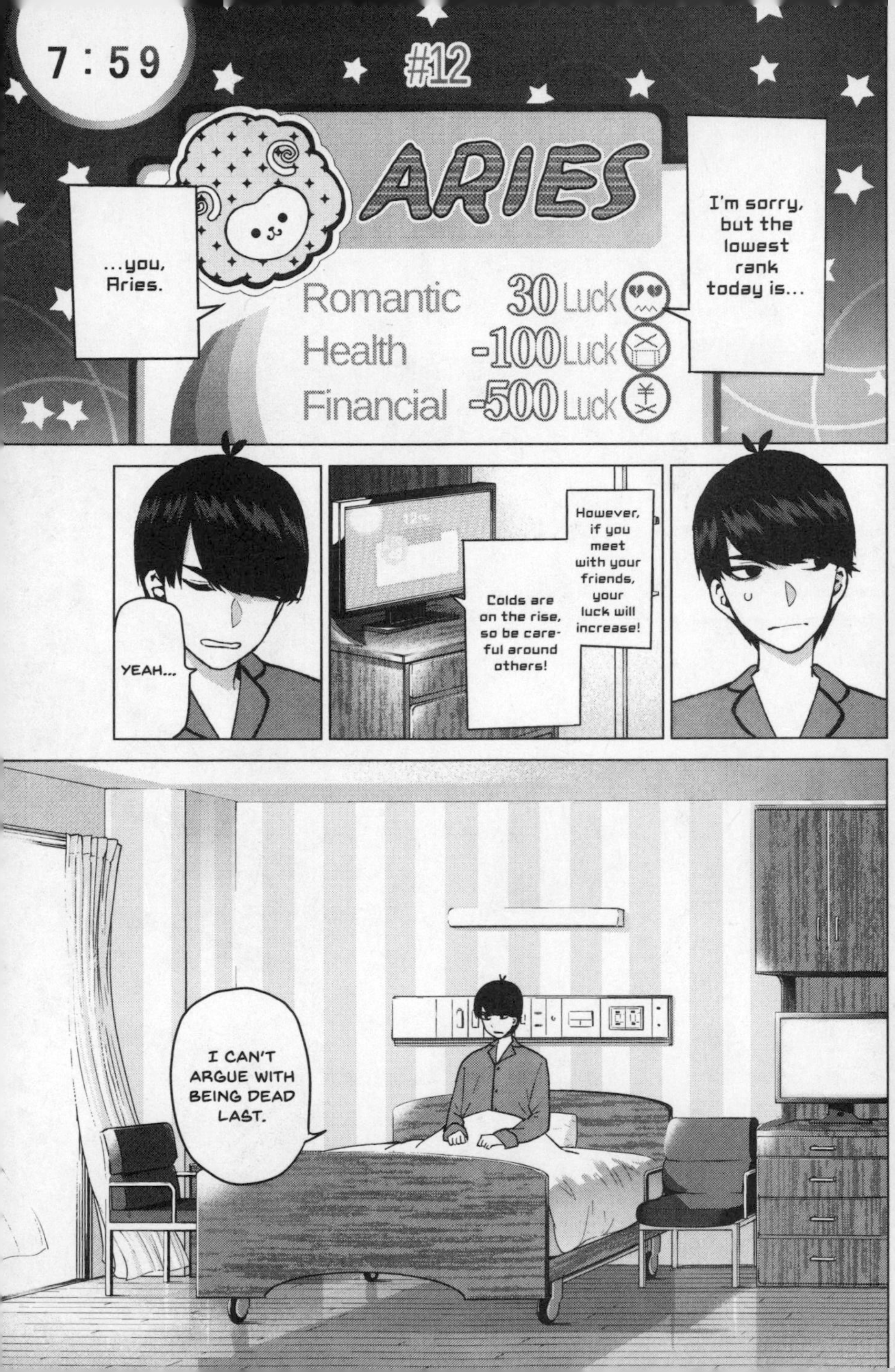
7:59
#12
I'm sorry, but the lowest rank today is...
ARIES
Romantic 30 Luck
Health -100 Luck
Financial -500 Luck
...you, Aries.
However, if you meet with your friends, your luck will increase!
Colds are on the rise, so be careful around others!
YEAH...
I CAN'T ARGUE WITH BEING DEAD LAST.

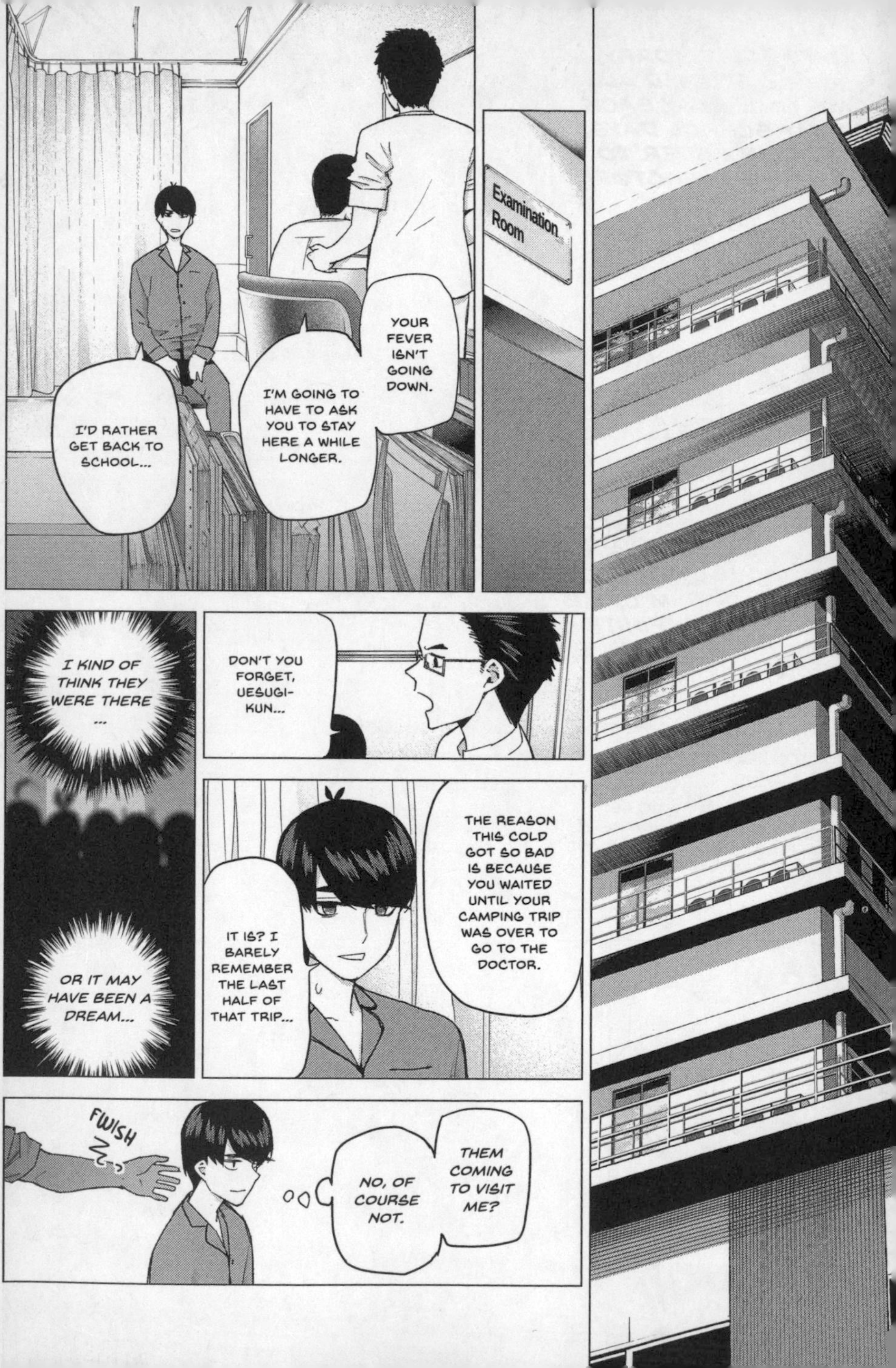
Examination Room
YOUR FEVER ISN'T GOING DOWN.
I'M GOING TO HAVE TO ASK YOU TO STAY HERE A WHILE LONGER.
I'D RATHER GET BACK TO SCHOOL...
DON'T YOU FORGET, UESUGI-KUN...
THE REASON THIS COLD GOT SO BAD IS BECAUSE YOU WAITED UNTIL YOUR CAMPING TRIP WAS OVER TO GO TO THE DOCTOR.
IT IS? I BARELY REMEMBER THE LAST HALF OF THAT TRIP...
I KIND OF THINK THEY WERE THERE ...
OR IT MAY HAVE BEEN A DREAM...
THEM COMING TO VISIT ME?
NO, OF COURSE NOT.
FWISH

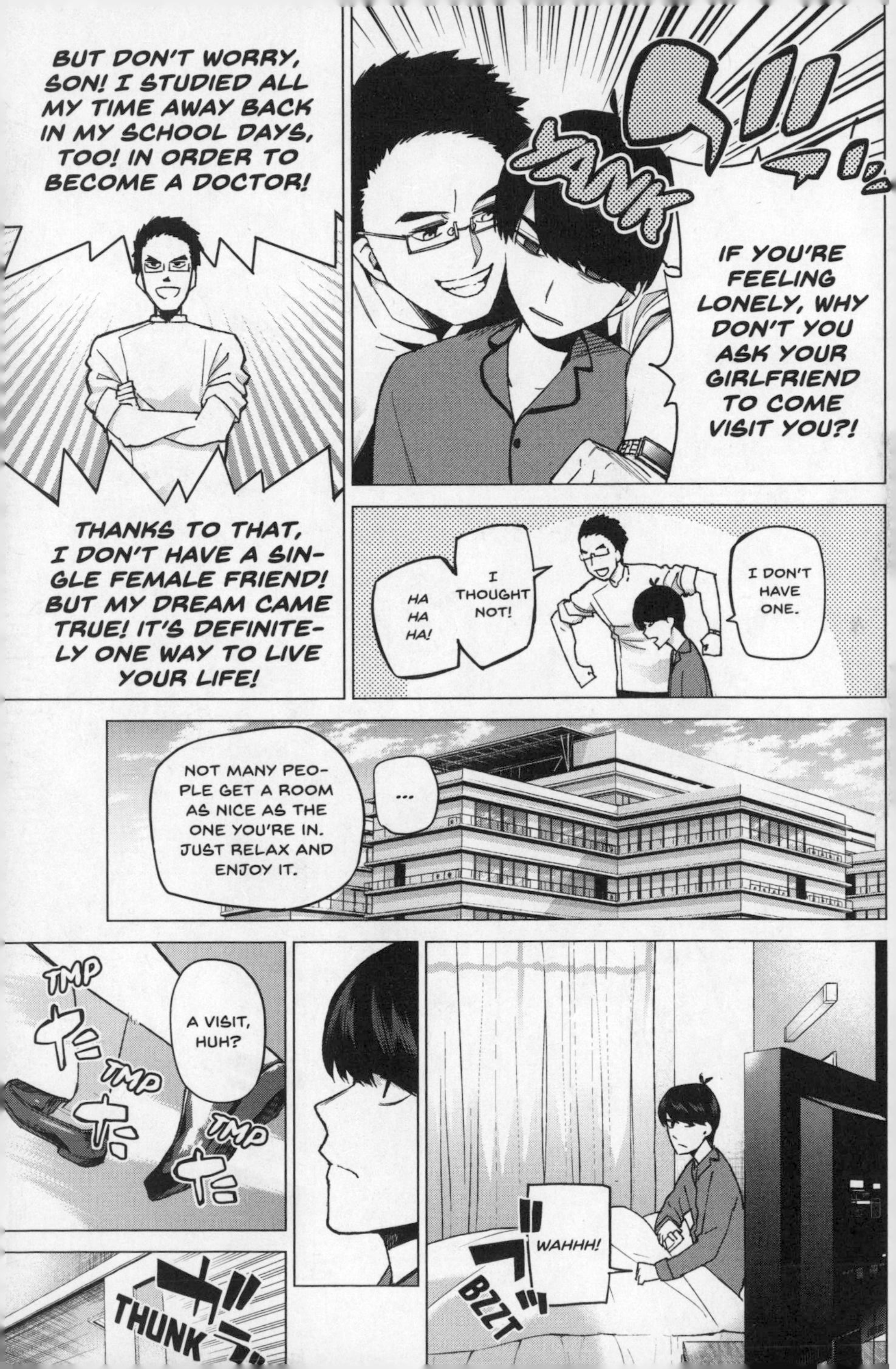

YANK
IF YOU'RE FEELING LONELY, WHY DON'T YOU ASK YOUR GIRLFRIEND TO COME VISIT YOU?!
I DON'T HAVE ONE.
I THOUGHT NOT!
HA HA HA!
BUT DON'T WORRY, SON! I STUDIED ALL MY TIME AWAY BACK IN MY SCHOOL DAYS, TOO! IN ORDER TO BECOME A DOCTOR!
THANKS TO THAT, I DON'T HAVE A SINGLE FEMALE FRIEND! BUT MY DREAM CAME TRUE! IT'S DEFINITELY ONE WAY TO LIVE YOUR LIFE!
...
NOT MANY PEOPLE GET A ROOM AS NICE AS THE ONE YOU'RE IN. JUST RELAX AND ENJOY IT.
WAHHH!
BZZT
TMP
A VISIT, HUH?
TMP
TMP
THUNK

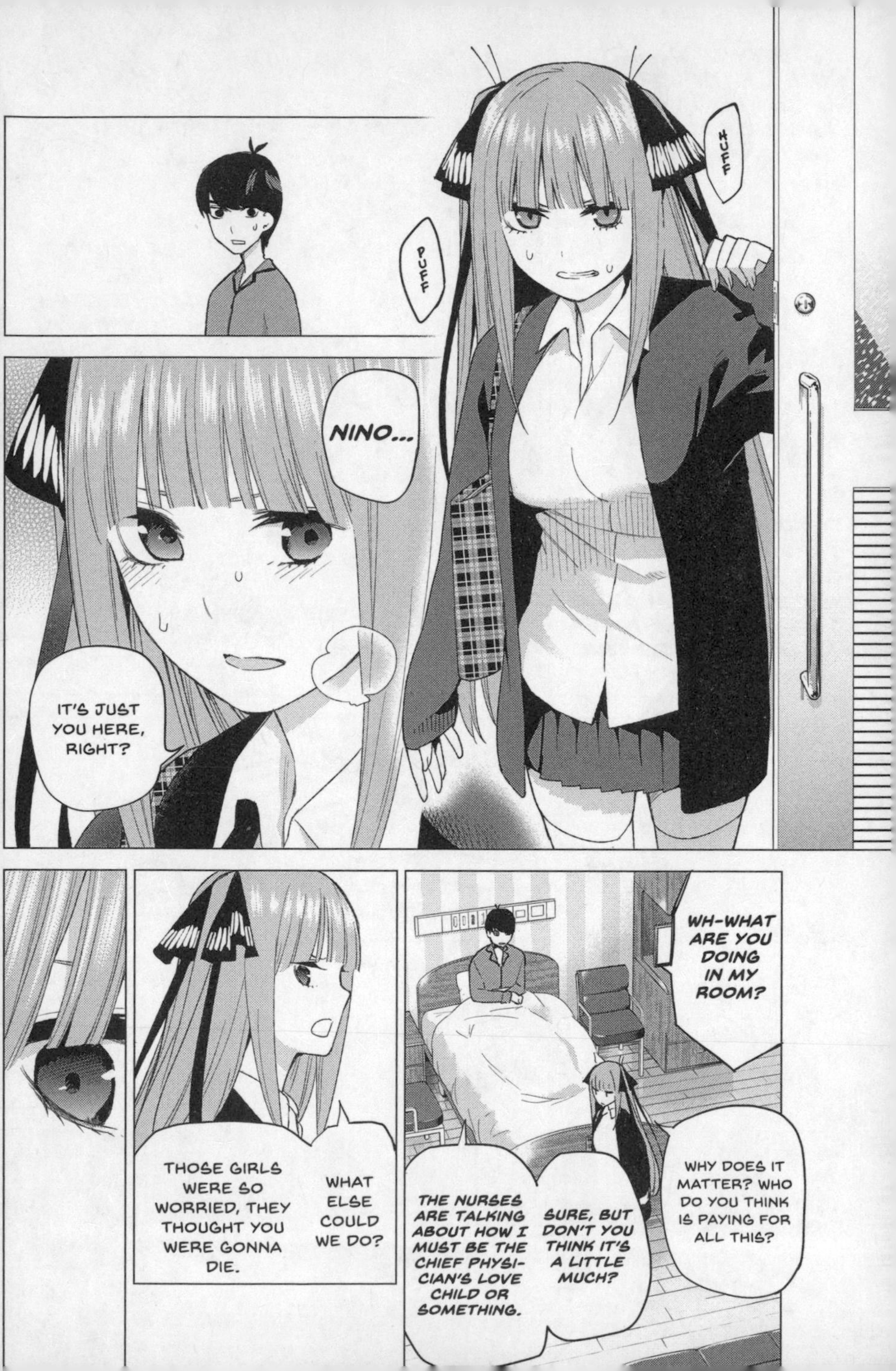
HUFF
PUFF
NINO...
IT'S JUST YOU HERE, RIGHT?
WH-WHAT ARE YOU DOING IN MY ROOM?
WHY DOES IT MATTER? WHO DO YOU THINK IS PAYING FOR ALL THIS?
SURE, BUT DON'T YOU THINK IT'S A LITTLE MUCH?
THE NURSES ARE TALKING ABOUT HOW I MUST BE THE CHIEF PHYSICIAN'S LOVE CHILD OR SOMETHING.
WHAT ELSE COULD WE DO?
THOSE GIRLS WERE SO WORRIED, THEY THOUGHT YOU WERE GONNA DIE.

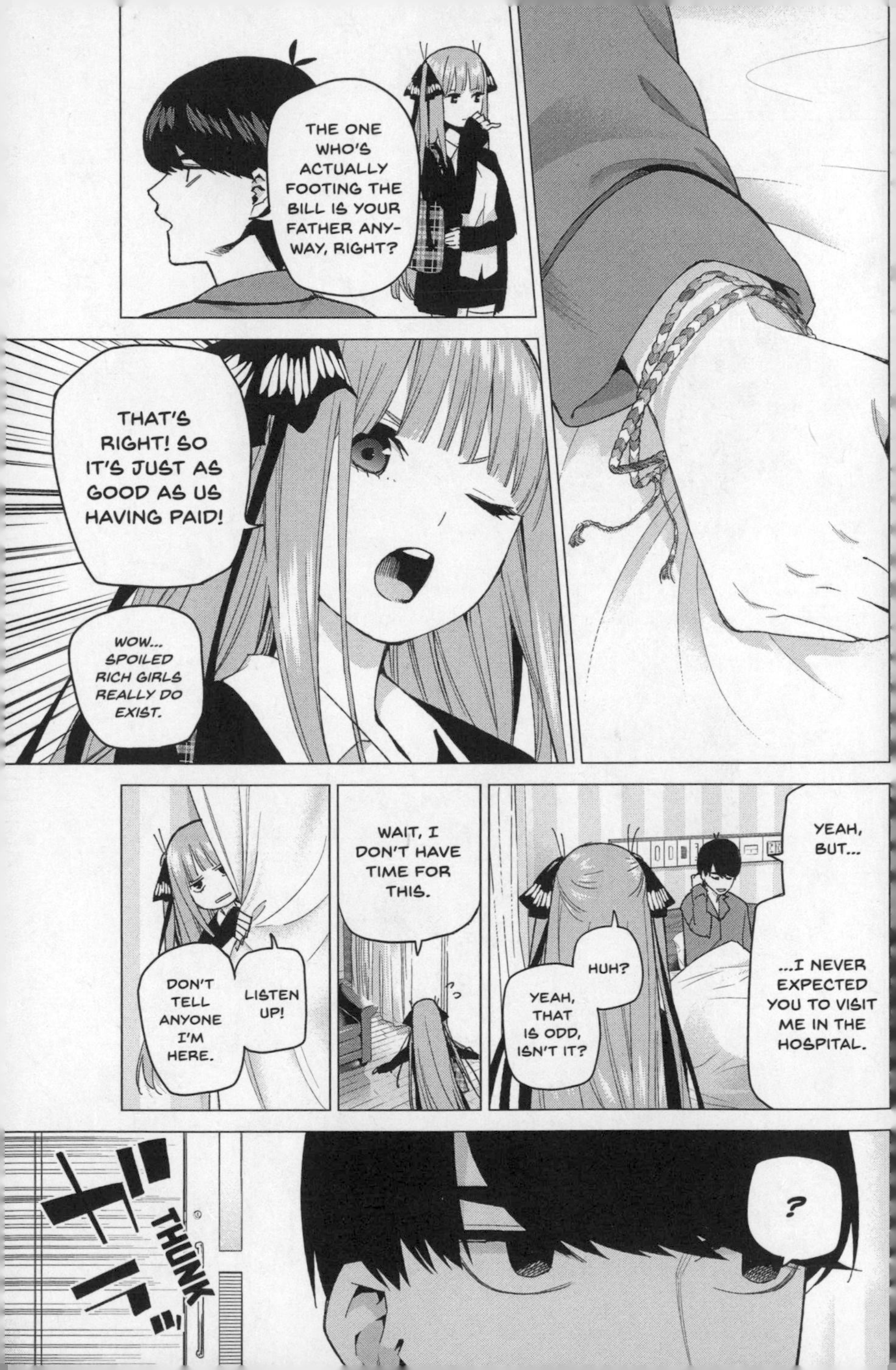
THE ONE WHO'S ACTUALLY FOOTING THE BILL IS YOUR FATHER ANYWAY, RIGHT?
THAT'S RIGHT! SO IT'S JUST AS GOOD AS US HAVING PAID!
WOW... SPOILED RICH GIRLS REALLY DO EXIST.
YEAH, BUT...
...I NEVER EXPECTED YOU TO VISIT ME IN THE HOSPITAL.
HUH?
YEAH, THAT IS ODD, ISN'T IT?
WAIT, I DON'T HAVE TIME FOR THIS.
LISTEN UP!
DON'T TELL ANYONE I'M HERE.
?
THUNK

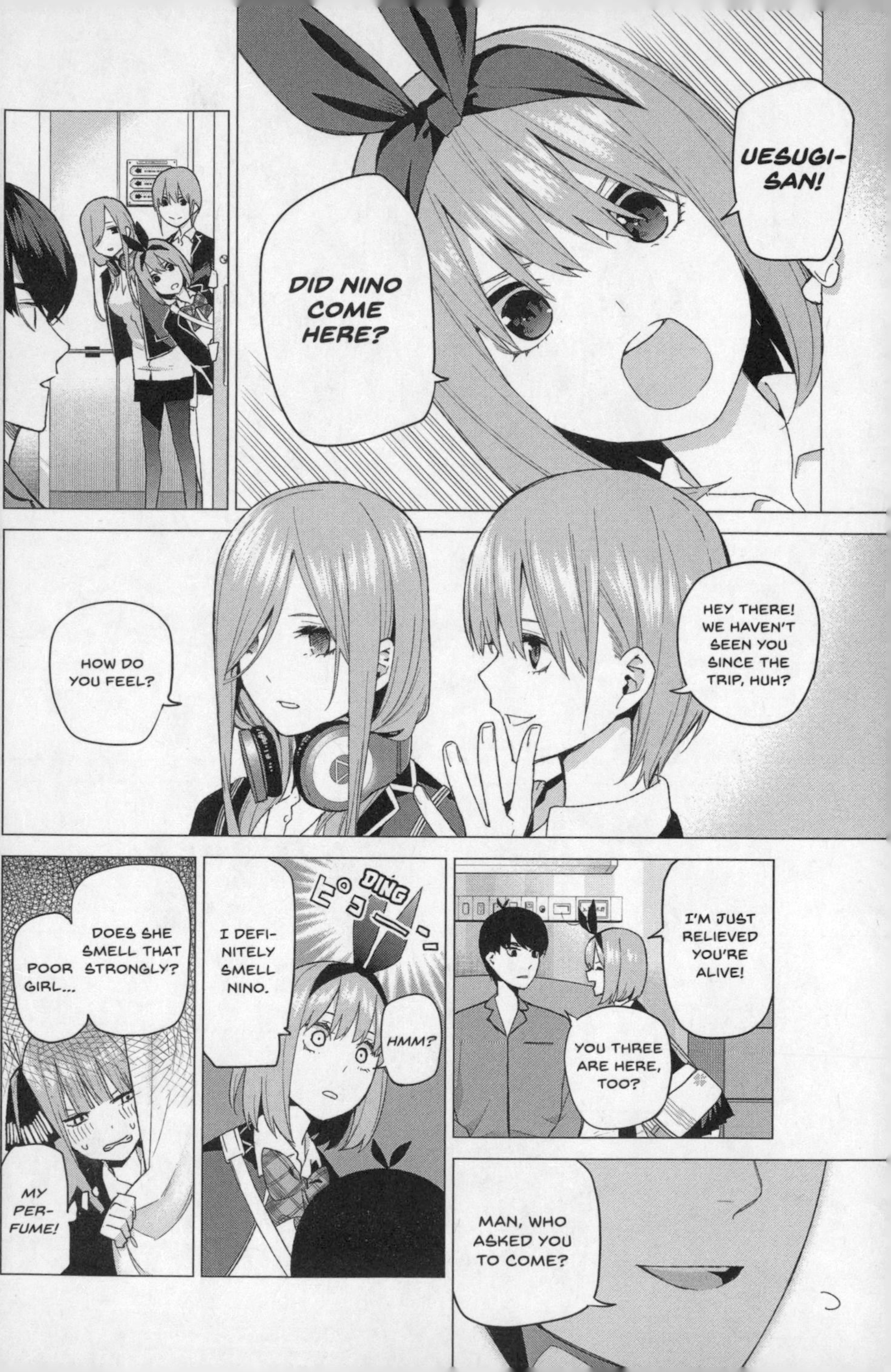
UESUGI-SAN!
DID NINO COME HERE?
HEY THERE! WE HAVEN'T SEEN YOU SINCE THE TRIP, HUH?
HOW DO YOU FEEL?
I'M JUST RELIEVED YOU'RE ALIVE!
YOU THREE ARE HERE, TOO?
MAN, WHO ASKED YOU TO COME?
DING
I DEFINITELY SMELL NINO.
HMM?
DOES SHE SMELL THAT STRONGLY?
POOR GIRL...
MY PERFUME!

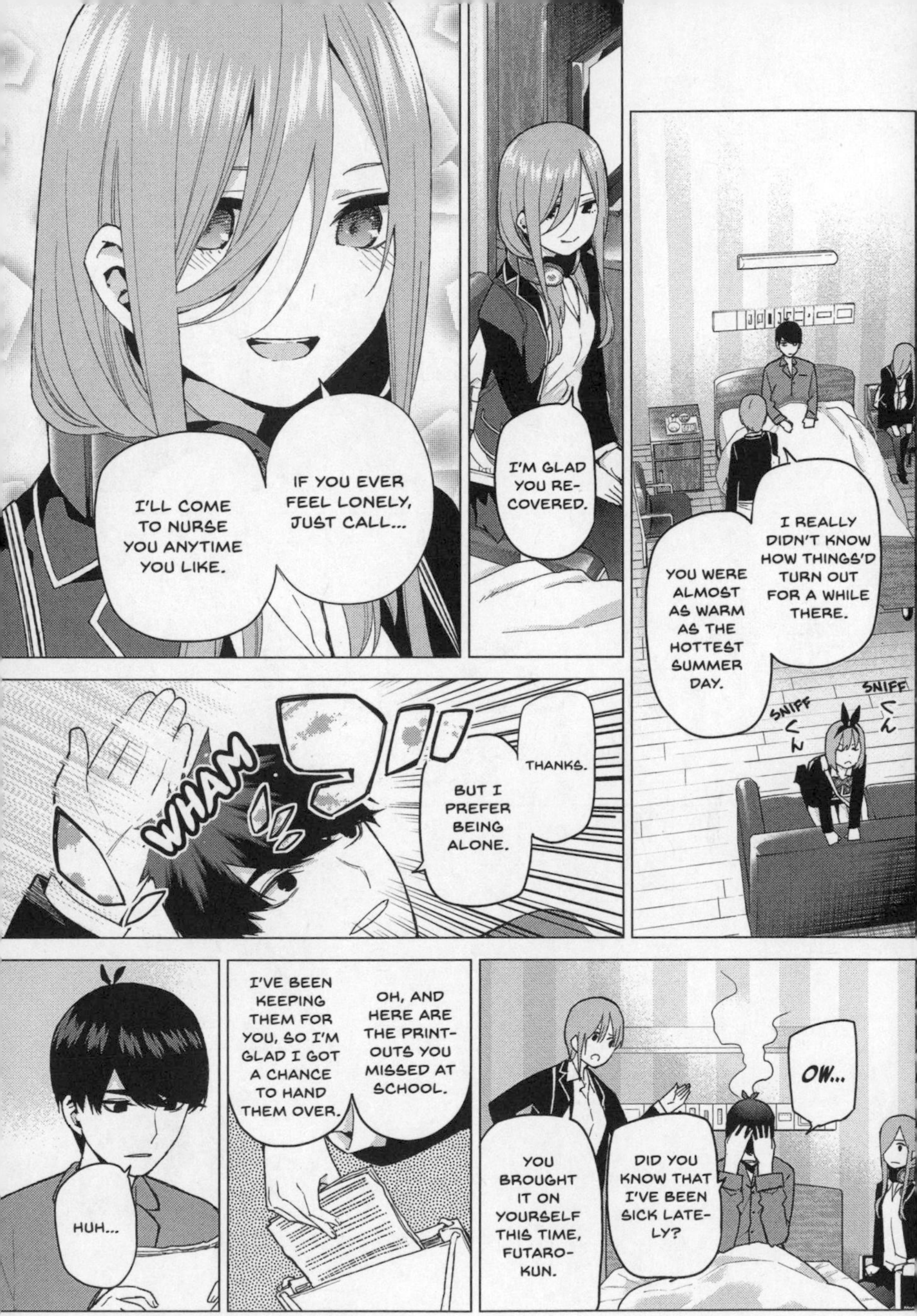
I REALLY DIDN'T KNOW HOW THINGS'D TURN OUT FOR A WHILE THERE.
YOU WERE ALMOST AS WARM AS THE HOTTEST SUMMER DAY.
SNIFF くん
SNIFF くん
I'M GLAD YOU RE-COVERED.
IF YOU EVER FEEL LONELY, JUST CALL...
I'LL COME TO NURSE YOU ANYTIME YOU LIKE.
THANKS.
BUT I PREFER BEING ALONE.
WHAM
OW...
DID YOU KNOW THAT I'VE BEEN SICK LATE-LY?
YOU BROUGHT IT ON YOURSELF THIS TIME, FUTARO-KUN.
OH, AND HERE ARE THE PRINT-OUTS YOU MISSED AT SCHOOL.
I'VE BEEN KEEPING THEM FOR YOU, SO I'M GLAD I GOT A CHANCE TO HAND THEM OVER.
HUH...

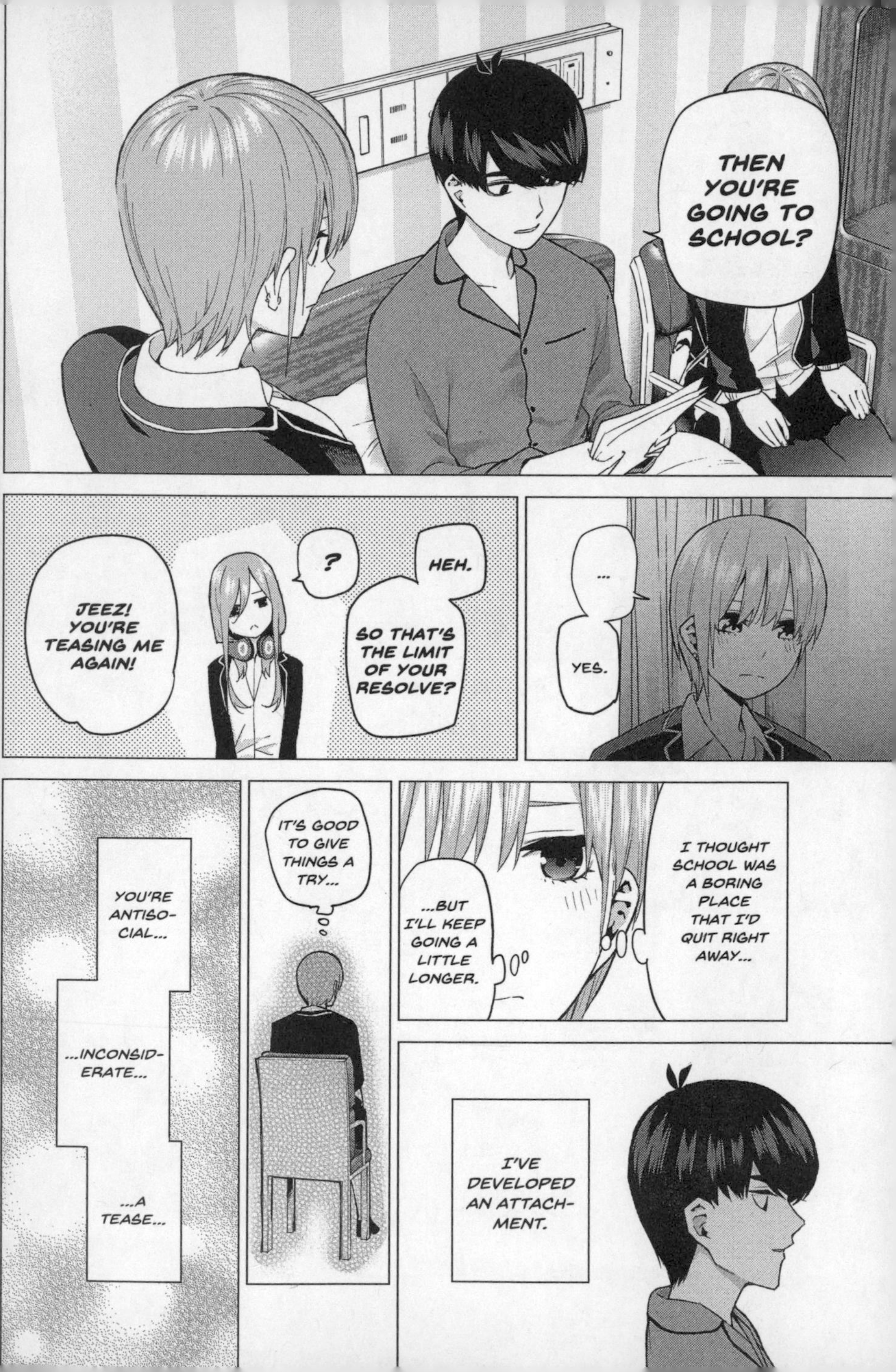
THEN YOU'RE GOING TO SCHOOL?
...
YES.
HEH.
SO THAT'S THE LIMIT OF YOUR RESOLVE?
?
JEEZ! YOU'RE TEASING ME AGAIN!
I THOUGHT SCHOOL WAS A BORING PLACE THAT I'D QUIT RIGHT AWAY...
...BUT I'LL KEEP GOING A LITTLE LONGER.
IT'S GOOD TO GIVE THINGS A TRY...
I'VE DEVELOPED AN ATTACHMENT.
YOU'RE ANTISOCIAL...
...INCONSIDERATE...
...A TEASE...

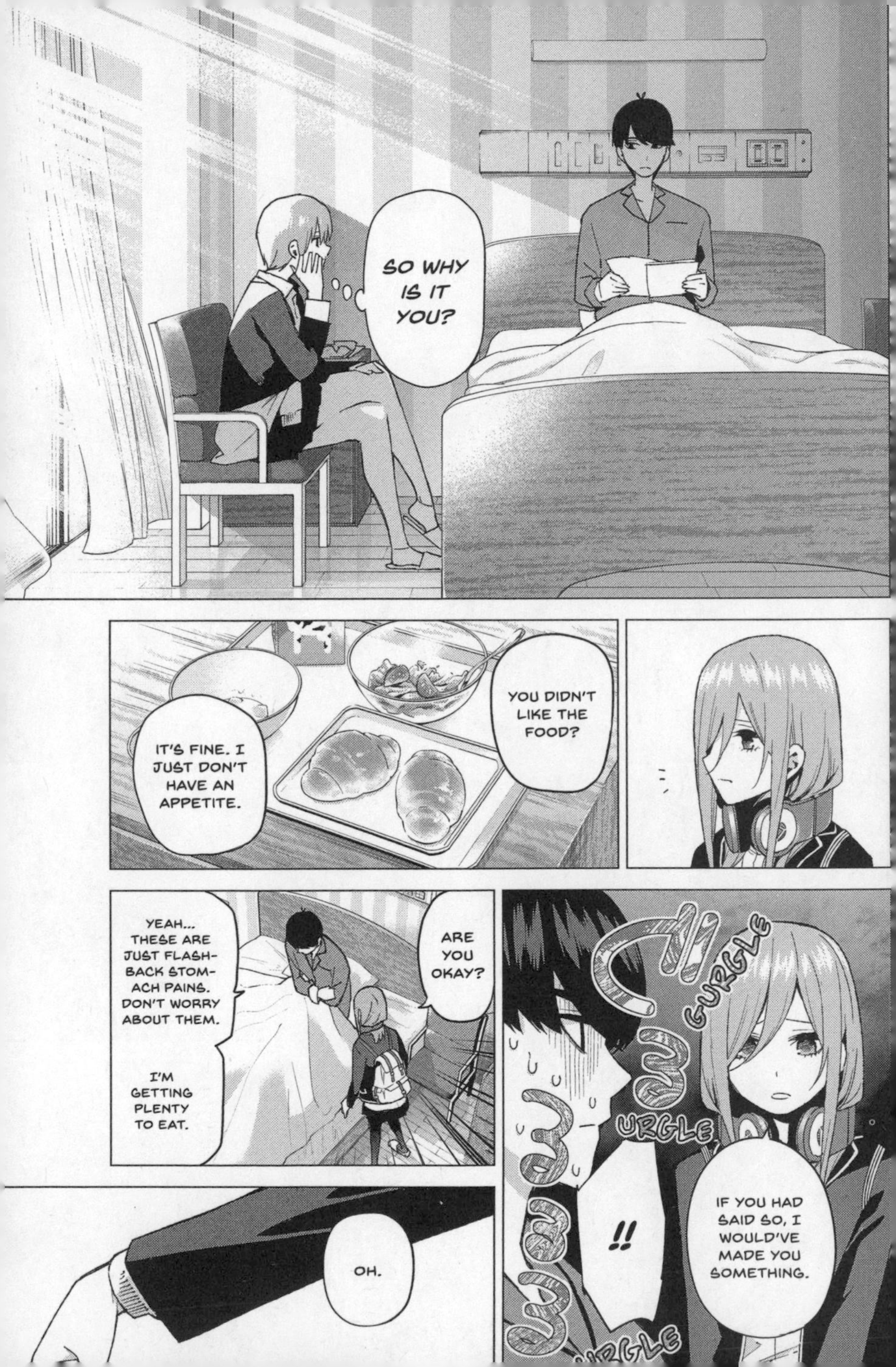
SO WHY IS IT YOU?
YOU DIDN'T LIKE THE FOOD?
IT'S FINE. I JUST DON'T HAVE AN APPETITE.
GURGLE
URGLE
!!
IF YOU HAD SAID SO, I WOULD'VE MADE YOU SOMETHING.
URGLE
ARE YOU OKAY?
YEAH... THESE ARE JUST FLASH-BACK STOMACH PAINS. DON'T WORRY ABOUT THEM.
I'M GETTING PLENTY TO EAT.
OH.

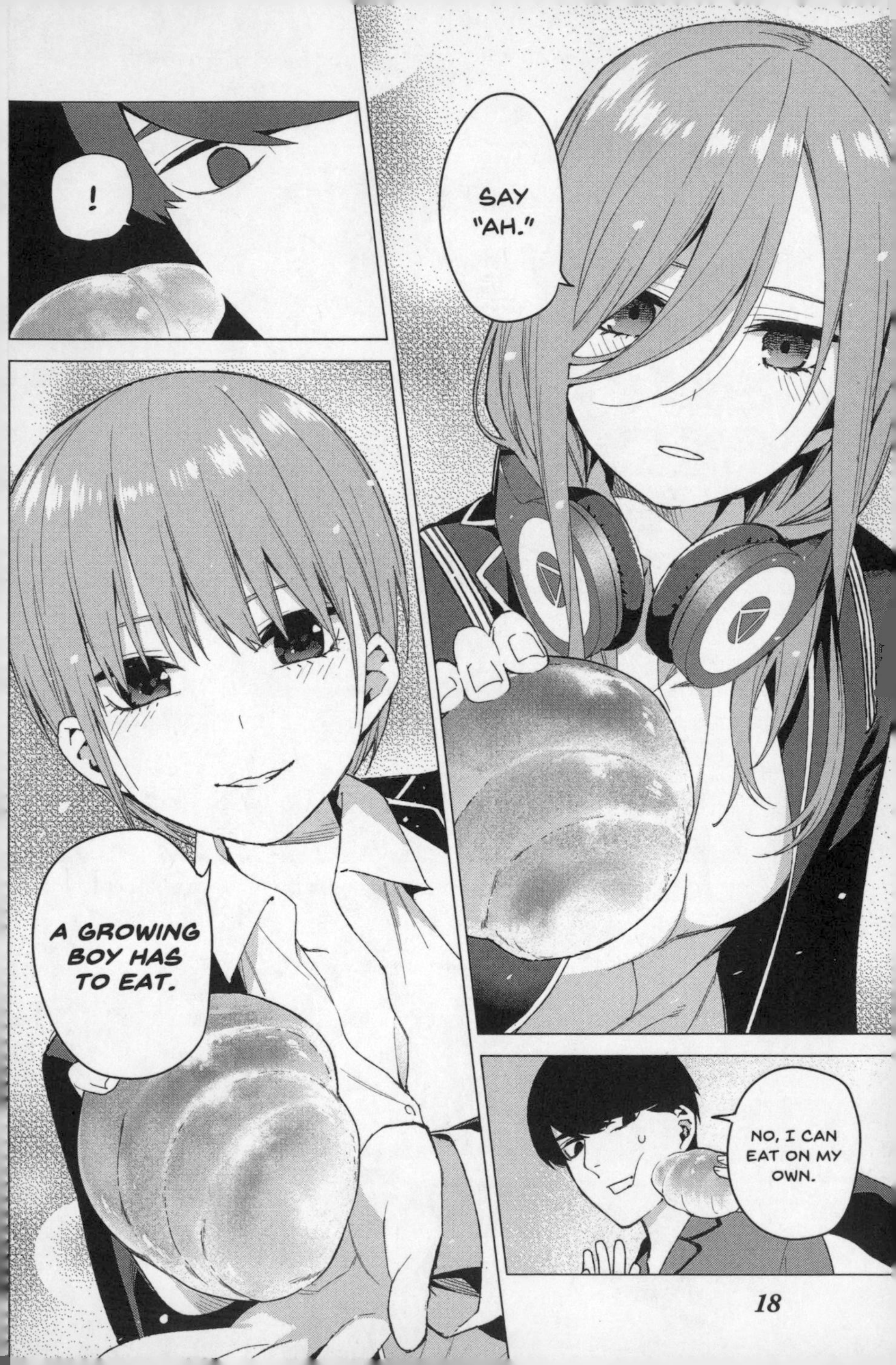
SAY "AH."
!
A GROWING BOY HAS TO EAT.
NO, I CAN EAT ON MY OWN.

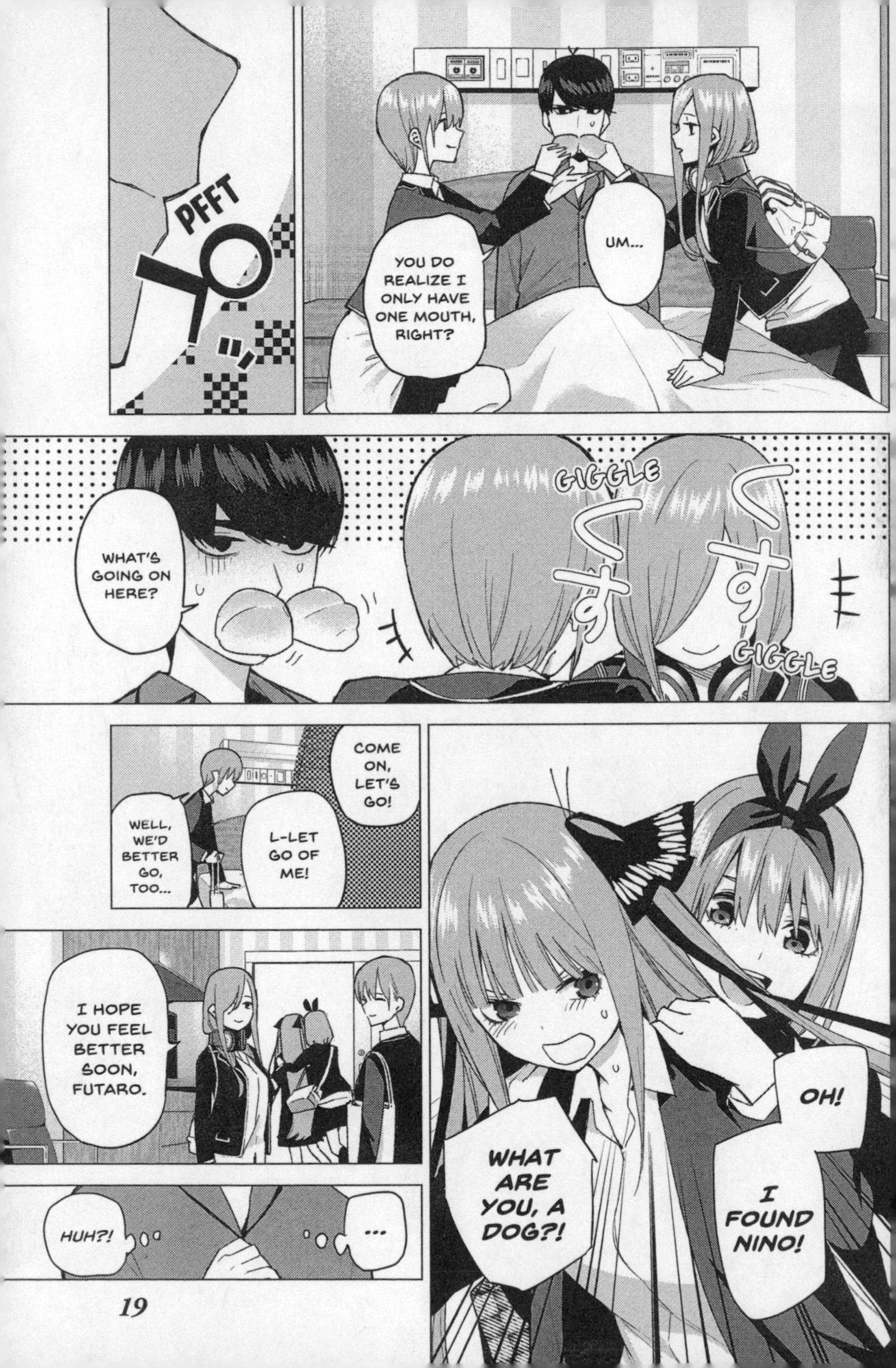
UM...
YOU DO REALIZE I ONLY HAVE ONE MOUTH, RIGHT?
PFFT
くす
GIGGLE
くす
GIGGLE
WHAT'S GOING ON HERE?
OH!
I FOUND NINO!
WHAT ARE YOU, A DOG?!
COME ON, LET'S GO!
L-LET GO OF ME!
WELL, WE'D BETTER GO, TOO...
I HOPE YOU FEEL BETTER SOON, FUTARO.
...
HUH?!

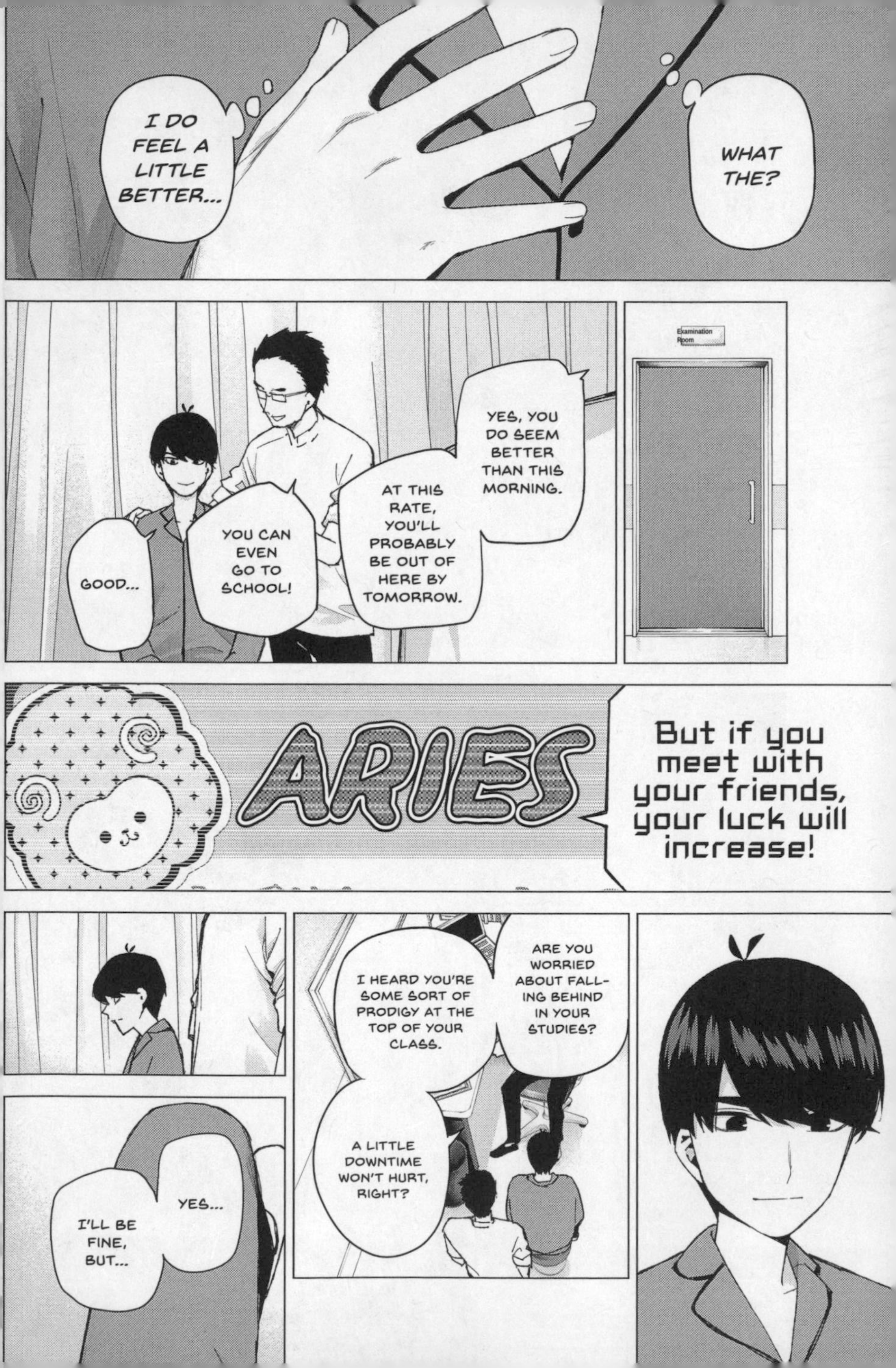
WHAT THE?
I DO FEEL A LITTLE BETTER...
Examination Room
YES, YOU DO SEEM BETTER THAN THIS MORNING.
AT THIS RATE, YOU'LL PROBABLY BE OUT OF HERE BY TOMORROW.
YOU CAN EVEN GO TO SCHOOL!
GOOD...
But if you meet with your friends, your luck will increase!
ARIES
ARE YOU WORRIED ABOUT FALLING BEHIND IN YOUR STUDIES?
I HEARD YOU'RE SOME SORT OF PRODIGY AT THE TOP OF YOUR CLASS.
A LITTLE DOWNTIME WON'T HURT, RIGHT?
YES...
I'LL BE FINE, BUT...

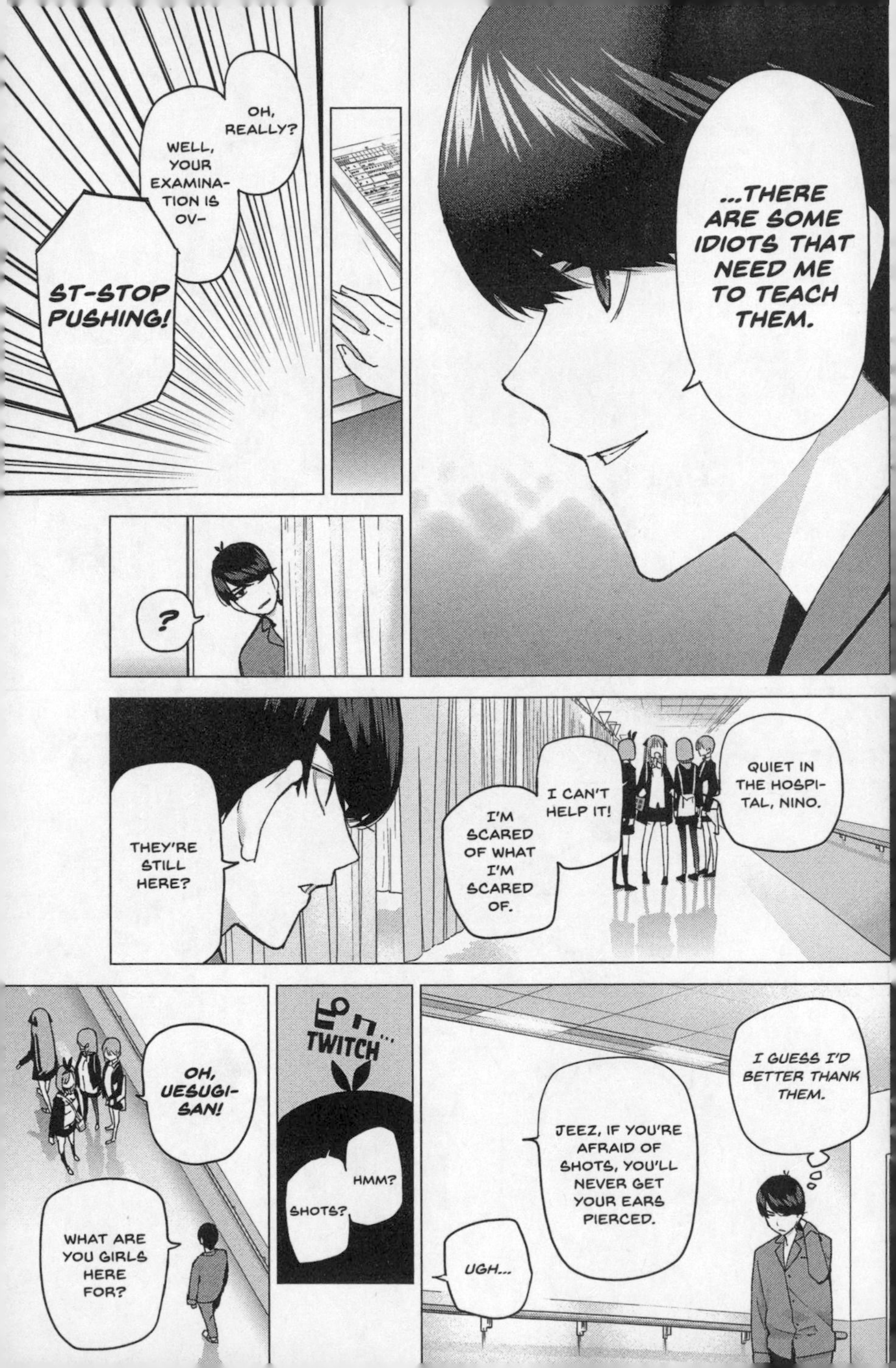
...THERE ARE SOME IDIOTS THAT NEED ME TO TEACH THEM.
OH, REALLY? WELL, YOUR EXAMINATION IS OV-
ST-STOP PUSHING!
?
QUIET IN THE HOSPITAL, NINO.
I CAN'T HELP IT!
I'M SCARED OF WHAT I'M SCARED OF.
THEY'RE STILL HERE?
I GUESS I'D BETTER THANK THEM.
JEEZ, IF YOU'RE AFRAID OF SHOTS, YOU'LL NEVER GET YOUR EARS PIERCED.
UGH...
ピク…
TWITCH
HMM?
SHOTS?
OH, UESUGI-SAN!
WHAT ARE YOU GIRLS HERE FOR?

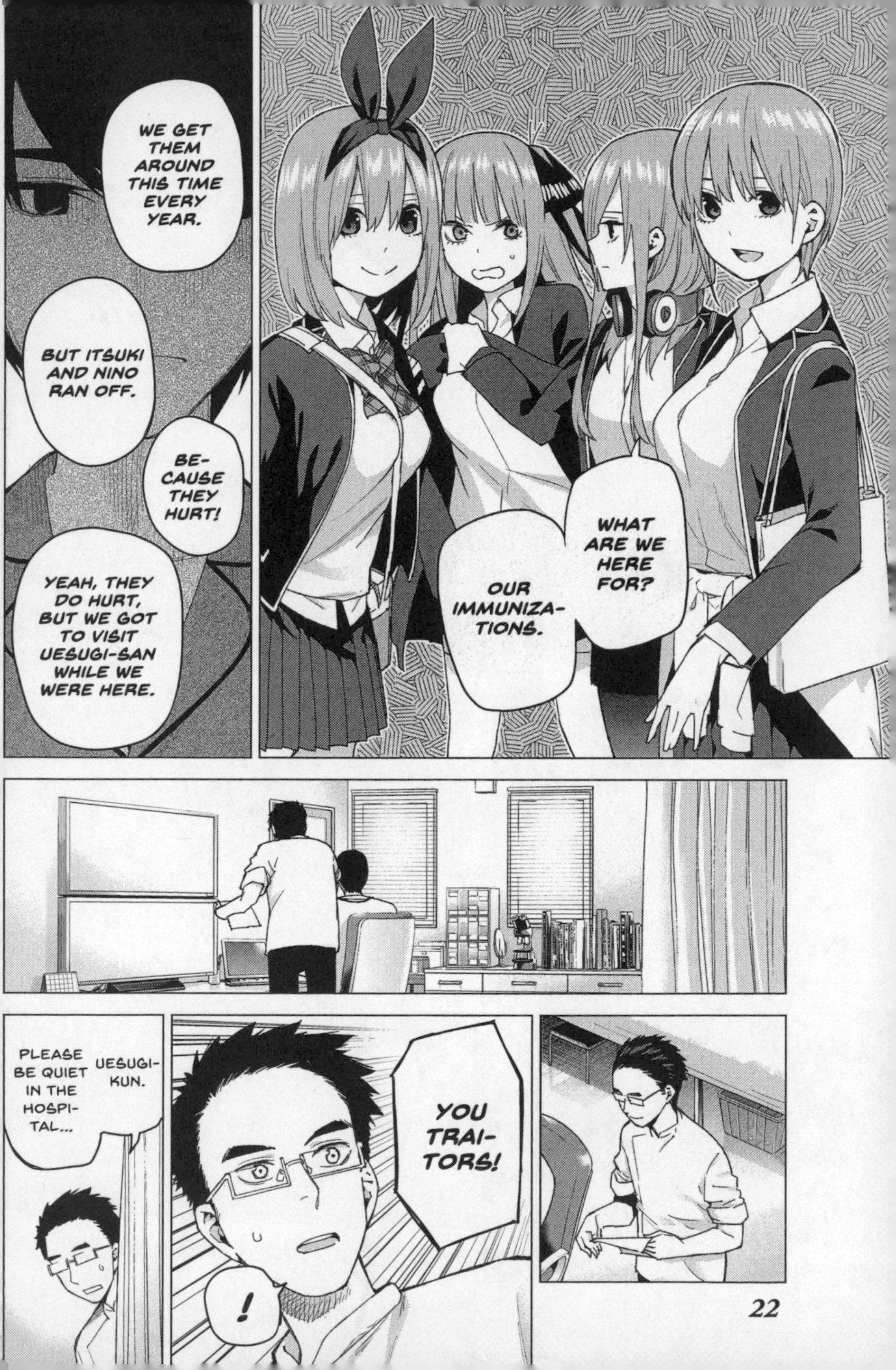
WHAT ARE WE HERE FOR?
OUR IMMUNIZA-TIONS.
WE GET THEM AROUND THIS TIME EVERY YEAR.
BUT ITSUKI AND NINO RAN OFF.
BE-CAUSE THEY HURT!
YEAH, THEY DO HURT, BUT WE GOT TO VISIT UESUGI-SAN WHILE WE WERE HERE.
YOU TRAI-TORS!
!
UESUGI-KUN.
PLEASE BE QUIET IN THE HOSPI-TAL...

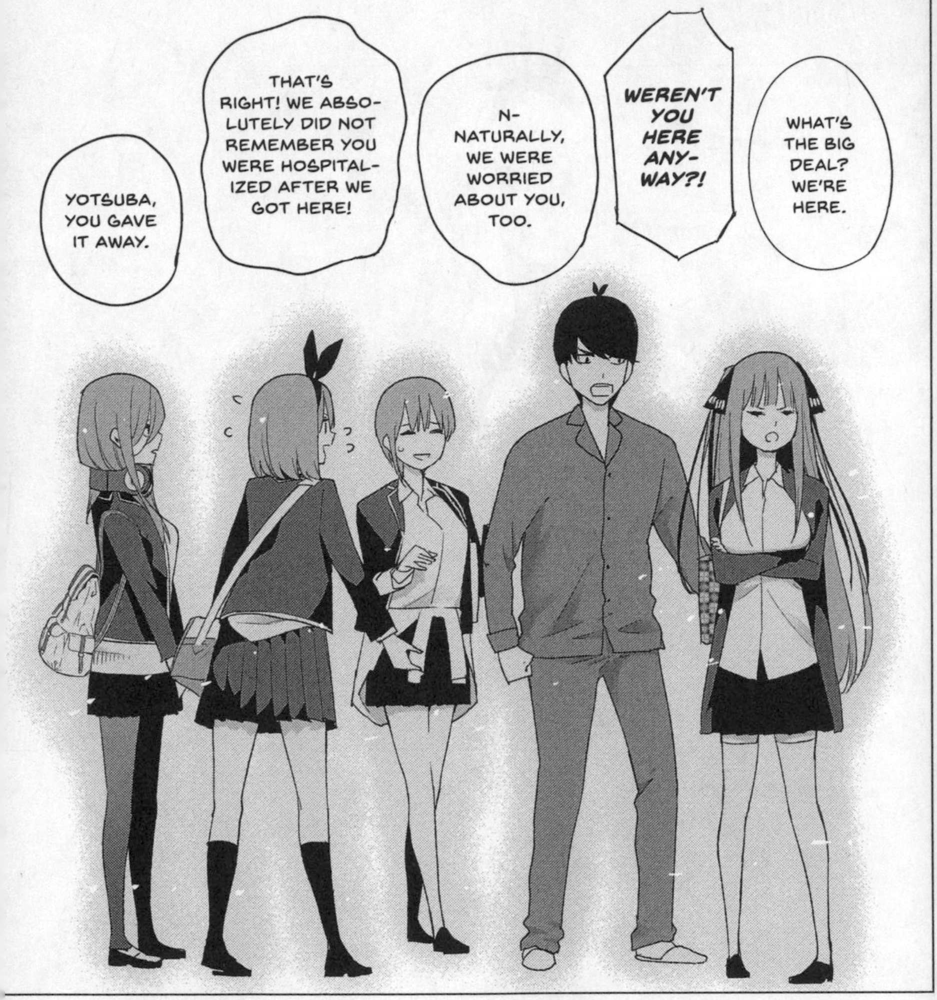
WHAT'S THE BIG DEAL? WE'RE HERE.
WEREN'T YOU HERE ANY-WAY?!
N-NATURALLY, WE WERE WORRIED ABOUT YOU, TOO.
THAT'S RIGHT! WE ABSO-LUTELY DID NOT REMEMBER YOU WERE HOSPITAL-IZED AFTER WE GOT HERE!
YOTSUBA, YOU GAVE IT AWAY.
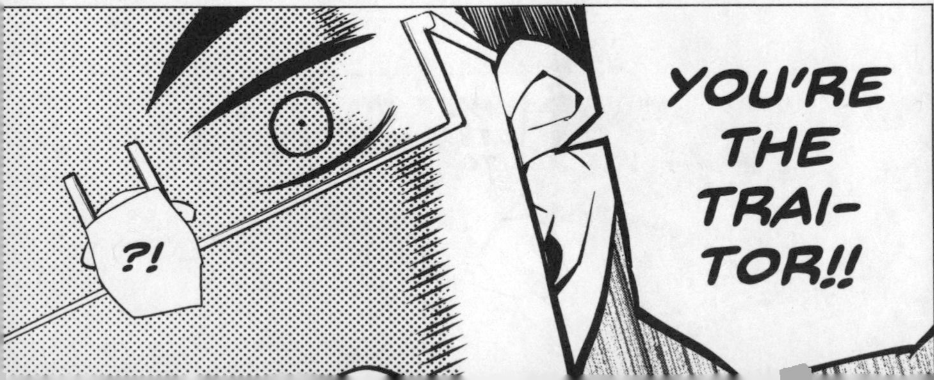
YOU'RE THE TRAI-TOR!!
?!

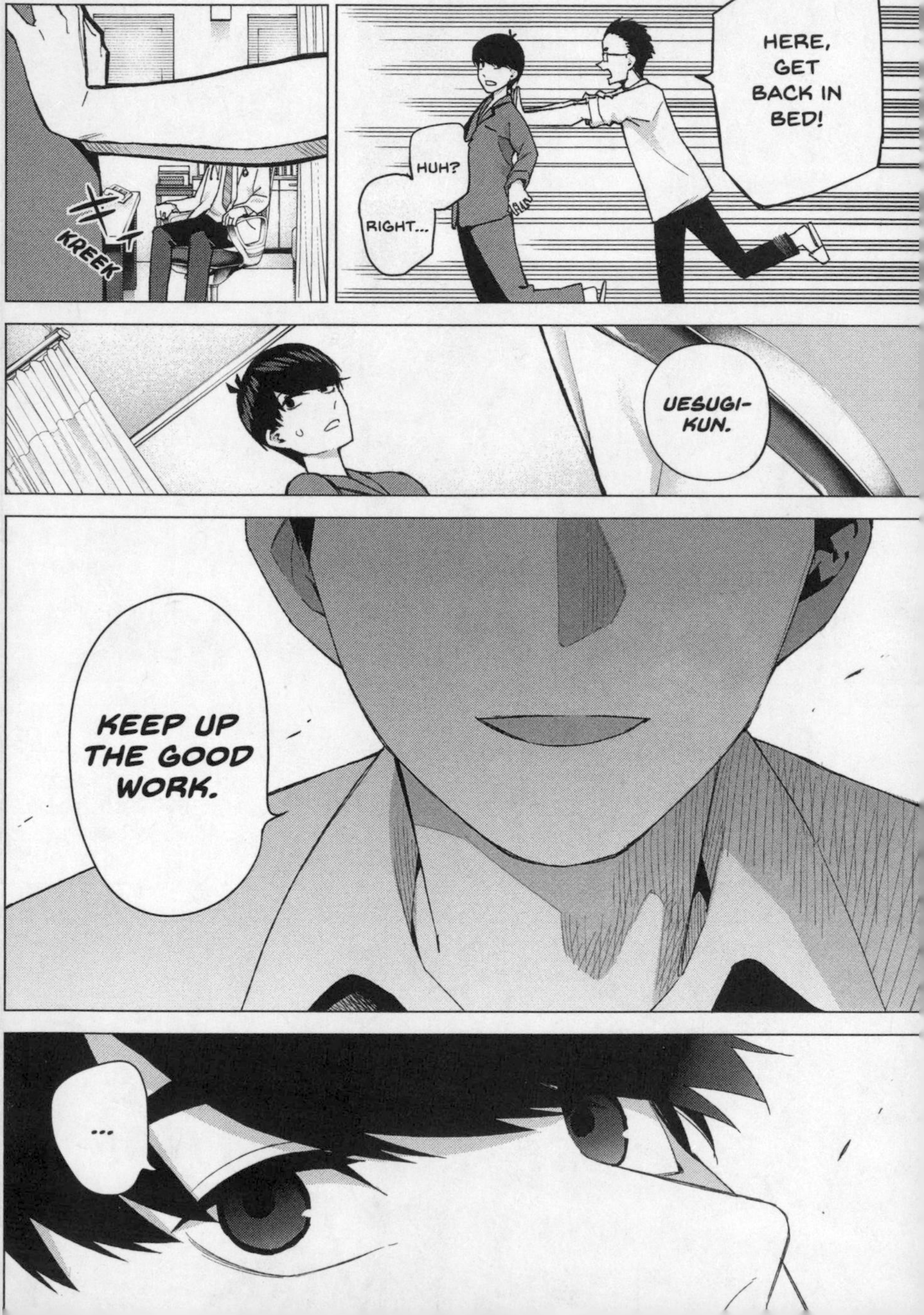
HERE, GET BACK IN BED!
HUH?
RIGHT...
KREEK
UESUGI-KUN.
KEEP UP THE GOOD WORK.
...

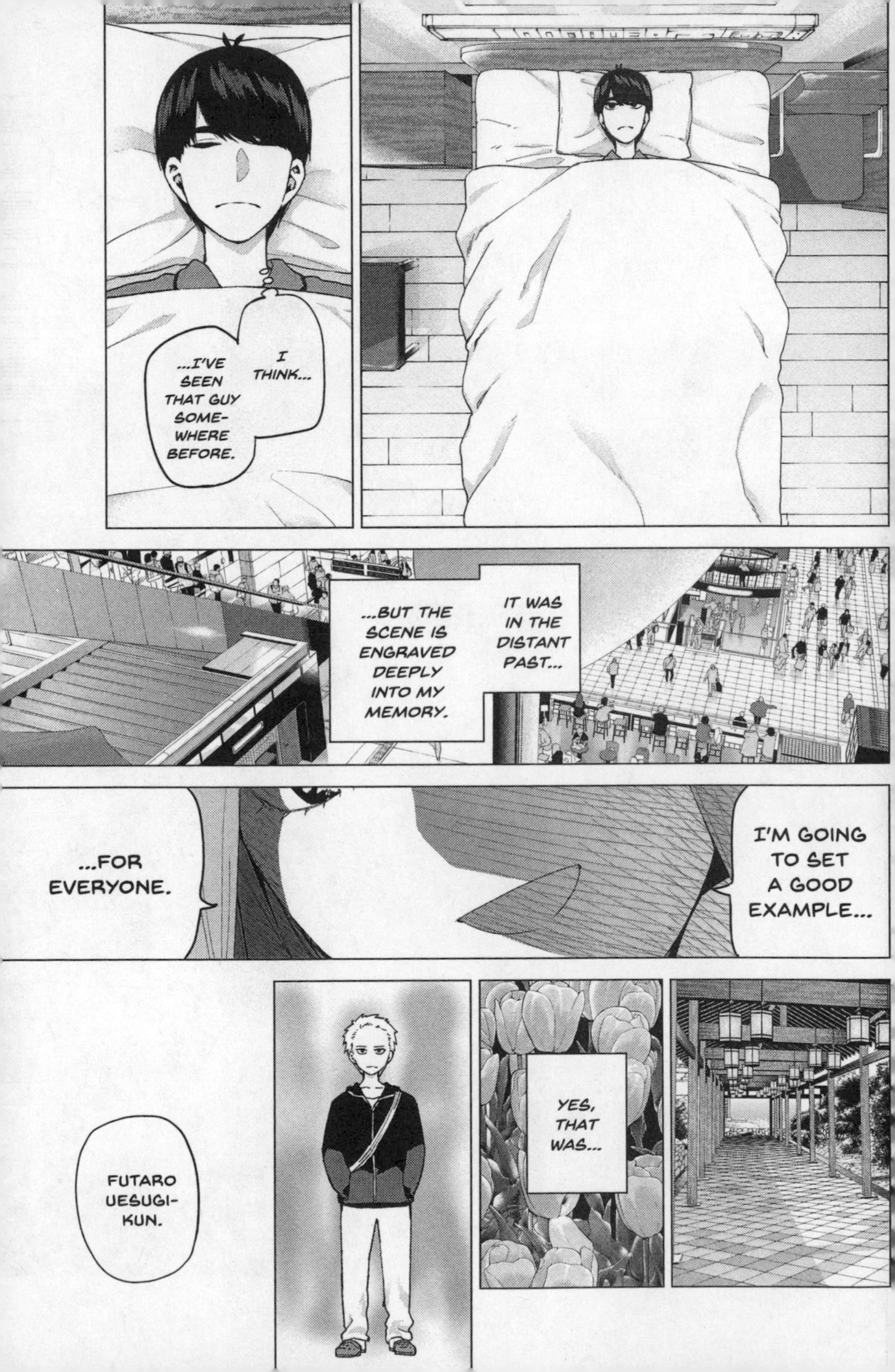
I THINK...
...I'VE SEEN THAT GUY SOME-WHERE BEFORE.
IT WAS IN THE DISTANT PAST...
...BUT THE SCENE IS ENGRAVED DEEPLY INTO MY MEMORY.
I'M GOING TO SET A GOOD EXAMPLE...
...FOR EVERYONE.
YES, THAT WAS...
FUTARO UESUGI-KUN.

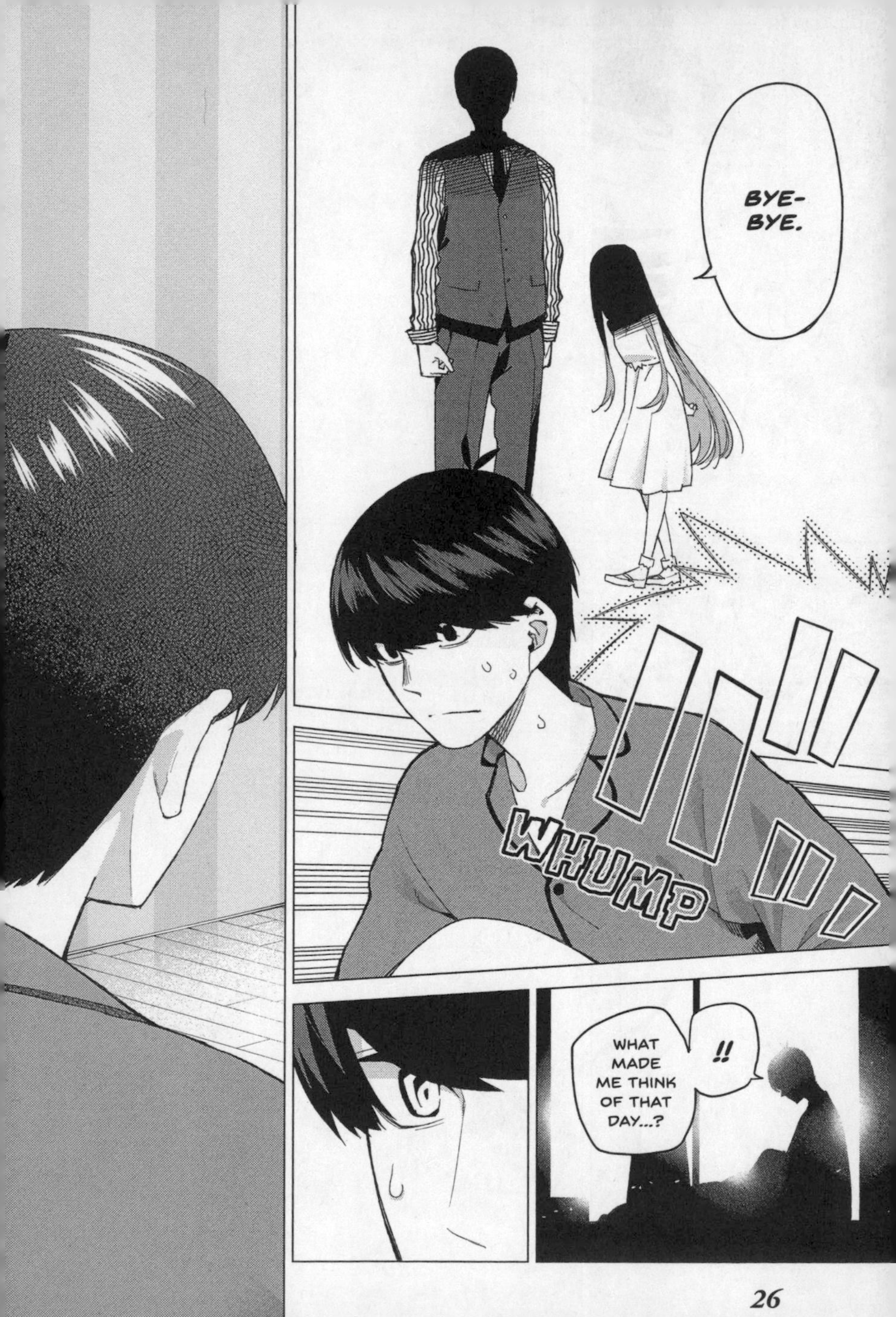
BYE-BYE.
WHUMP
!!
WHAT MADE ME THINK OF THAT DAY...?

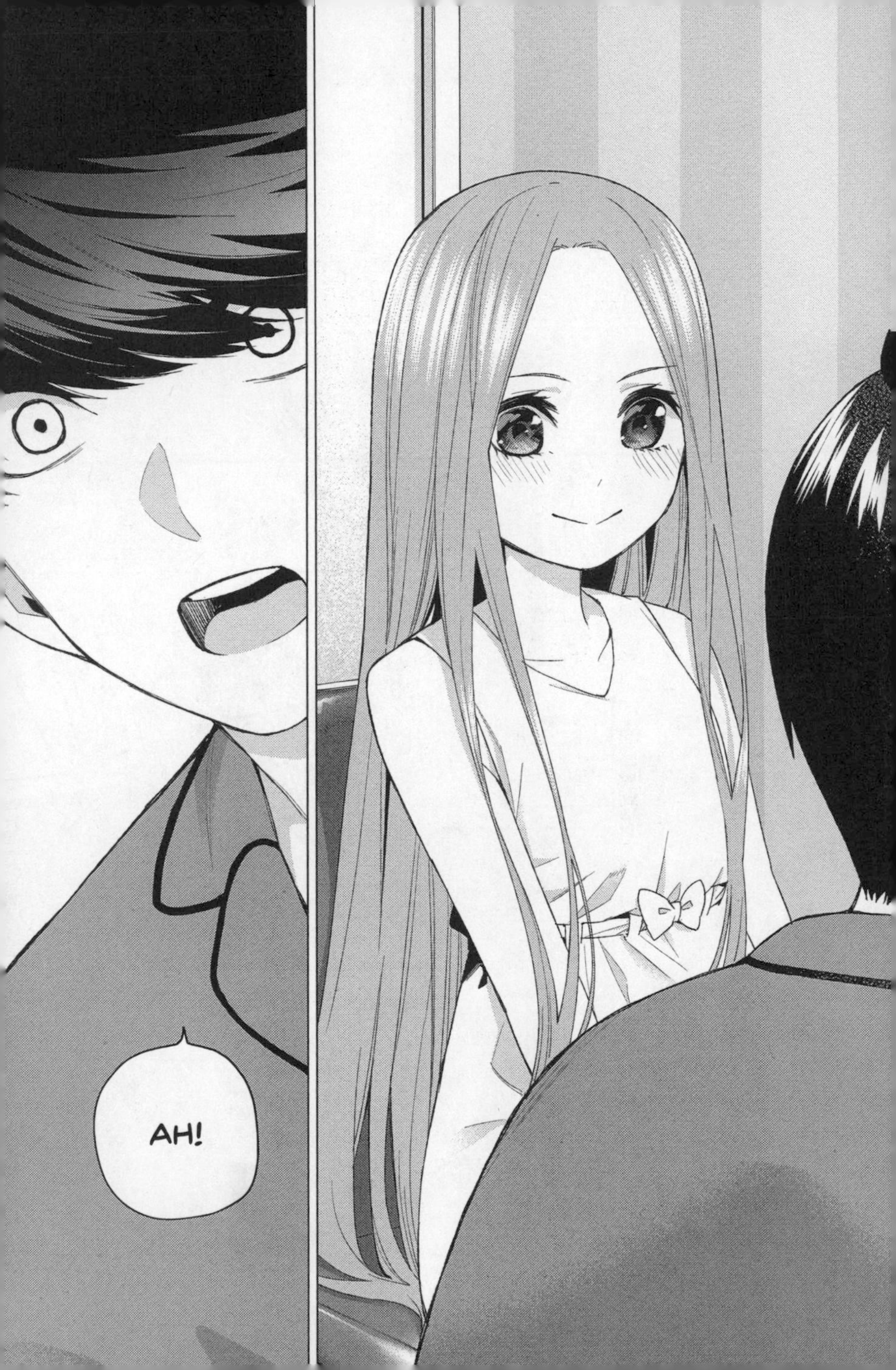
AH!

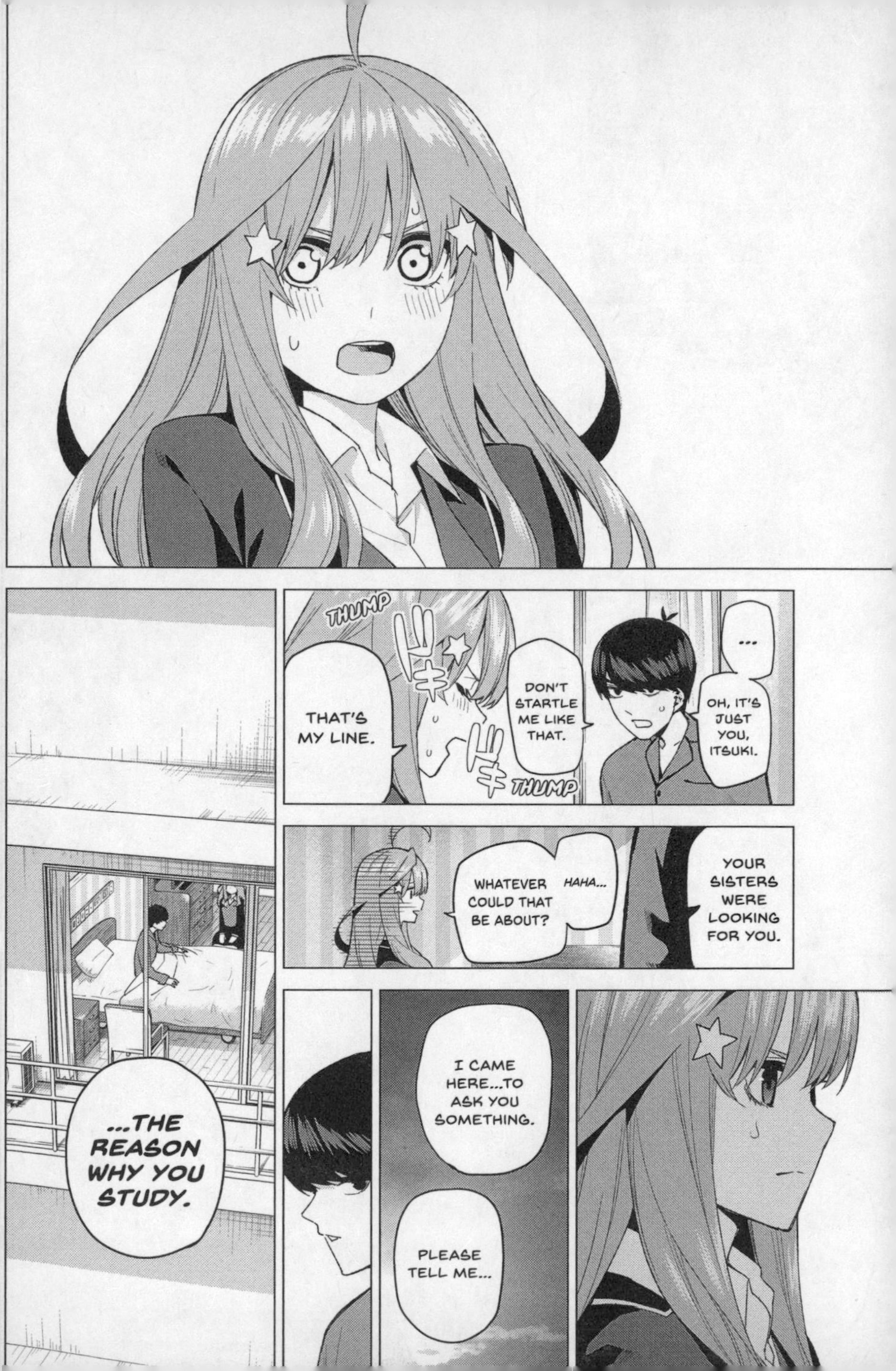
...
OH, IT'S JUST YOU, ITSUKI.
DON'T STARTLE ME LIKE THAT.
THUMP
THUMP
THAT'S MY LINE.
YOUR SISTERS WERE LOOKING FOR YOU.
HAHA...
WHATEVER COULD THAT BE ABOUT?
I CAME HERE...TO ASK YOU SOMETHING.
PLEASE TELL ME...
...THE REASON WHY YOU STUDY.

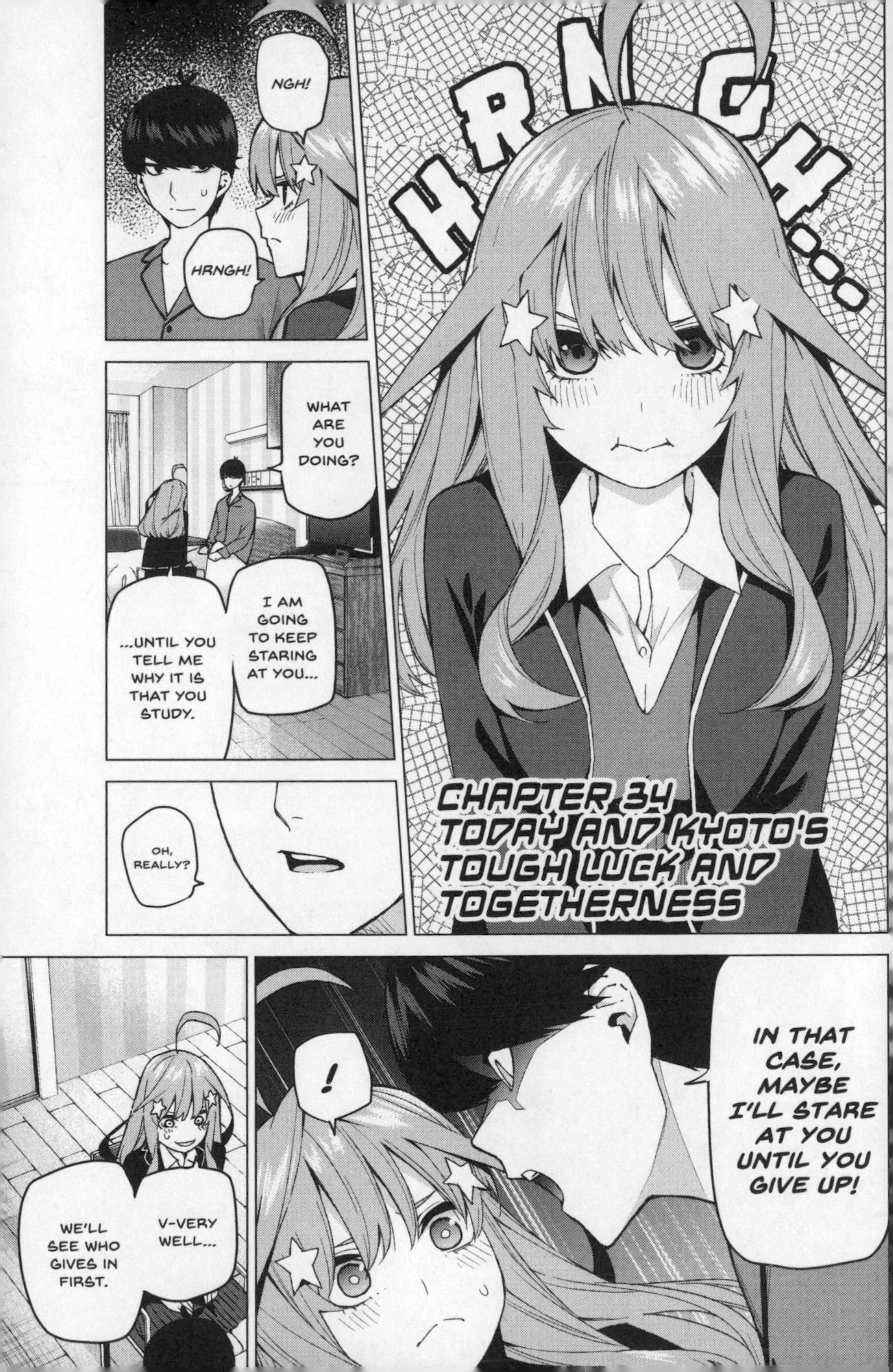
HRNGH...
CHAPTER 34
TODAY AND KYOTO'S TOUGH LUCK AND TOGETHERNESS
NGH!
HRNGH!
WHAT ARE YOU DOING?
I AM GOING TO KEEP STARING AT YOU...
...UNTIL YOU TELL ME WHY IT IS THAT YOU STUDY.
OH, REALLY?
IN THAT CASE, MAYBE I'LL STARE AT YOU UNTIL YOU GIVE UP!
!
V-VERY WELL...
WE'LL SEE WHO GIVES IN FIRST.

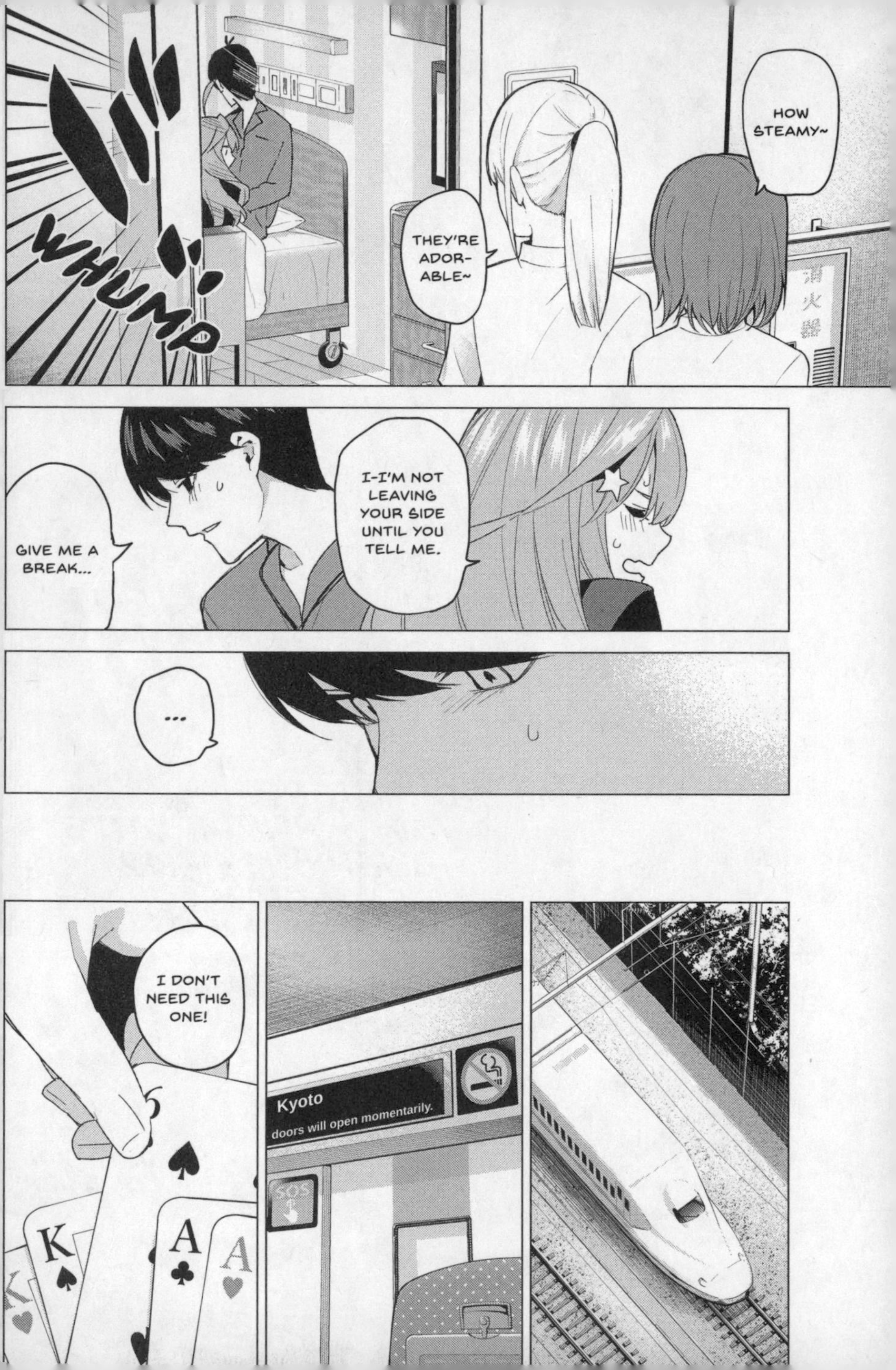
HOW STEAMY~
THEY'RE ADOR-ABLE~
WHUMP
I-I'M NOT LEAVING YOUR SIDE UNTIL YOU TELL ME.
GIVE ME A BREAK...
...
Kyoto
doors will open momentarily.
SOS
I DON'T NEED THIS ONE!

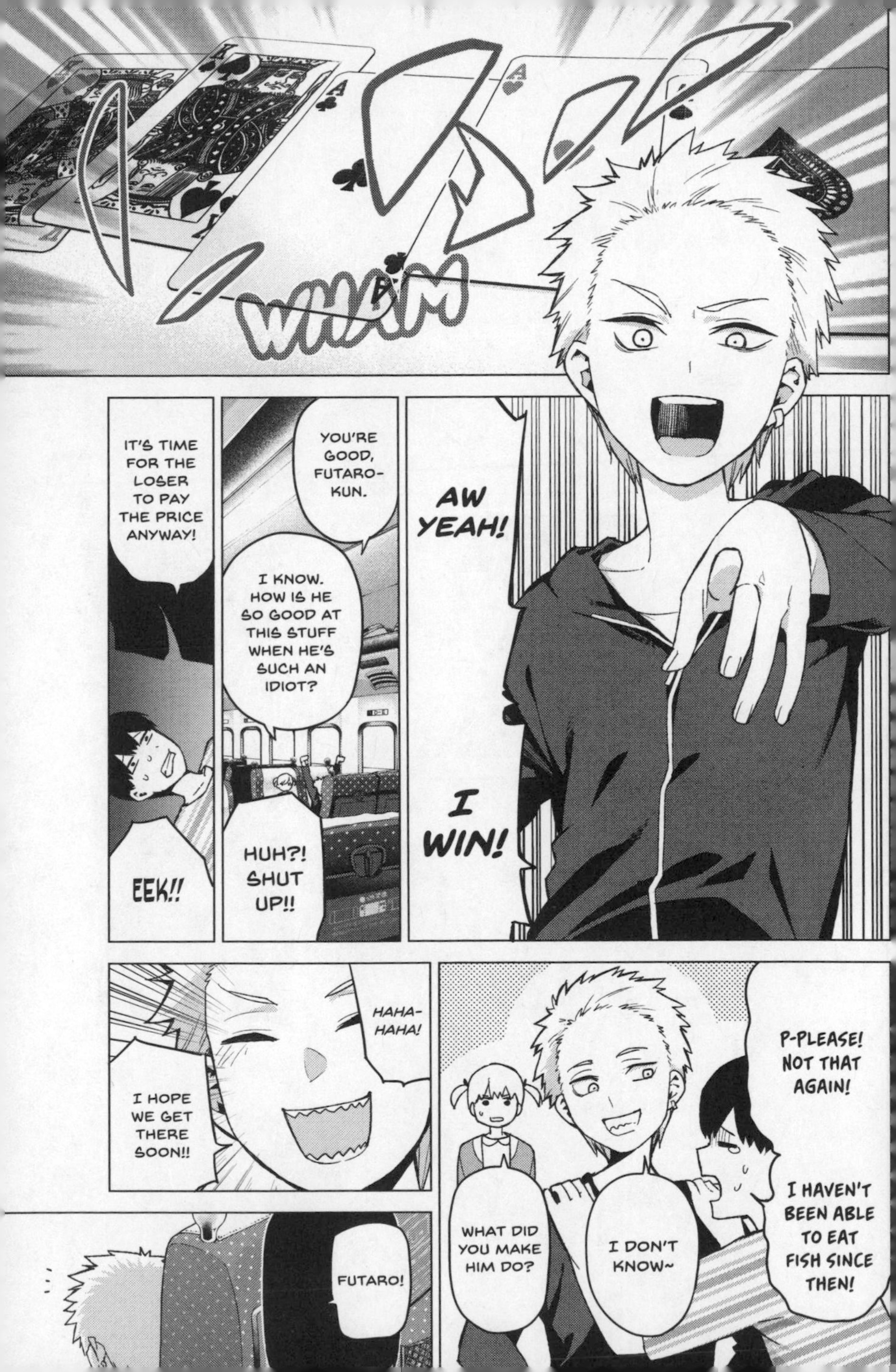
WHAM
AW YEAH!
I WIN!
YOU'RE GOOD, FUTARO-KUN.
I KNOW. HOW IS HE SO GOOD AT THIS STUFF WHEN HE'S SUCH AN IDIOT?
HUH?! SHUT UP!!
IT'S TIME FOR THE LOSER TO PAY THE PRICE ANYWAY!
EEK!!
P-PLEASE! NOT THAT AGAIN!
I HAVEN'T BEEN ABLE TO EAT FISH SINCE THEN!
I DON'T KNOW~
WHAT DID YOU MAKE HIM DO?
HAHA-HAHA!
I HOPE WE GET THERE SOON!!
FUTARO!

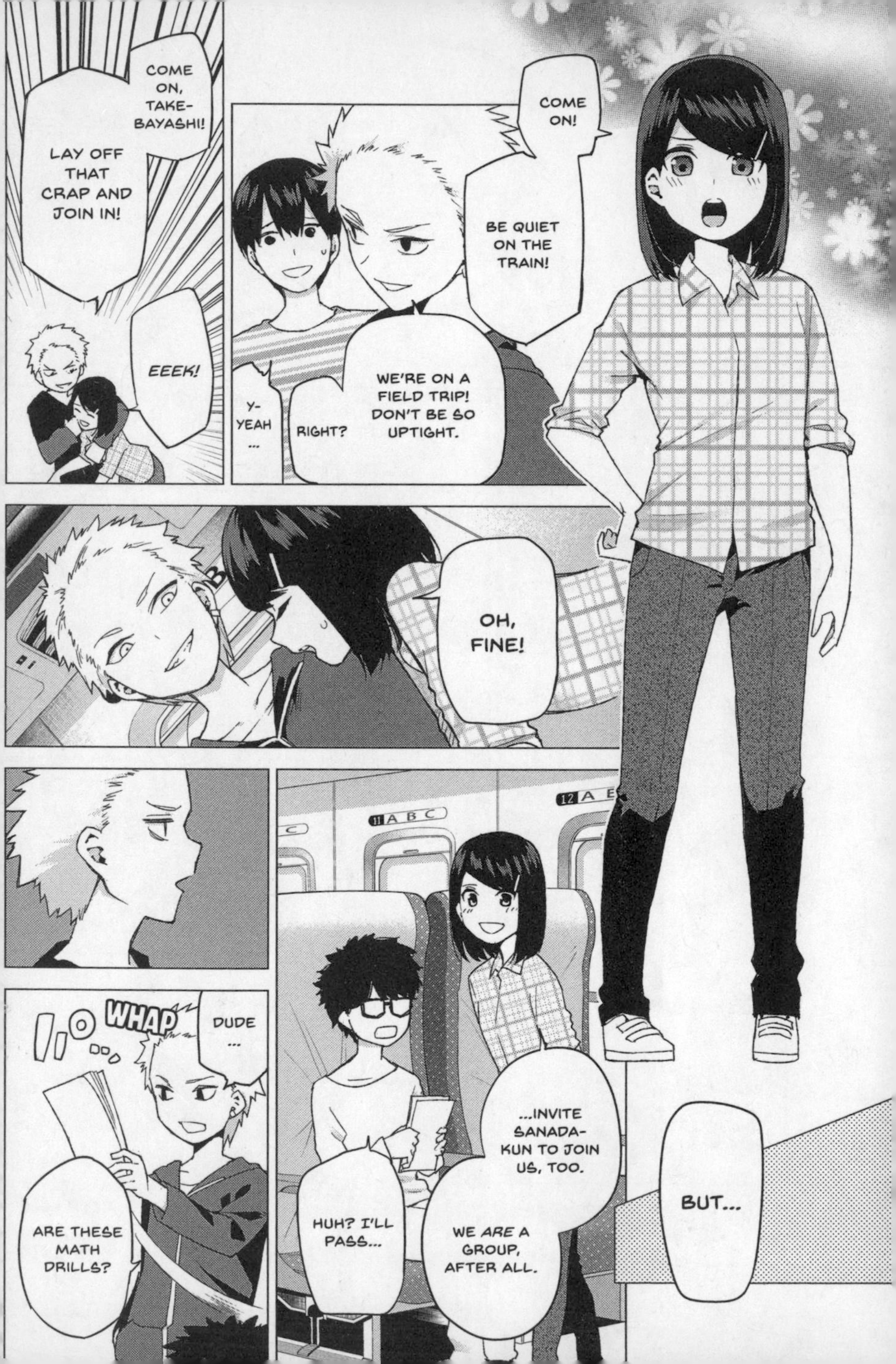
BE QUIET ON THE TRAIN!
COME ON!
WE'RE ON A FIELD TRIP! DON'T BE SO UPTIGHT.
RIGHT?
Y-YEAH ...
COME ON, TAKE-BAYASHI!
LAY OFF THAT CRAP AND JOIN IN!
EEEK!
OH, FINE!
BUT...
...INVITE SANADA-KUN TO JOIN US, TOO.
WE *ARE* A GROUP, AFTER ALL.
HUH? I'LL PASS...
WHAP
DUDE ...
ARE THESE MATH DRILLS?

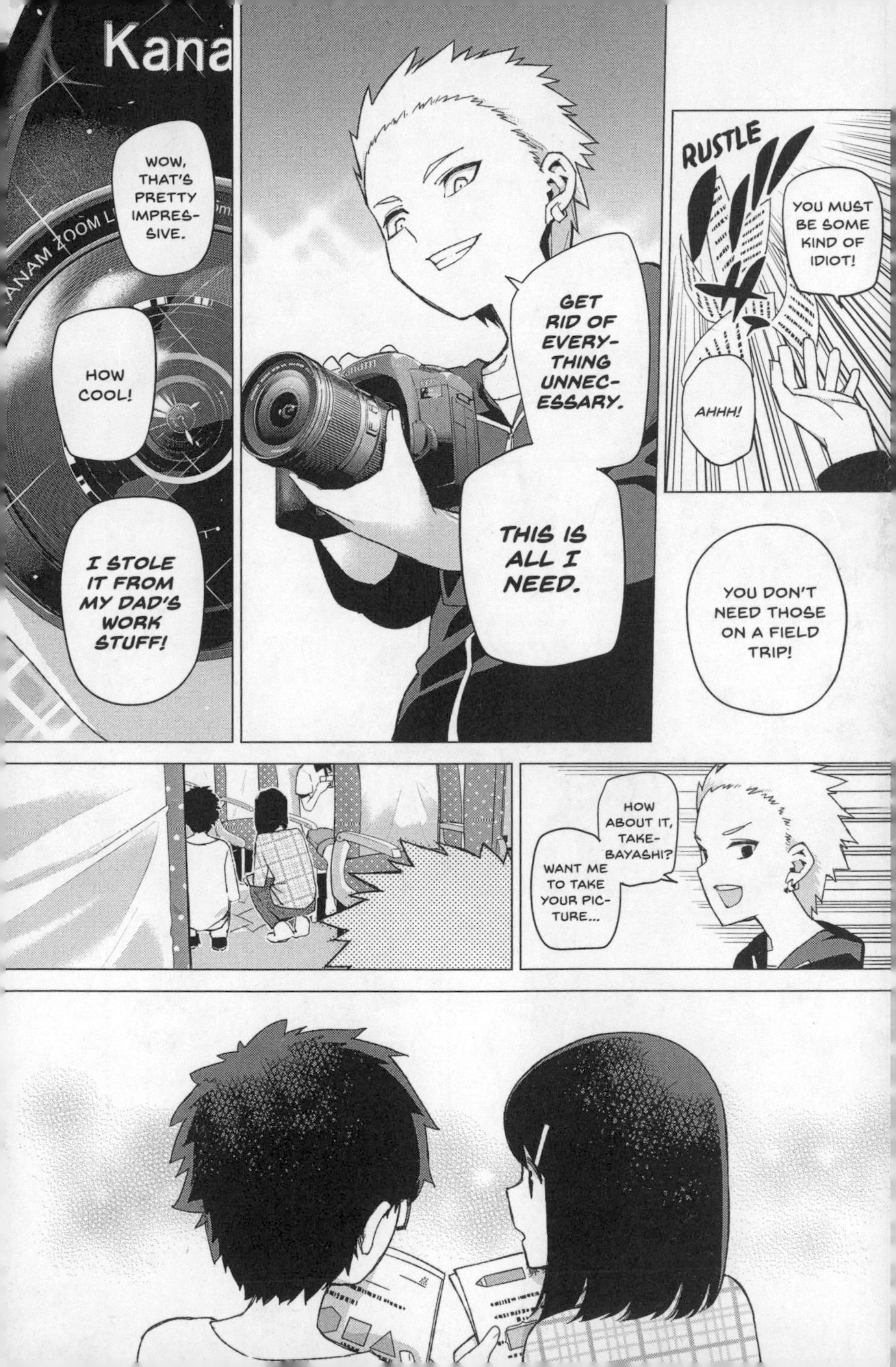
RUSTLE
YOU MUST BE SOME KIND OF IDIOT!
AHHH!
YOU DON'T NEED THOSE ON A FIELD TRIP!
GET RID OF EVERYTHING UNNECESSARY.
THIS IS ALL I NEED.
Kana
WOW, THAT'S PRETTY IMPRESSIVE.
HOW COOL!
I STOLE IT FROM MY DAD'S WORK STUFF!
HOW ABOUT IT, TAKEBAYASHI?
WANT ME TO TAKE YOUR PICTURE...

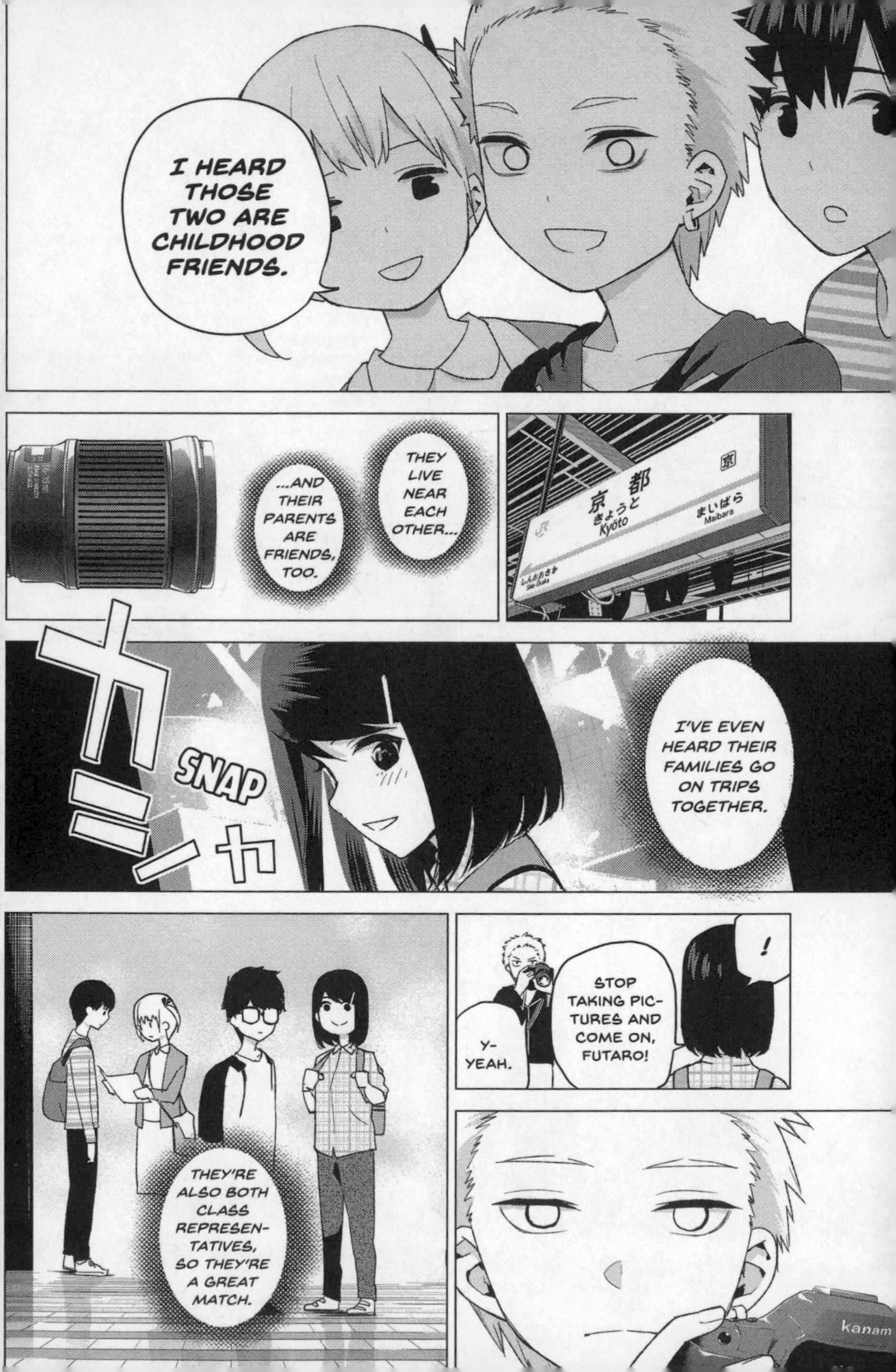
I HEARD THOSE TWO ARE CHILDHOOD FRIENDS.
京都
きょうと
Kyōto
まいばら
Maibara
しんおおさか
THEY LIVE NEAR EACH OTHER...
...AND THEIR PARENTS ARE FRIENDS, TOO.
I'VE EVEN HEARD THEIR FAMILIES GO ON TRIPS TOGETHER.
SNAP
!
STOP TAKING PIC-TURES AND COME ON, FUTARO!
Y- YEAH.
THEY'RE ALSO BOTH CLASS REPRESEN-TATIVES, SO THEY'RE A GREAT MATCH.

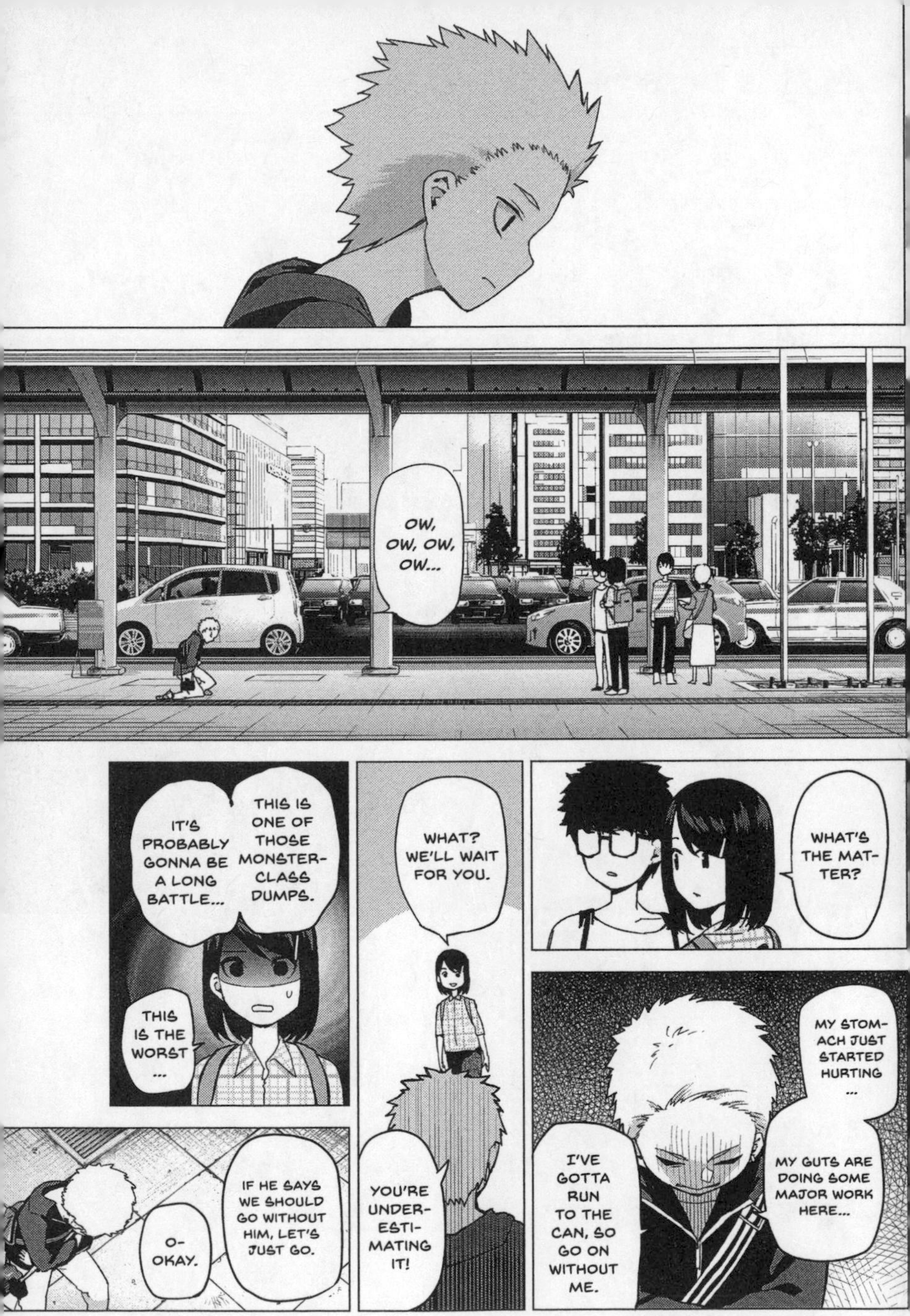

OW, OW, OW, OW...
WHAT'S THE MATTER?
MY STOMACH JUST STARTED HURTING...
MY GUTS ARE DOING SOME MAJOR WORK HERE...
I'VE GOTTA RUN TO THE CAN, SO GO ON WITHOUT ME.
WHAT? WE'LL WAIT FOR YOU.
YOU'RE UNDERESTIMATING IT!
THIS IS ONE OF THOSE MONSTER-CLASS DUMPS.
IT'S PROBABLY GONNA BE A LONG BATTLE...
THIS IS THE WORST...
IF HE SAYS WE SHOULD GO WITHOUT HIM, LET'S JUST GO.
O-OKAY.

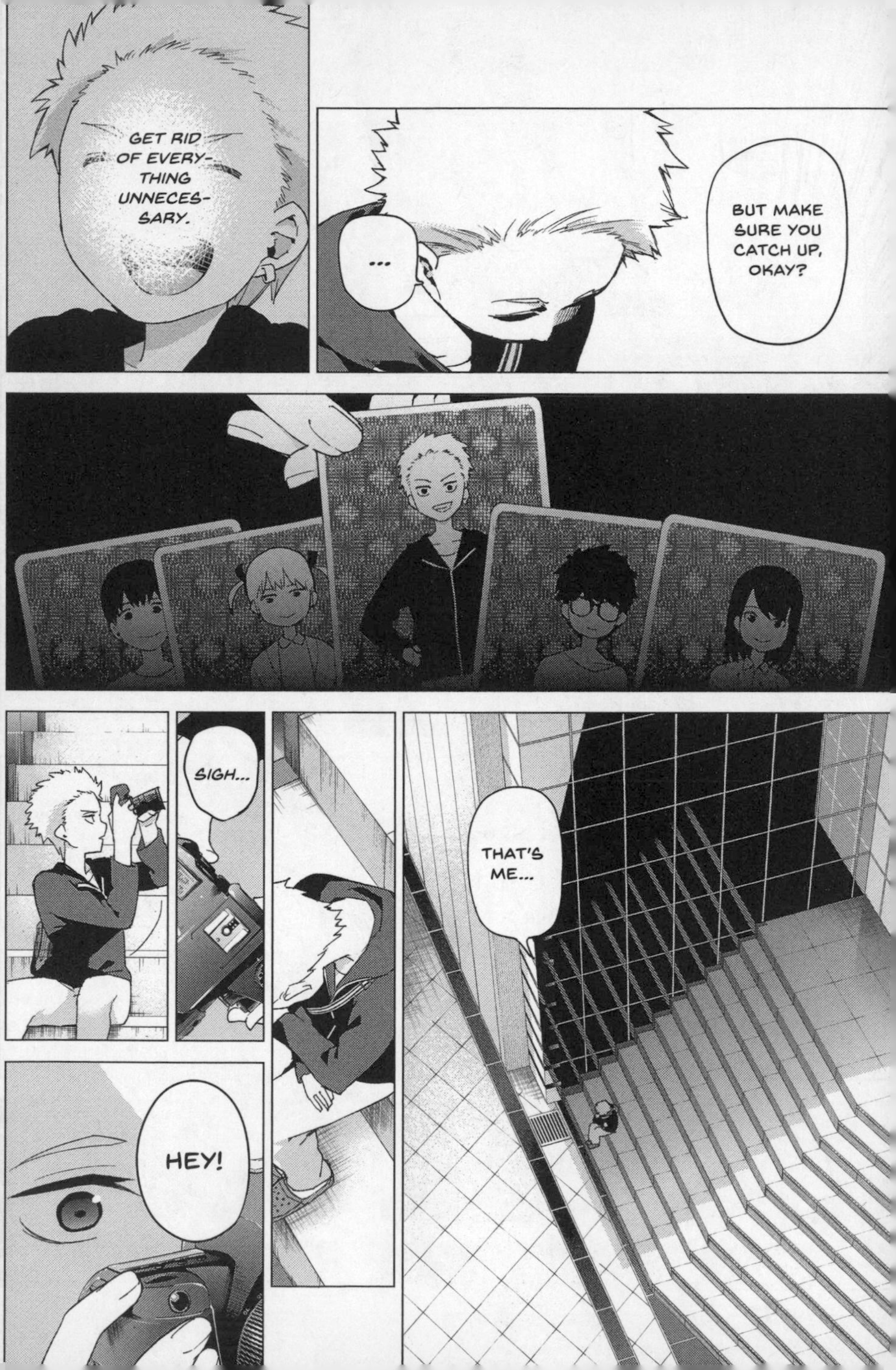
BUT MAKE SURE YOU CATCH UP, OKAY?
...
GET RID OF EVERY-THING UNNECES-SARY.
THAT'S ME...
SIGH...
HEY!

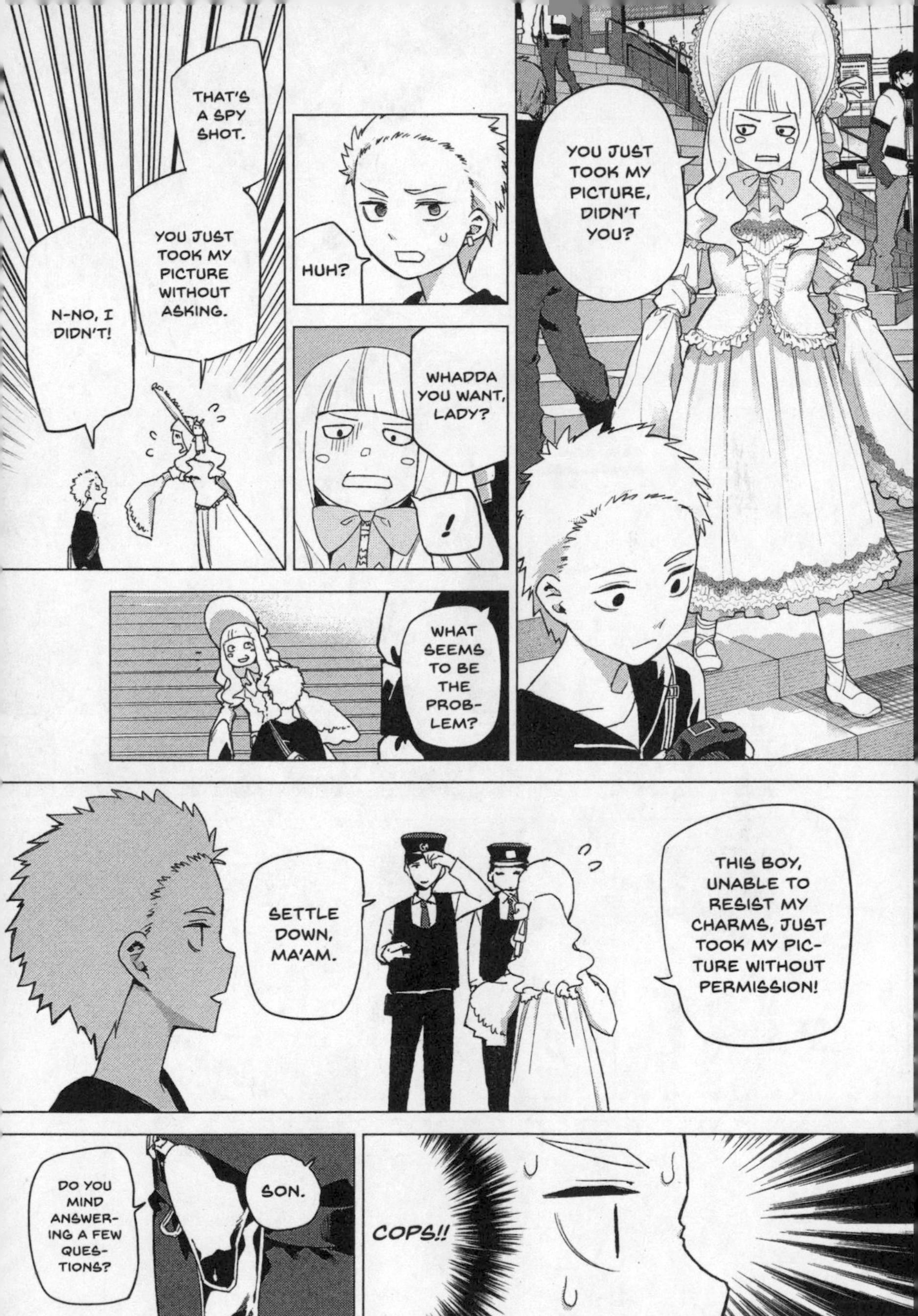
YOU JUST TOOK MY PICTURE, DIDN'T YOU?
HUH?
WHADDA YOU WANT, LADY?
!
THAT'S A SPY SHOT.
YOU JUST TOOK MY PICTURE WITHOUT ASKING.
N-NO, I DIDN'T!
WHAT SEEMS TO BE THE PROBLEM?
THIS BOY, UNABLE TO RESIST MY CHARMS, JUST TOOK MY PICTURE WITHOUT PERMISSION!
SETTLE DOWN, MA'AM.
COPS!!
SON.
DO YOU MIND ANSWERING A FEW QUESTIONS?

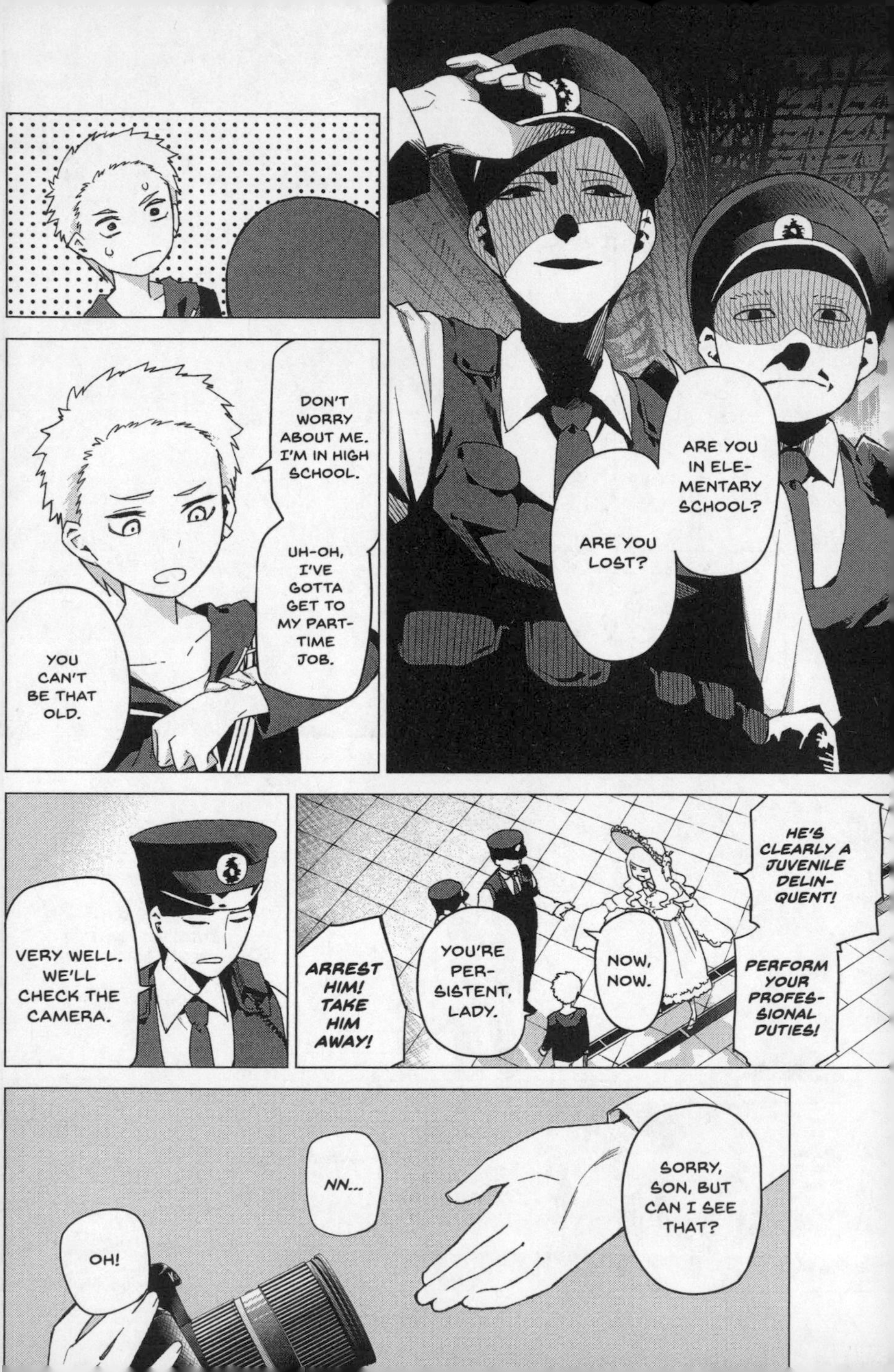
ARE YOU IN ELEMENTARY SCHOOL?
ARE YOU LOST?
DON'T WORRY ABOUT ME. I'M IN HIGH SCHOOL.
UH-OH, I'VE GOTTA GET TO MY PART-TIME JOB.
YOU CAN'T BE THAT OLD.
HE'S CLEARLY A JUVENILE DELINQUENT!
PERFORM YOUR PROFESSIONAL DUTIES!
NOW, NOW.
YOU'RE PERSISTENT, LADY.
ARREST HIM! TAKE HIM AWAY!
VERY WELL. WE'LL CHECK THE CAMERA.
SORRY, SON, BUT CAN I SEE THAT?
NN...
OH!

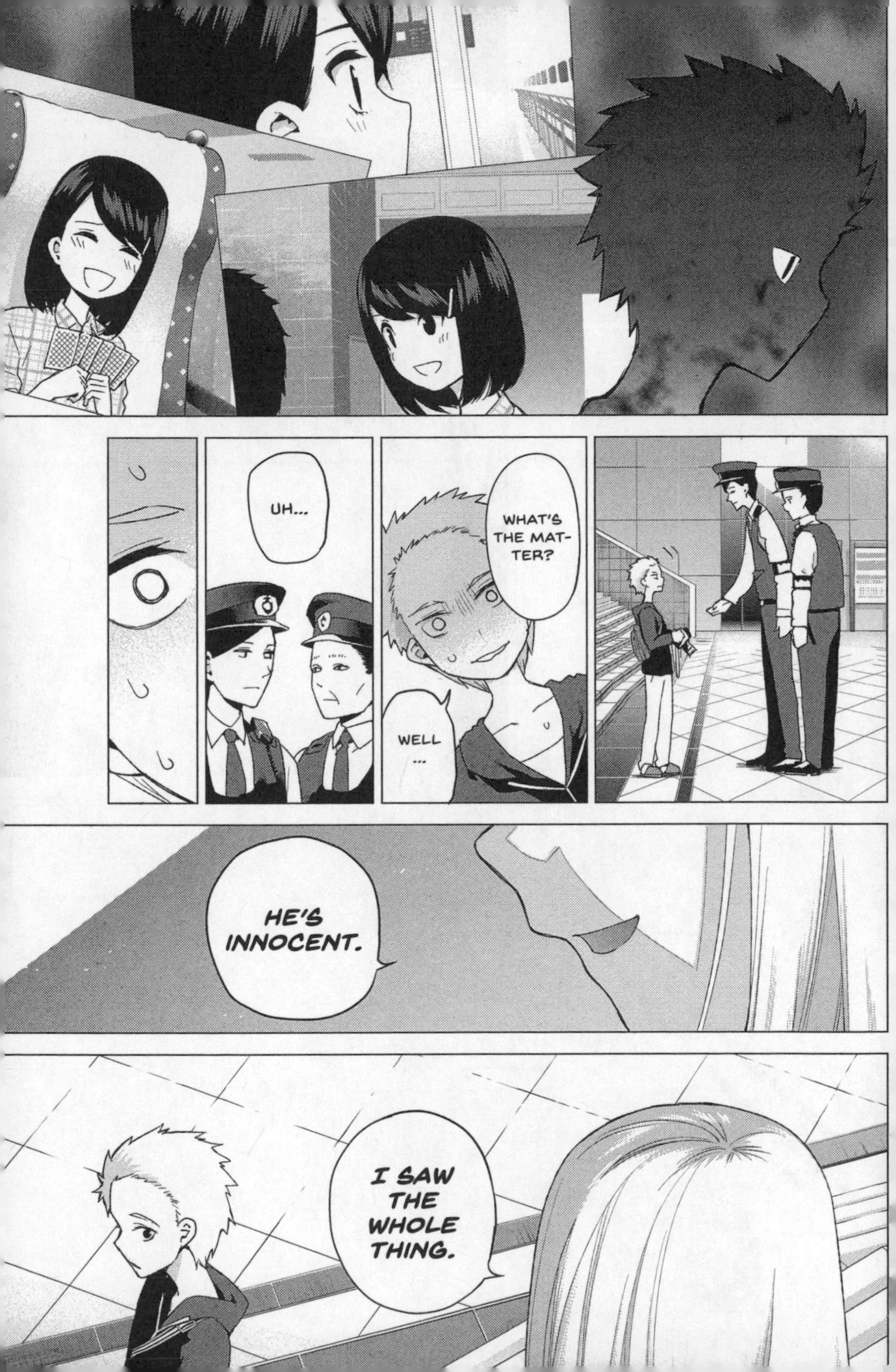
WHAT'S THE MAT-TER?
WELL ...
UH...
HE'S INNOCENT.
I SAW THE WHOLE THING.

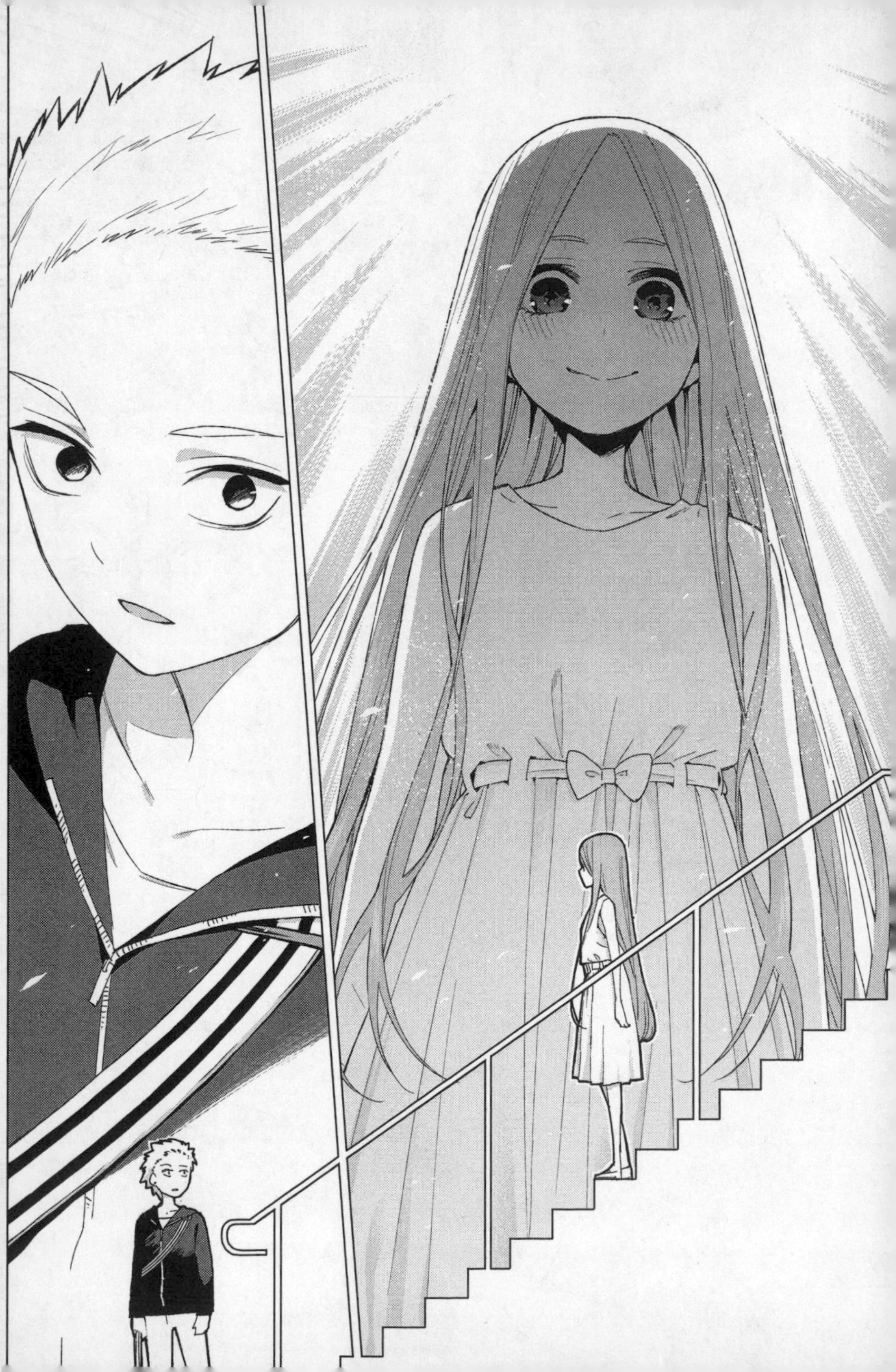

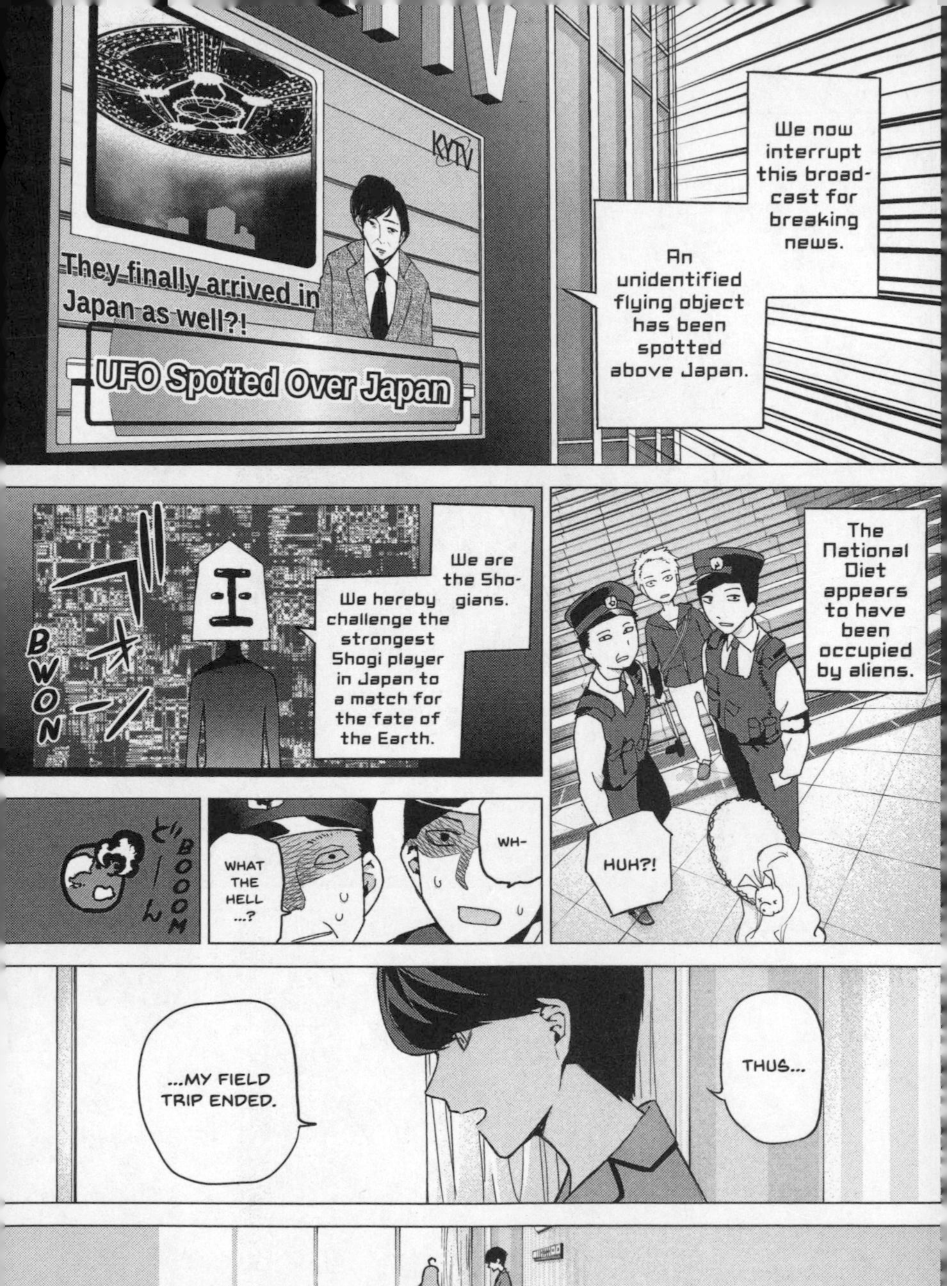

We now interrupt this broadcast for breaking news.
An unidentified flying object has been spotted above Japan.
KYTV
They finally arrived in Japan as well?!
UFO Spotted Over Japan
The National Diet appears to have been occupied by aliens.
HUH?!
We are the Shogians.
We hereby challenge the strongest Shogi player in Japan to a match for the fate of the Earth.
BWON
WH-
WHAT THE HELL ...?
BOOOM
THUS...
...MY FIELD TRIP ENDED.

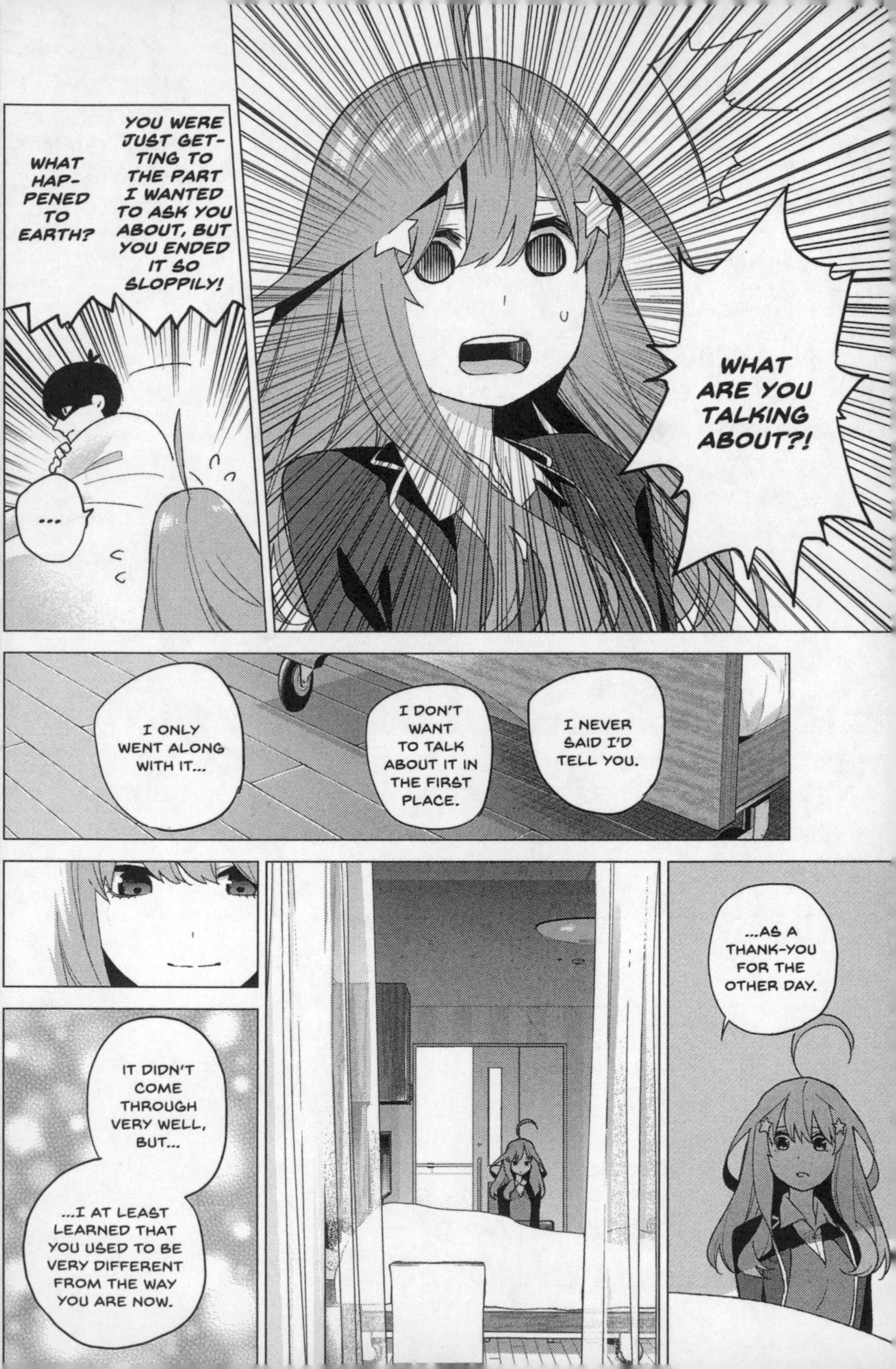
WHAT ARE YOU TALKING ABOUT?!
YOU WERE JUST GETTING TO THE PART I WANTED TO ASK YOU ABOUT, BUT YOU ENDED IT SO SLOPPILY!
WHAT HAPPENED TO EARTH?
...
I NEVER SAID I'D TELL YOU.
I DON'T WANT TO TALK ABOUT IT IN THE FIRST PLACE.
I ONLY WENT ALONG WITH IT...
...AS A THANK-YOU FOR THE OTHER DAY.
IT DIDN'T COME THROUGH VERY WELL, BUT...
...I AT LEAST LEARNED THAT YOU USED TO BE VERY DIFFERENT FROM THE WAY YOU ARE NOW.

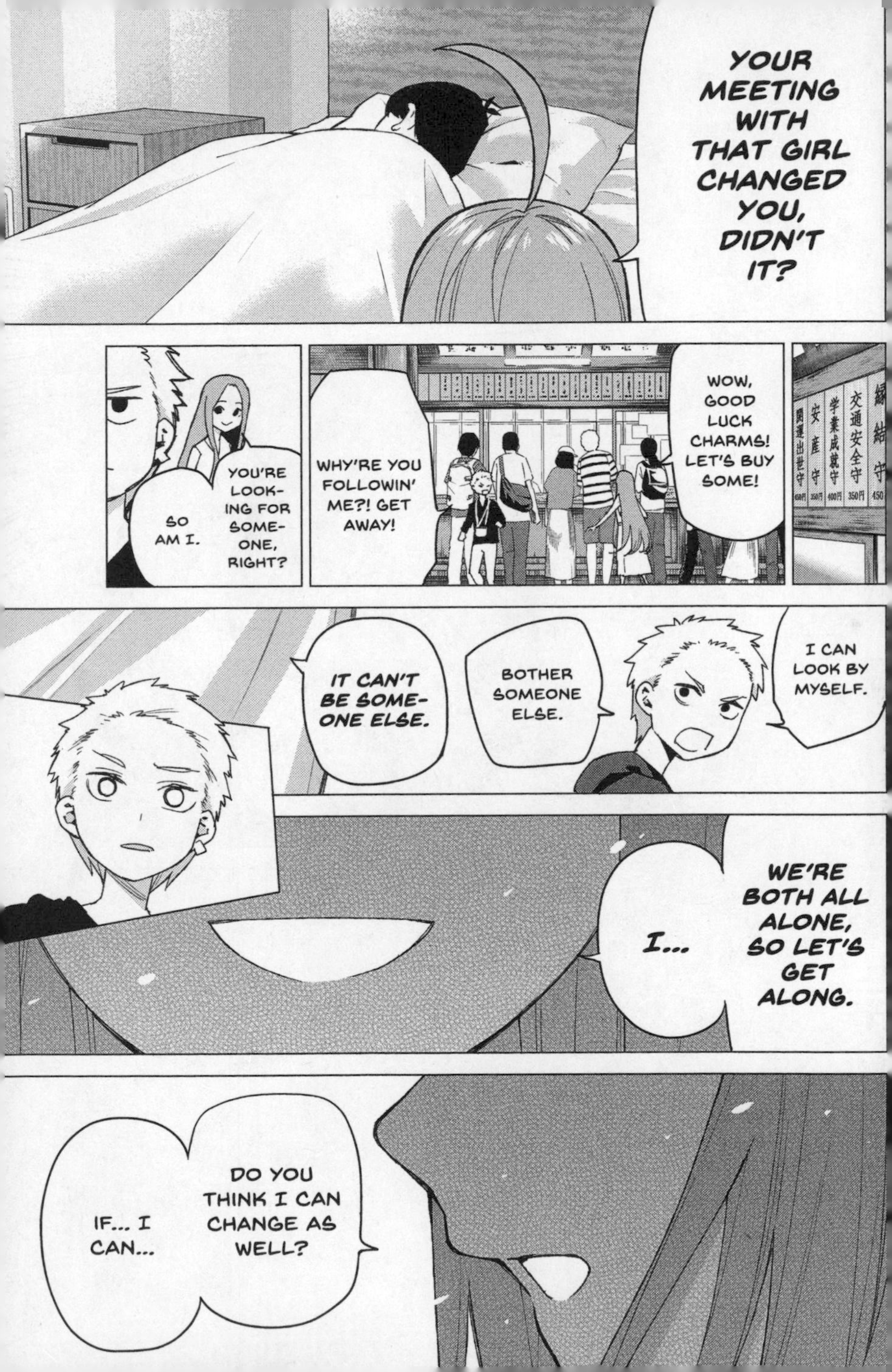
YOUR MEETING WITH THAT GIRL CHANGED YOU, DIDN'T IT?
WOW, GOOD LUCK CHARMS! LET'S BUY SOME!
WHY'RE YOU FOLLOWIN' ME?! GET AWAY!
YOU'RE LOOKING FOR SOMEONE, RIGHT?
SO AM I.
I CAN LOOK BY MYSELF.
BOTHER SOMEONE ELSE.
IT CAN'T BE SOMEONE ELSE.
WE'RE BOTH ALL ALONE, SO LET'S GET ALONG.
I...
DO YOU THINK I CAN CHANGE AS WELL?
IF... I CAN...

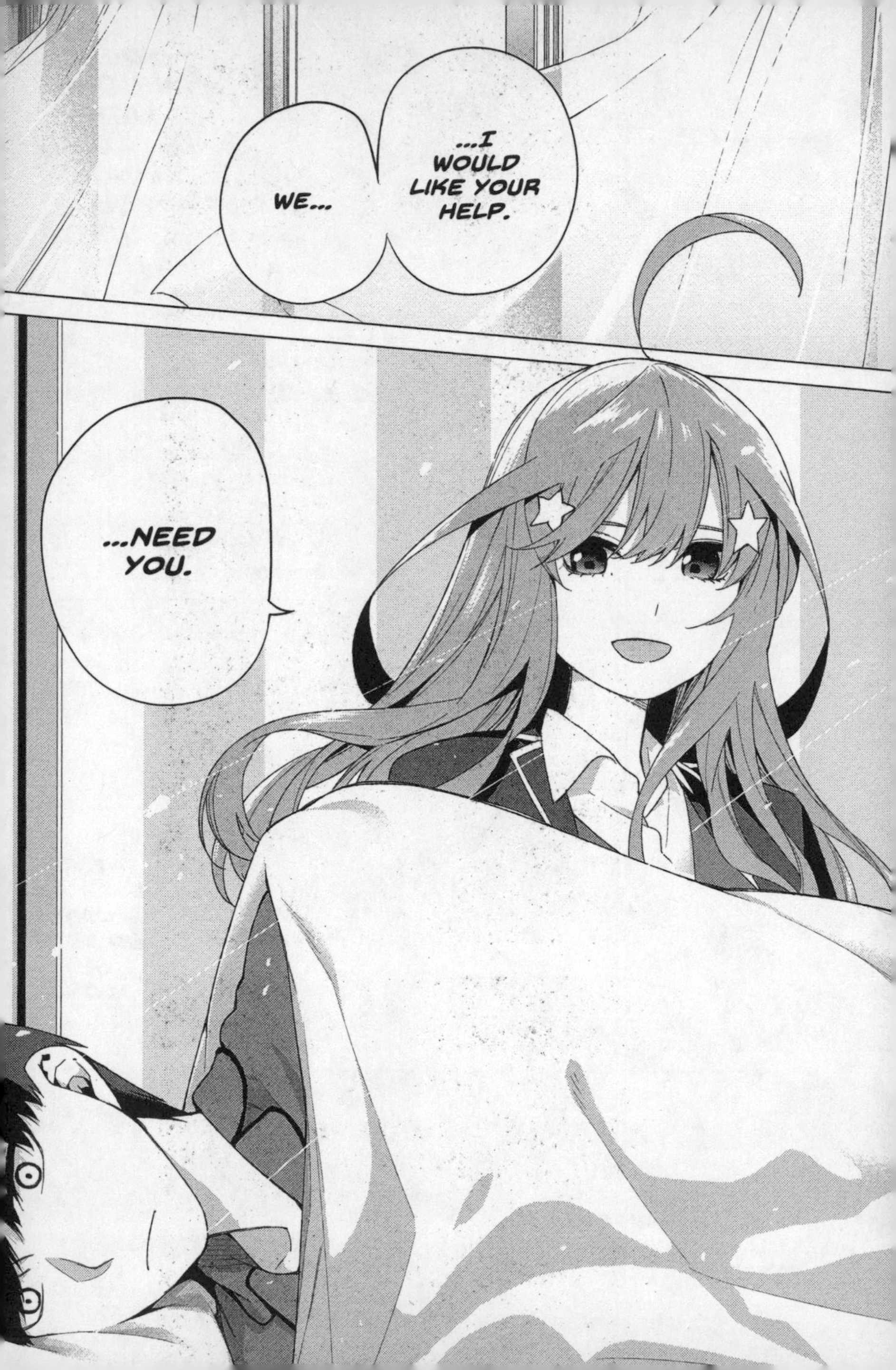
...I WOULD LIKE YOUR HELP.
WE...
...NEED YOU.

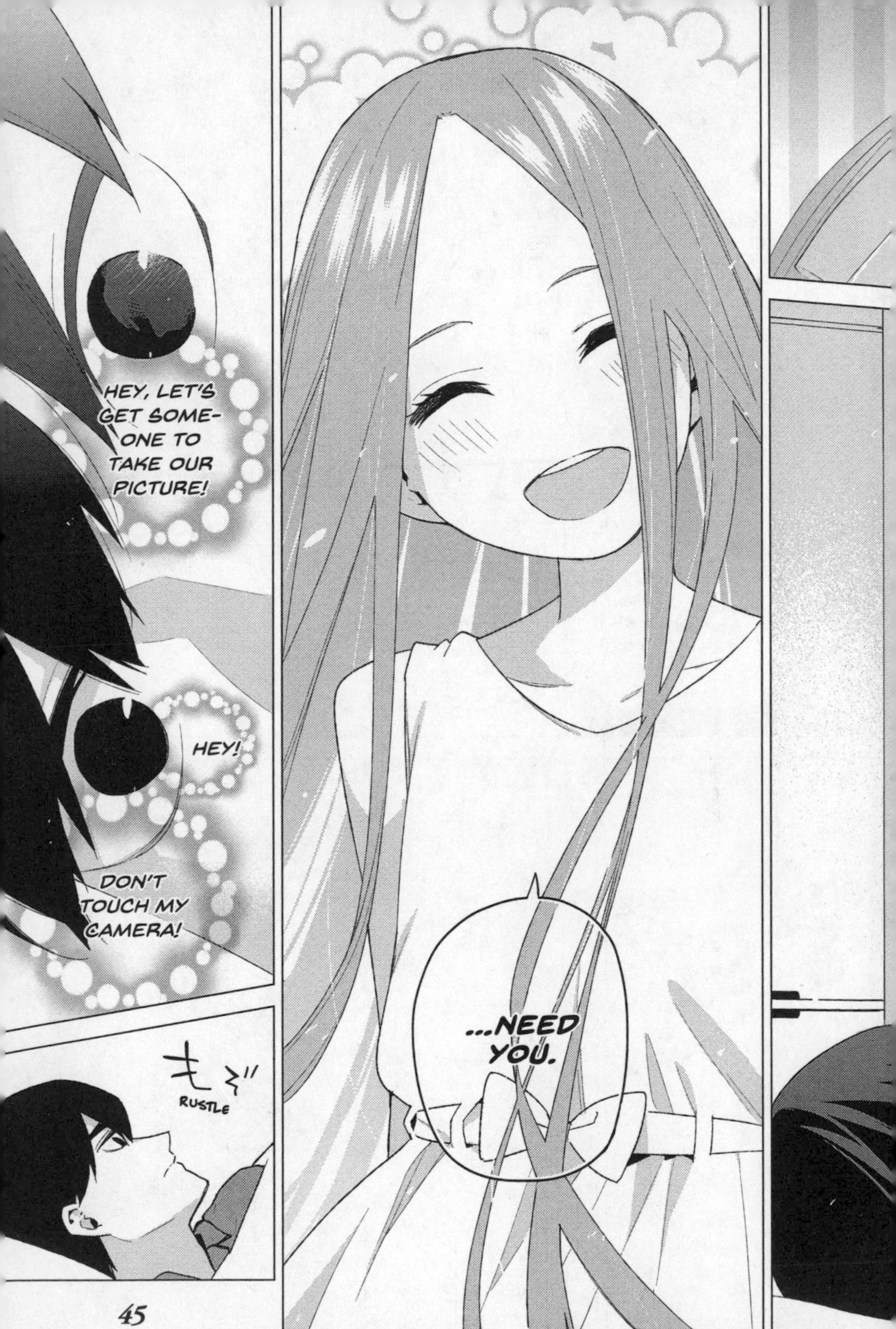
...NEED YOU.
HEY, LET'S GET SOME-ONE TO TAKE OUR PICTURE!
HEY!
DON'T TOUCH MY CAMERA!
もぞ
RUSTLE

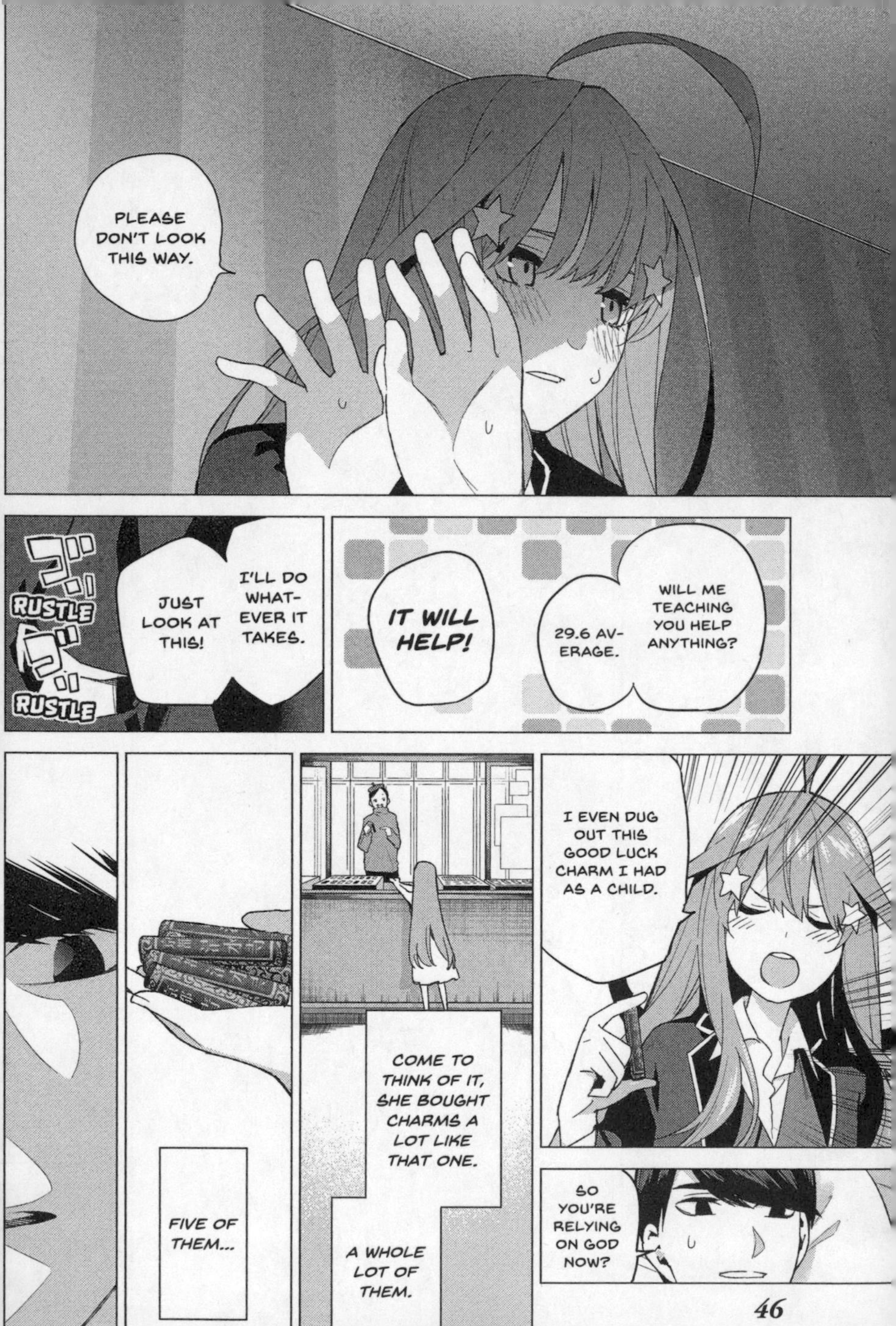
PLEASE DON'T LOOK THIS WAY.
WILL ME TEACHING YOU HELP ANYTHING?
29.6 AVERAGE.
IT WILL HELP!
I'LL DO WHATEVER IT TAKES.
JUST LOOK AT THIS!
RUSTLE
RUSTLE
I EVEN DUG OUT THIS GOOD LUCK CHARM I HAD AS A CHILD.
SO YOU'RE RELYING ON GOD NOW?
COME TO THINK OF IT, SHE BOUGHT CHARMS A LOT LIKE THAT ONE.
A WHOLE LOT OF THEM.
FIVE OF THEM...

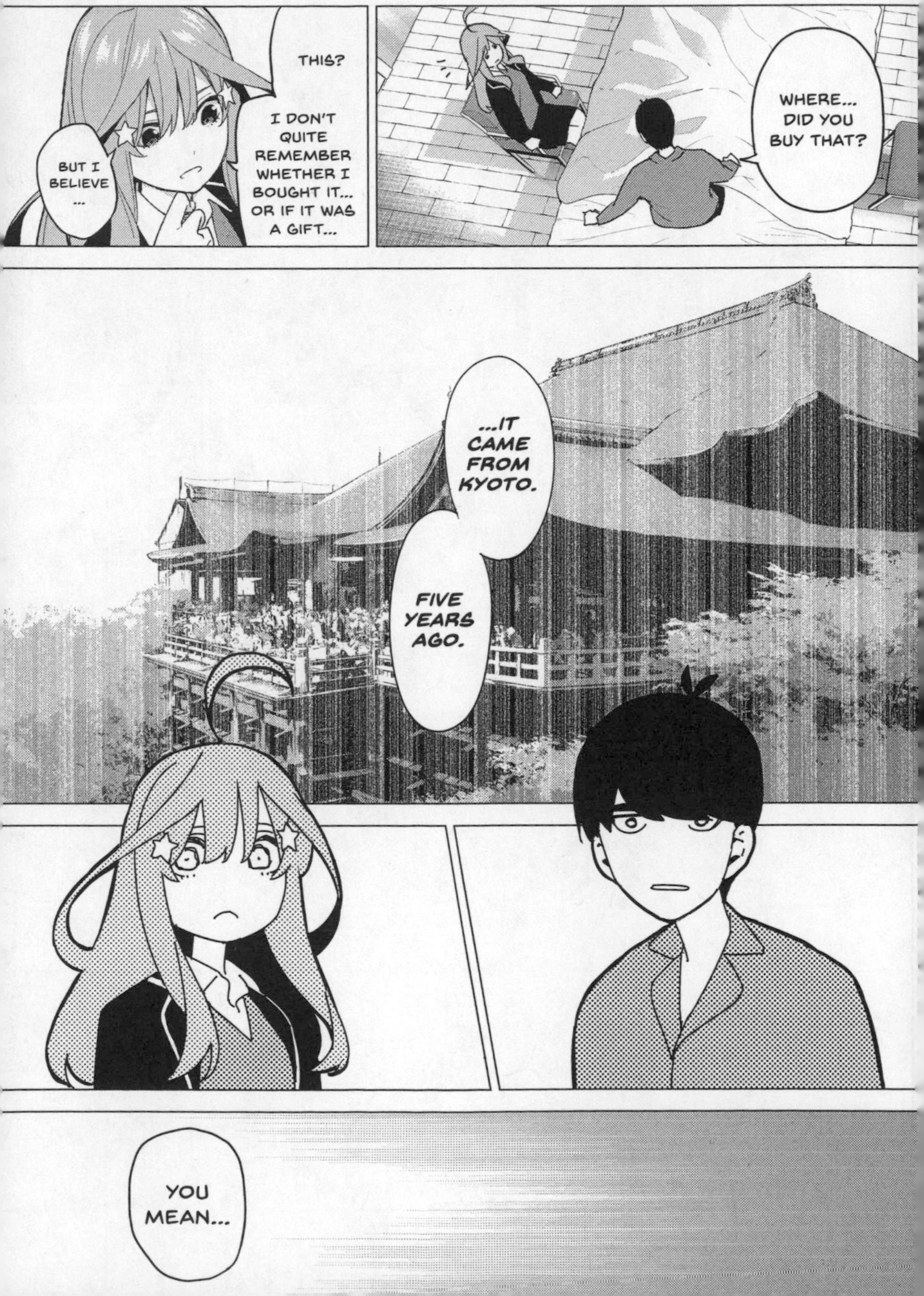
WHERE... DID YOU BUY THAT?
THIS?
I DON'T QUITE REMEMBER WHETHER I BOUGHT IT... OR IF IT WAS A GIFT...
BUT I BELIEVE ...
...IT CAME FROM KYOTO.
FIVE YEARS AGO.
YOU MEAN...

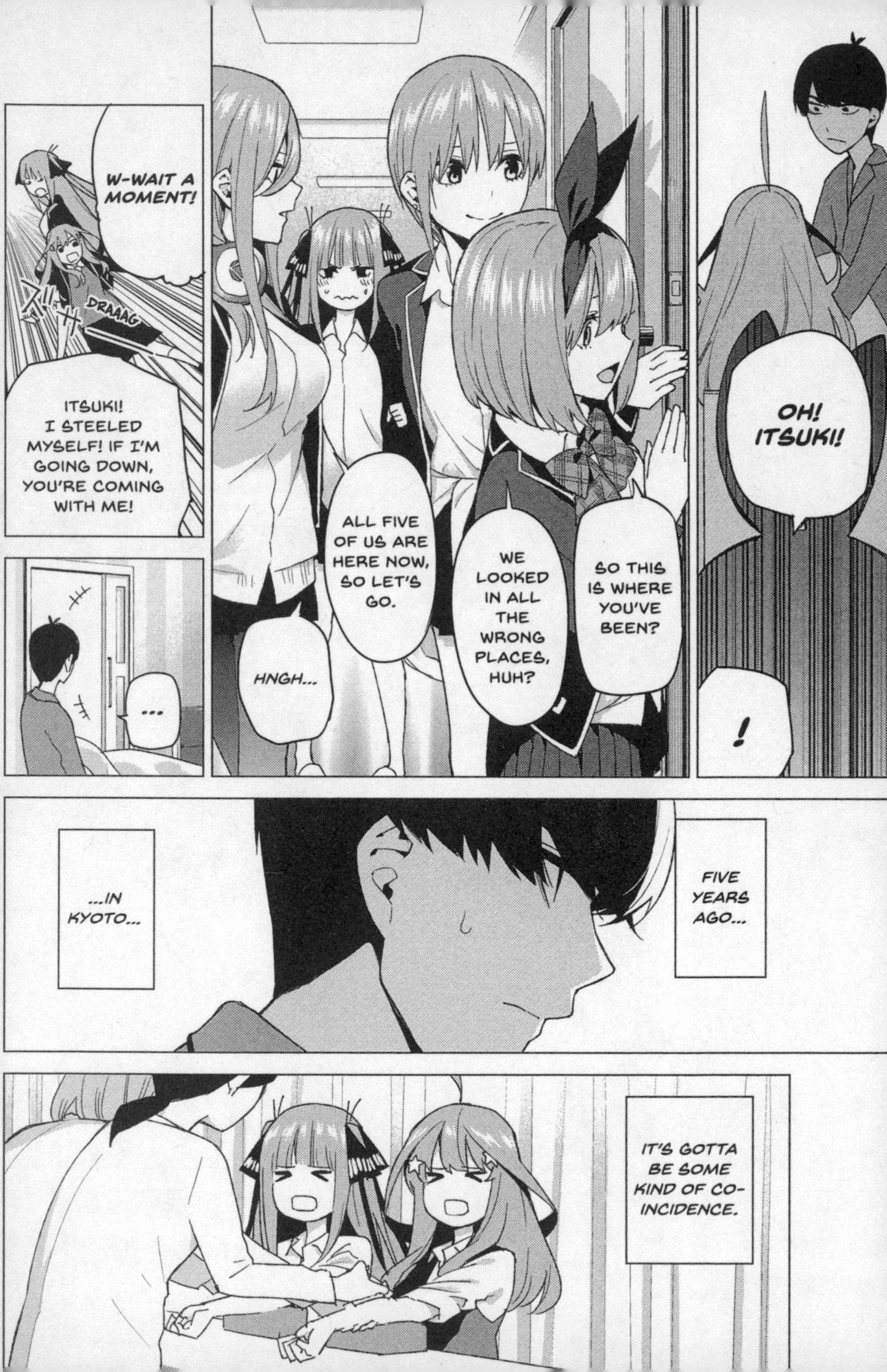
OH! ITSUKI!
!
SO THIS IS WHERE YOU'VE BEEN?
WE LOOKED IN ALL THE WRONG PLACES, HUH?
ALL FIVE OF US ARE HERE NOW, SO LET'S GO.
HNGH...
W-WAIT A MOMENT!
DRAAAG
ITSUKI! I STEELED MYSELF! IF I'M GOING DOWN, YOU'RE COMING WITH ME!
...
FIVE YEARS AGO...
...IN KYOTO...
IT'S GOTTA BE SOME KIND OF CO-INCIDENCE.

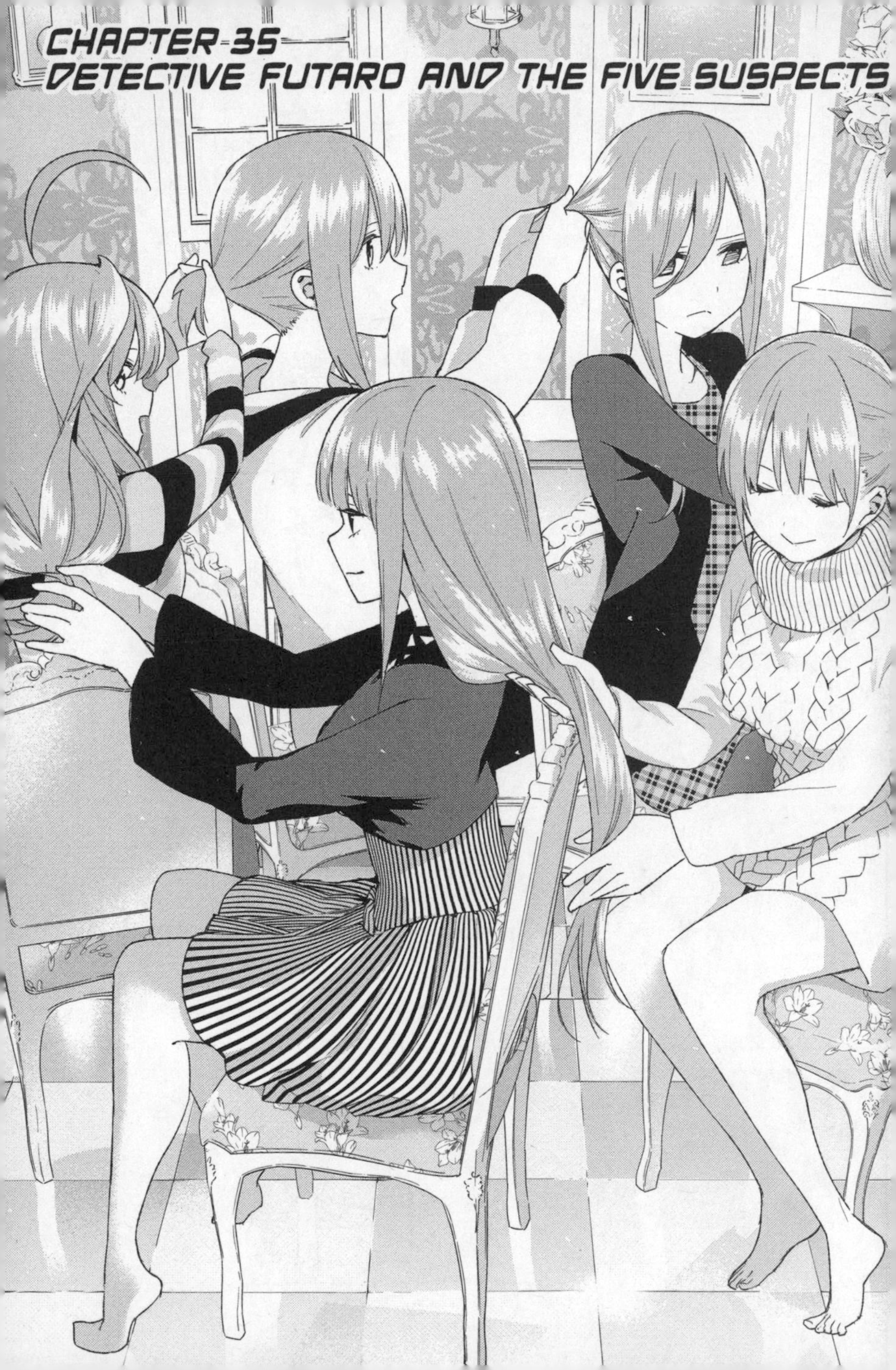
CHAPTER 35
DETECTIVE FUTARO AND THE FIVE SUSPECTS

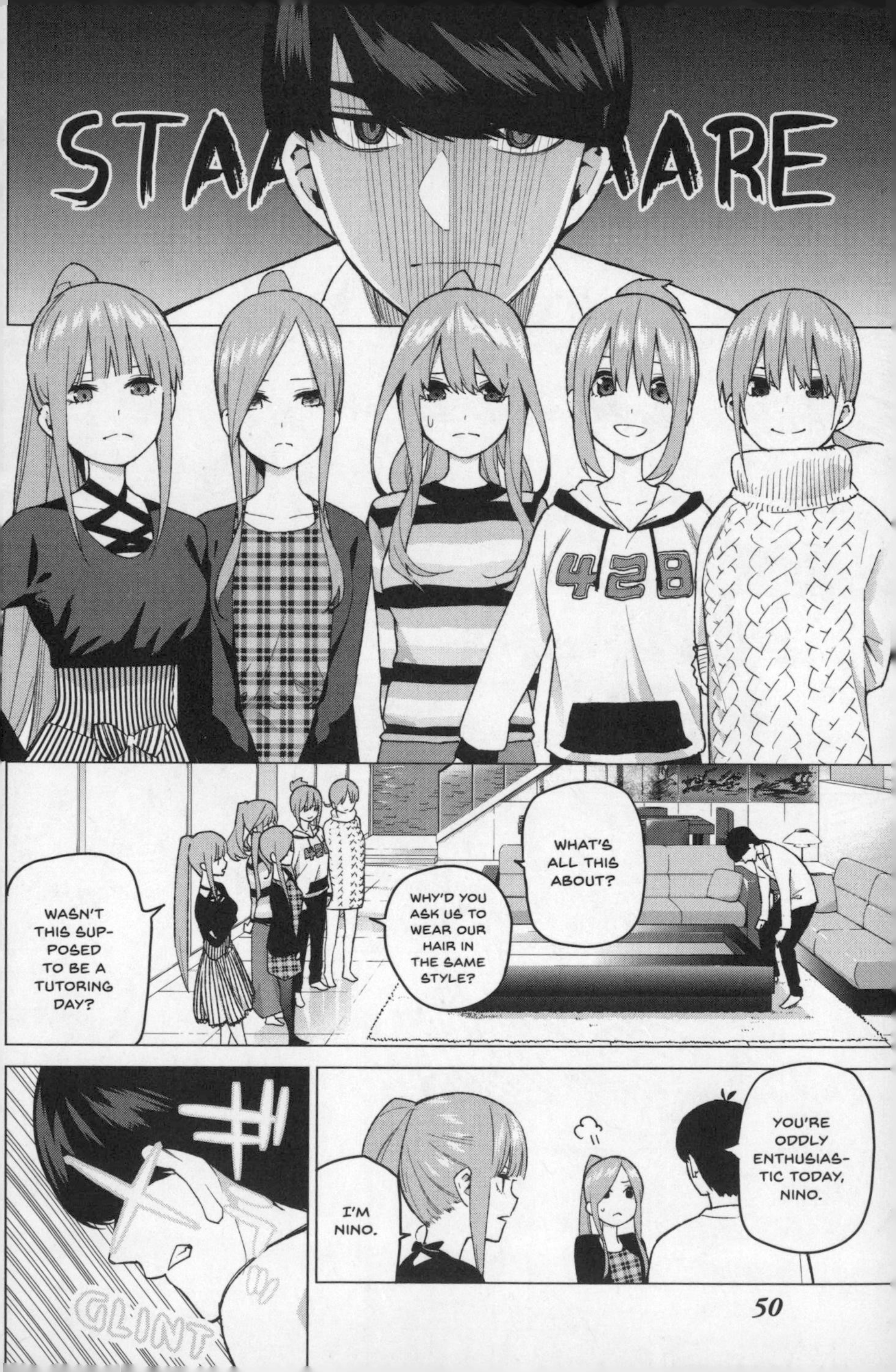
STAA AARE
WHAT'S ALL THIS ABOUT?
WHY'D YOU ASK US TO WEAR OUR HAIR IN THE SAME STYLE?
WASN'T THIS SUP-POSED TO BE A TUTORING DAY?
YOU'RE ODDLY ENTHUSIAS-TIC TODAY, NINO.
I'M NINO.
GLINT

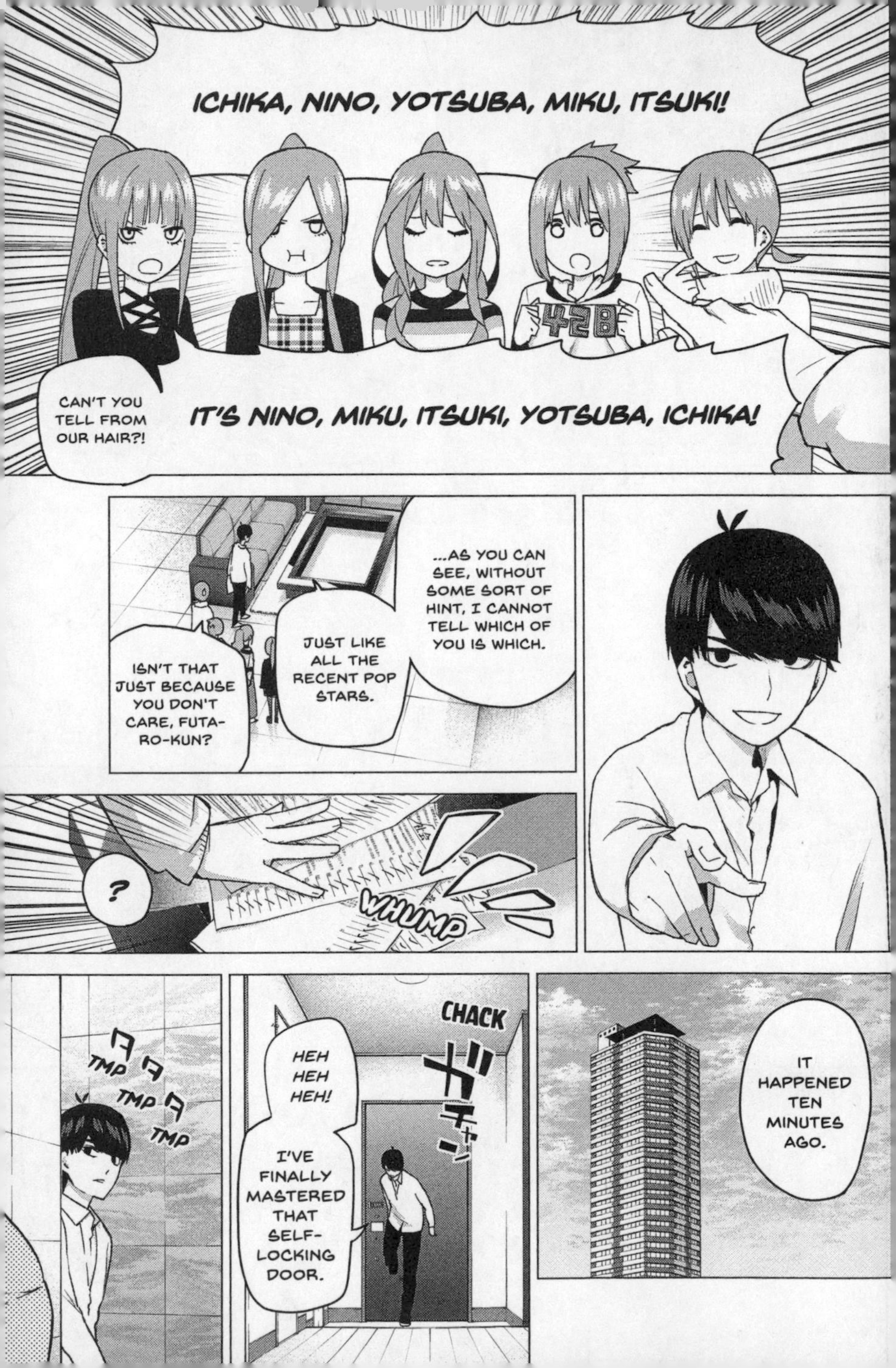
ICHIKA, NINO, YOTSUBA, MIKU, ITSUKI!
IT'S NINO, MIKU, ITSUKI, YOTSUBA, ICHIKA!
CAN'T YOU TELL FROM OUR HAIR?!
...AS YOU CAN SEE, WITHOUT SOME SORT OF HINT, I CANNOT TELL WHICH OF YOU IS WHICH.
JUST LIKE ALL THE RECENT POP STARS.
ISN'T THAT JUST BECAUSE YOU DON'T CARE, FUTA-RO-KUN?
?
WHUMP
IT HAPPENED TEN MINUTES AGO.
CHACK
HEH HEH HEH!
I'VE FINALLY MASTERED THAT SELF-LOCKING DOOR.
TMP
TMP
TMP

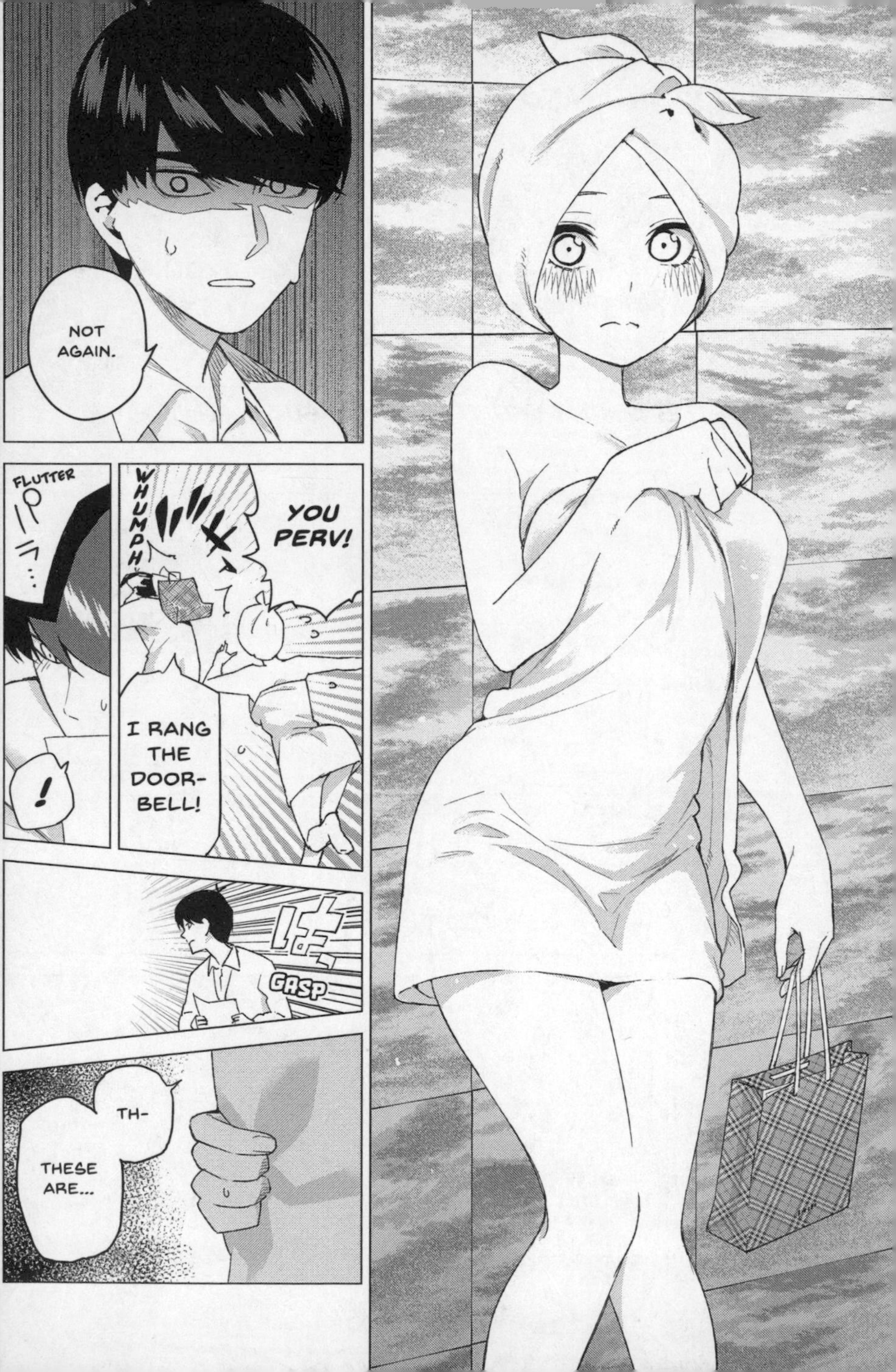
NOT AGAIN.
YOU PERV!
WHUMPH
I RANG THE DOOR-BELL!
FLUTTER
!
GASP
TH-
THESE ARE...

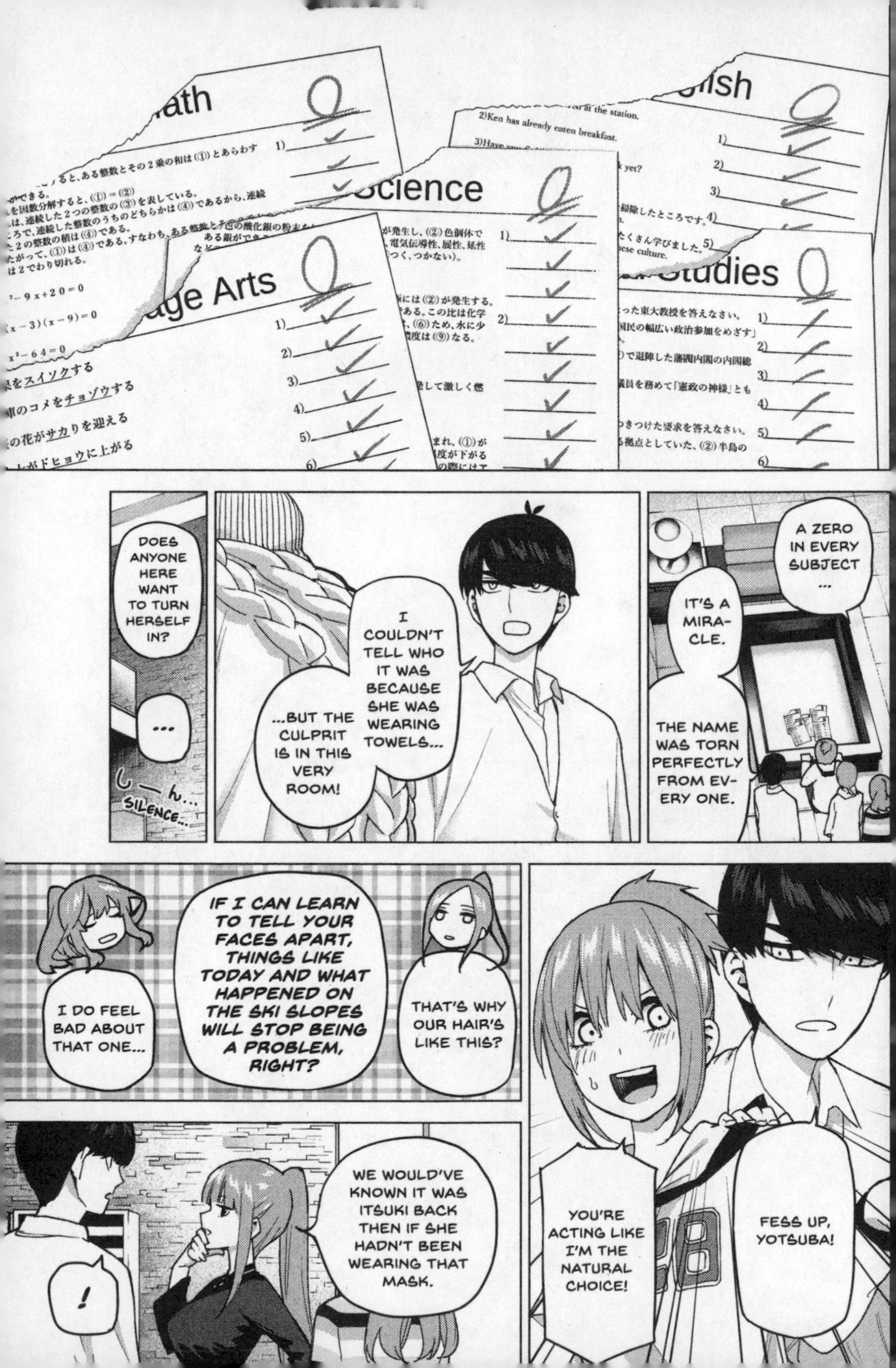
Science
2)Ken has already eaten breakfast.
A ZERO IN EVERY SUBJECT...
IT'S A MIRACLE.
THE NAME WAS TORN PERFECTLY FROM EVERY ONE.
I COULDN'T TELL WHO IT WAS BECAUSE SHE WAS WEARING TOWELS...
...BUT THE CULPRIT IS IN THIS VERY ROOM!
DOES ANYONE HERE WANT TO TURN HERSELF IN?
...
しーん…
SILENCE...
FESS UP, YOTSUBA!
YOU'RE ACTING LIKE I'M THE NATURAL CHOICE!
IF I CAN LEARN TO TELL YOUR FACES APART, THINGS LIKE TODAY AND WHAT HAPPENED ON THE SKI SLOPES WILL STOP BEING A PROBLEM, RIGHT?
THAT'S WHY OUR HAIR'S LIKE THIS?
I DO FEEL BAD ABOUT THAT ONE...
WE WOULD'VE KNOWN IT WAS ITSUKI BACK THEN IF SHE HADN'T BEEN WEARING THAT MASK.
!

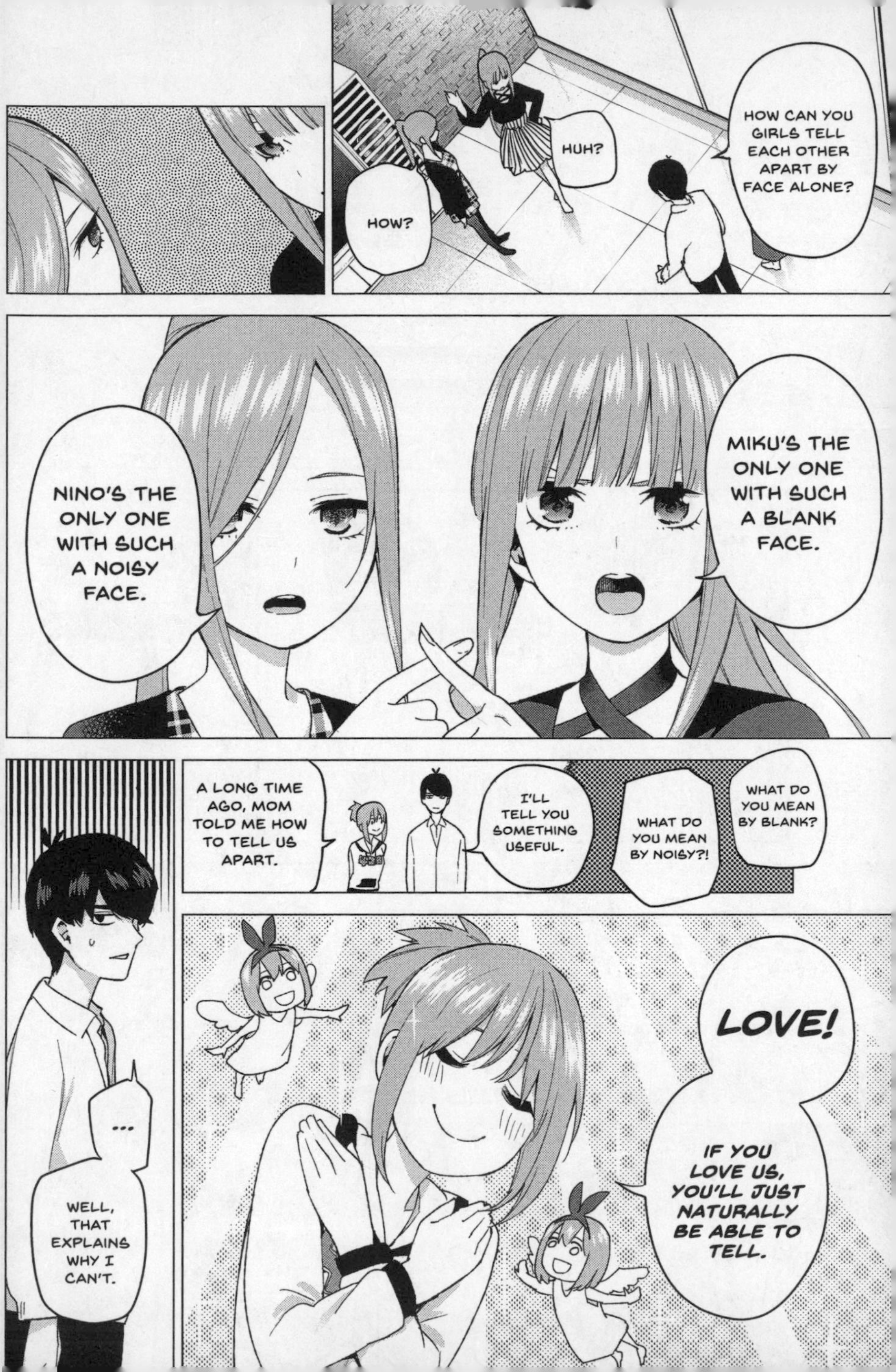

HOW CAN YOU GIRLS TELL EACH OTHER APART BY FACE ALONE?
HUH?
HOW?
MIKU'S THE ONLY ONE WITH SUCH A BLANK FACE.
NINO'S THE ONLY ONE WITH SUCH A NOISY FACE.
WHAT DO YOU MEAN BY BLANK?
WHAT DO YOU MEAN BY NOISY?!
I'LL TELL YOU SOMETHING USEFUL.
A LONG TIME AGO, MOM TOLD ME HOW TO TELL US APART.
LOVE!
IF YOU LOVE US, YOU'LL JUST NATURALLY BE ABLE TO TELL.
...
WELL, THAT EXPLAINS WHY I CAN'T.

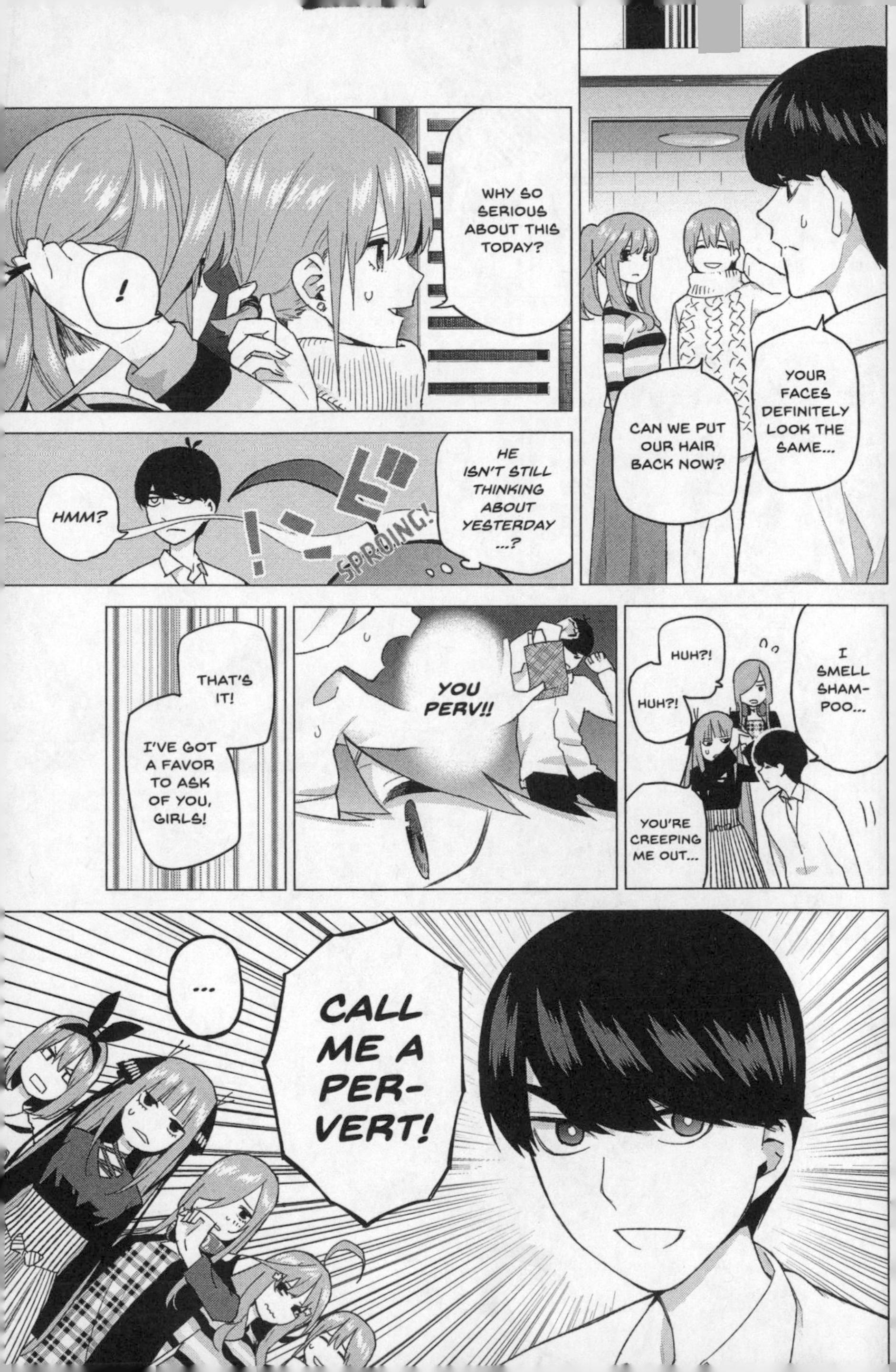
YOUR FACES DEFINITELY LOOK THE SAME...
CAN WE PUT OUR HAIR BACK NOW?
WHY SO SERIOUS ABOUT THIS TODAY?
!
HE ISN'T STILL THINKING ABOUT YESTERDAY ...?
SPROING!
HMM?
I SMELL SHAMPOO...
HUH?!
HUH?!
YOU'RE CREEPING ME OUT...
YOU PERV!!
THAT'S IT!
I'VE GOT A FAVOR TO ASK OF YOU, GIRLS!
CALL ME A PER-VERT!
...

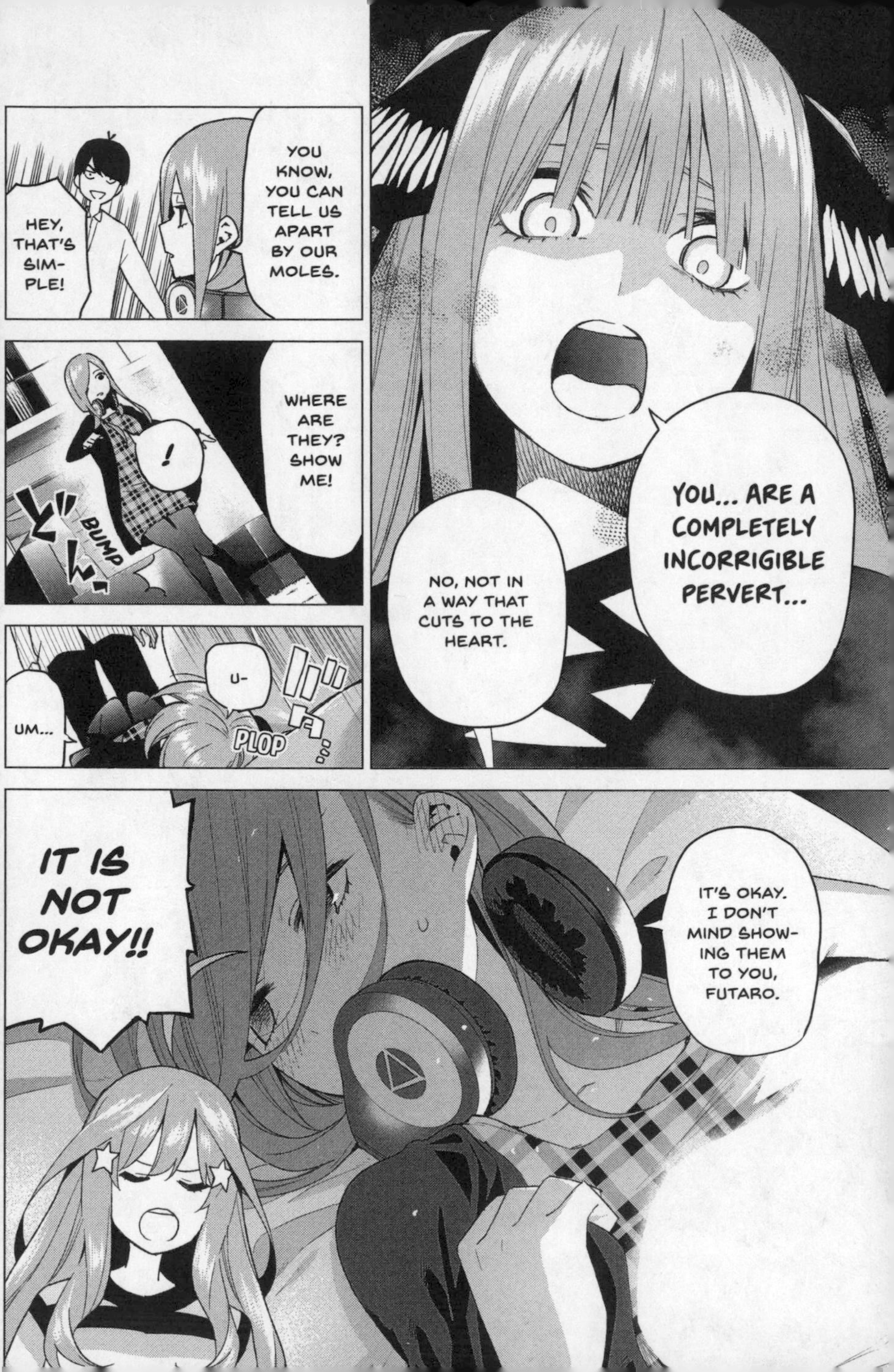
YOU... ARE A COMPLETELY INCORRIGIBLE PERVERT...
NO, NOT IN A WAY THAT CUTS TO THE HEART.
YOU KNOW, YOU CAN TELL US APART BY OUR MOLES.
HEY, THAT'S SIM-PLE!
WHERE ARE THEY? SHOW ME!
!
BUMP
U-
PLOP
UM...
IT'S OKAY. I DON'T MIND SHOWING THEM TO YOU, FUTARO.
IT IS NOT OKAY!!

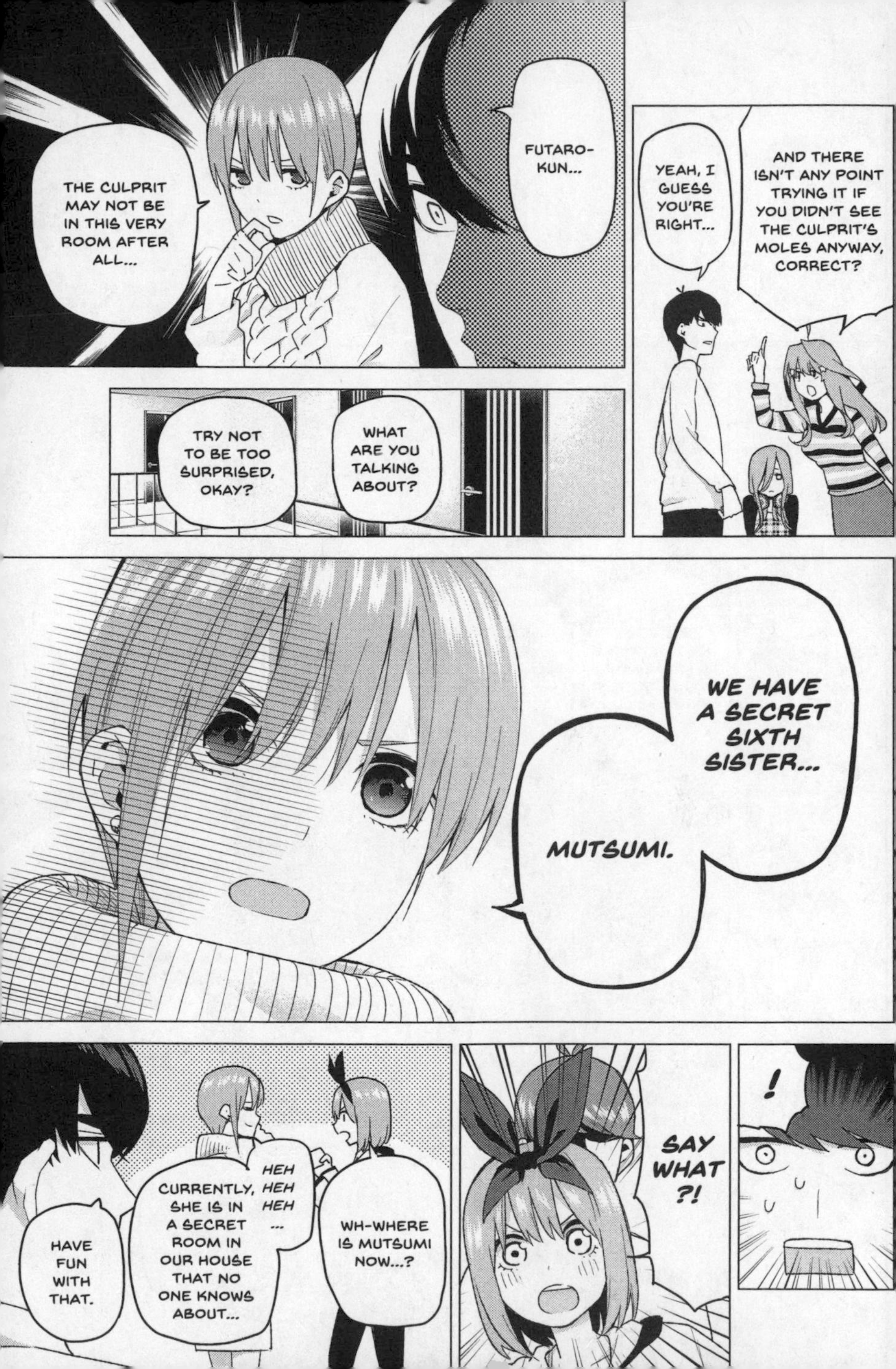
AND THERE ISN'T ANY POINT TRYING IT IF YOU DIDN'T SEE THE CULPRIT'S MOLES ANYWAY, CORRECT?
YEAH, I GUESS YOU'RE RIGHT...
FUTARO-KUN...
THE CULPRIT MAY NOT BE IN THIS VERY ROOM AFTER ALL...
WHAT ARE YOU TALKING ABOUT?
TRY NOT TO BE TOO SURPRISED, OKAY?
WE HAVE A SECRET SIXTH SISTER...
MUTSUMI.
!
SAY WHAT?!
WH-WHERE IS MUTSUMI NOW...?
HEH HEH HEH ...
CURRENTLY, SHE IS IN A SECRET ROOM IN OUR HOUSE THAT NO ONE KNOWS ABOUT...
HAVE FUN WITH THAT.

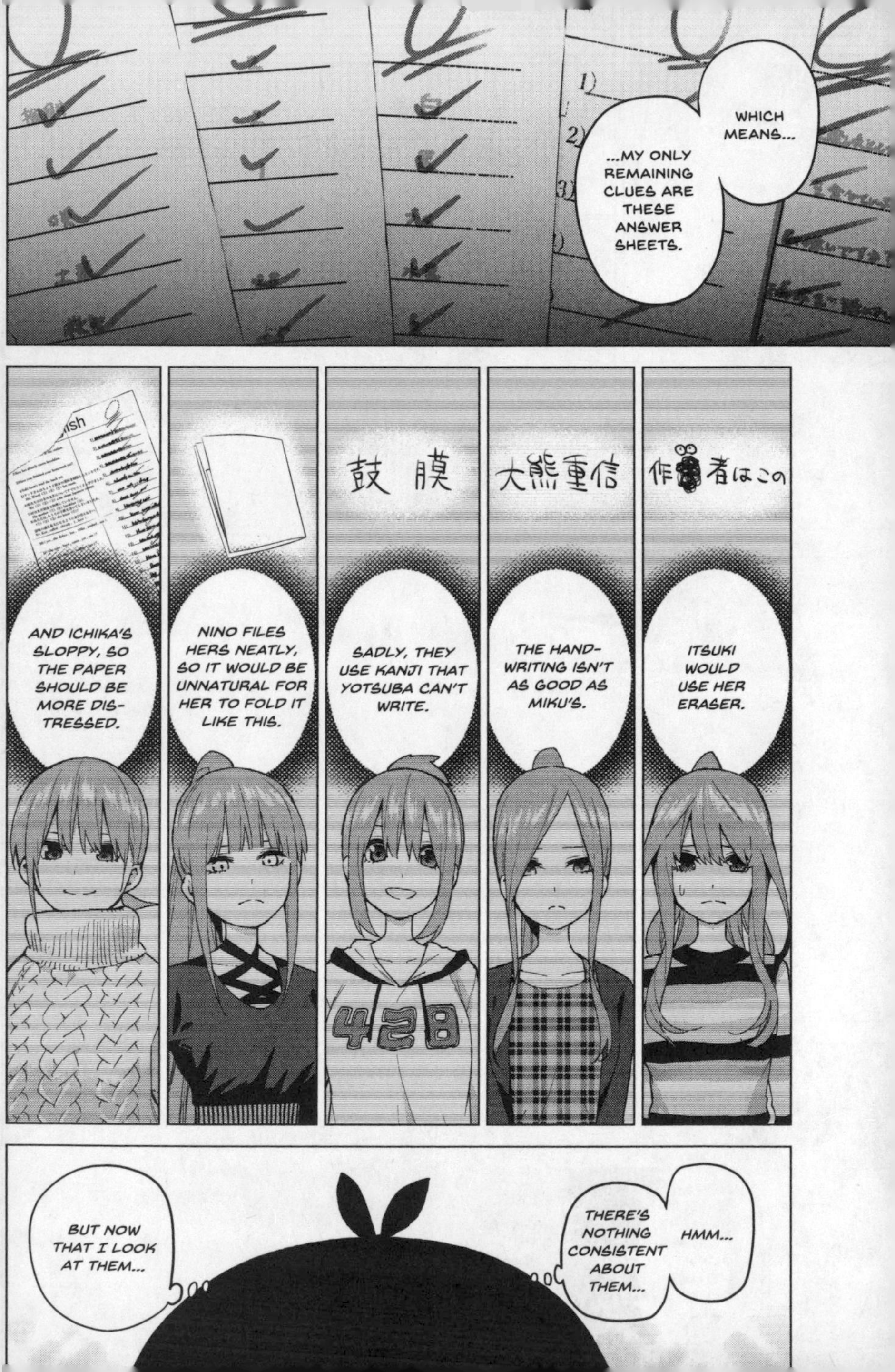
WHICH MEANS...
...MY ONLY REMAINING CLUES ARE THESE ANSWER SHEETS.
作者はこの
ITSUKI WOULD USE HER ERASER.
大熊重信
THE HAND-WRITING ISN'T AS GOOD AS MIKU'S.
鼓 膜
SADLY, THEY USE KANJI THAT YOTSUBA CAN'T WRITE.
NINO FILES HERS NEATLY, SO IT WOULD BE UNNATURAL FOR HER TO FOLD IT LIKE THIS.
AND ICHIKA'S SLOPPY, SO THE PAPER SHOULD BE MORE DIS-TRESSED.
HMM...
THERE'S NOTHING CONSISTENT ABOUT THEM...
BUT NOW THAT I LOOK AT THEM...

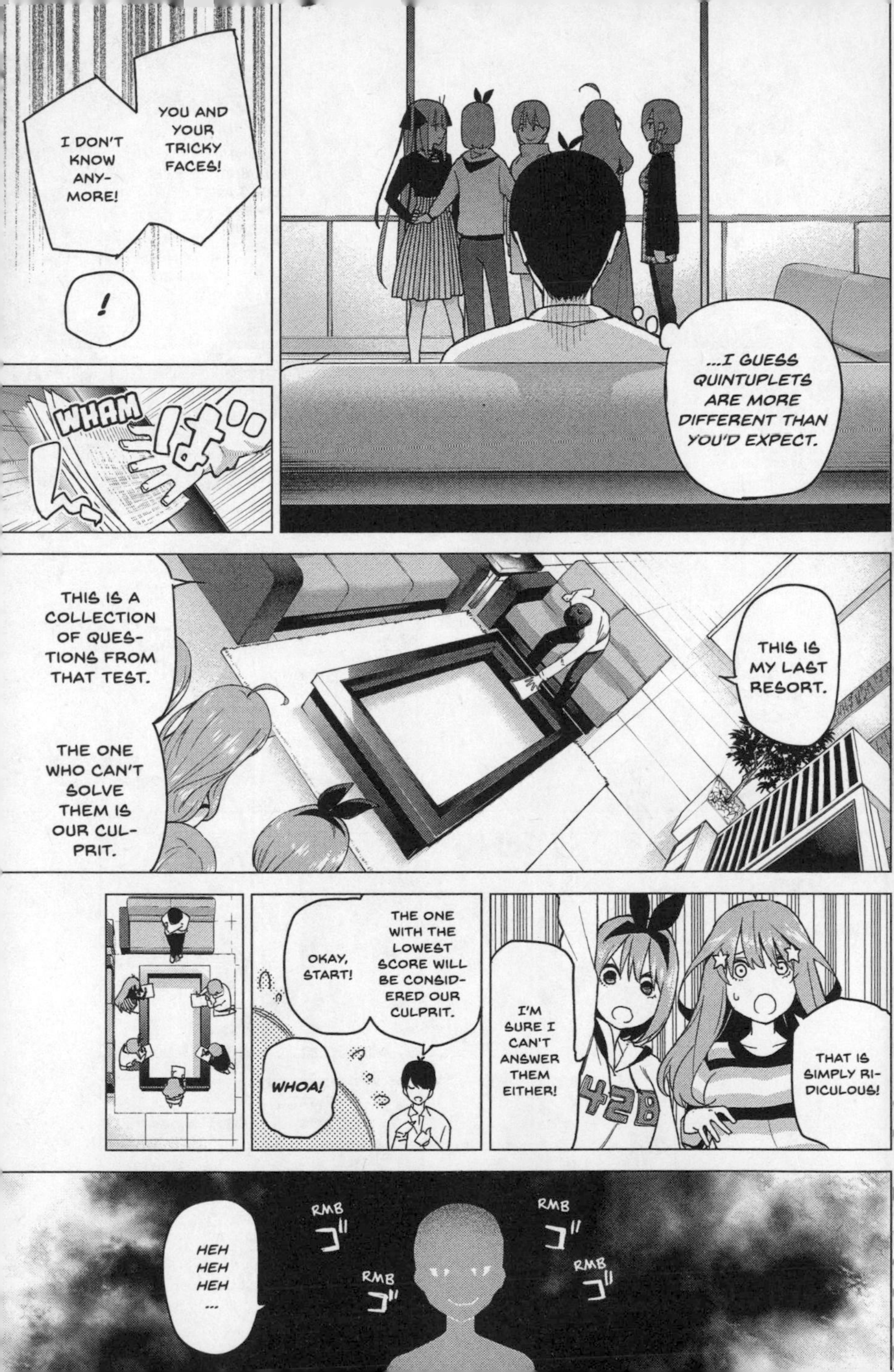
...I GUESS QUINTUPLETS ARE MORE DIFFERENT THAN YOU'D EXPECT.
YOU AND YOUR TRICKY FACES!
I DON'T KNOW ANY-MORE!
!
WHAM
THIS IS MY LAST RESORT.
THIS IS A COLLECTION OF QUES-TIONS FROM THAT TEST.
THE ONE WHO CAN'T SOLVE THEM IS OUR CUL-PRIT.
THAT IS SIMPLY RI-DICULOUS!
I'M SURE I CAN'T ANSWER THEM EITHER!
THE ONE WITH THE LOWEST SCORE WILL BE CONSID-ERED OUR CULPRIT.
OKAY, START!
WHOA!
RMB ゴ
RMB ゴ
RMB ゴ
RMB ゴ
HEH HEH HEH ...

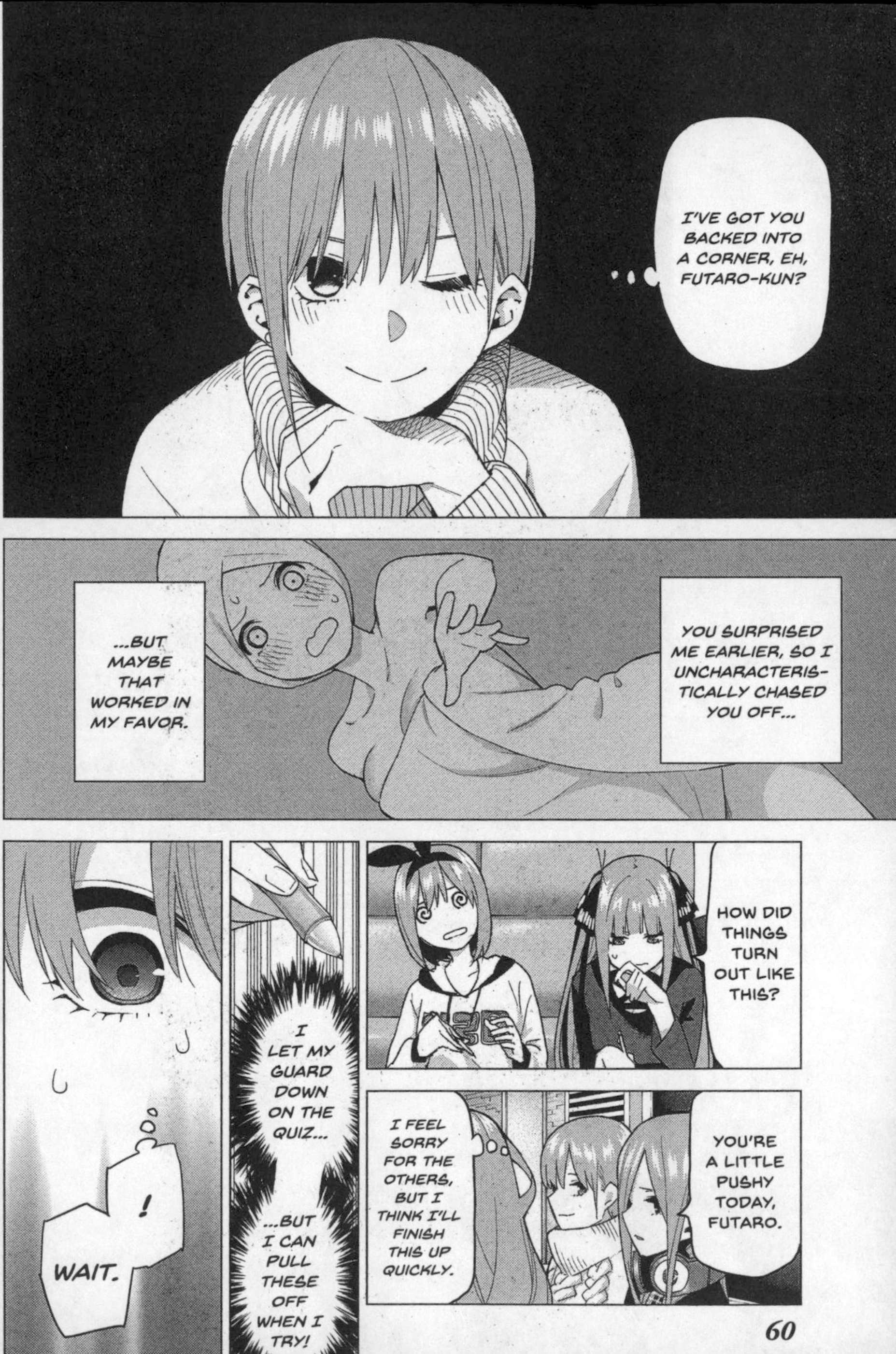

I'VE GOT YOU BACKED INTO A CORNER, EH, FUTARO-KUN?
YOU SURPRISED ME EARLIER, SO I UNCHARACTERIS-TICALLY CHASED YOU OFF...
...BUT MAYBE THAT WORKED IN MY FAVOR.
HOW DID THINGS TURN OUT LIKE THIS?
YOU'RE A LITTLE PUSHY TODAY, FUTARO.
I FEEL SORRY FOR THE OTHERS, BUT I THINK I'LL FINISH THIS UP QUICKLY.
I LET MY GUARD DOWN ON THE QUIZ...
...BUT I CAN PULL THESE OFF WHEN I TRY!
!
WAIT.

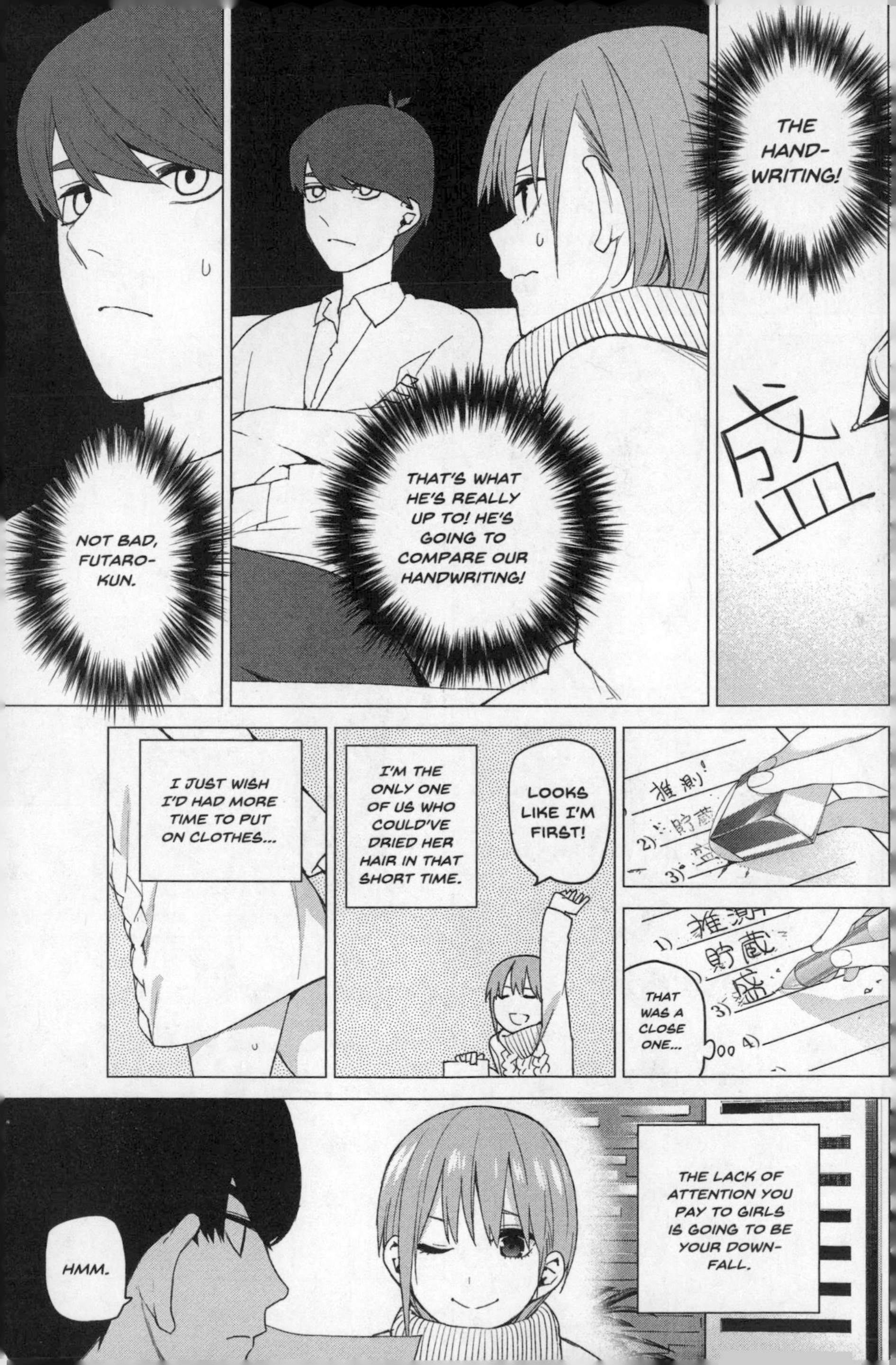
THE HAND-WRITING!
THAT'S WHAT HE'S REALLY UP TO! HE'S GOING TO COMPARE OUR HANDWRITING!
NOT BAD, FUTARO-KUN.
THAT WAS A CLOSE ONE...
LOOKS LIKE I'M FIRST!
I'M THE ONLY ONE OF US WHO COULD'VE DRIED HER HAIR IN THAT SHORT TIME.
I JUST WISH I'D HAD MORE TIME TO PUT ON CLOTHES...
THE LACK OF ATTENTION YOU PAY TO GIRLS IS GOING TO BE YOUR DOWN-FALL.
HMM.

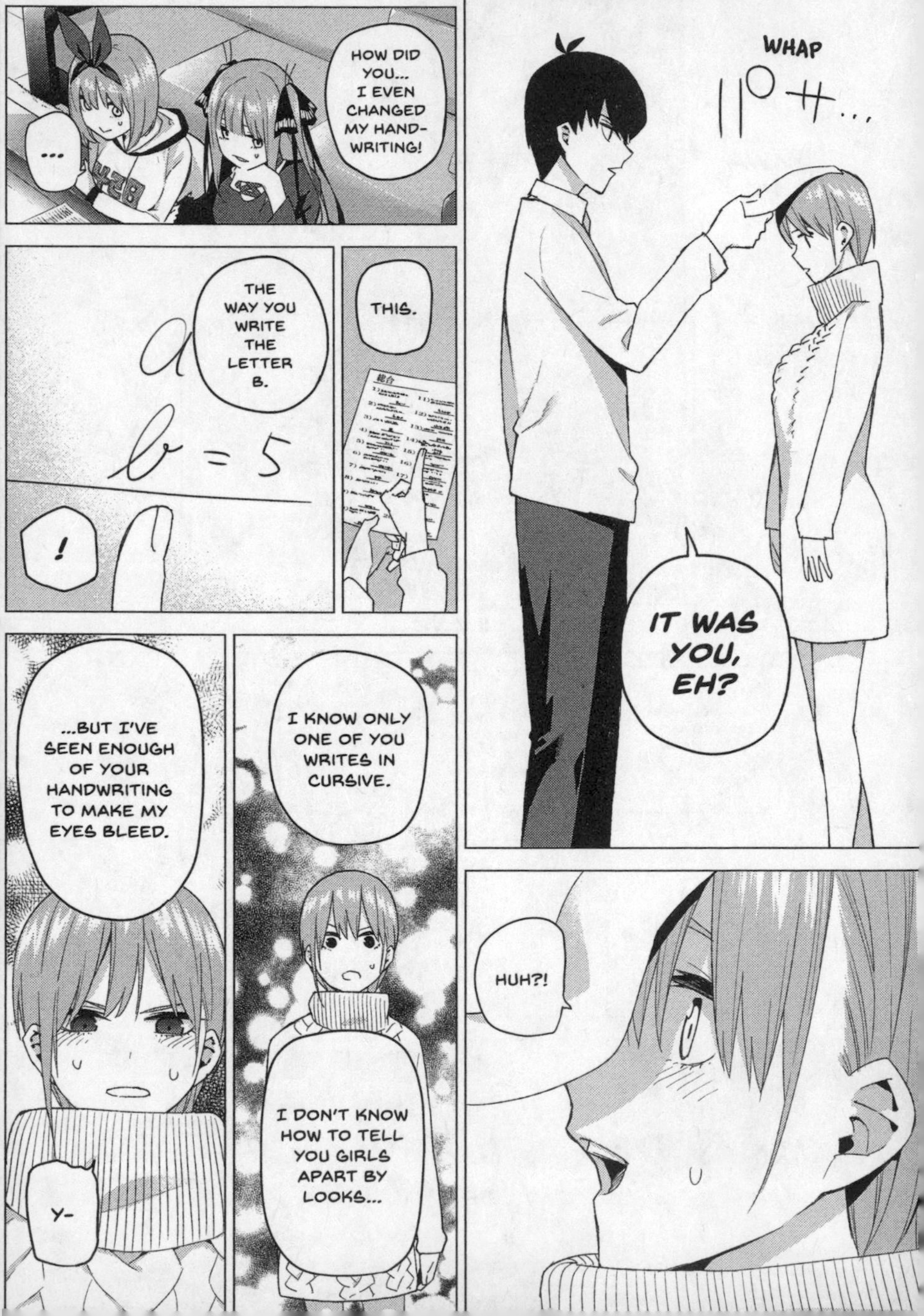
WHAP
IT WAS YOU, EH?
HUH?!
HOW DID YOU... I EVEN CHANGED MY HAND-WRITING!
...
THIS.
THE WAY YOU WRITE THE LETTER B.
!
I KNOW ONLY ONE OF YOU WRITES IN CURSIVE.
I DON'T KNOW HOW TO TELL YOU GIRLS APART BY LOOKS...
...BUT I'VE SEEN ENOUGH OF YOUR HANDWRITING TO MAKE MY EYES BLEED.
Y-

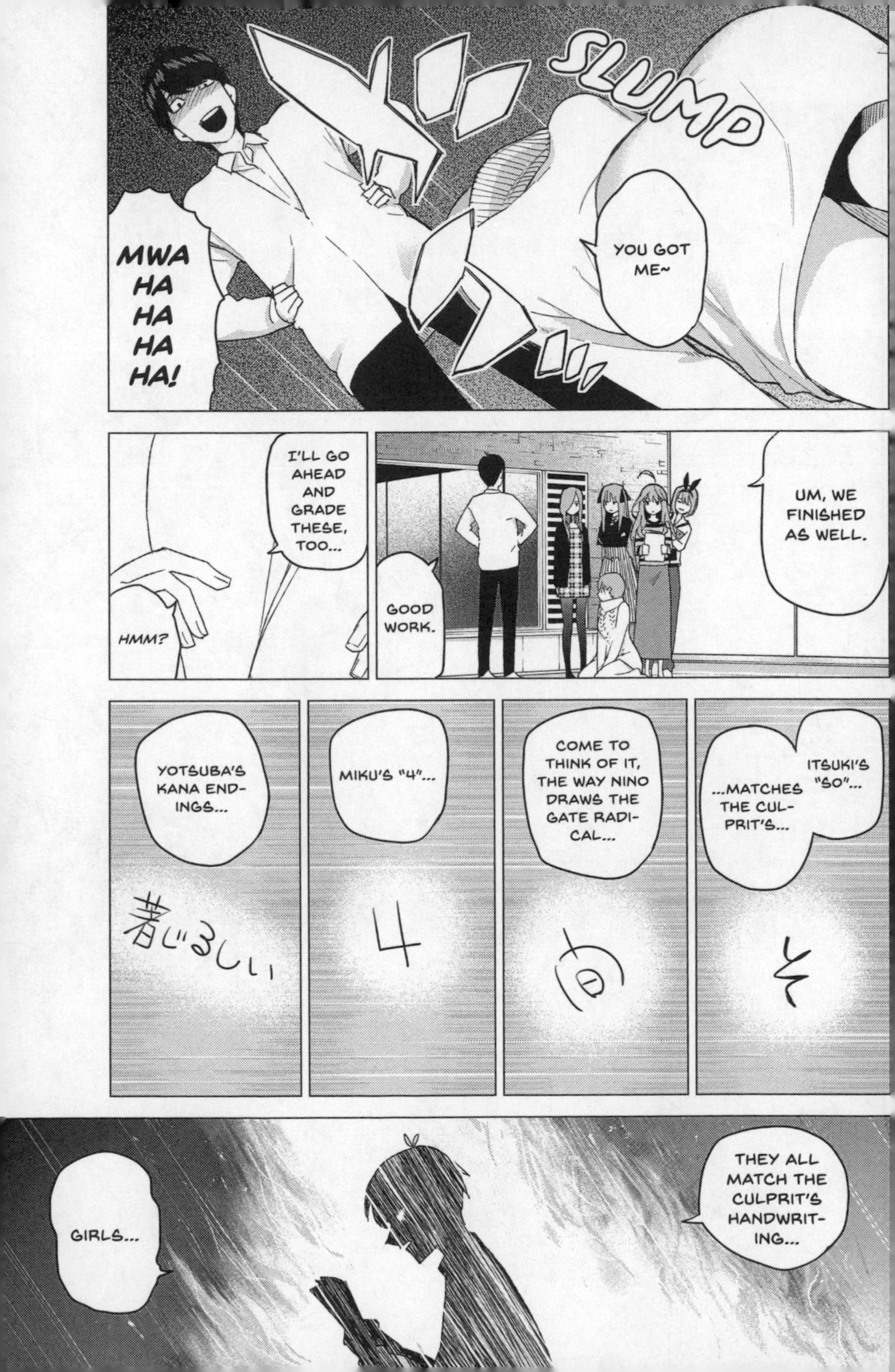
SLUMP
YOU GOT ME~
MWA HA HA HA HA!
UM, WE FINISHED AS WELL.
GOOD WORK.
I'LL GO AHEAD AND GRADE THESE, TOO...
HMM?
ITSUKI'S "SO"...
...MATCHES THE CULPRIT'S...
COME TO THINK OF IT, THE WAY NINO DRAWS THE GATE RADICAL...
MIKU'S "4"...
YOTSUBA'S KANA ENDINGS...
THEY ALL MATCH THE CULPRIT'S HANDWRITING...
GIRLS...

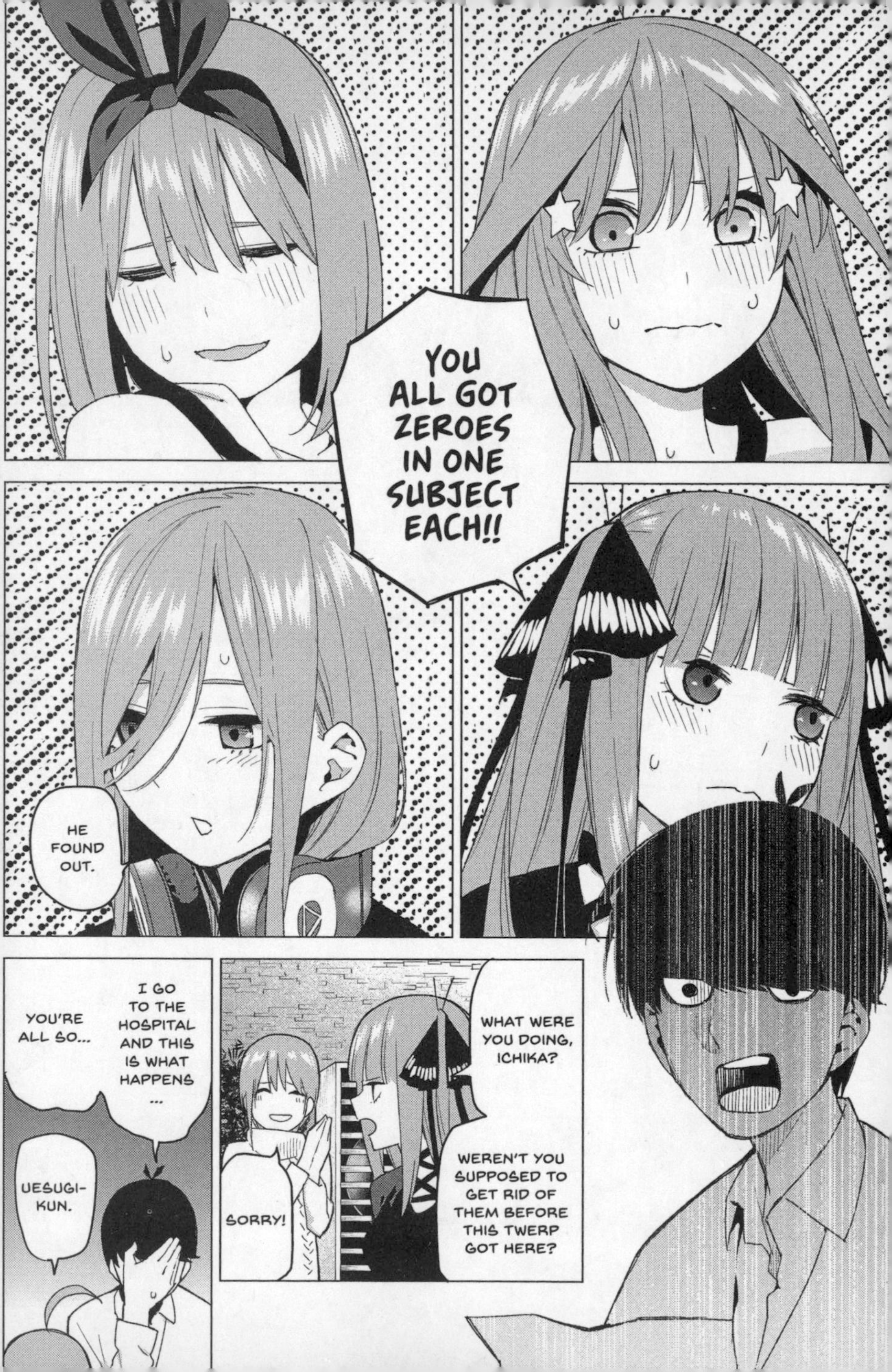
YOU ALL GOT ZEROES IN ONE SUBJECT EACH!!
HE FOUND OUT.
WHAT WERE YOU DOING, ICHIKA?
WEREN'T YOU SUPPOSED TO GET RID OF THEM BEFORE THIS TWERP GOT HERE?
SORRY!
I GO TO THE HOSPITAL AND THIS IS WHAT HAPPENS ...
YOU'RE ALL SO...
UESUGI-KUN.

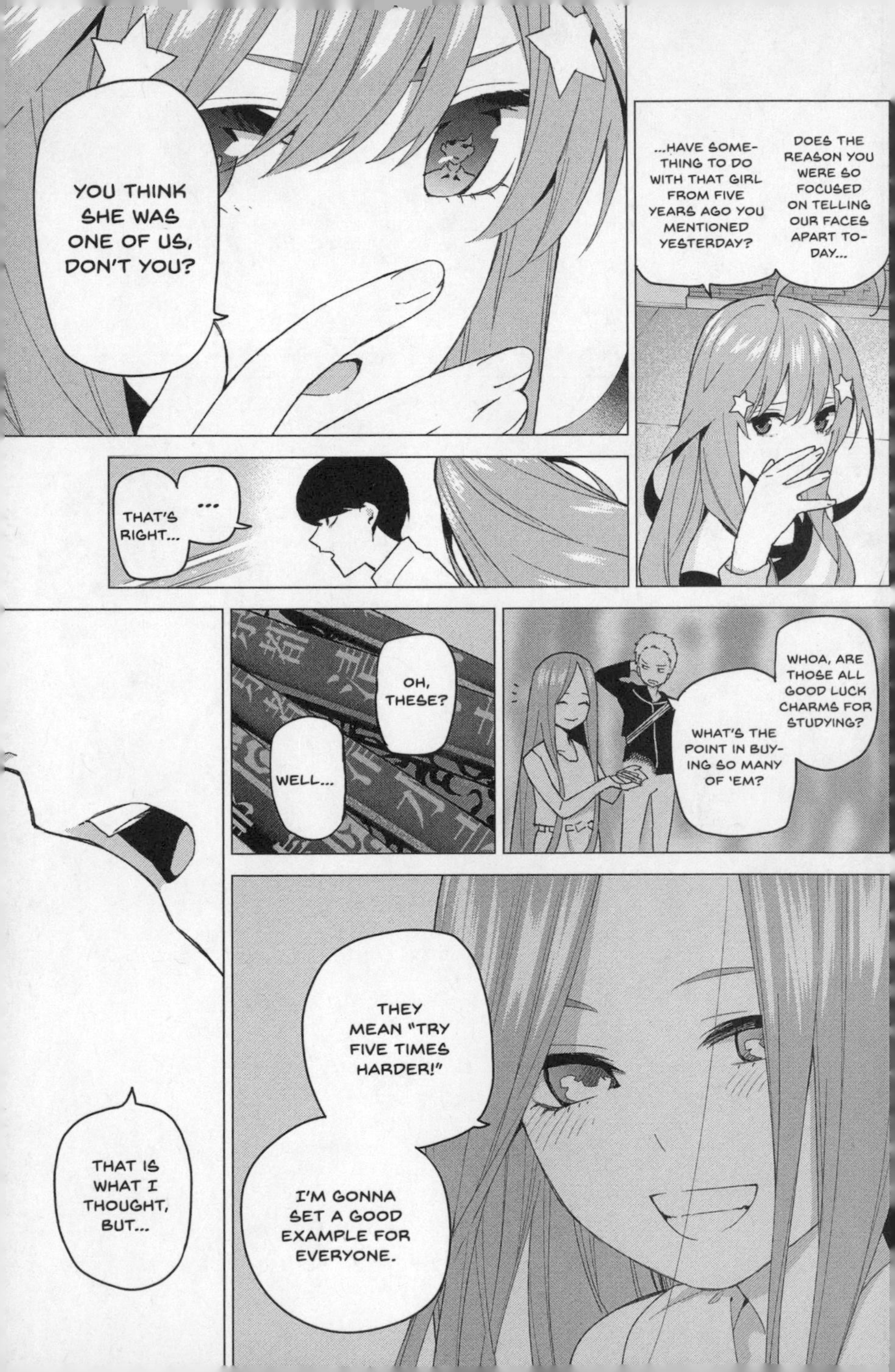
DOES THE REASON YOU WERE SO FOCUSED ON TELLING OUR FACES APART TO-DAY...
...HAVE SOME-THING TO DO WITH THAT GIRL FROM FIVE YEARS AGO YOU MENTIONED YESTERDAY?
YOU THINK SHE WAS ONE OF US, DON'T YOU?
...
THAT'S RIGHT...
WHOA, ARE THOSE ALL GOOD LUCK CHARMS FOR STUDYING?
WHAT'S THE POINT IN BUY-ING SO MANY OF 'EM?
OH, THESE?
WELL...
THEY MEAN "TRY FIVE TIMES HARDER!"
I'M GONNA SET A GOOD EXAMPLE FOR EVERYONE.
THAT IS WHAT I THOUGHT, BUT...

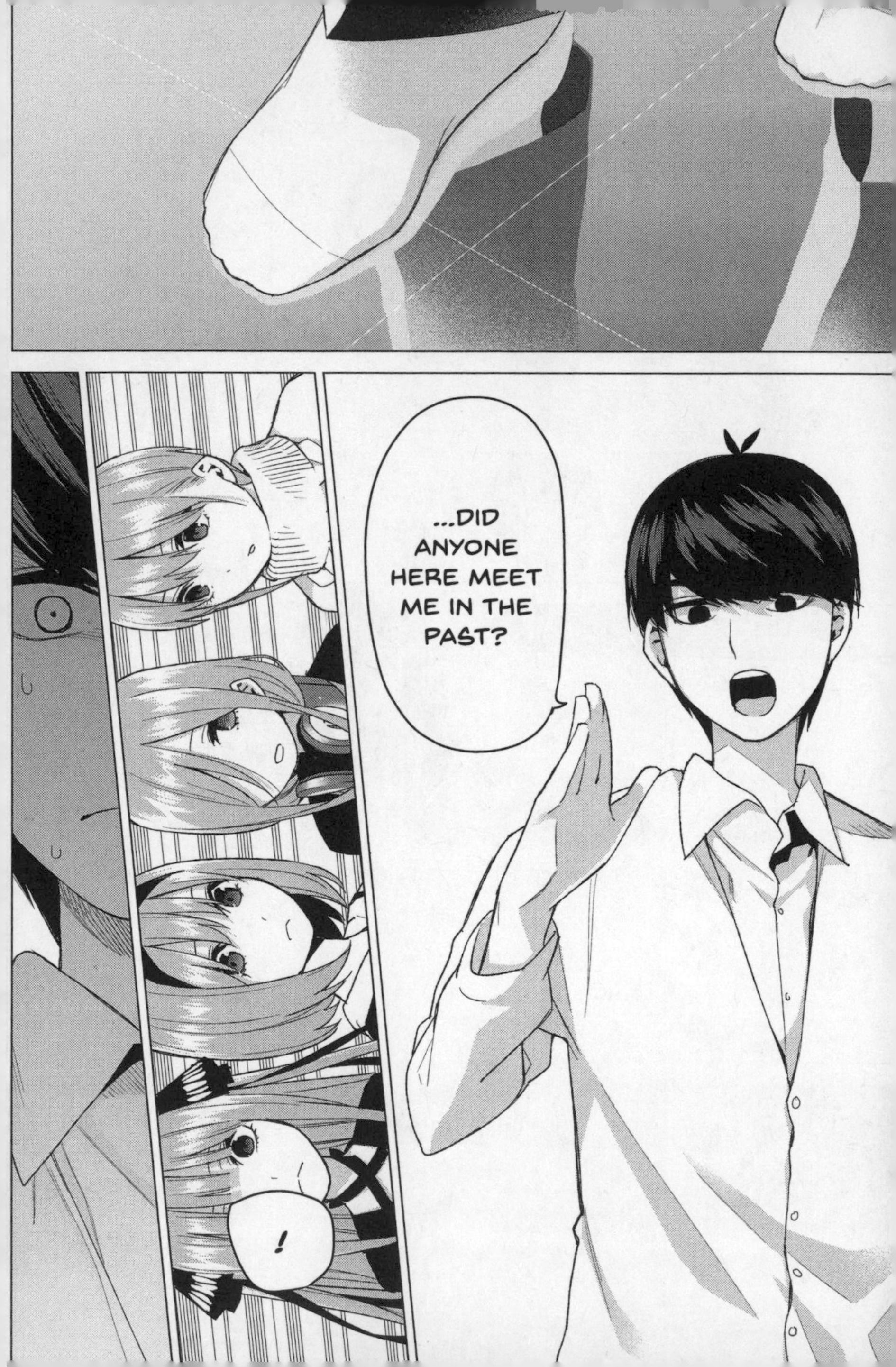
...DID ANYONE HERE MEET ME IN THE PAST?
!

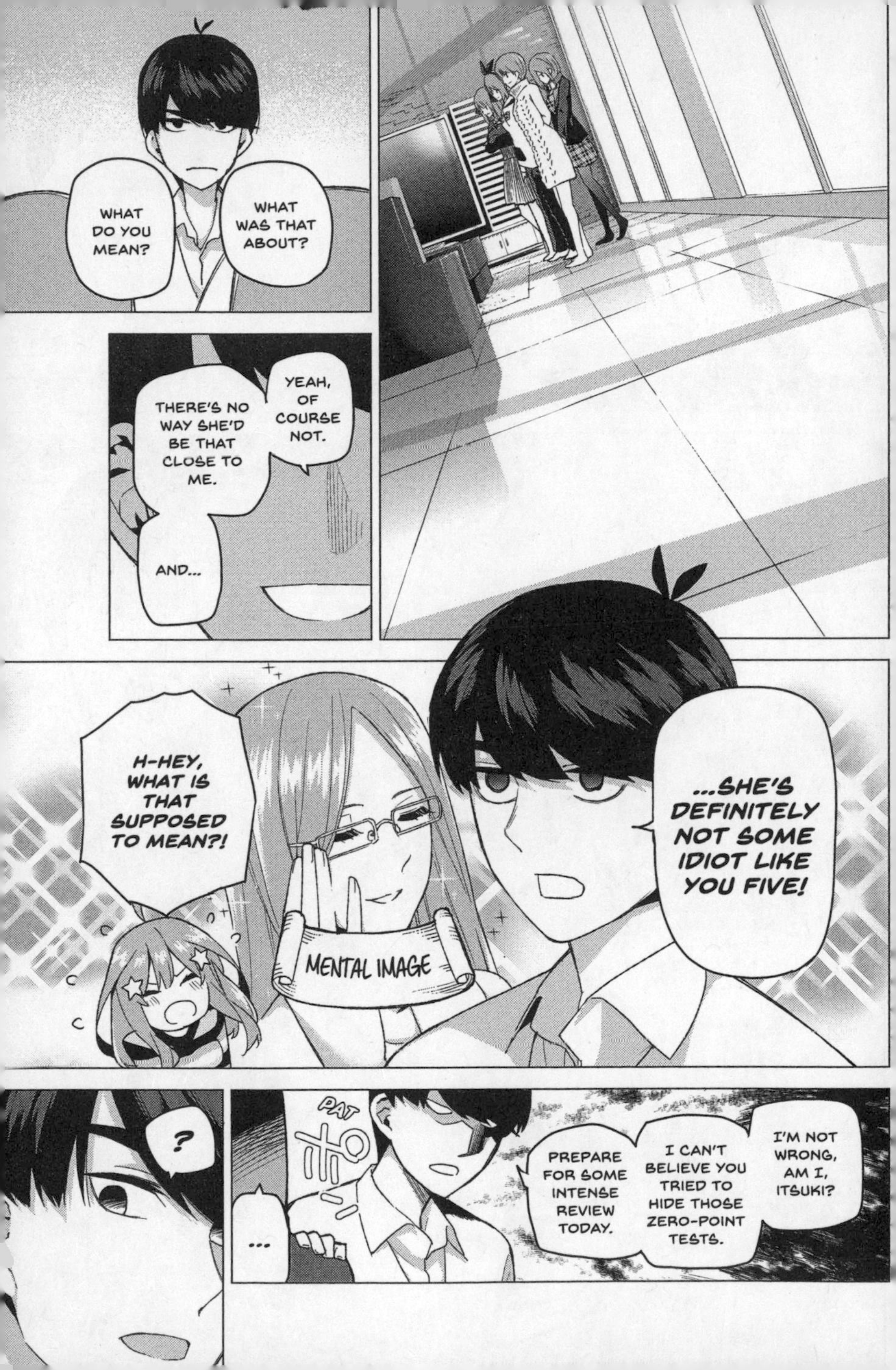
WHAT WAS THAT ABOUT?
WHAT DO YOU MEAN?
YEAH, OF COURSE NOT.
THERE'S NO WAY SHE'D BE THAT CLOSE TO ME.
AND...
...SHE'S DEFINITELY NOT SOME IDIOT LIKE YOU FIVE!
MENTAL IMAGE
H-HEY, WHAT IS THAT SUPPOSED TO MEAN?!
I'M NOT WRONG, AM I, ITSUKI?
I CAN'T BELIEVE YOU TRIED TO HIDE THOSE ZERO-POINT TESTS.
PREPARE FOR SOME INTENSE REVIEW TODAY.
PAT
...
?

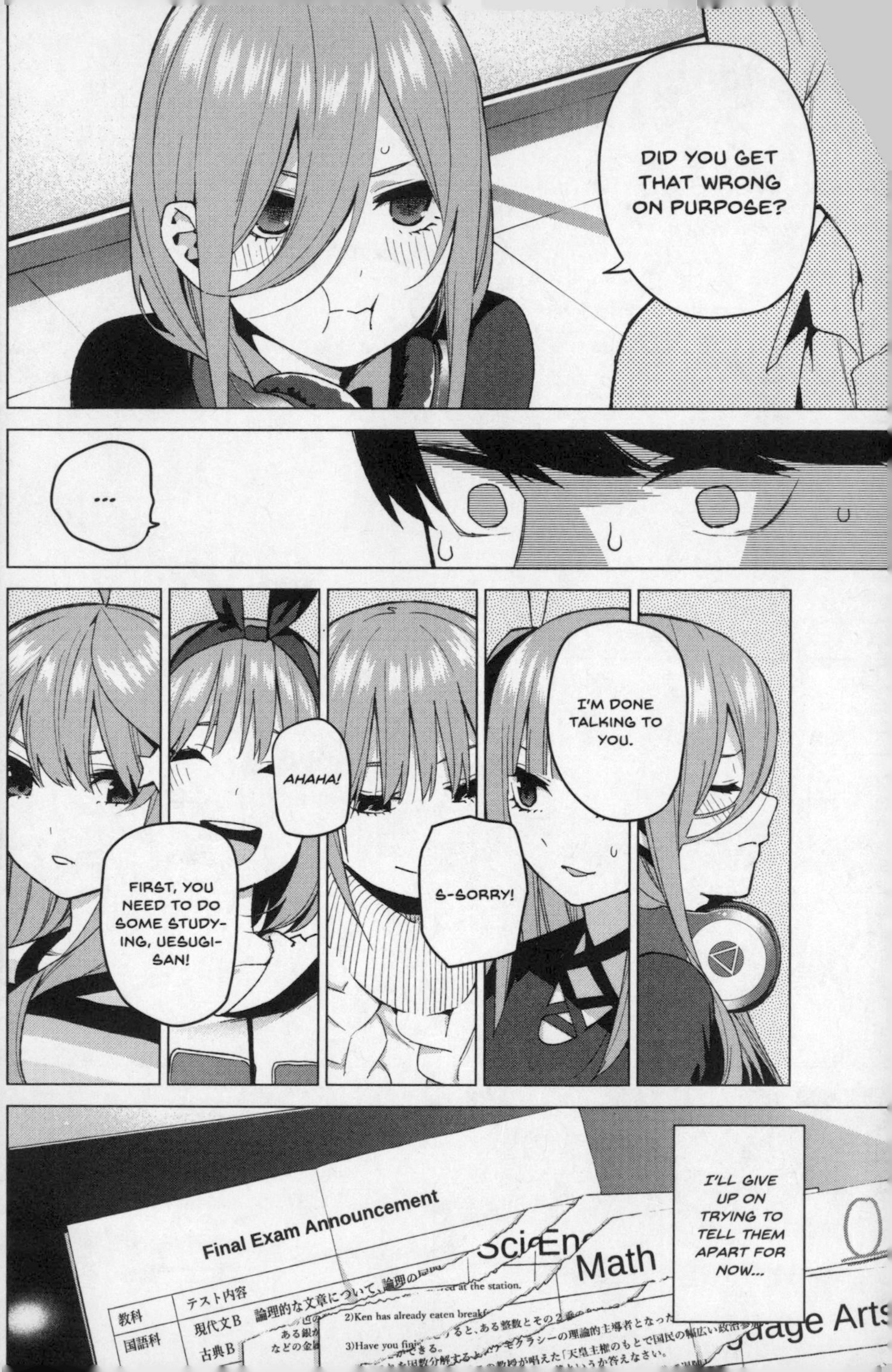
DID YOU GET THAT WRONG ON PURPOSE?
...
I'M DONE TALKING TO YOU.
S-SORRY!
AHAHA!
FIRST, YOU NEED TO DO SOME STUDYING, UESUGI-SAN!
I'LL GIVE UP ON TRYING TO TELL THEM APART FOR NOW...
Final Exam Announcement
Math

# CHAPTER 36
# THE LABOR THANKSGIVING TOUR ①

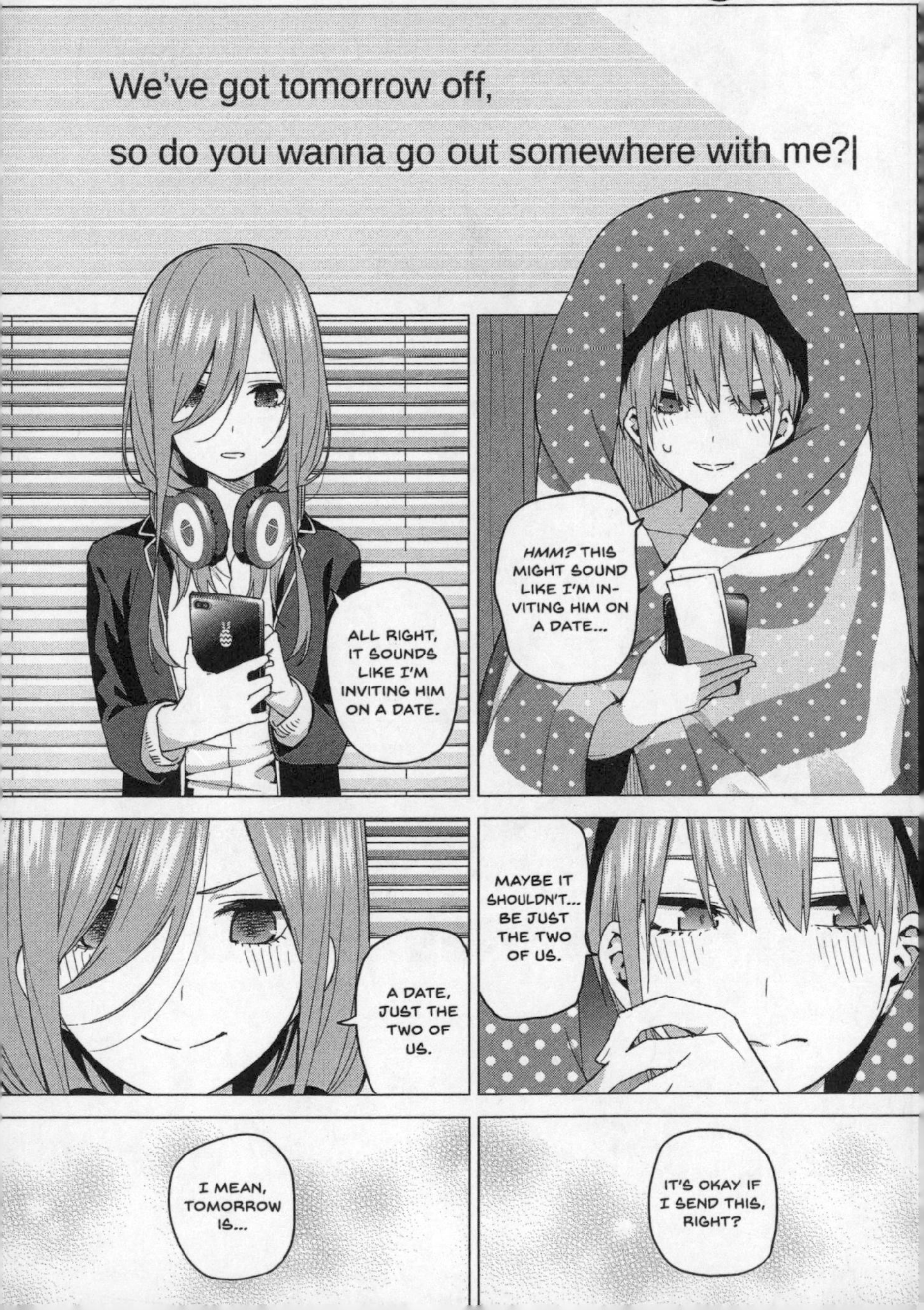
We've got tomorrow off,
so do you wanna go out somewhere with me?|
HMM? THIS MIGHT SOUND LIKE I'M INVITING HIM ON A DATE...
ALL RIGHT, IT SOUNDS LIKE I'M INVITING HIM ON A DATE.
MAYBE IT SHOULDN'T... BE JUST THE TWO OF US.
A DATE, JUST THE TWO OF US.
IT'S OKAY IF I SEND THIS, RIGHT?
I MEAN, TOMORROW IS...

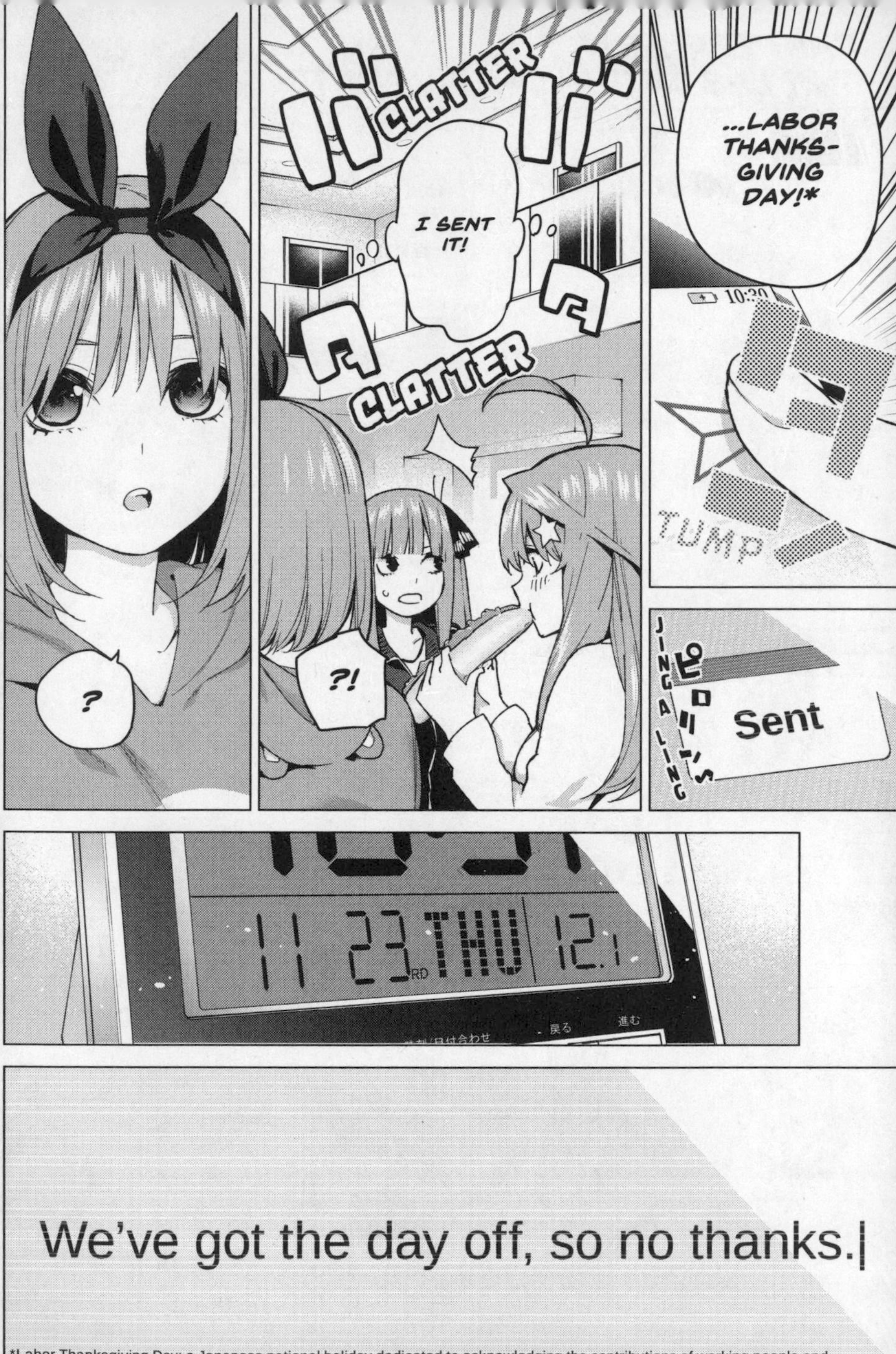

...LABOR THANKS-GIVING DAY!*
10:30
TUMP
JINGALING
Sent
CLATTER
I SENT IT!
CLATTER
?!
?
11 23RD THU 12.1
戻る
進む
We've got the day off, so no thanks.


*Labor Thanksgiving Day: a Japanese national holiday dedicated to acknowledging the contributions of working people and thanking others. Held annually on November 23rd.

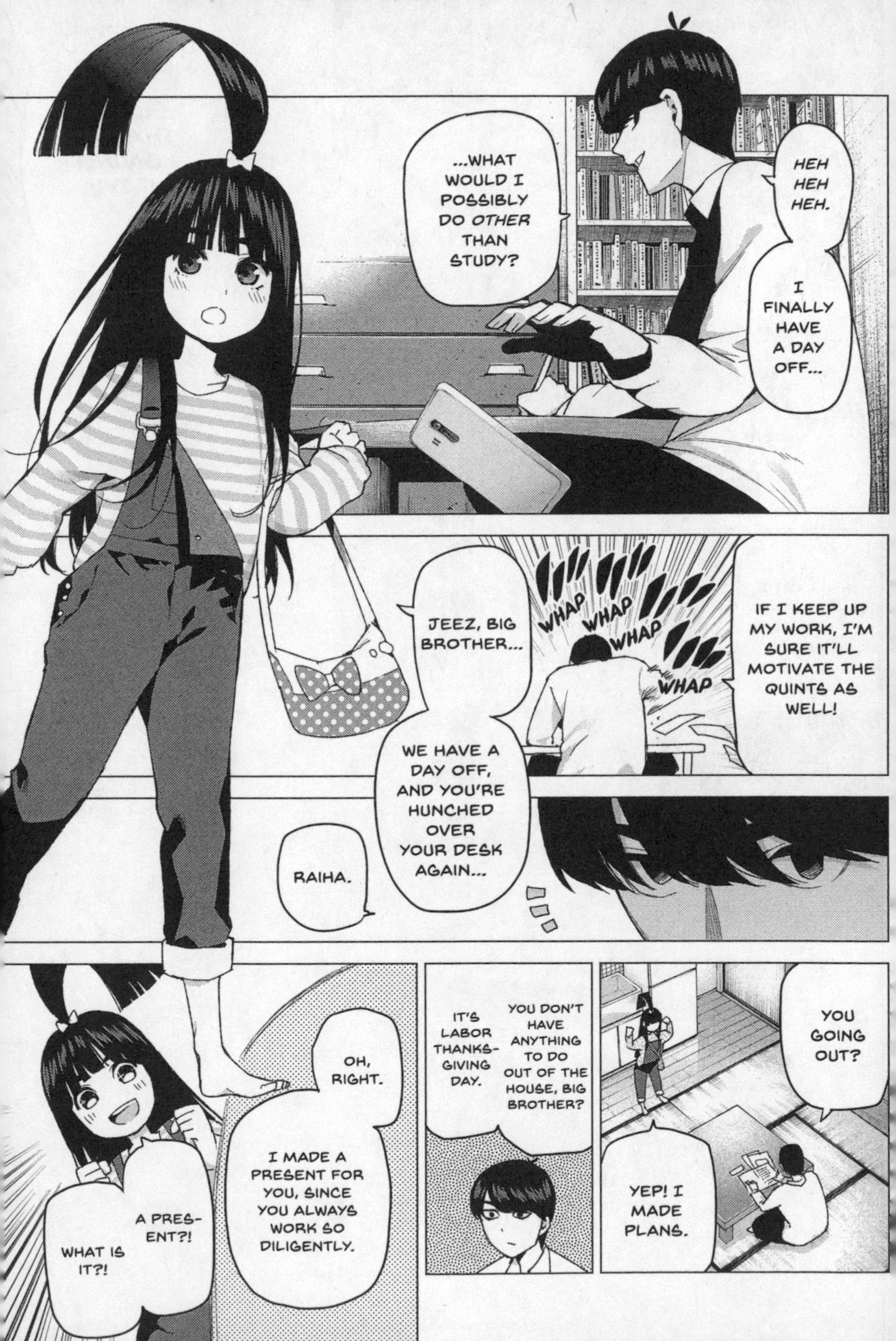
HEH HEH HEH.
I FINALLY HAVE A DAY OFF...
...WHAT WOULD I POSSIBLY DO *OTHER* THAN STUDY?
IF I KEEP UP MY WORK, I'M SURE IT'LL MOTIVATE THE QUINTS AS WELL!
WHAP
WHAP
WHAP
WHAP
JEEZ, BIG BROTHER...
WE HAVE A DAY OFF, AND YOU'RE HUNCHED OVER YOUR DESK AGAIN...
RAIHA.
YOU GOING OUT?
YEP! I MADE PLANS.
YOU DON'T HAVE ANYTHING TO DO OUT OF THE HOUSE, BIG BROTHER?
IT'S LABOR THANKSGIVING DAY.
OH, RIGHT.
I MADE A PRESENT FOR YOU, SINCE YOU ALWAYS WORK SO DILIGENTLY.
A PRESENT?!
WHAT IS IT?!

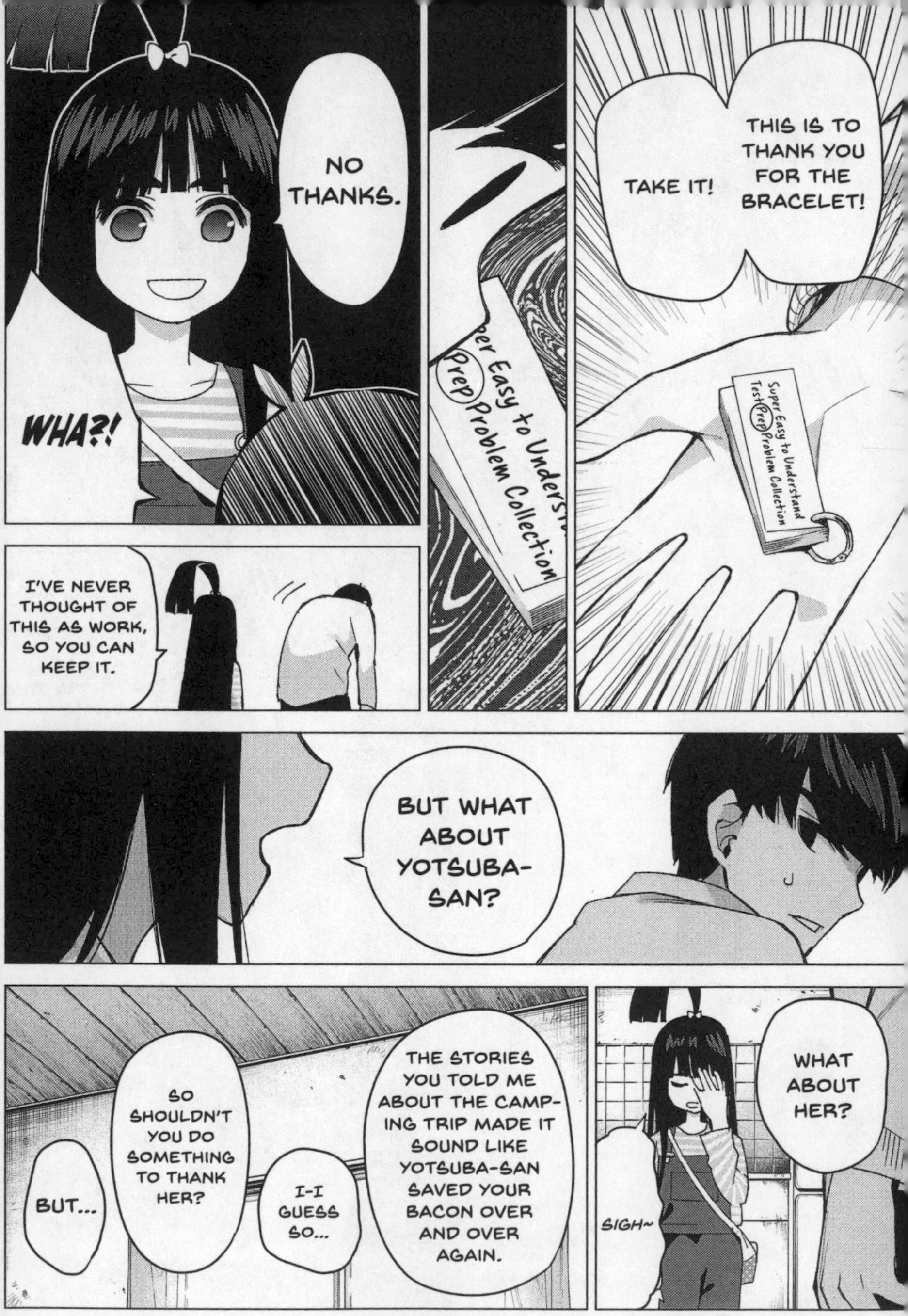
THIS IS TO THANK YOU FOR THE BRACELET!
TAKE IT!
Super Easy to Understand Test Prep Problem Collection
per Easy to Underst
Prep Problem Collection
NO THANKS.
WHA?!
I'VE NEVER THOUGHT OF THIS AS WORK, SO YOU CAN KEEP IT.
BUT WHAT ABOUT YOTSUBA-SAN?
WHAT ABOUT HER?
SIGH~
THE STORIES YOU TOLD ME ABOUT THE CAMPING TRIP MADE IT SOUND LIKE YOTSUBA-SAN SAVED YOUR BACON OVER AND OVER AGAIN.
I-I GUESS SO...
SO SHOULDN'T YOU DO SOMETHING TO THANK HER?
BUT...

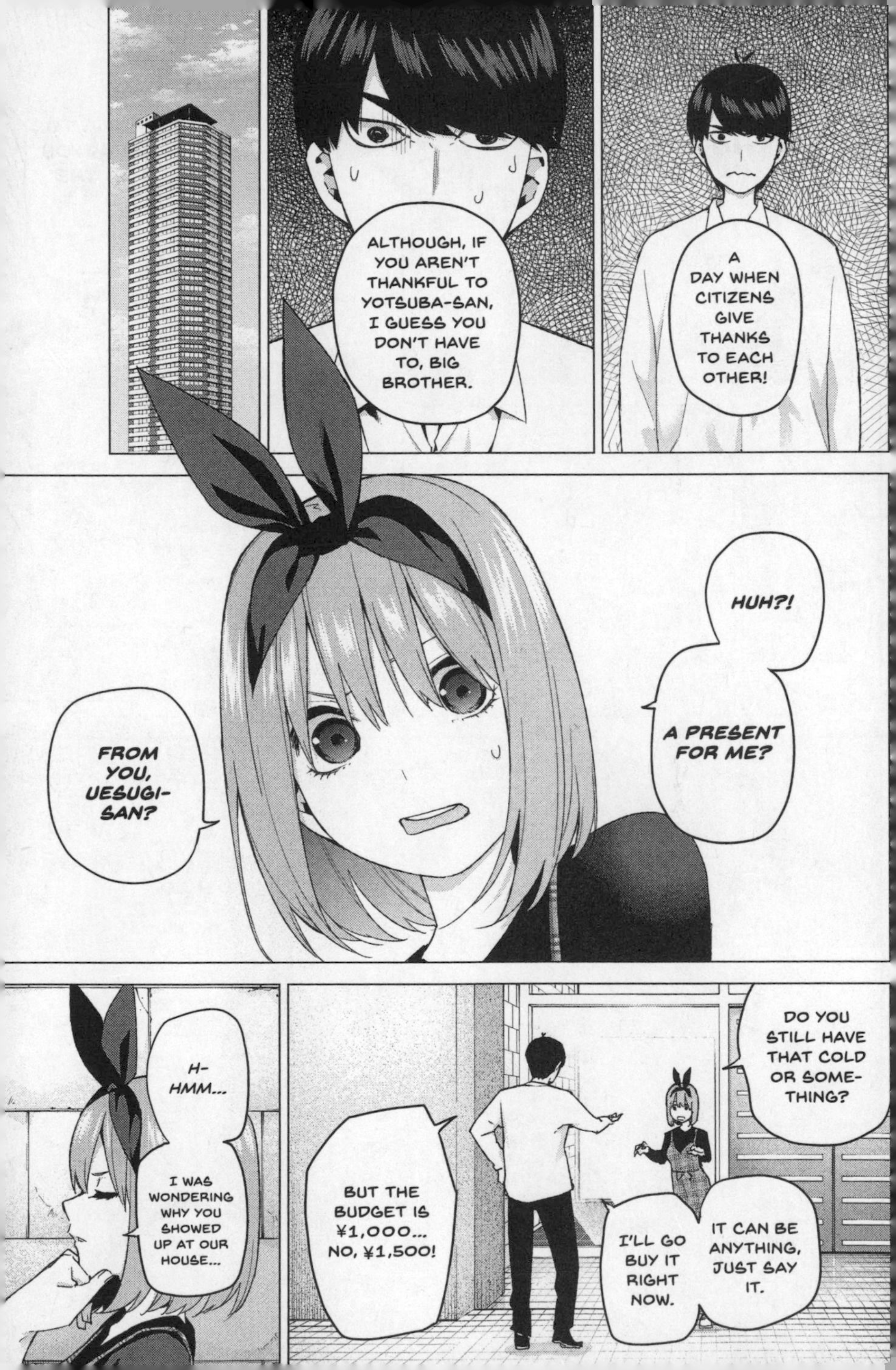
A DAY WHEN CITIZENS GIVE THANKS TO EACH OTHER!
ALTHOUGH, IF YOU AREN'T THANKFUL TO YOTSUBA-SAN, I GUESS YOU DON'T HAVE TO, BIG BROTHER.
HUH?!
A PRESENT FOR ME?
FROM YOU, UESUGI-SAN?
DO YOU STILL HAVE THAT COLD OR SOME-THING?
IT CAN BE ANYTHING, JUST SAY IT.
I'LL GO BUY IT RIGHT NOW.
BUT THE BUDGET IS ¥1,000... NO, ¥1,500!
H-HMM...
I WAS WONDERING WHY YOU SHOWED UP AT OUR HOUSE...

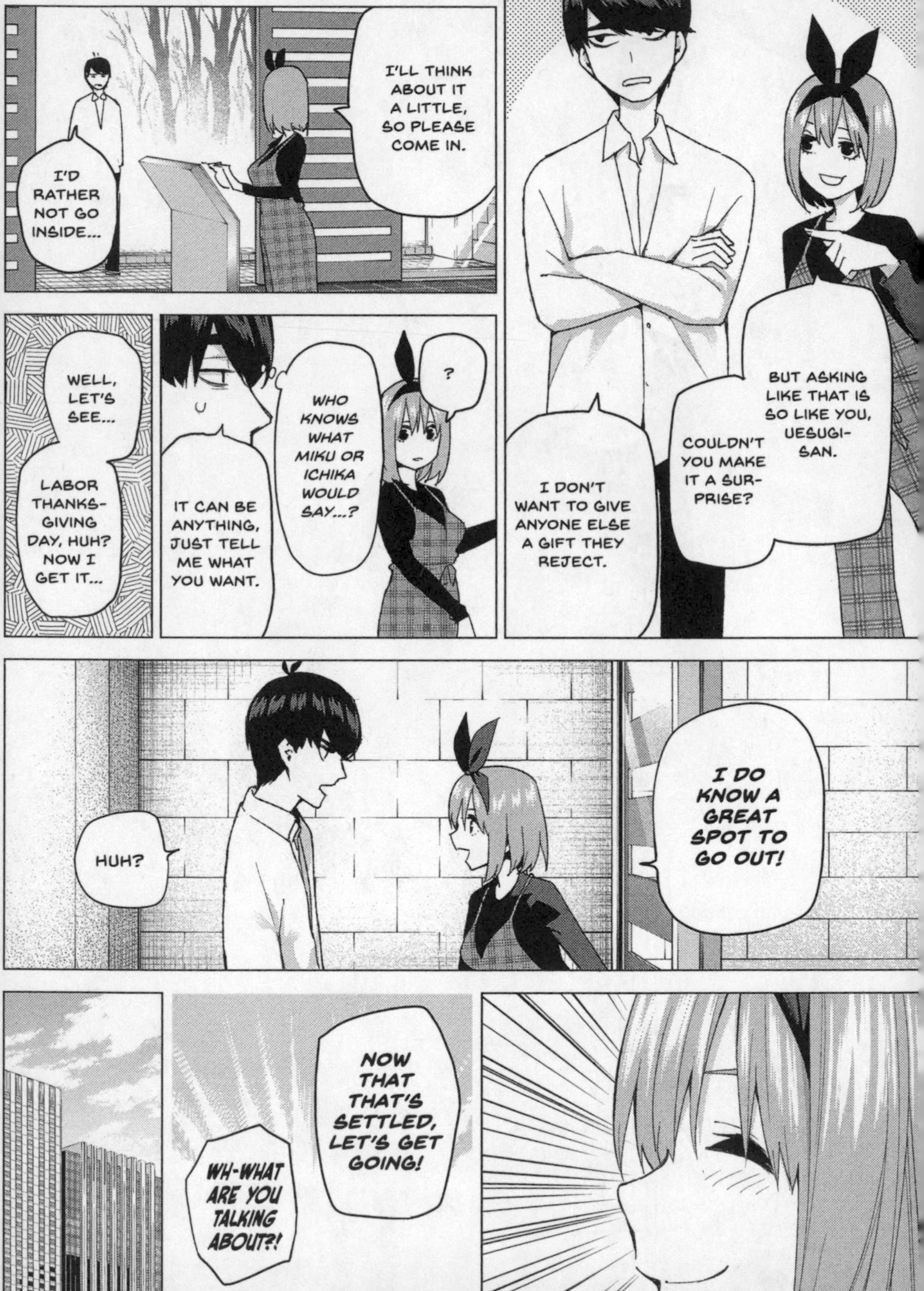
BUT ASKING LIKE THAT IS SO LIKE YOU, UESUGI-SAN.
COULDN'T YOU MAKE IT A SURPRISE?
I DON'T WANT TO GIVE ANYONE ELSE A GIFT THEY REJECT.
I'LL THINK ABOUT IT A LITTLE, SO PLEASE COME IN.
I'D RATHER NOT GO INSIDE...
?
WHO KNOWS WHAT MIKU OR ICHIKA WOULD SAY...?
IT CAN BE ANYTHING, JUST TELL ME WHAT YOU WANT.
WELL, LET'S SEE...
LABOR THANKSGIVING DAY, HUH? NOW I GET IT...
I DO KNOW A GREAT SPOT TO GO OUT!
HUH?
NOW THAT THAT'S SETTLED, LET'S GET GOING!
WH-WHAT ARE YOU TALKING ABOUT?!

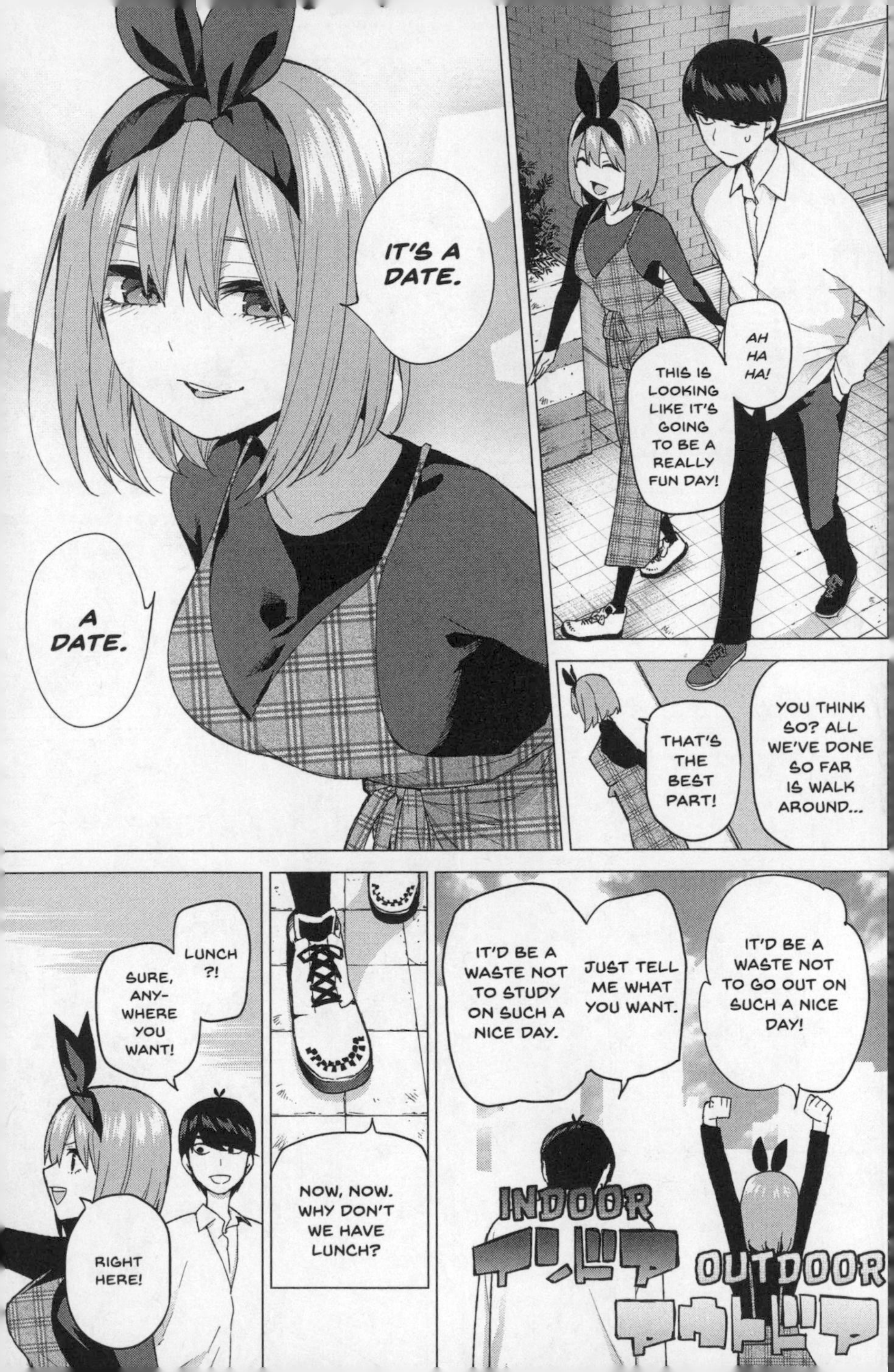
AH HA HA!
THIS IS LOOKING LIKE IT'S GOING TO BE A REALLY FUN DAY!
YOU THINK SO? ALL WE'VE DONE SO FAR IS WALK AROUND...
THAT'S THE BEST PART!
IT'S A DATE.
A DATE.
IT'D BE A WASTE NOT TO GO OUT ON SUCH A NICE DAY!
JUST TELL ME WHAT YOU WANT.
IT'D BE A WASTE NOT TO STUDY ON SUCH A NICE DAY.
OUTDOOR
INDOOR
NOW, NOW. WHY DON'T WE HAVE LUNCH?
LUNCH?!
SURE, ANYWHERE YOU WANT!
RIGHT HERE!

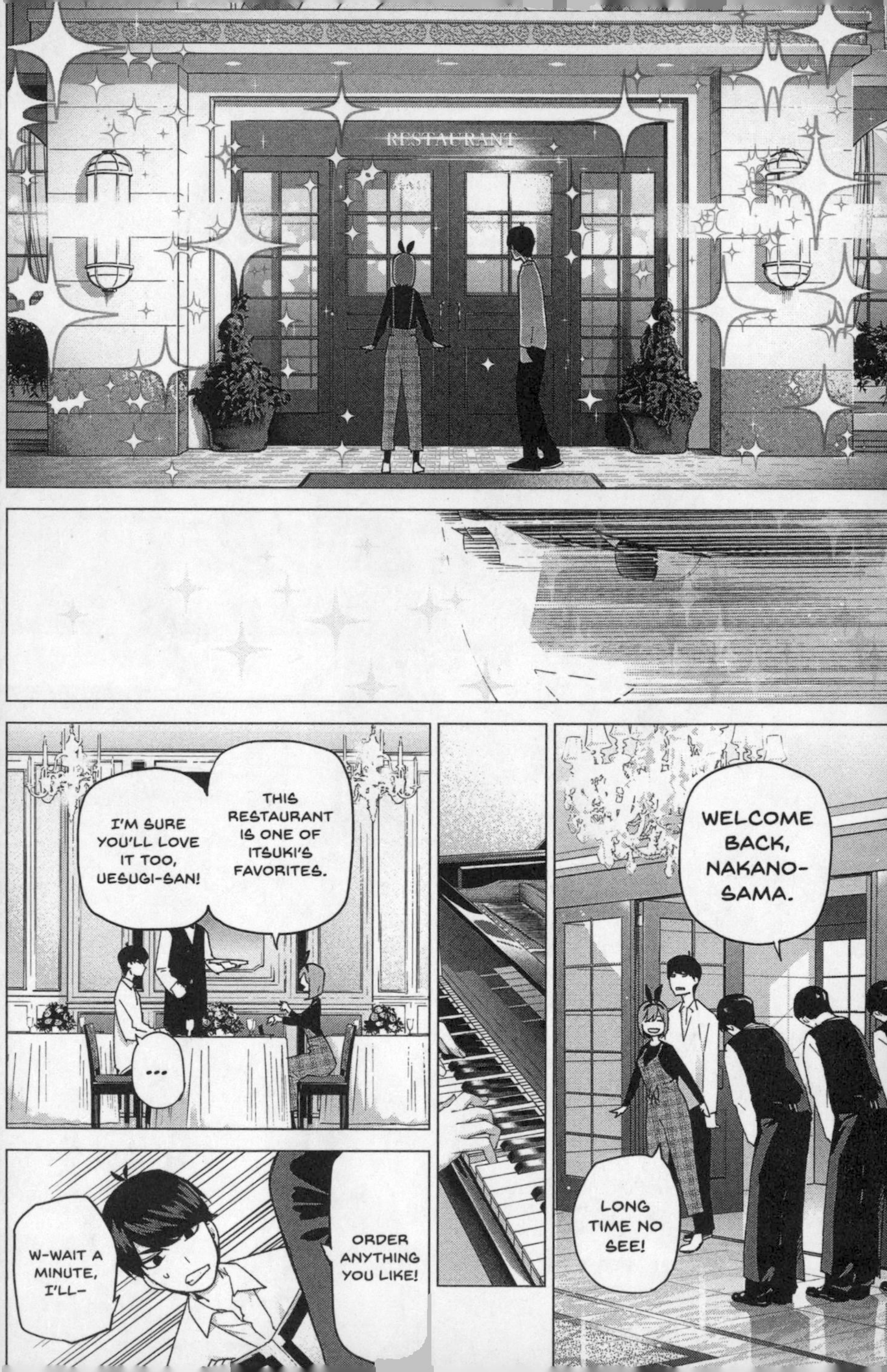
RESTAURANT
WELCOME BACK, NAKANO-SAMA.
LONG TIME NO SEE!
THIS RESTAURANT IS ONE OF ITSUKI'S FAVORITES.
I'M SURE YOU'LL LOVE IT TOO, UESUGI-SAN!
...
ORDER ANYTHING YOU LIKE!
W-WAIT A MINUTE, I'LL-

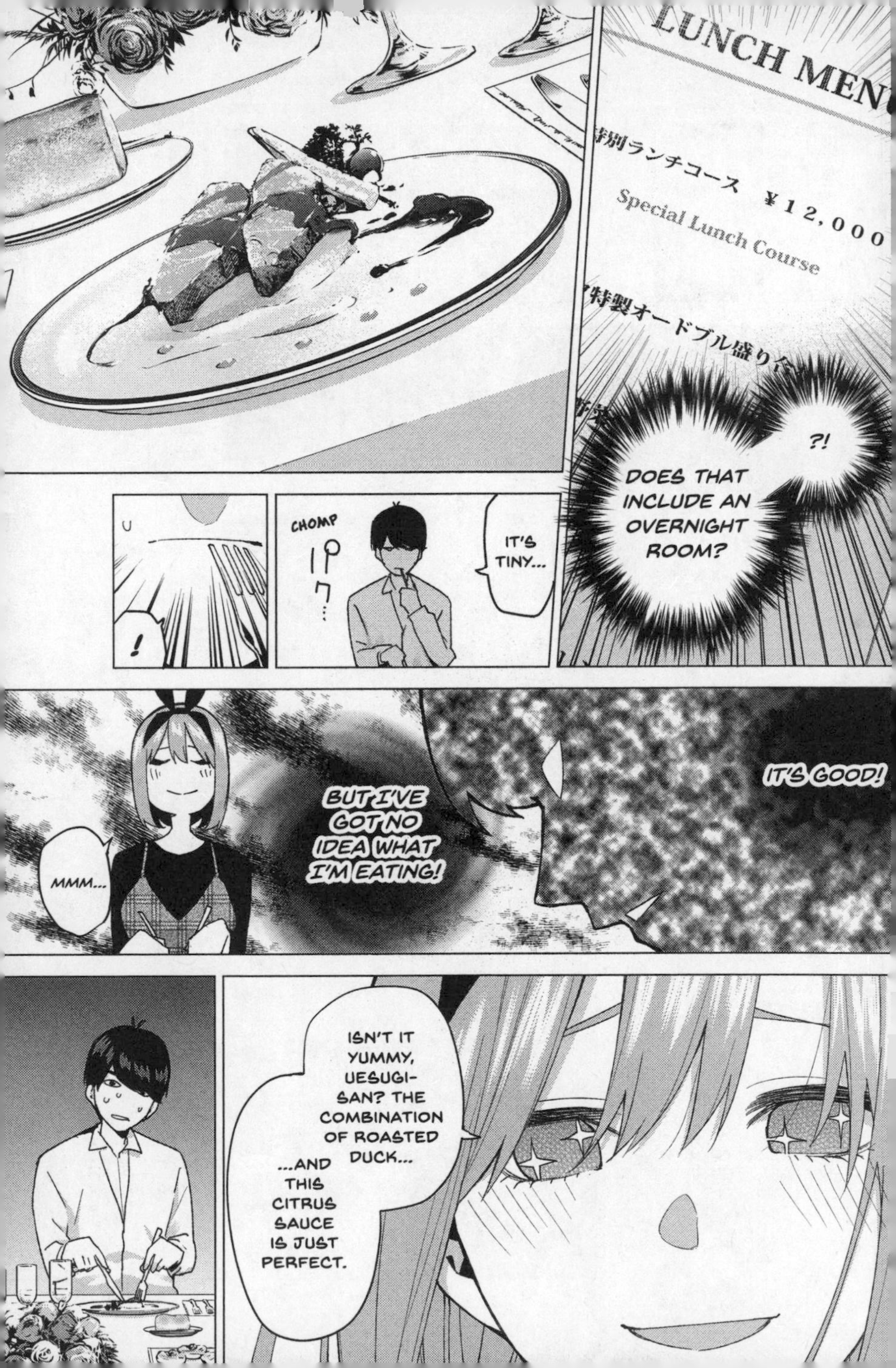
LUNCH MEN
特別ランチコース ¥12,000
Special Lunch Course
特製オードブル盛り
?!
DOES THAT INCLUDE AN OVERNIGHT ROOM?
IT'S TINY...
CHOMP
!
IT'S GOOD!
BUT I'VE GOT NO IDEA WHAT I'M EATING!
MMM...
ISN'T IT YUMMY, UESUGI-SAN? THE COMBINATION OF ROASTED DUCK...
...AND THIS CITRUS SAUCE IS JUST PERFECT.

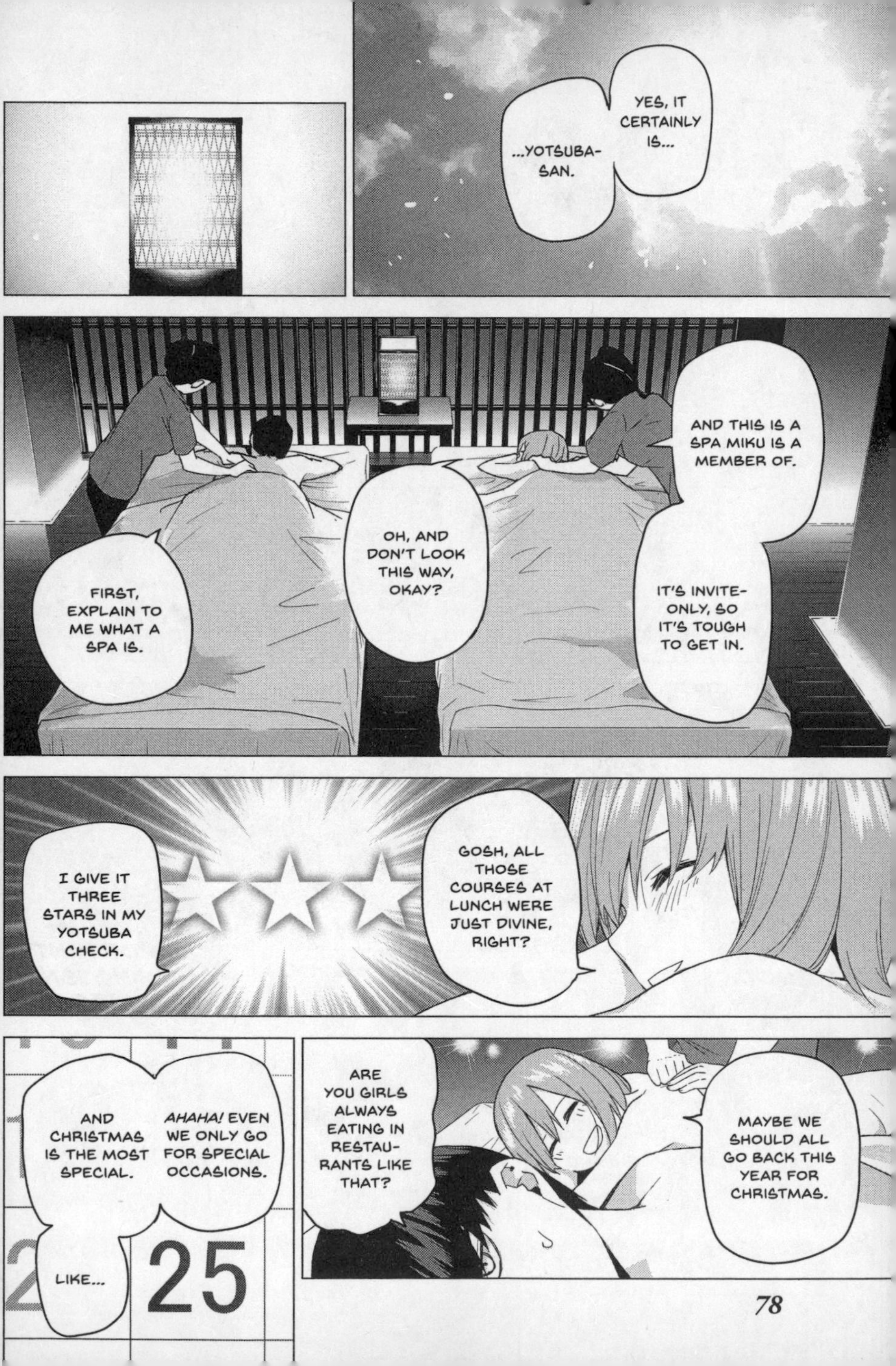
YES, IT CERTAINLY IS...
...YOTSUBA-SAN.
AND THIS IS A SPA MIKU IS A MEMBER OF.
IT'S INVITE-ONLY, SO IT'S TOUGH TO GET IN.
OH, AND DON'T LOOK THIS WAY, OKAY?
FIRST, EXPLAIN TO ME WHAT A SPA IS.
GOSH, ALL THOSE COURSES AT LUNCH WERE JUST DIVINE, RIGHT?
I GIVE IT THREE STARS IN MY YOTSUBA CHECK.
MAYBE WE SHOULD ALL GO BACK THIS YEAR FOR CHRISTMAS.
ARE YOU GIRLS ALWAYS EATING IN RESTAURANTS LIKE THAT?
*AHAHA!* EVEN WE ONLY GO FOR SPECIAL OCCASIONS.
AND CHRISTMAS IS THE MOST SPECIAL.
LIKE...
25

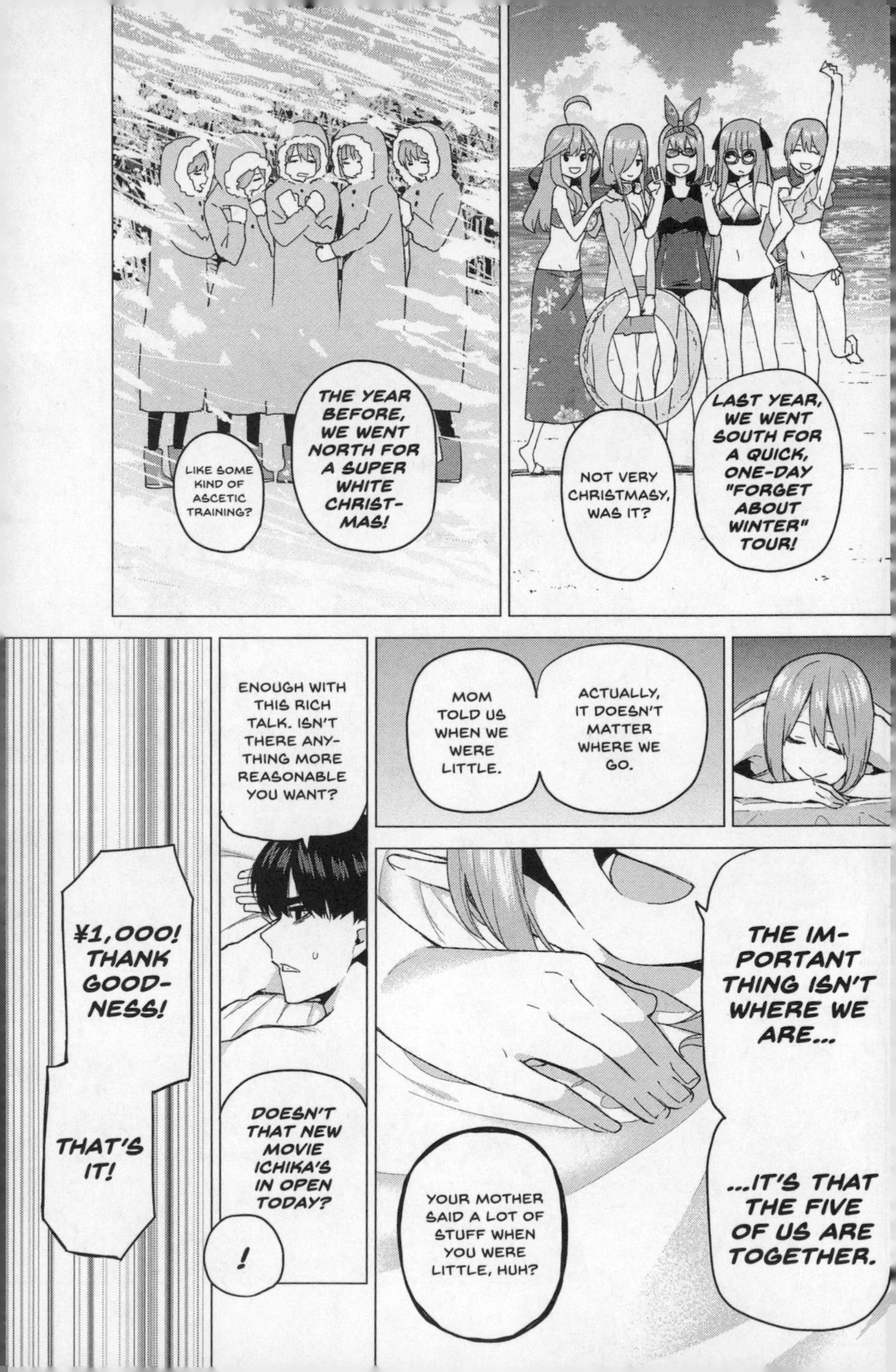
LAST YEAR, WE WENT SOUTH FOR A QUICK, ONE-DAY "FORGET ABOUT WINTER" TOUR!
NOT VERY CHRISTMASY, WAS IT?
THE YEAR BEFORE, WE WENT NORTH FOR A SUPER WHITE CHRIST-MAS!
LIKE SOME KIND OF ASCETIC TRAINING?
ACTUALLY, IT DOESN'T MATTER WHERE WE GO.
MOM TOLD US WHEN WE WERE LITTLE.
THE IM-PORTANT THING ISN'T WHERE WE ARE...
...IT'S THAT THE FIVE OF US ARE TOGETHER.
YOUR MOTHER SAID A LOT OF STUFF WHEN YOU WERE LITTLE, HUH?
ENOUGH WITH THIS RICH TALK. ISN'T THERE ANY-THING MORE REASONABLE YOU WANT?
DOESN'T THAT NEW MOVIE ICHIKA'S IN OPEN TODAY?
!
¥1,000! THANK GOOD-NESS!
THAT'S IT!

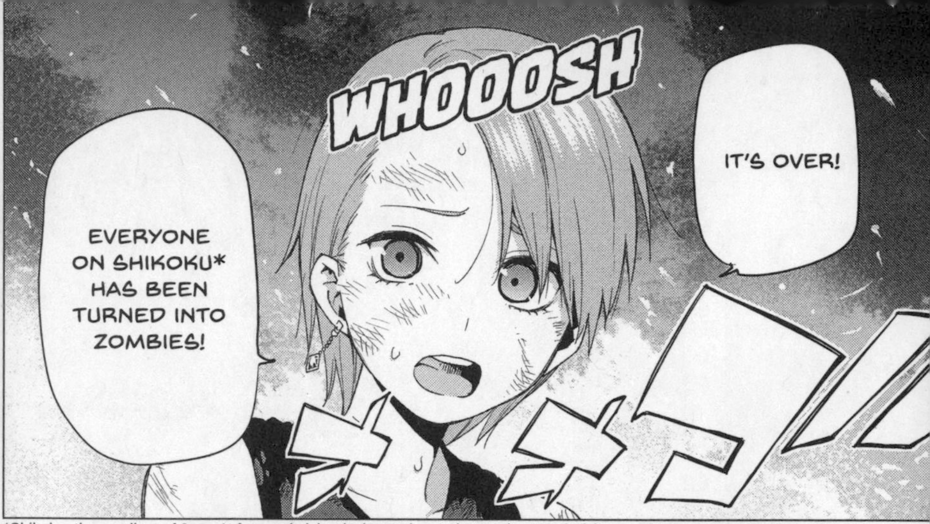
IT'S OVER!
WHOOOSH
EVERYONE ON SHIKOKU* HAS BEEN TURNED INTO ZOMBIES!
*Shikoku: the smallest of Japan's four main islands, located near the southern end of the country.

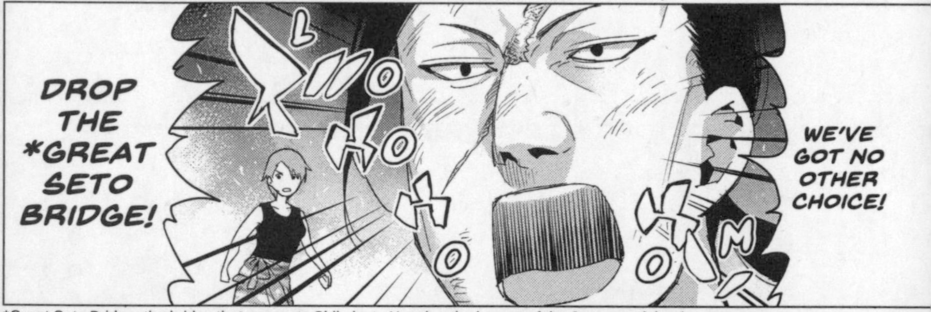
WE'VE GOT NO OTHER CHOICE!
DROP THE *GREAT SETO BRIDGE!
*Great Seto Bridge: the bridge that connects Shikoku to Honshu, the largest of the Japanese islands.

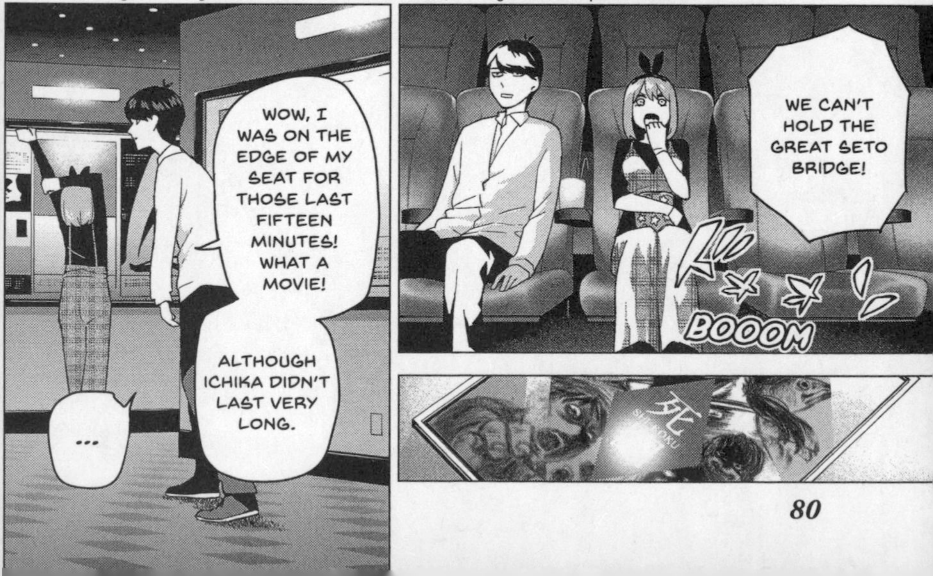
WE CAN'T HOLD THE GREAT SETO BRIDGE!
BOOOM
WOW, I WAS ON THE EDGE OF MY SEAT FOR THOSE LAST FIFTEEN MINUTES! WHAT A MOVIE!
ALTHOUGH ICHIKA DIDN'T LAST VERY LONG.
...

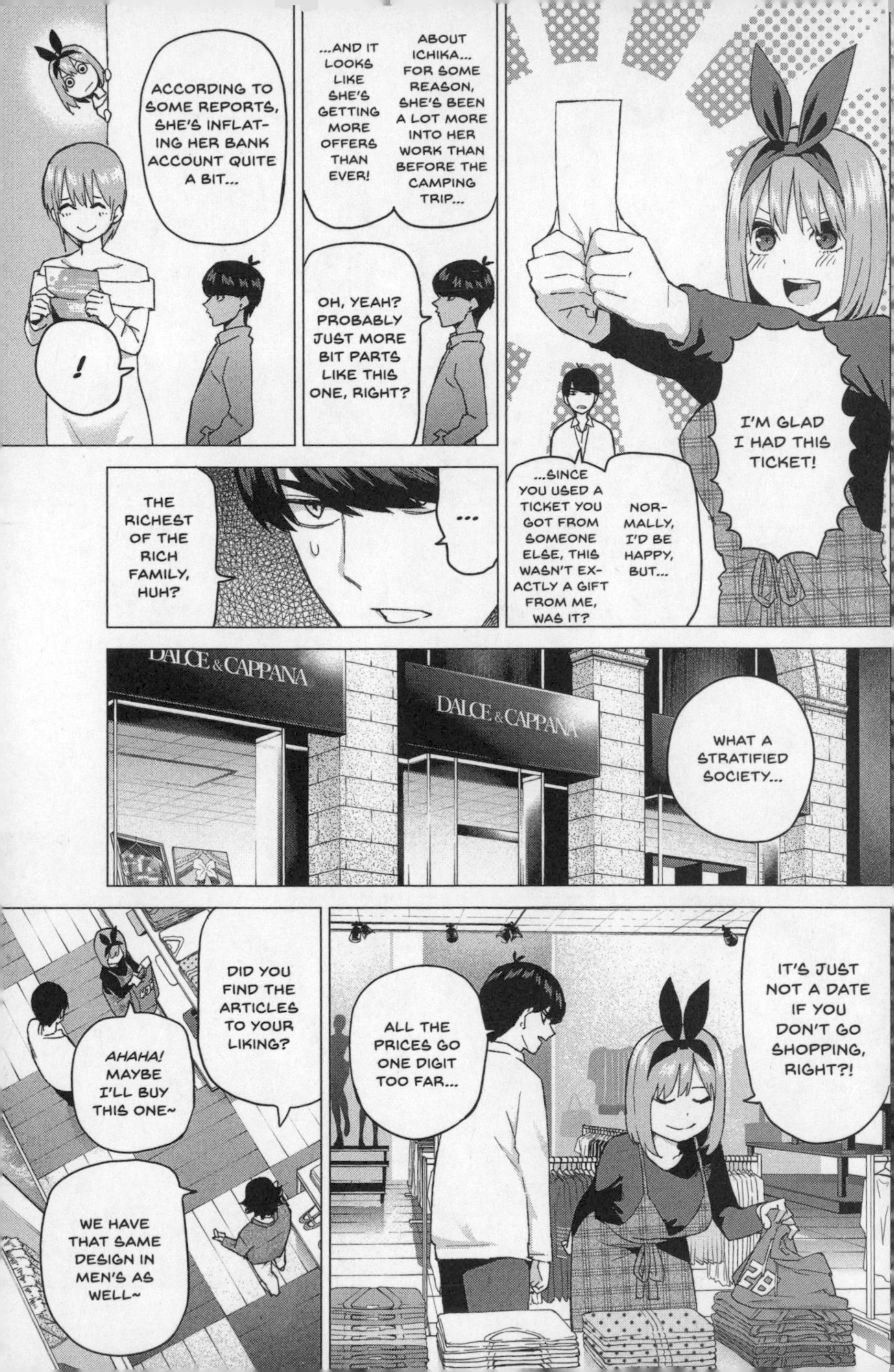
I'M GLAD I HAD THIS TICKET!
NORMALLY, I'D BE HAPPY, BUT... ...SINCE YOU USED A TICKET YOU GOT FROM SOMEONE ELSE, THIS WASN'T EXACTLY A GIFT FROM ME, WAS IT?
ABOUT ICHIKA... FOR SOME REASON, SHE'S BEEN A LOT MORE INTO HER WORK THAN BEFORE THE CAMPING TRIP... ...AND IT LOOKS LIKE SHE'S GETTING MORE OFFERS THAN EVER!
OH, YEAH? PROBABLY JUST MORE BIT PARTS LIKE THIS ONE, RIGHT?
ACCORDING TO SOME REPORTS, SHE'S INFLATING HER BANK ACCOUNT QUITE A BIT...
!
...
THE RICHEST OF THE RICH FAMILY, HUH?
DALCE & CAPPANA
DALCE & CAPPANA
WHAT A STRATIFIED SOCIETY...
IT'S JUST NOT A DATE IF YOU DON'T GO SHOPPING, RIGHT?!
ALL THE PRICES GO ONE DIGIT TOO FAR...
DID YOU FIND THE ARTICLES TO YOUR LIKING?
AHAHA! MAYBE I'LL BUY THIS ONE~
WE HAVE THAT SAME DESIGN IN MEN'S AS WELL~

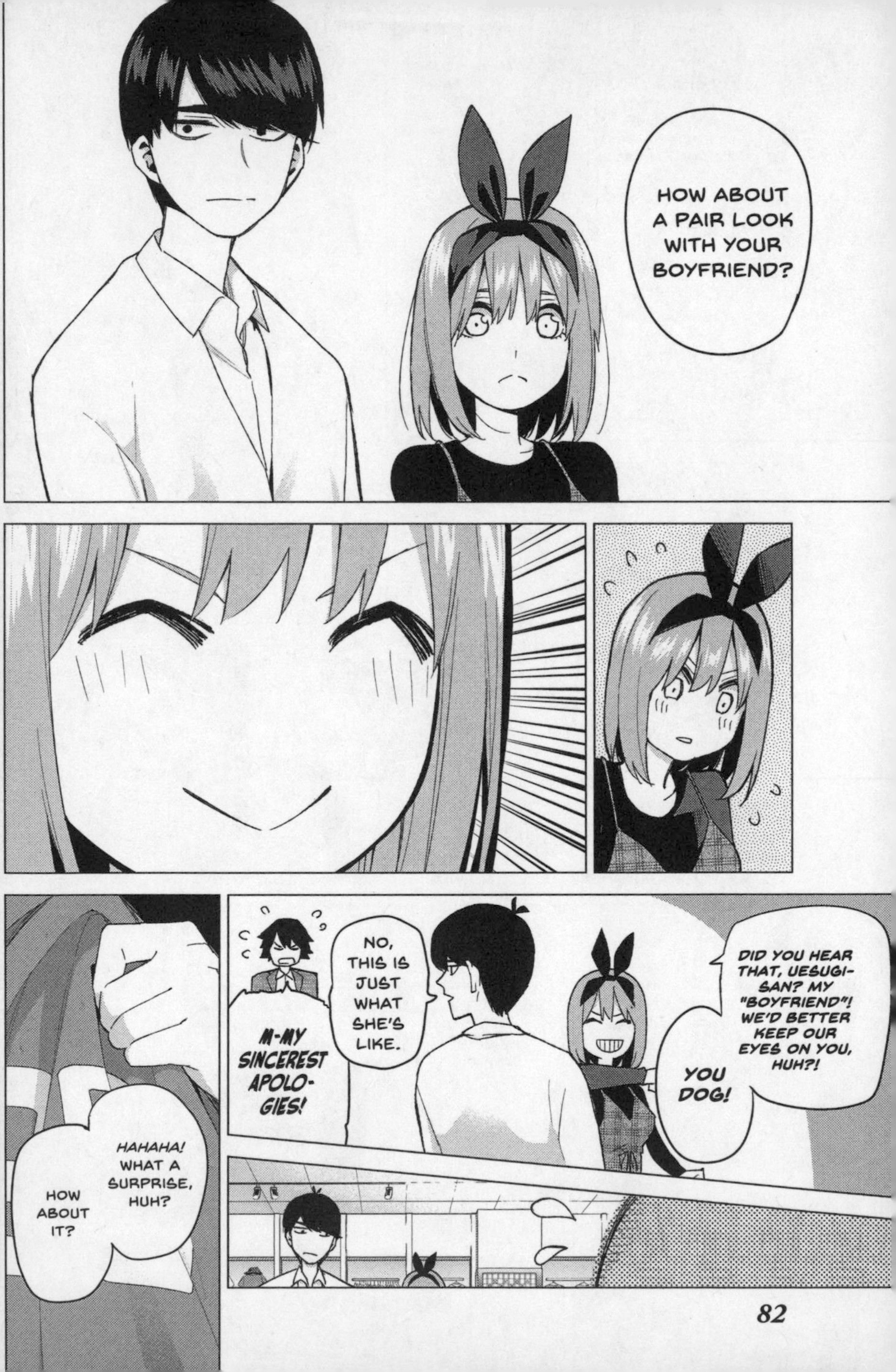
HOW ABOUT A PAIR LOOK WITH YOUR BOYFRIEND?
DID YOU HEAR THAT, UESUGI-SAN? MY "BOYFRIEND"! WE'D BETTER KEEP OUR EYES ON YOU, HUH?!
YOU DOG!
NO, THIS IS JUST WHAT SHE'S LIKE.
M-MY SINCEREST APOLO-GIES!
HAHAHA! WHAT A SURPRISE, HUH?
HOW ABOUT IT?

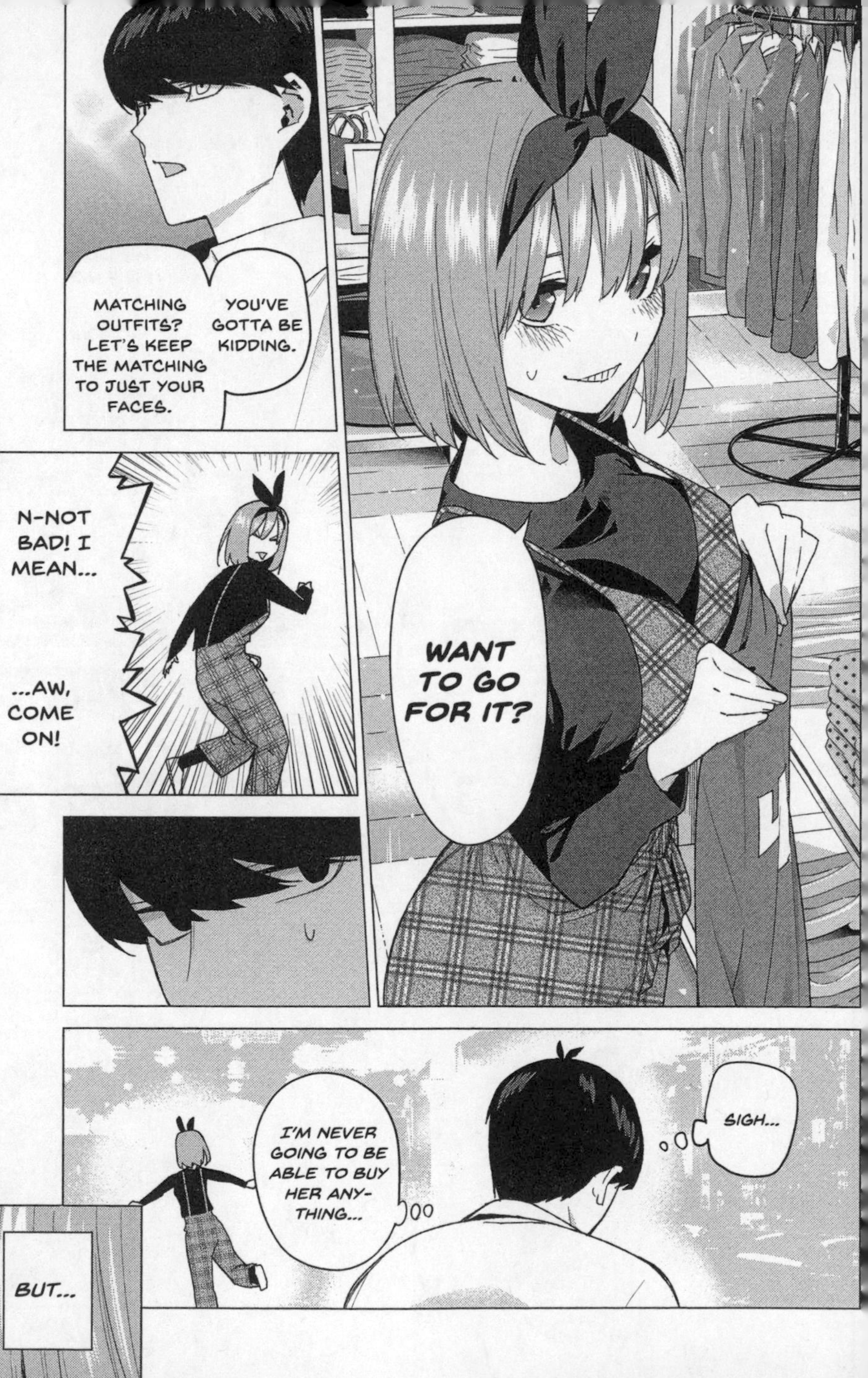
WANT TO GO FOR IT?
YOU'VE GOTTA BE KIDDING.
MATCHING OUTFITS? LET'S KEEP THE MATCHING TO JUST YOUR FACES.
N-NOT BAD! I MEAN...
...AW, COME ON!
SIGH...
I'M NEVER GOING TO BE ABLE TO BUY HER ANY-THING...
BUT...

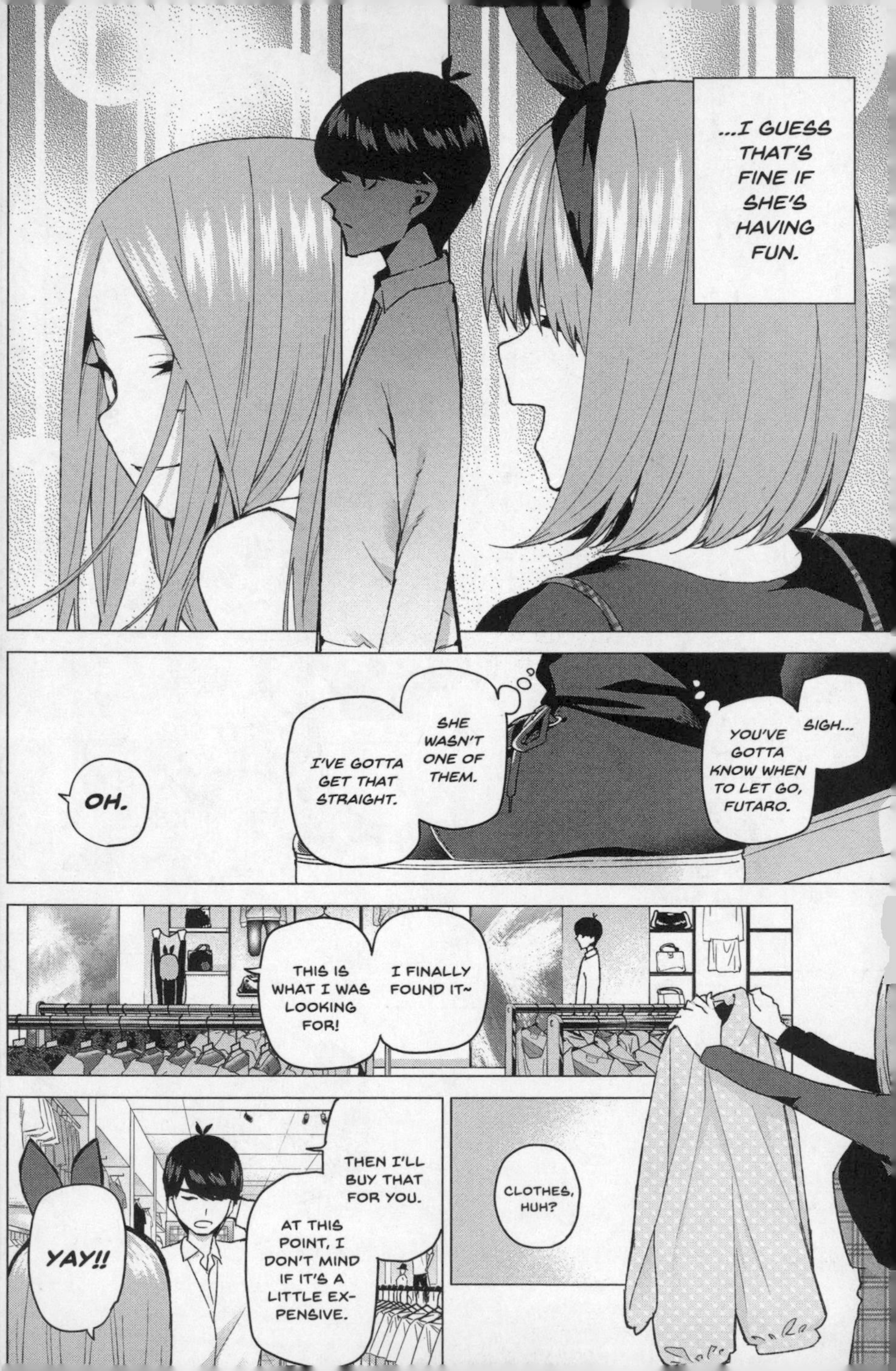
...I GUESS THAT'S FINE IF SHE'S HAVING FUN.
SIGH...
YOU'VE GOTTA KNOW WHEN TO LET GO, FUTARO.
SHE WASN'T ONE OF THEM.
I'VE GOTTA GET THAT STRAIGHT.
OH.
I FINALLY FOUND IT~
THIS IS WHAT I WAS LOOKING FOR!
CLOTHES, HUH?
THEN I'LL BUY THAT FOR YOU.
AT THIS POINT, I DON'T MIND IF IT'S A LITTLE EX-PENSIVE.
YAY!!

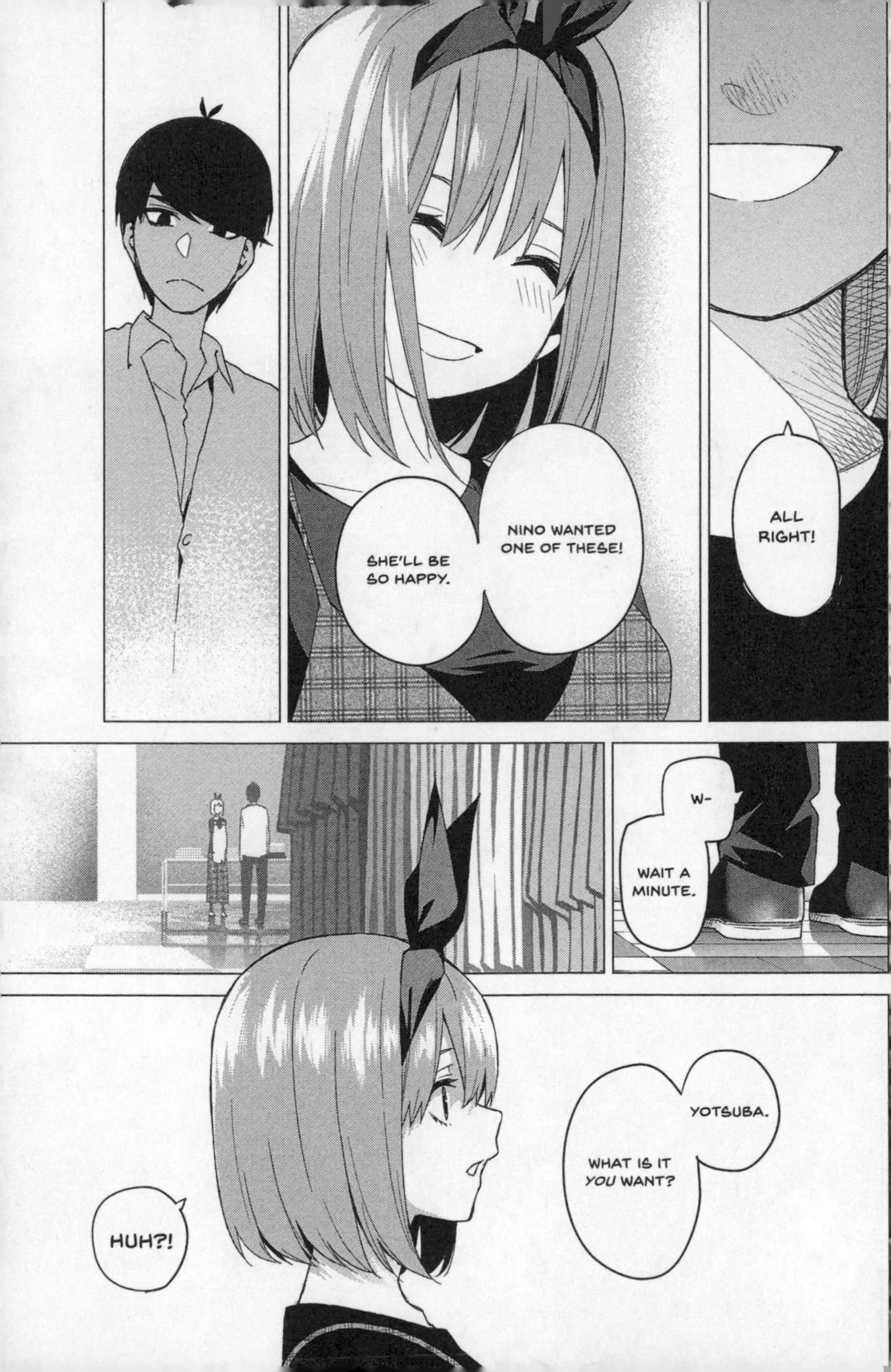
ALL RIGHT!
NINO WANTED ONE OF THESE!
SHE'LL BE SO HAPPY.
W-
WAIT A MINUTE.
YOTSUBA.
WHAT IS IT *YOU* WANT?
HUH?!

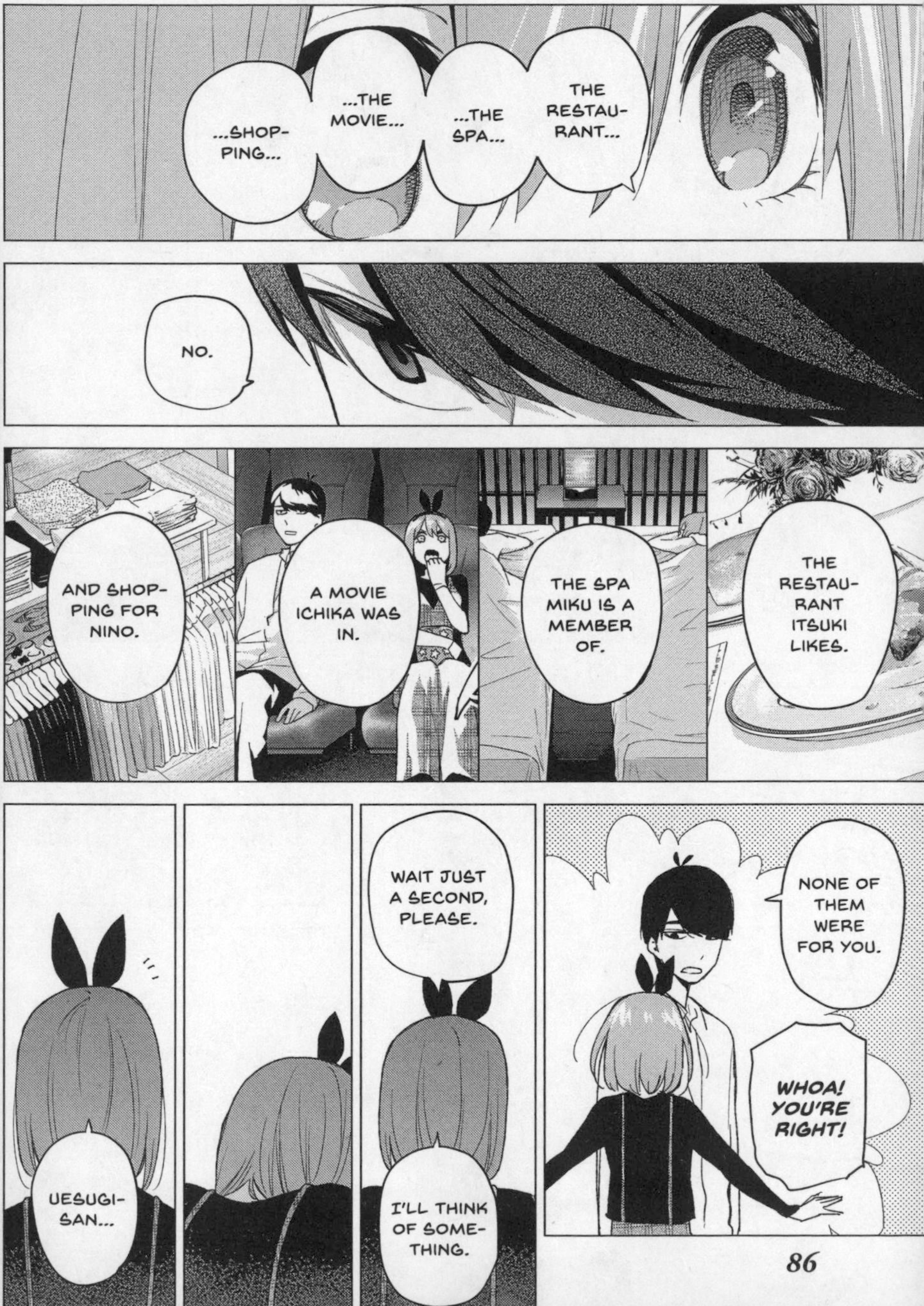
THE RESTAU-RANT...
...THE SPA...
...THE MOVIE...
...SHOP-PING...
NO.
THE RESTAU-RANT ITSUKI LIKES.
THE SPA MIKU IS A MEMBER OF.
A MOVIE ICHIKA WAS IN.
AND SHOP-PING FOR NINO.
NONE OF THEM WERE FOR YOU.
WHOA! YOU'RE RIGHT!
WAIT JUST A SECOND, PLEASE.
I'LL THINK OF SOME-THING.
UESUGI-SAN...

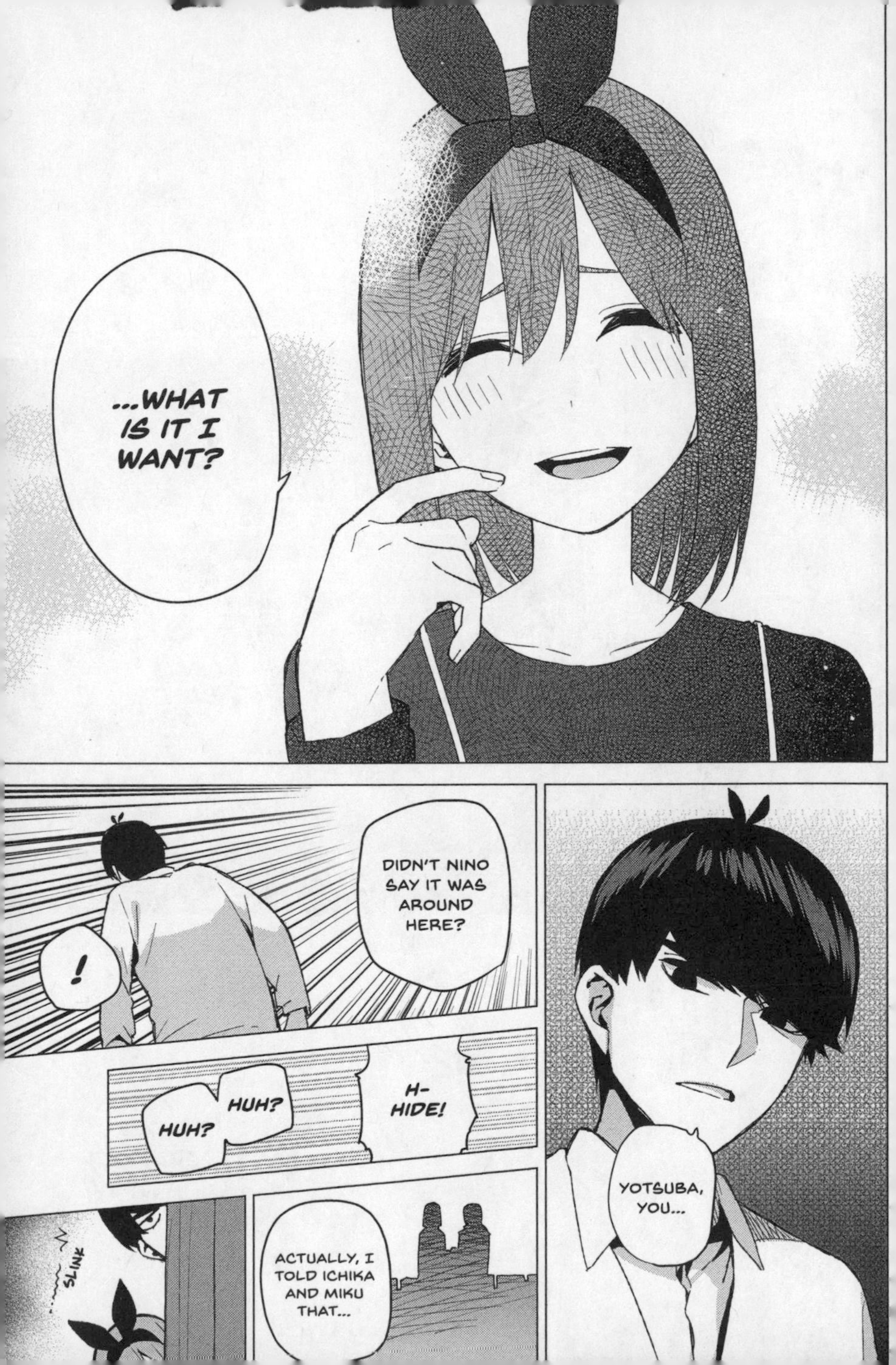
...WHAT IS IT I WANT?
YOTSUBA, YOU...
DIDN'T NINO SAY IT WAS AROUND HERE?
!
H- HIDE!
HUH?
HUH?
ACTUALLY, I TOLD ICHIKA AND MIKU THAT...
SLINK

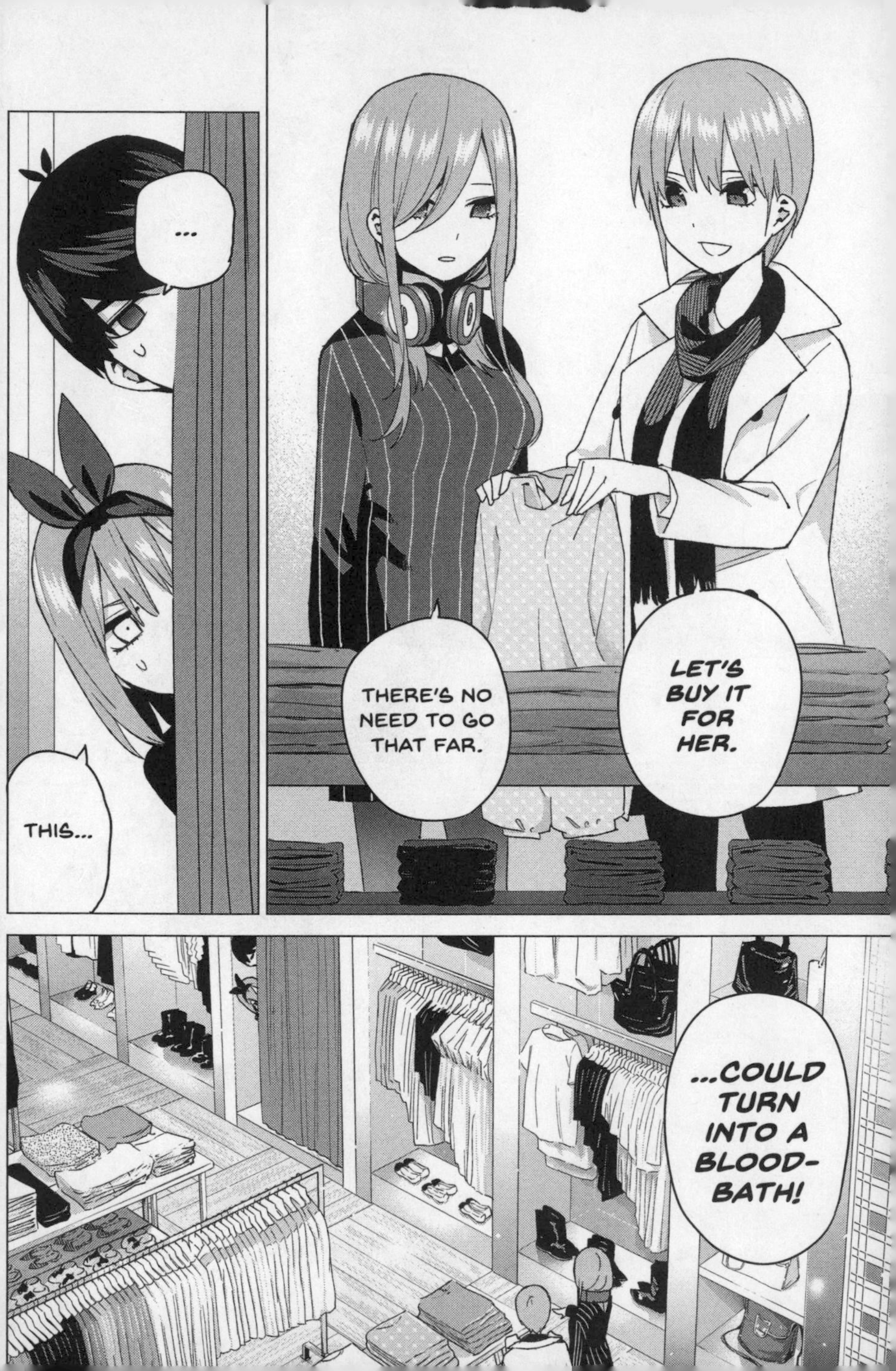
LET'S BUY IT FOR HER.
THERE'S NO NEED TO GO THAT FAR.
...
THIS...
...COULD TURN INTO A BLOOD-BATH!

# CHAPTER 37
# THE LABOR THANKSGIVING TOUR ②

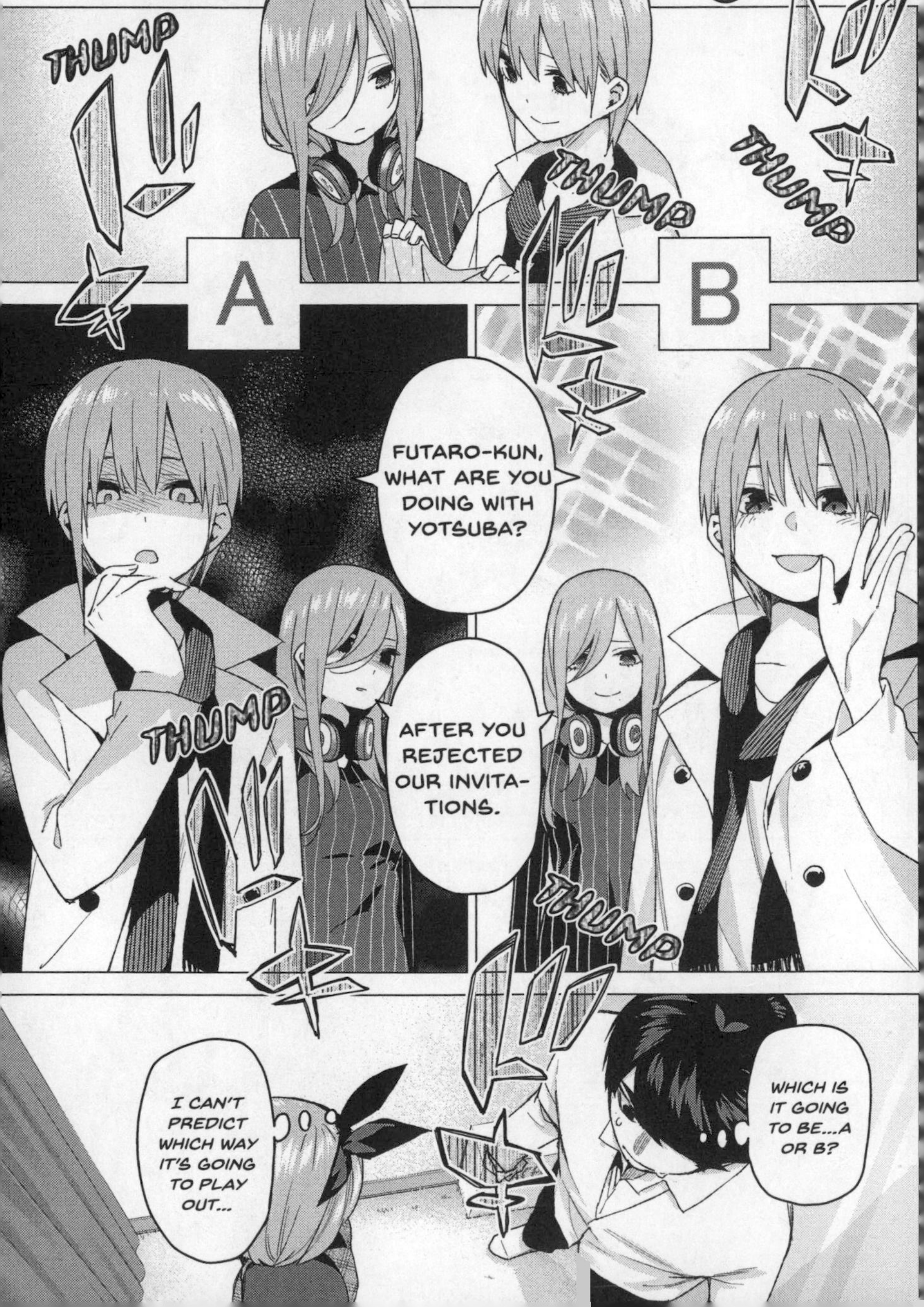

THUMP
THUMP
THUMP
B
A
FUTARO-KUN, WHAT ARE YOU DOING WITH YOTSUBA?
AFTER YOU REJECTED OUR INVITATIONS.
THUMP
THUMP
WHICH IS IT GOING TO BE...A OR B?
I CAN'T PREDICT WHICH WAY IT'S GOING TO PLAY OUT...

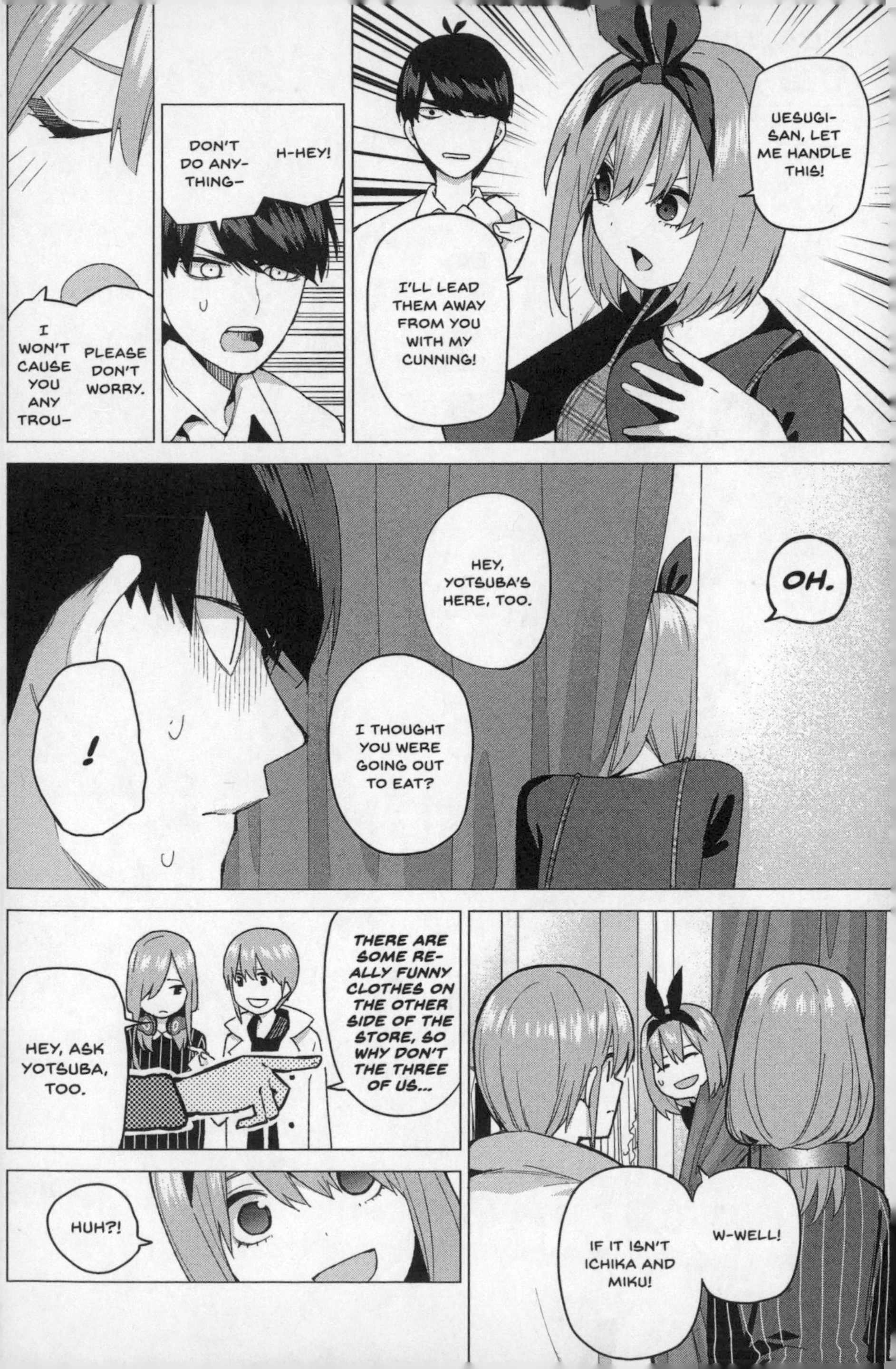
UESUGI-SAN, LET ME HANDLE THIS!
I'LL LEAD THEM AWAY FROM YOU WITH MY CUNNING!
H-HEY!
DON'T DO ANY-THING–
PLEASE DON'T WORRY.
I WON'T CAUSE YOU ANY TROU–
OH.
HEY, YOTSUBA'S HERE, TOO.
I THOUGHT YOU WERE GOING OUT TO EAT?
!
W-WELL!
IF IT ISN'T ICHIKA AND MIKU!
THERE ARE SOME RE-ALLY FUNNY CLOTHES ON THE OTHER SIDE OF THE STORE, SO WHY DON'T THE THREE OF US...
HEY, ASK YOTSUBA, TOO.
HUH?!

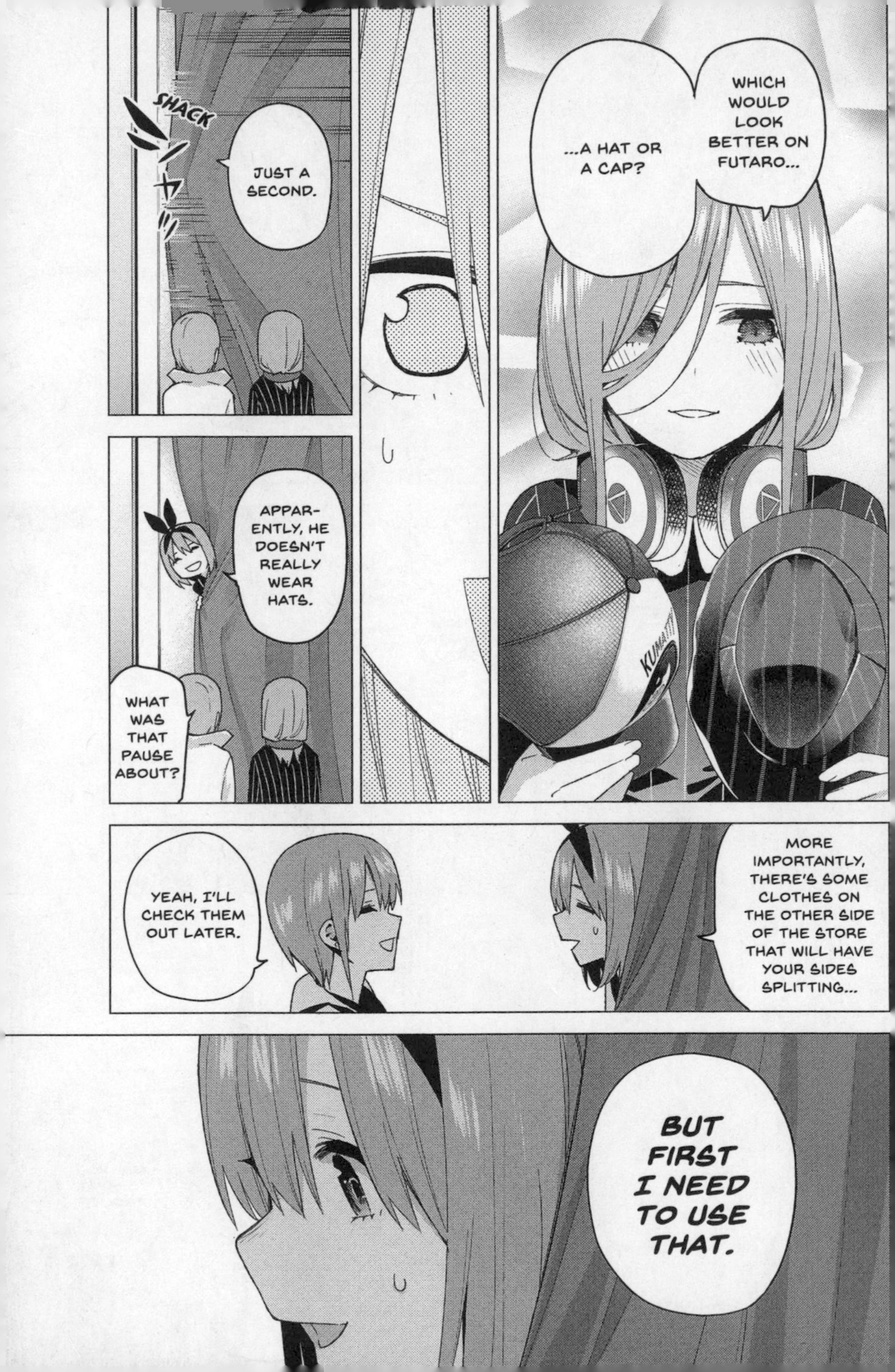
WHICH WOULD LOOK BETTER ON FUTARO...
...A HAT OR A CAP?
SHACK
JUST A SECOND.
APPAR-ENTLY, HE DOESN'T REALLY WEAR HATS.
WHAT WAS THAT PAUSE ABOUT?
MORE IMPORTANTLY, THERE'S SOME CLOTHES ON THE OTHER SIDE OF THE STORE THAT WILL HAVE YOUR SIDES SPLITTING...
YEAH, I'LL CHECK THEM OUT LATER.
BUT FIRST I NEED TO USE THAT.

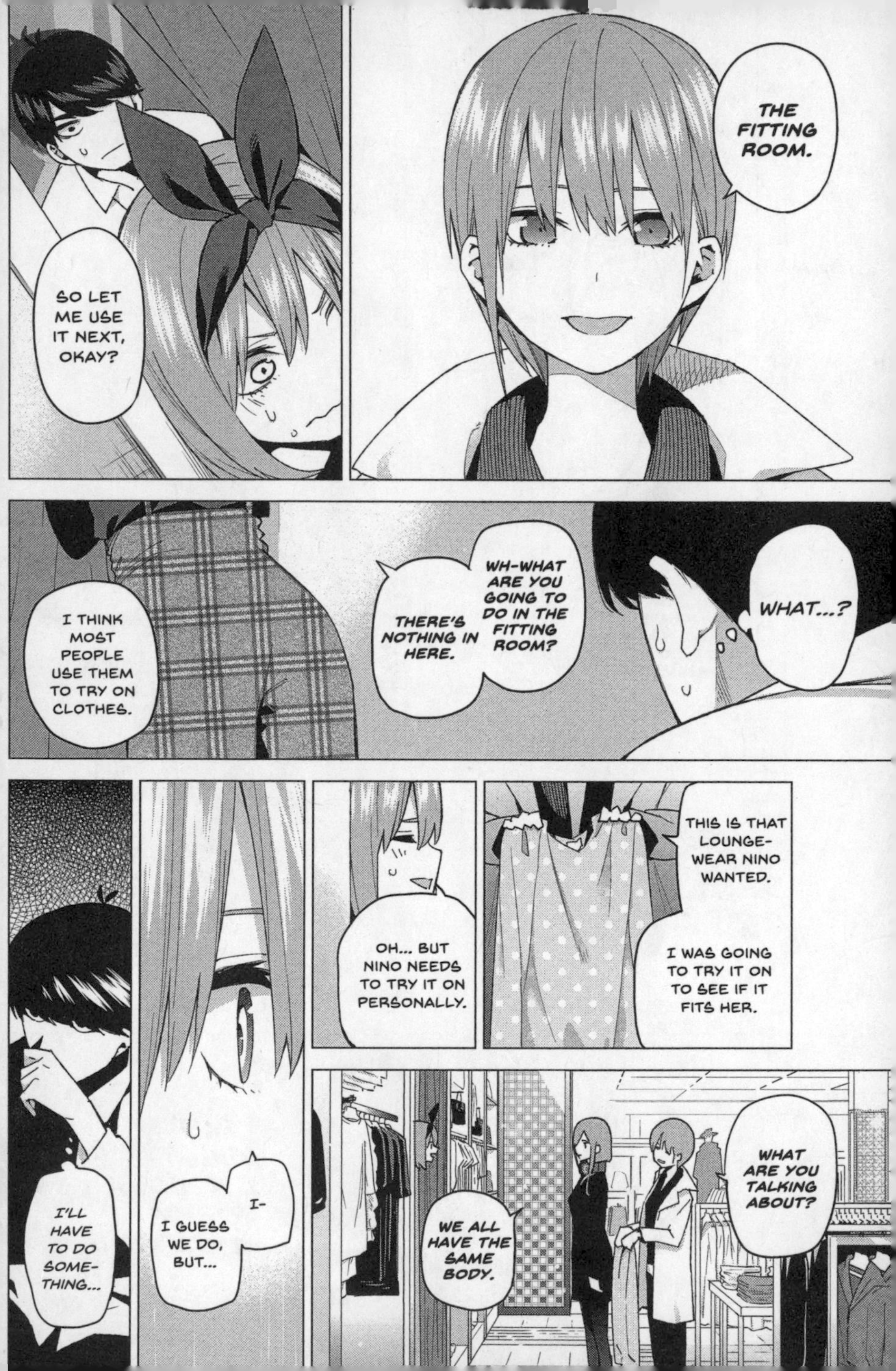
THE FITTING ROOM.
SO LET ME USE IT NEXT, OKAY?
WHAT...?
WH-WHAT ARE YOU GOING TO DO IN THE FITTING ROOM?
THERE'S NOTHING IN HERE.
I THINK MOST PEOPLE USE THEM TO TRY ON CLOTHES.
THIS IS THAT LOUNGE-WEAR NINO WANTED.
I WAS GOING TO TRY IT ON TO SEE IF IT FITS HER.
OH... BUT NINO NEEDS TO TRY IT ON PERSONALLY.
WHAT ARE YOU TALKING ABOUT?
WE ALL HAVE THE SAME BODY.
I-
I GUESS WE DO, BUT...
I'LL HAVE TO DO SOME-THING...

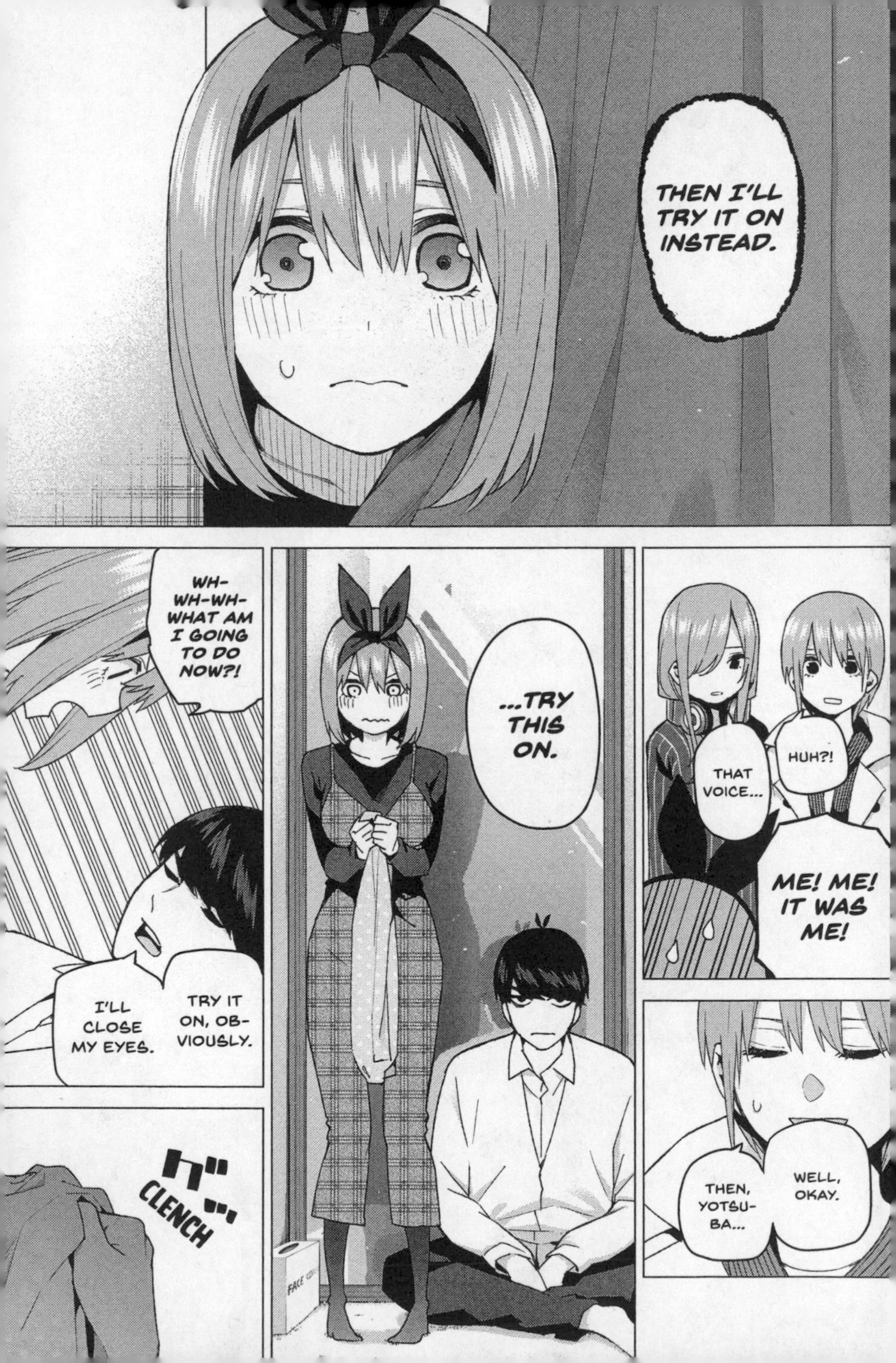
THEN I'LL TRY IT ON INSTEAD.
HUH?!
THAT VOICE...
ME! ME! IT WAS ME!
WELL, OKAY.
THEN, YOTSUBA...
...TRY THIS ON.
WH-WH-WH-WHAT AM I GOING TO DO NOW?!
TRY IT ON, OBVIOUSLY.
I'LL CLOSE MY EYES.
CLENCH

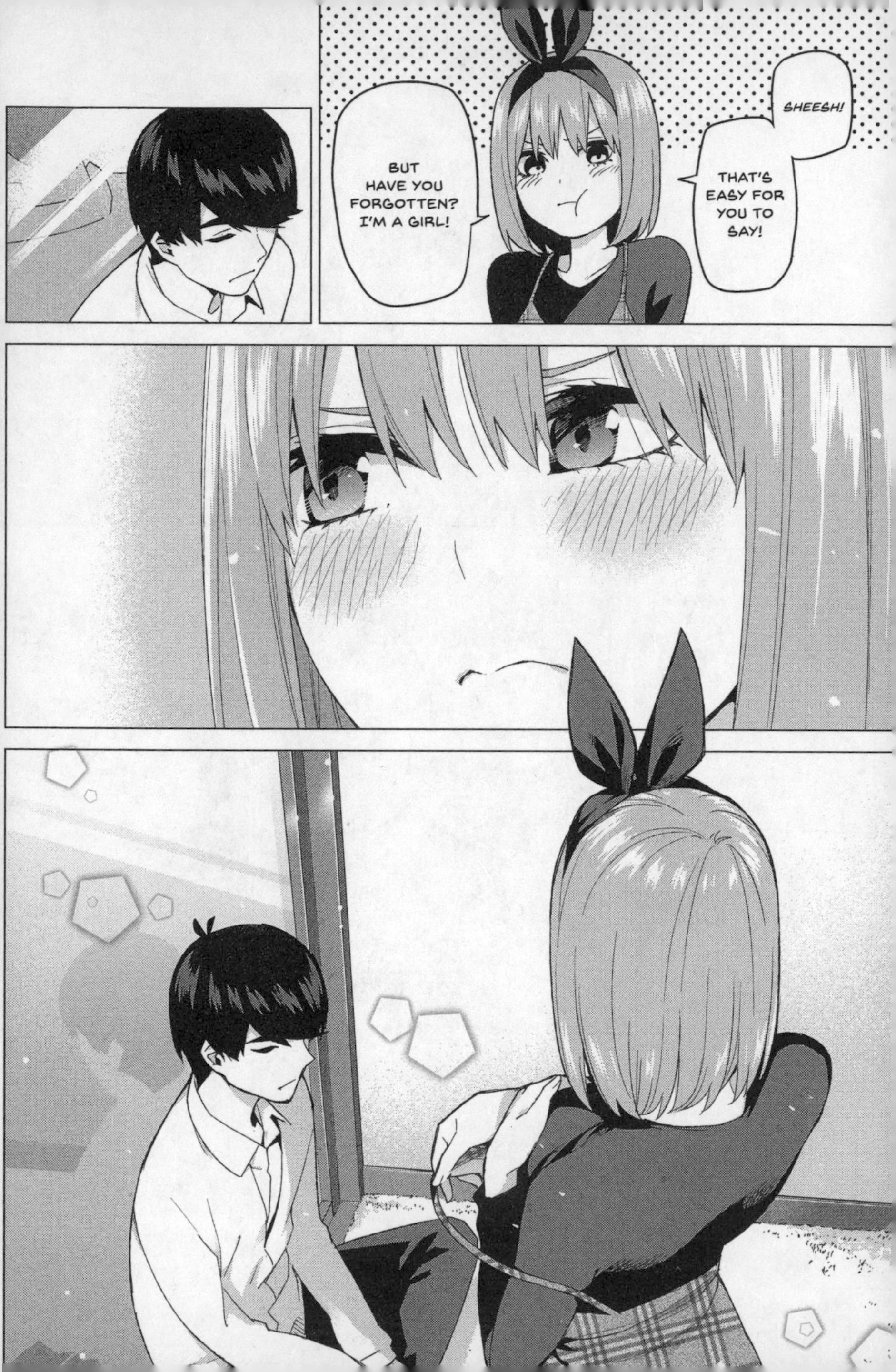
SHEESH!
THAT'S EASY FOR YOU TO SAY!
BUT HAVE YOU FORGOTTEN? I'M A GIRL!

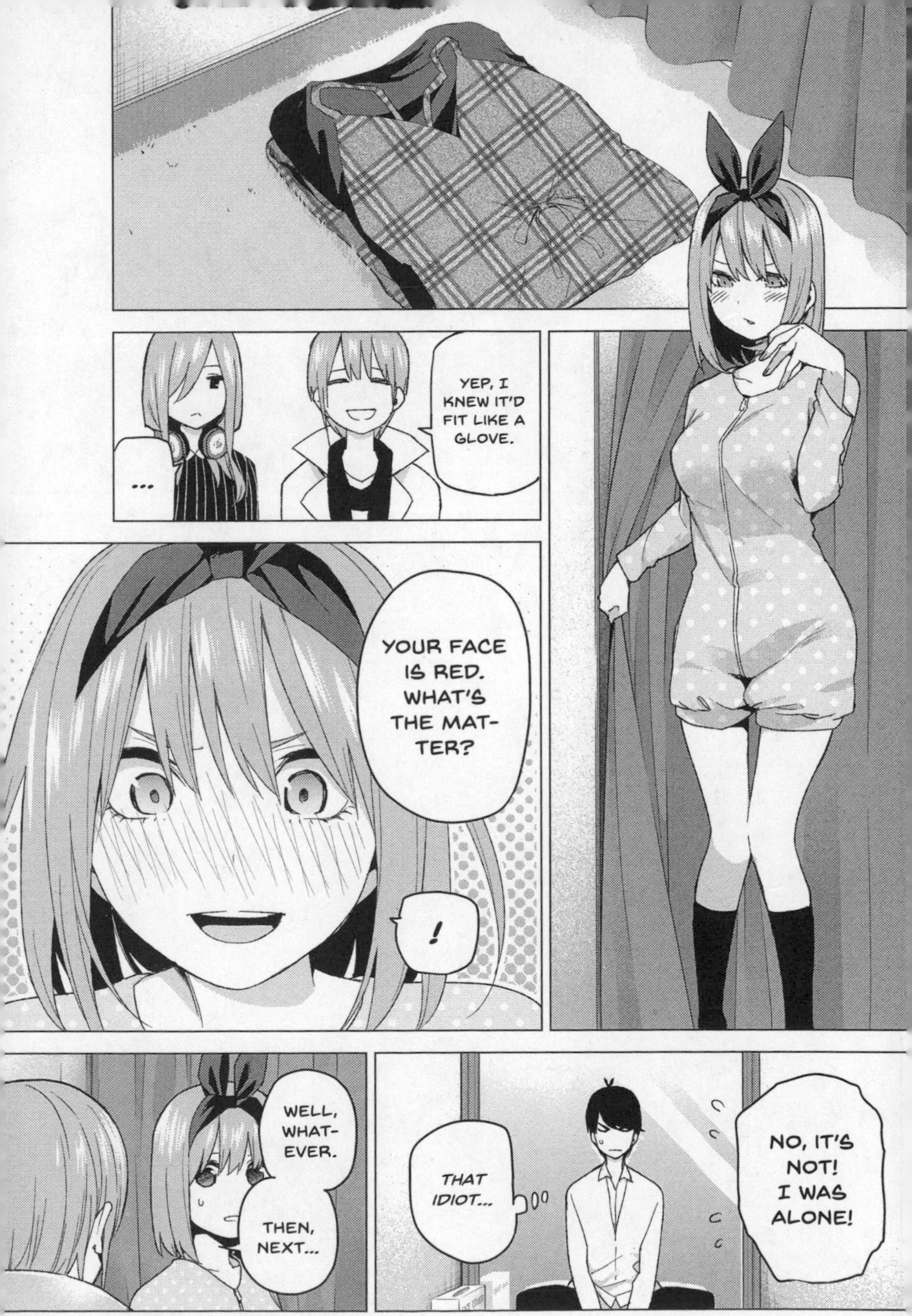
YEP, I KNEW IT'D FIT LIKE A GLOVE.
...
YOUR FACE IS RED. WHAT'S THE MAT-TER?
!
NO, IT'S NOT! I WAS ALONE!
THAT IDIOT...
WELL, WHAT-EVER.
THEN, NEXT...

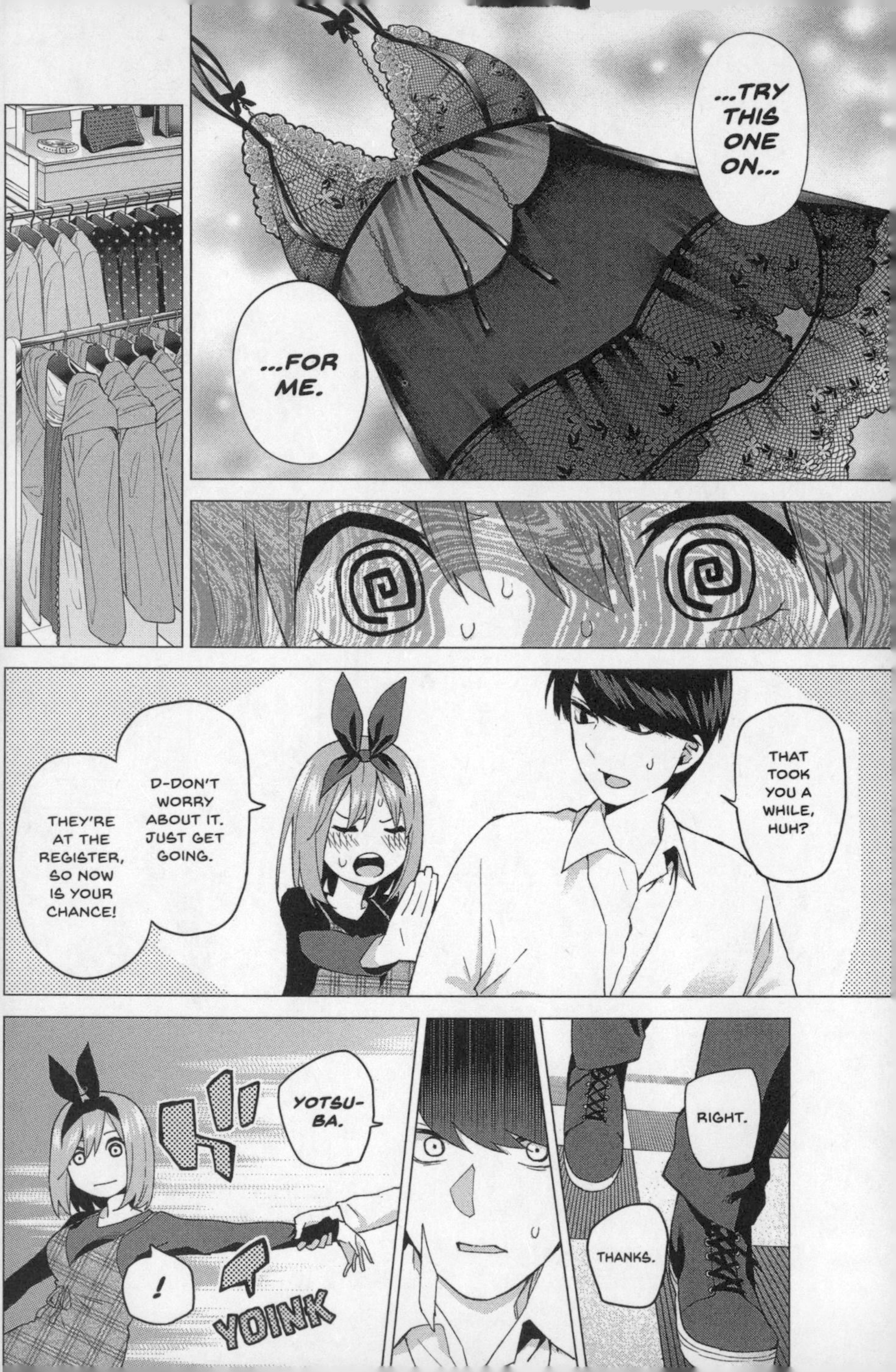
...TRY THIS ONE ON...
...FOR ME.
THAT TOOK YOU A WHILE, HUH?
D-DON'T WORRY ABOUT IT. JUST GET GOING.
THEY'RE AT THE REGISTER, SO NOW IS YOUR CHANCE!
RIGHT.
THANKS.
YOTSU-BA.
K!!
!
YOINK

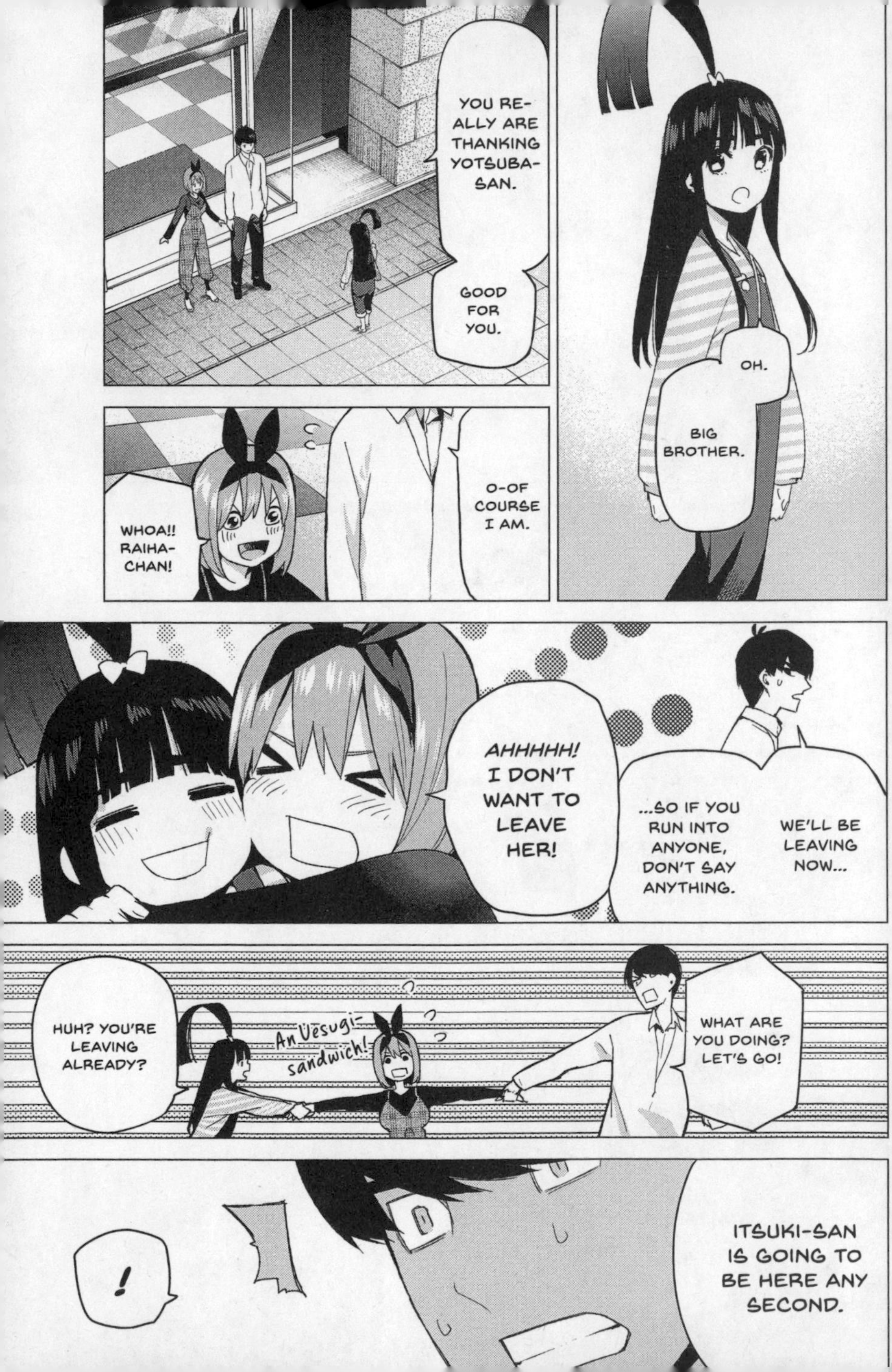
OH.
BIG BROTHER.
YOU RE-ALLY ARE THANKING YOTSUBA-SAN.
GOOD FOR YOU.
O-OF COURSE I AM.
WHOA!! RAIHA-CHAN!
WE'LL BE LEAVING NOW...
...SO IF YOU RUN INTO ANYONE, DON'T SAY ANYTHING.
AHHHHH! I DON'T WANT TO LEAVE HER!
WHAT ARE YOU DOING? LET'S GO!
An Uesugi sandwich!
HUH? YOU'RE LEAVING ALREADY?
ITSUKI-SAN IS GOING TO BE HERE ANY SECOND.
!

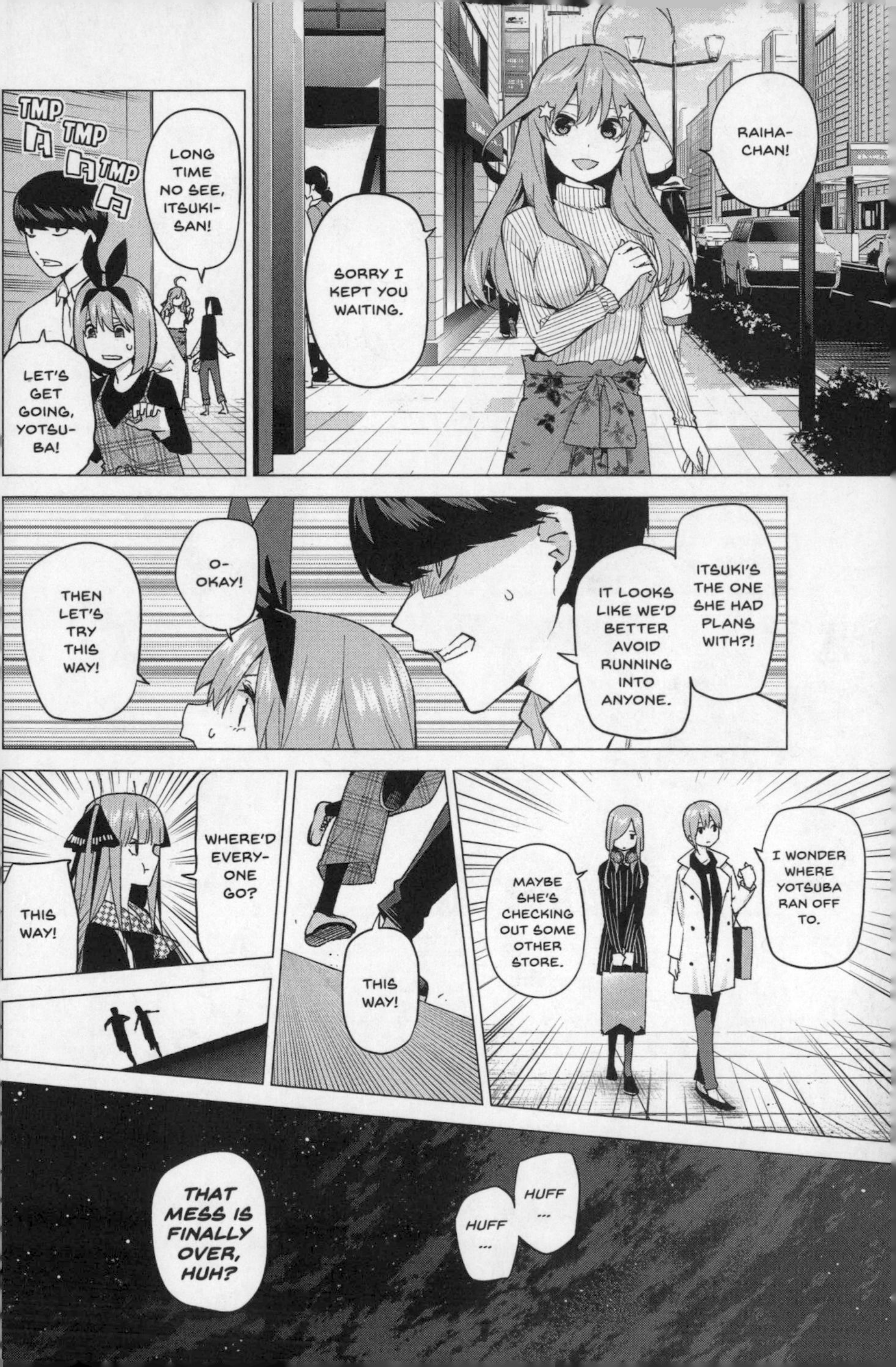
RAIHA-CHAN!
SORRY I KEPT YOU WAITING.
LONG TIME NO SEE, ITSUKI-SAN!
TMP TMP TMP
LET'S GET GOING, YOTSUBA!
ITSUKI'S THE ONE SHE HAD PLANS WITH?!
IT LOOKS LIKE WE'D BETTER AVOID RUNNING INTO ANYONE.
O-OKAY!
THEN LET'S TRY THIS WAY!
I WONDER WHERE YOTSUBA RAN OFF TO.
MAYBE SHE'S CHECKING OUT SOME OTHER STORE.
THIS WAY!
WHERE'D EVERY-ONE GO?
THIS WAY!
HUFF...
HUFF...
THAT MESS IS FINALLY OVER, HUH?

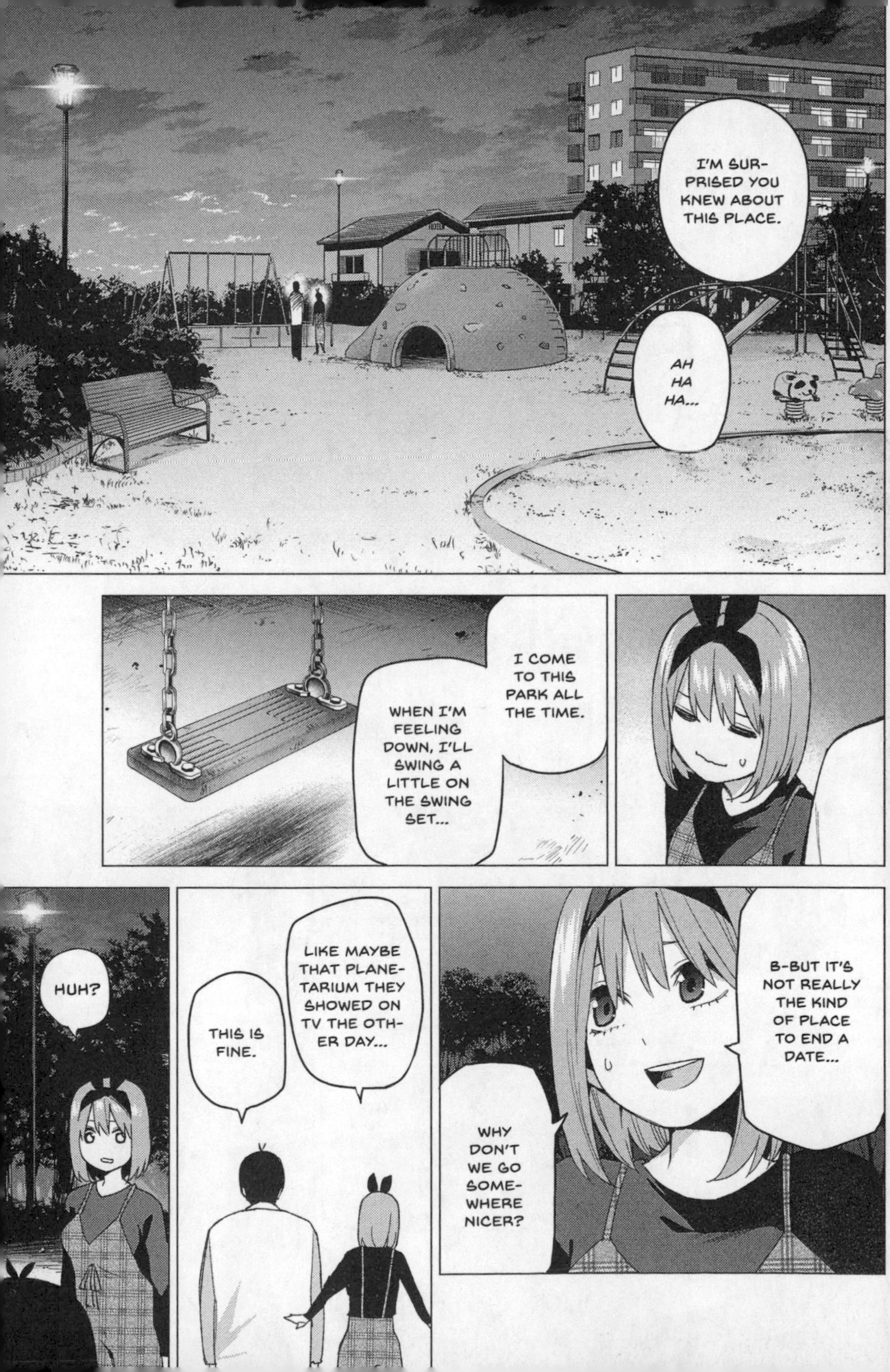
I'M SURPRISED YOU KNEW ABOUT THIS PLACE.
AH HA HA...
I COME TO THIS PARK ALL THE TIME.
WHEN I'M FEELING DOWN, I'LL SWING A LITTLE ON THE SWING SET...
B-BUT IT'S NOT REALLY THE KIND OF PLACE TO END A DATE...
WHY DON'T WE GO SOMEWHERE NICER?
LIKE MAYBE THAT PLANETARIUM THEY SHOWED ON TV THE OTHER DAY...
THIS IS FINE.
HUH?

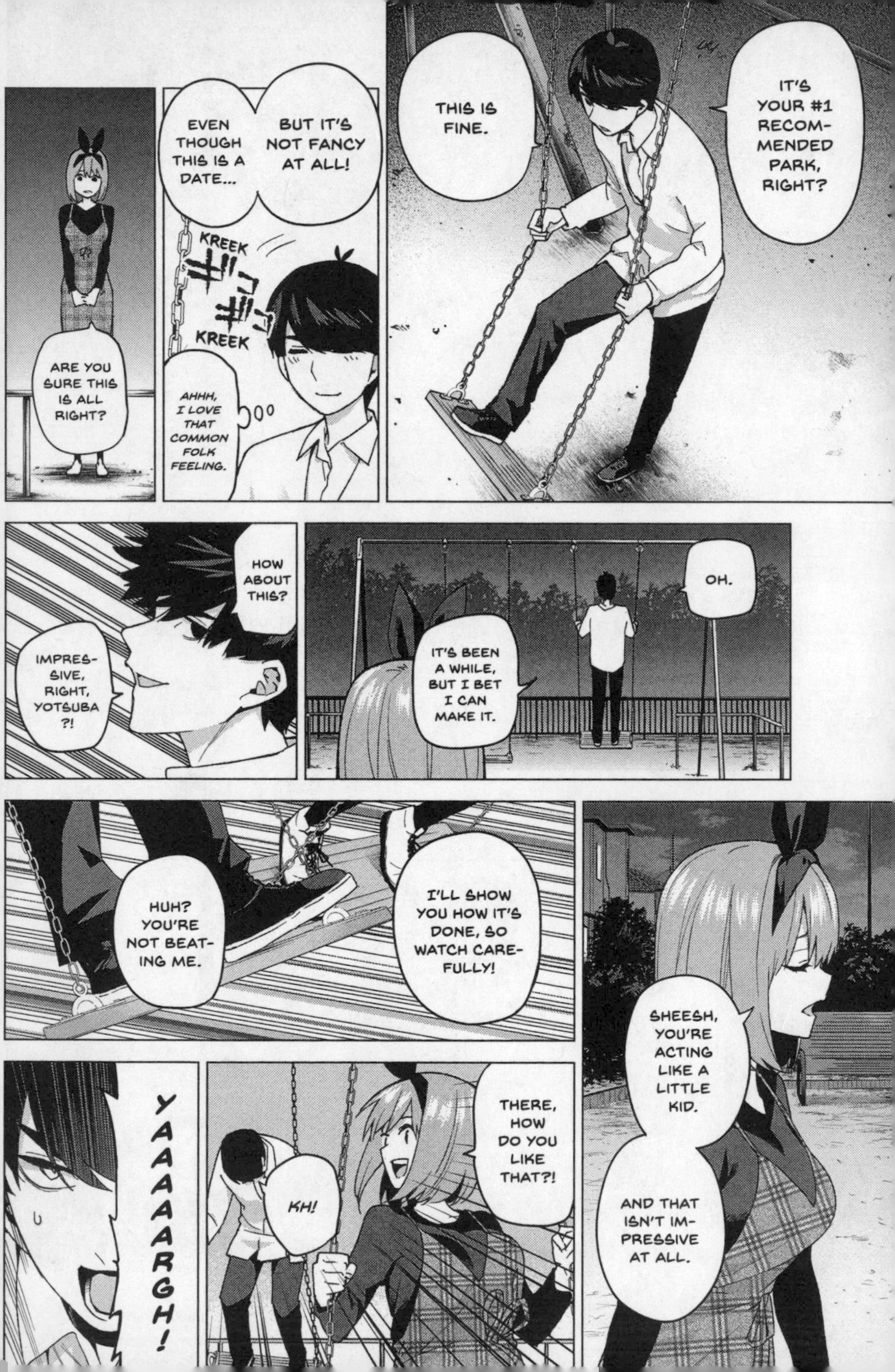
IT'S YOUR #1 RECOMMENDED PARK, RIGHT?
THIS IS FINE.
BUT IT'S NOT FANCY AT ALL!
EVEN THOUGH THIS IS A DATE...
KREEK
KREEK
AHHH, I LOVE THAT COMMON FOLK FEELING.
ARE YOU SURE THIS IS ALL RIGHT?
OH.
IT'S BEEN A WHILE, BUT I BET I CAN MAKE IT.
HOW ABOUT THIS?
IMPRESSIVE, RIGHT, YOTSUBA?!
SHEESH, YOU'RE ACTING LIKE A LITTLE KID.
AND THAT ISN'T IMPRESSIVE AT ALL.
I'LL SHOW YOU HOW IT'S DONE, SO WATCH CAREFULLY!
HUH? YOU'RE NOT BEATING ME.
THERE, HOW DO YOU LIKE THAT?!
KH!
YAAAAARGH!

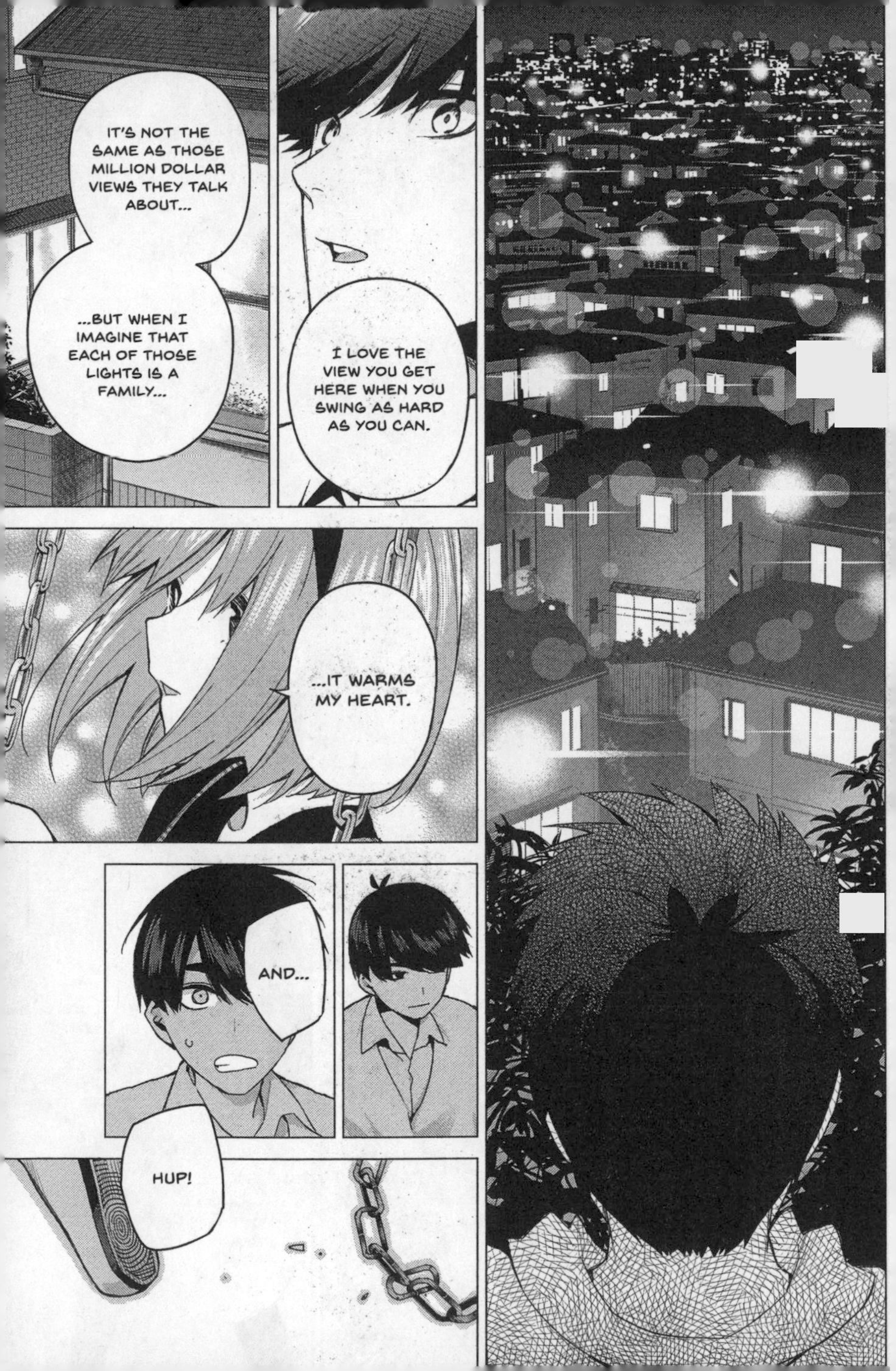
I LOVE THE VIEW YOU GET HERE WHEN YOU SWING AS HARD AS YOU CAN.
IT'S NOT THE SAME AS THOSE MILLION DOLLAR VIEWS THEY TALK ABOUT...
...BUT WHEN I IMAGINE THAT EACH OF THOSE LIGHTS IS A FAMILY...
...IT WARMS MY HEART.
AND...
HUP!

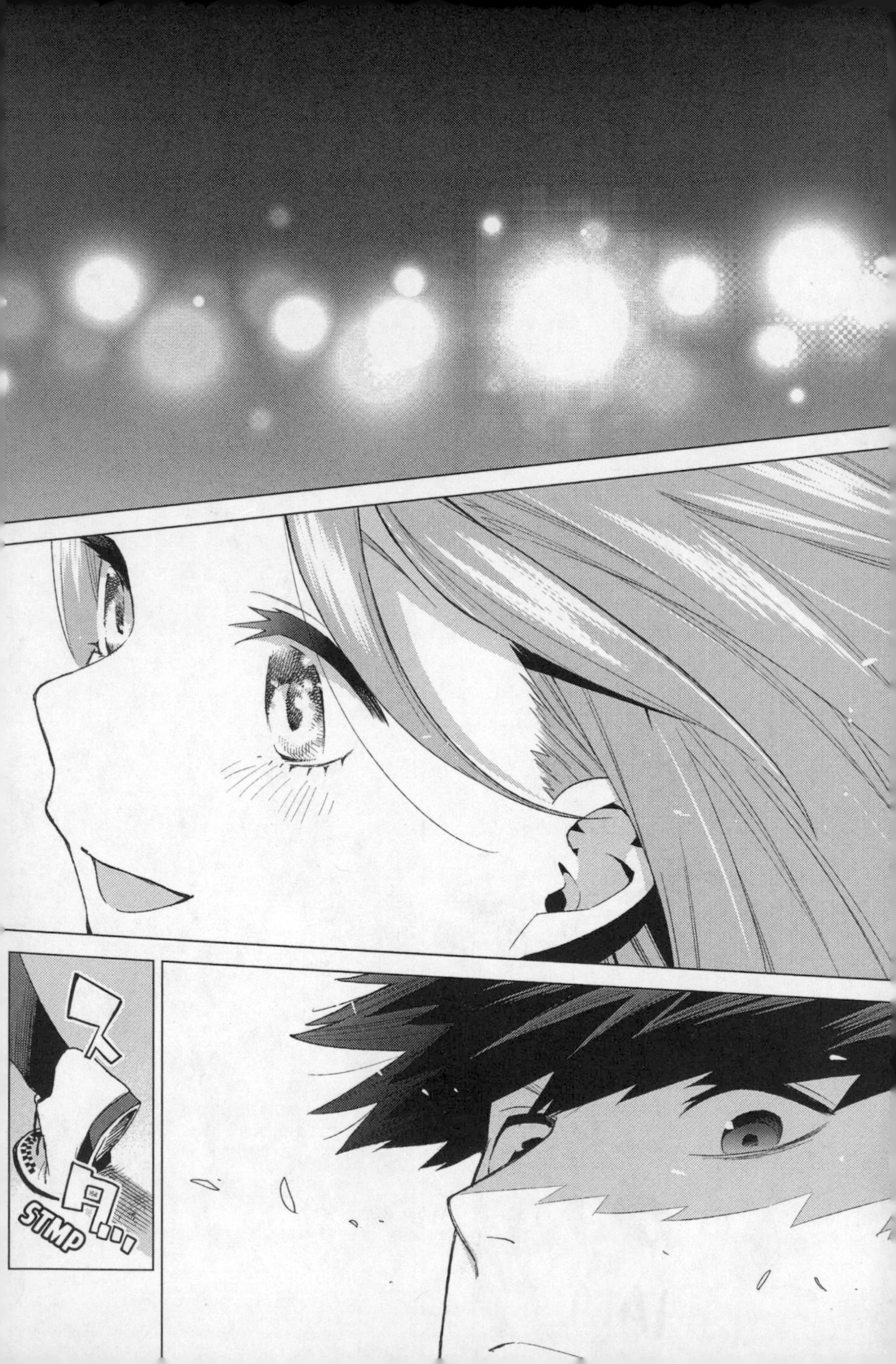
スタ…
STMP

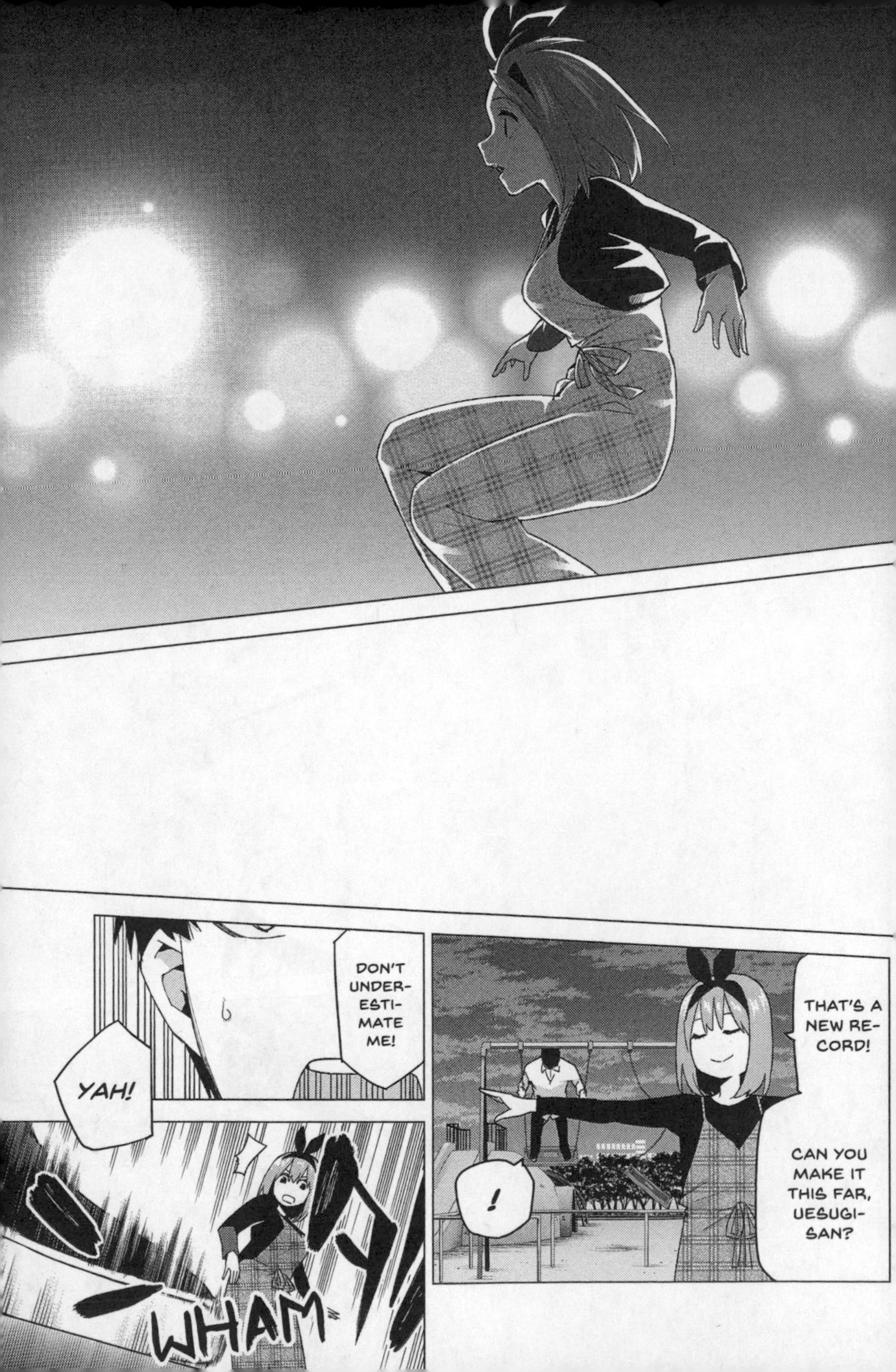
THAT'S A NEW RE-CORD!
CAN YOU MAKE IT THIS FAR, UESUGI-SAN?
!
DON'T UNDER-ESTI-MATE ME!
YAH!
WHAM

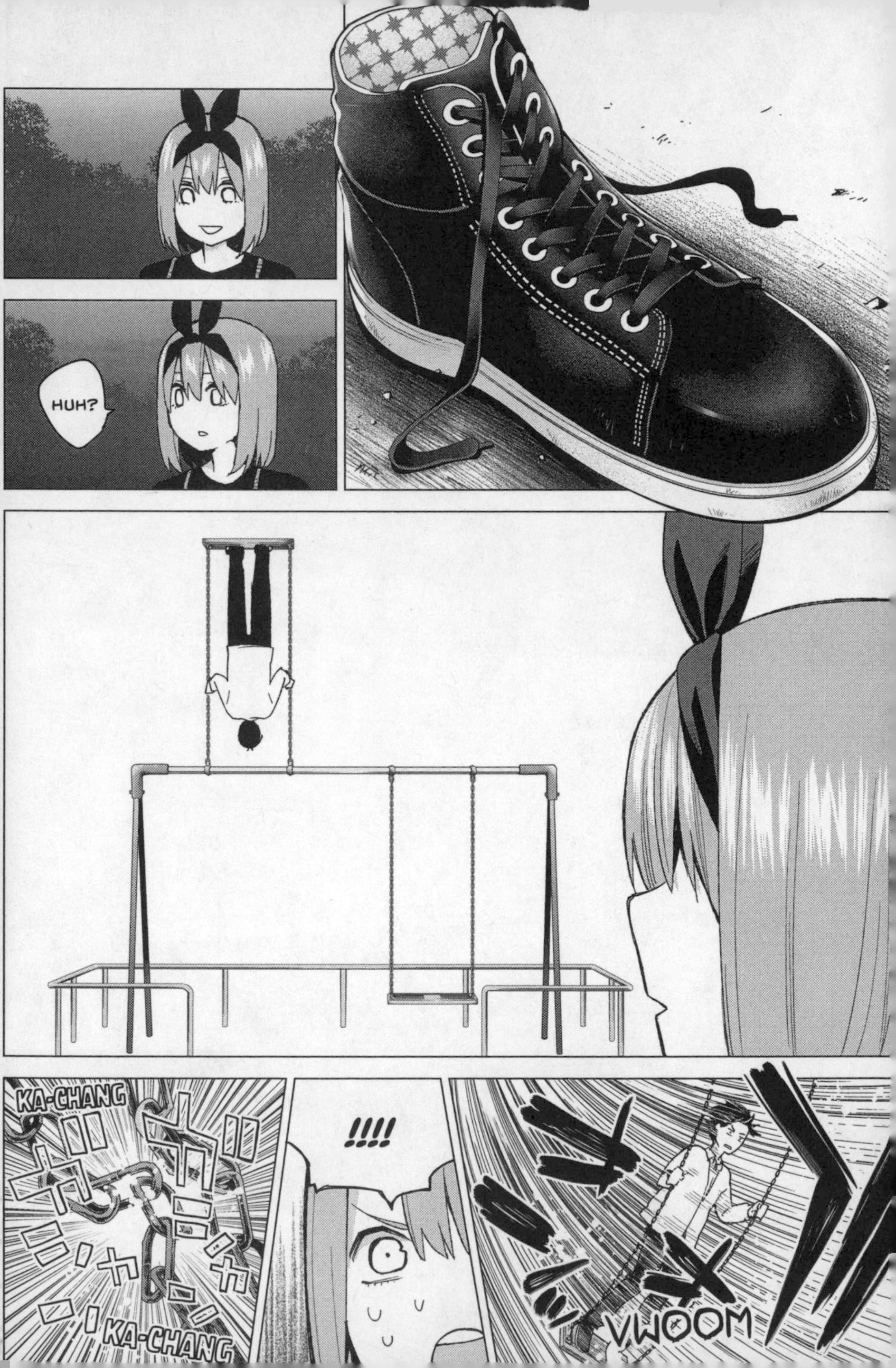
HUH?
VWOOM
!!!!
KA-CHANG
KA-CHANG

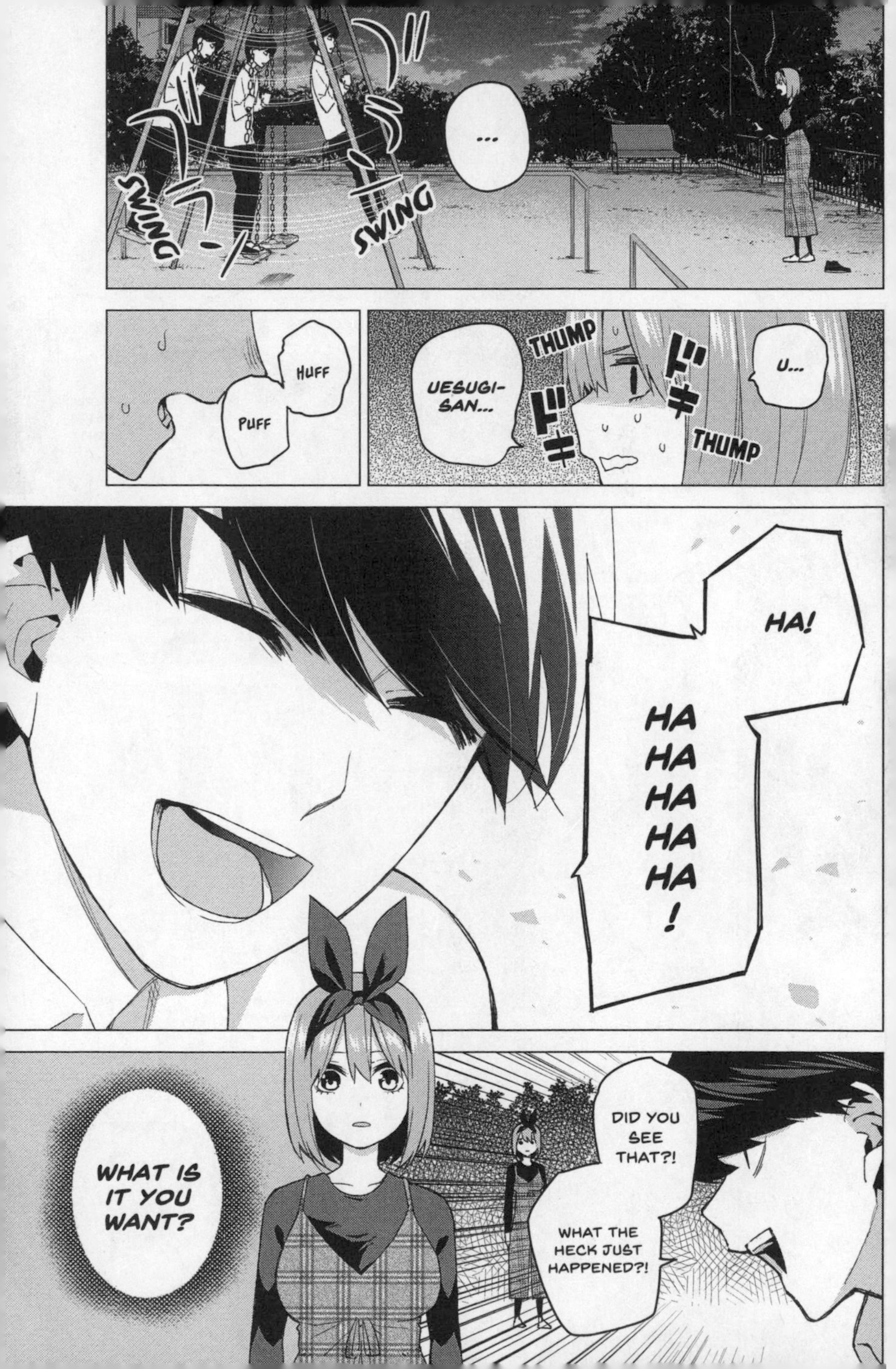
...
SWING
SWING
U...
THUMP
ドキ
ドキ
THUMP
UESUGI-SAN...
HUFF
PUFF
HA!
HA HA HA HA HA HA!
DID YOU SEE THAT?!
WHAT THE HECK JUST HAPPENED?!
WHAT IS IT YOU WANT?

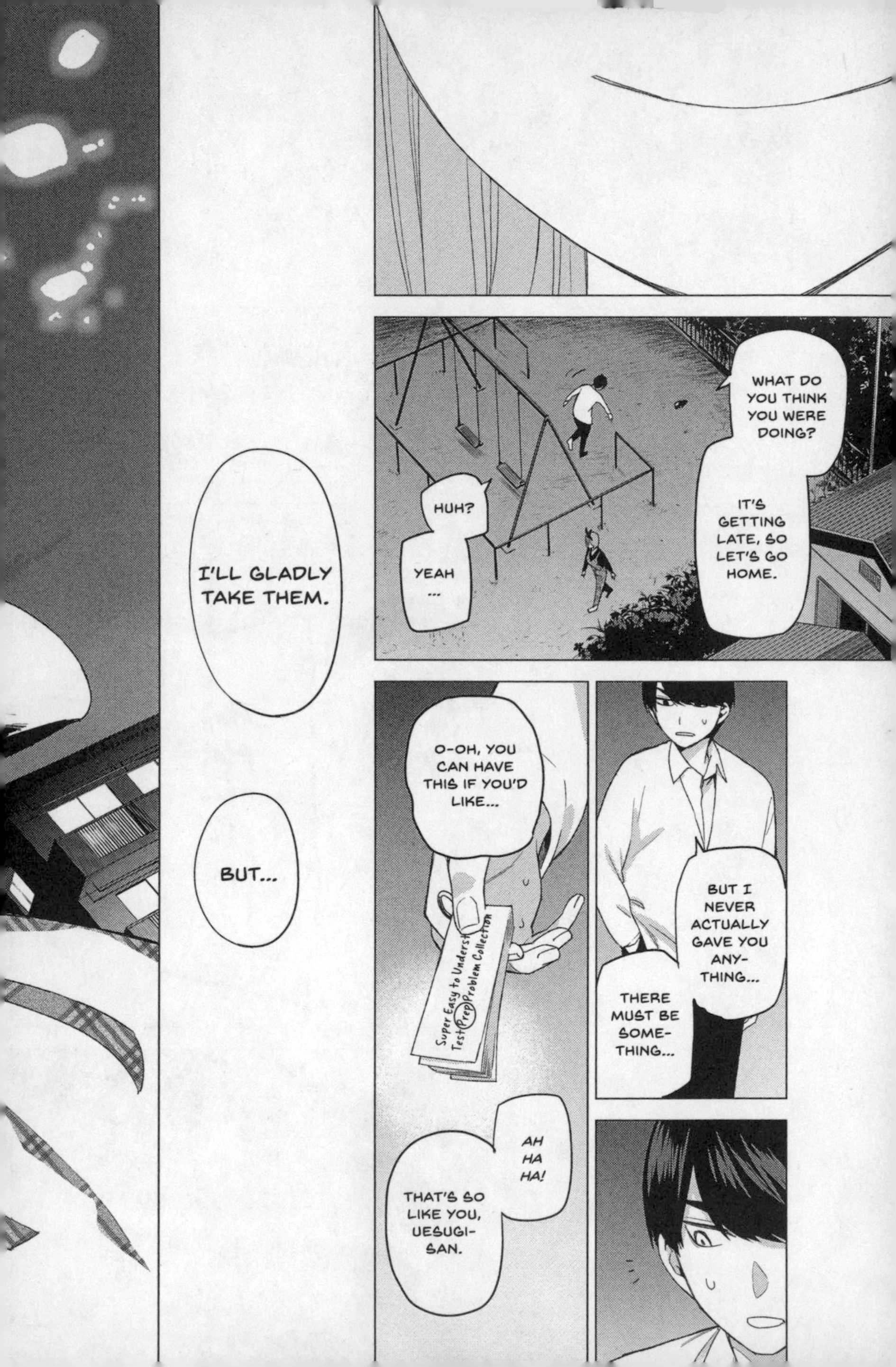
WHAT DO YOU THINK YOU WERE DOING?
IT'S GETTING LATE, SO LET'S GO HOME.
HUH?
YEAH...
BUT I NEVER ACTUALLY GAVE YOU ANYTHING...
THERE MUST BE SOME-THING...
O-OH, YOU CAN HAVE THIS IF YOU'D LIKE...
Super Easy to Underst
Test Prep Problem Collection
AH HA HA!
THAT'S SO LIKE YOU, UESUGI-SAN.
I'LL GLADLY TAKE THEM.
BUT...

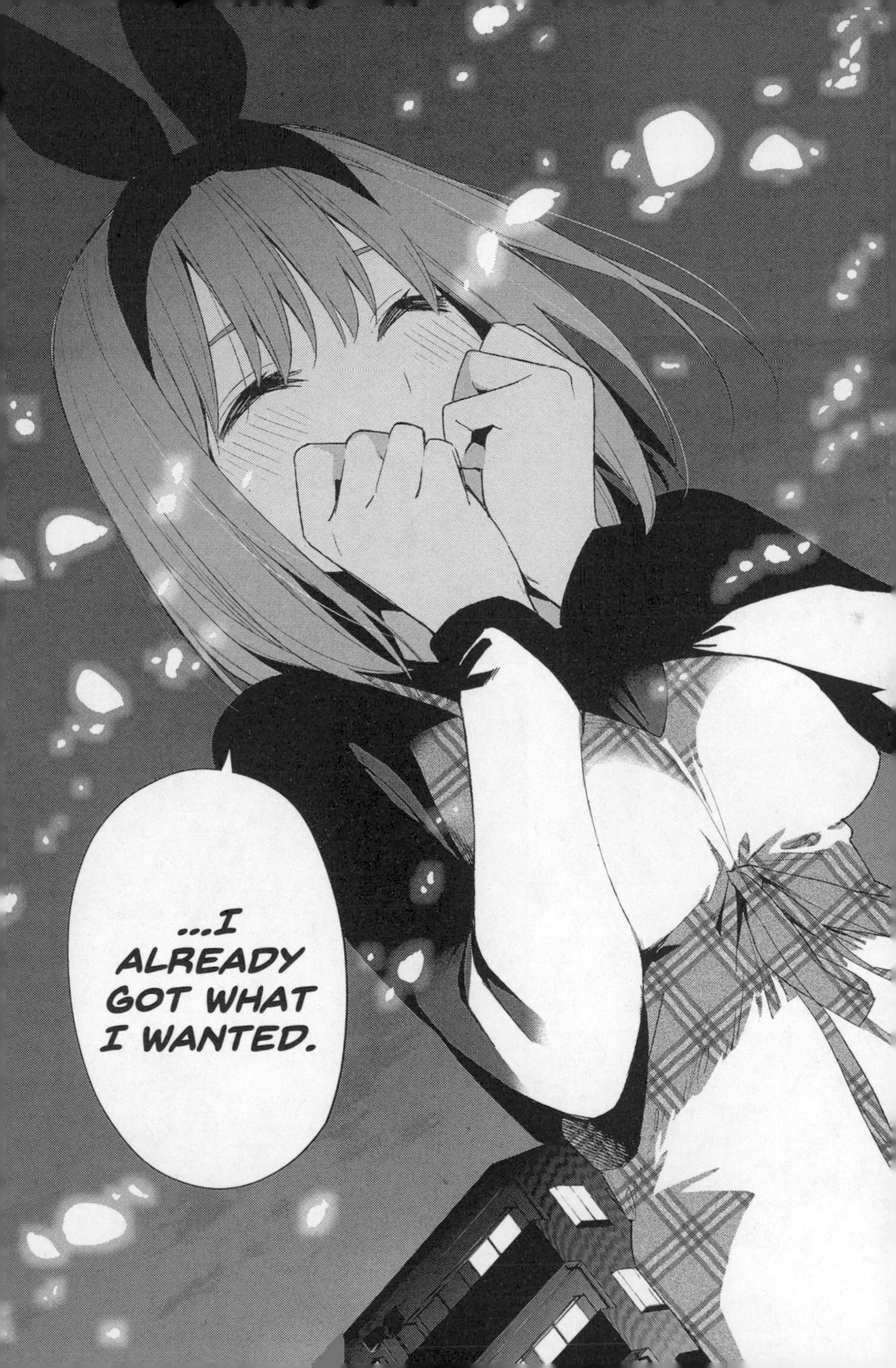
...I ALREADY GOT WHAT I WANTED.

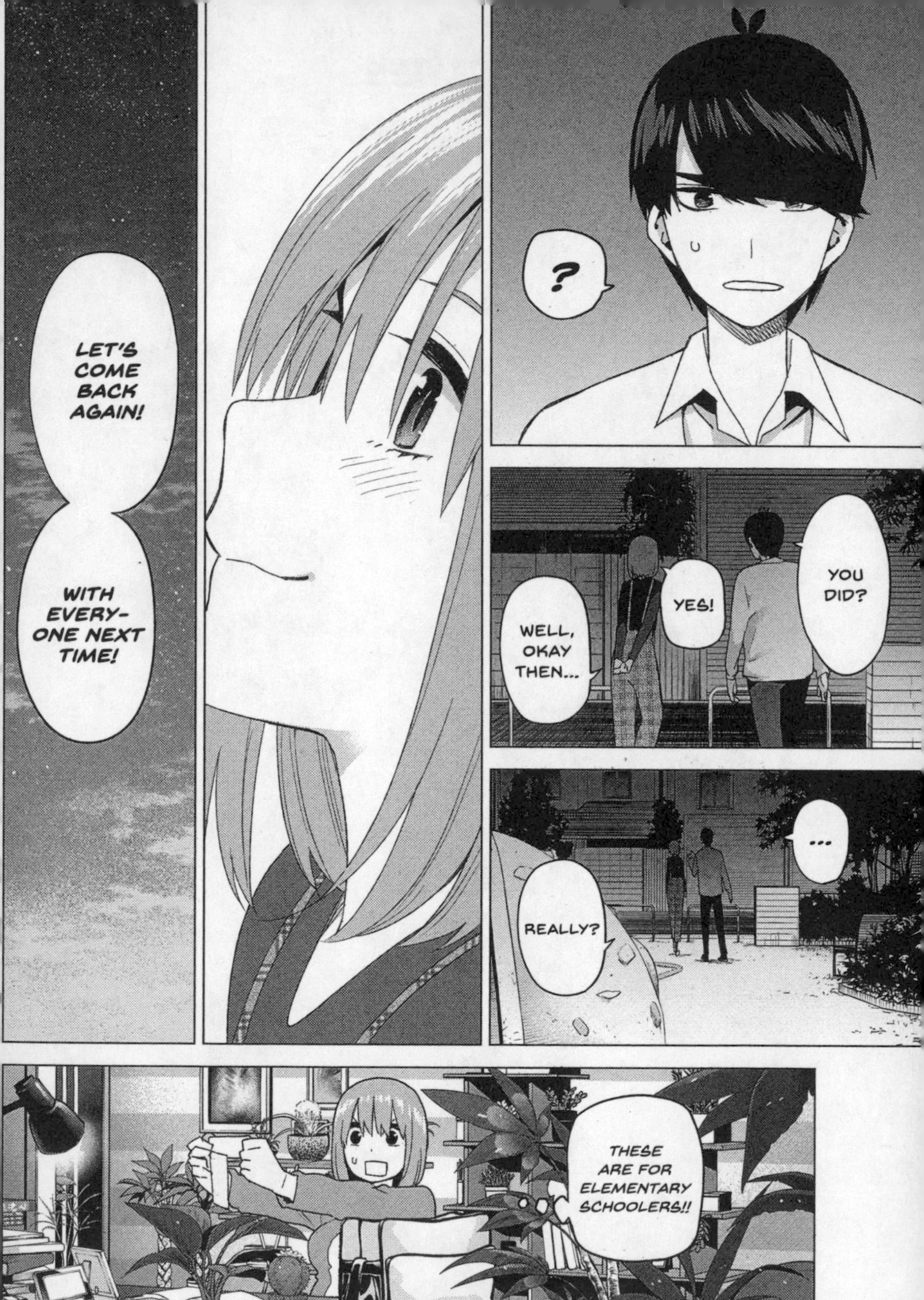
?
YOU DID?
YES!
WELL, OKAY THEN...
...
REALLY?
LET'S COME BACK AGAIN!
WITH EVERY-ONE NEXT TIME!
THESE ARE FOR ELEMENTARY SCHOOLERS!!

# CHAPTER 38
# THE LIVING ROOM CONFESSION

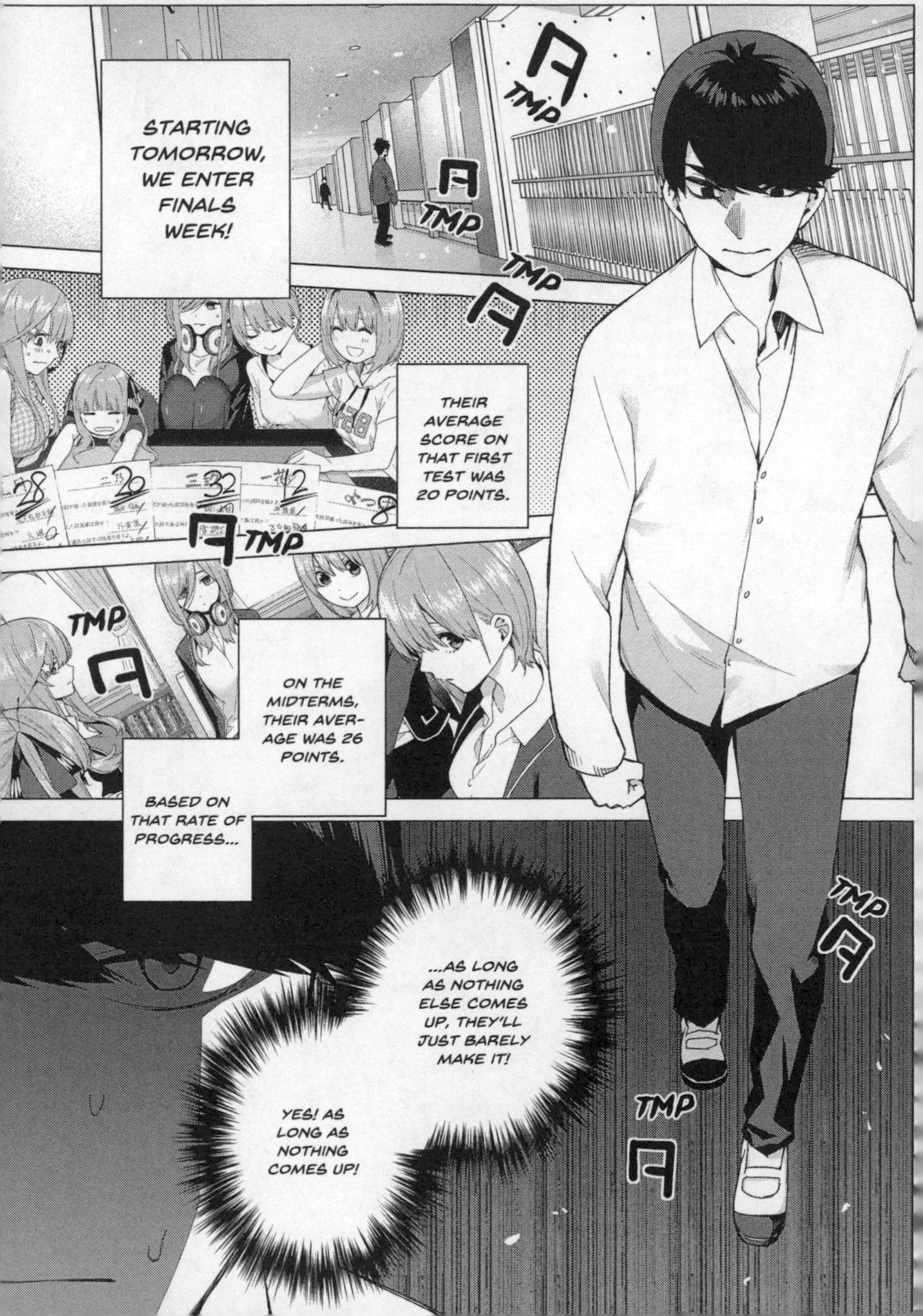
TMP
TMP
TMP
STARTING TOMORROW, WE ENTER FINALS WEEK!
THEIR AVERAGE SCORE ON THAT FIRST TEST WAS 20 POINTS.
TMP
TMP
ON THE MIDTERMS, THEIR AVERAGE WAS 26 POINTS.
BASED ON THAT RATE OF PROGRESS...
TMP
TMP
...AS LONG AS NOTHING ELSE COMES UP, THEY'LL JUST BARELY MAKE IT!
YES! AS LONG AS NOTHING COMES UP!

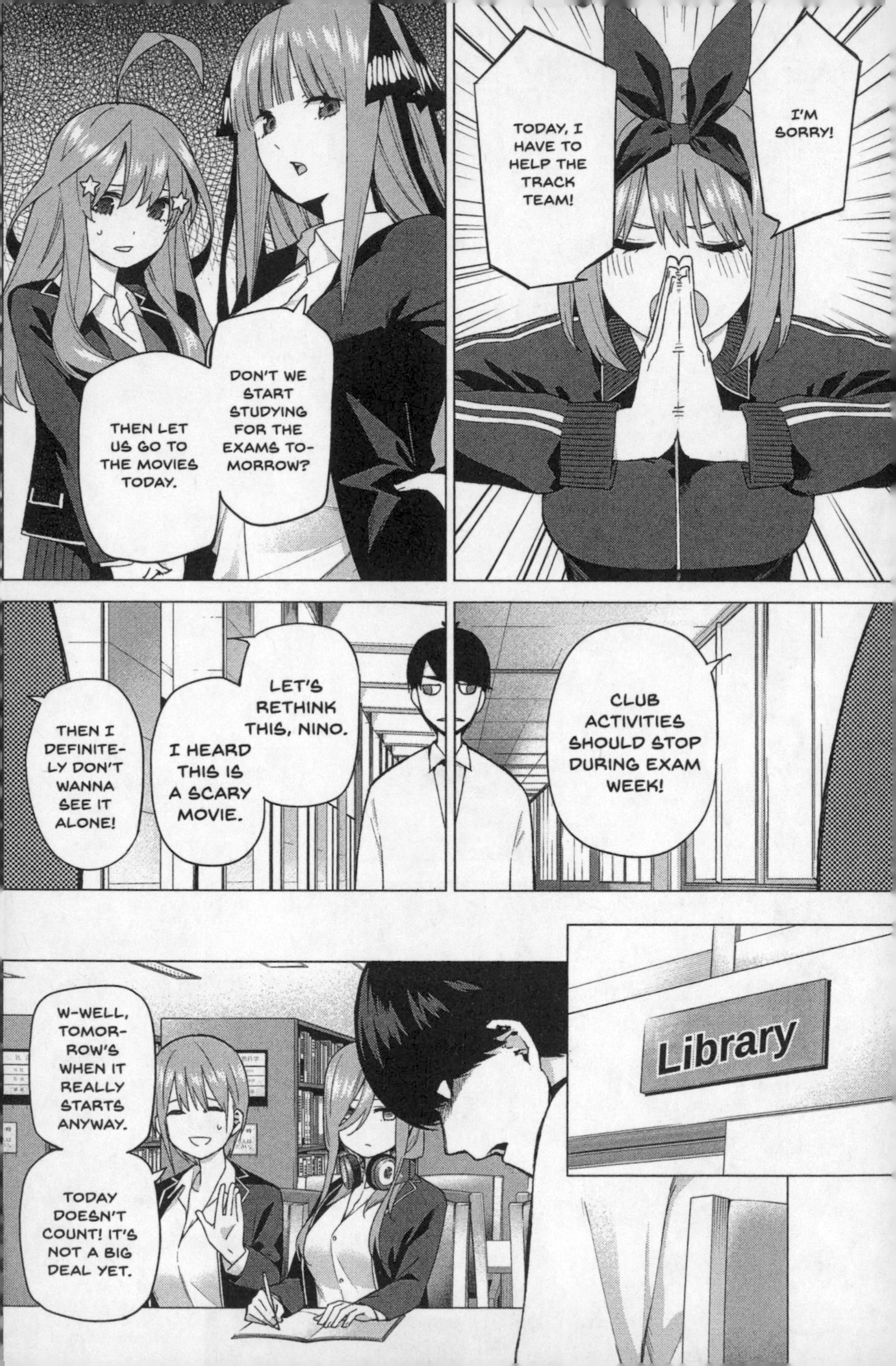
I'M SORRY!
TODAY, I HAVE TO HELP THE TRACK TEAM!
DON'T WE START STUDYING FOR THE EXAMS TO-MORROW?
THEN LET US GO TO THE MOVIES TODAY.
CLUB ACTIVITIES SHOULD STOP DURING EXAM WEEK!
LET'S RETHINK THIS, NINO.
I HEARD THIS IS A SCARY MOVIE.
THEN I DEFINITE-LY DON'T WANNA SEE IT ALONE!
Library
W-WELL, TOMOR-ROW'S WHEN IT REALLY STARTS ANYWAY.
TODAY DOESN'T COUNT! IT'S NOT A BIG DEAL YET.

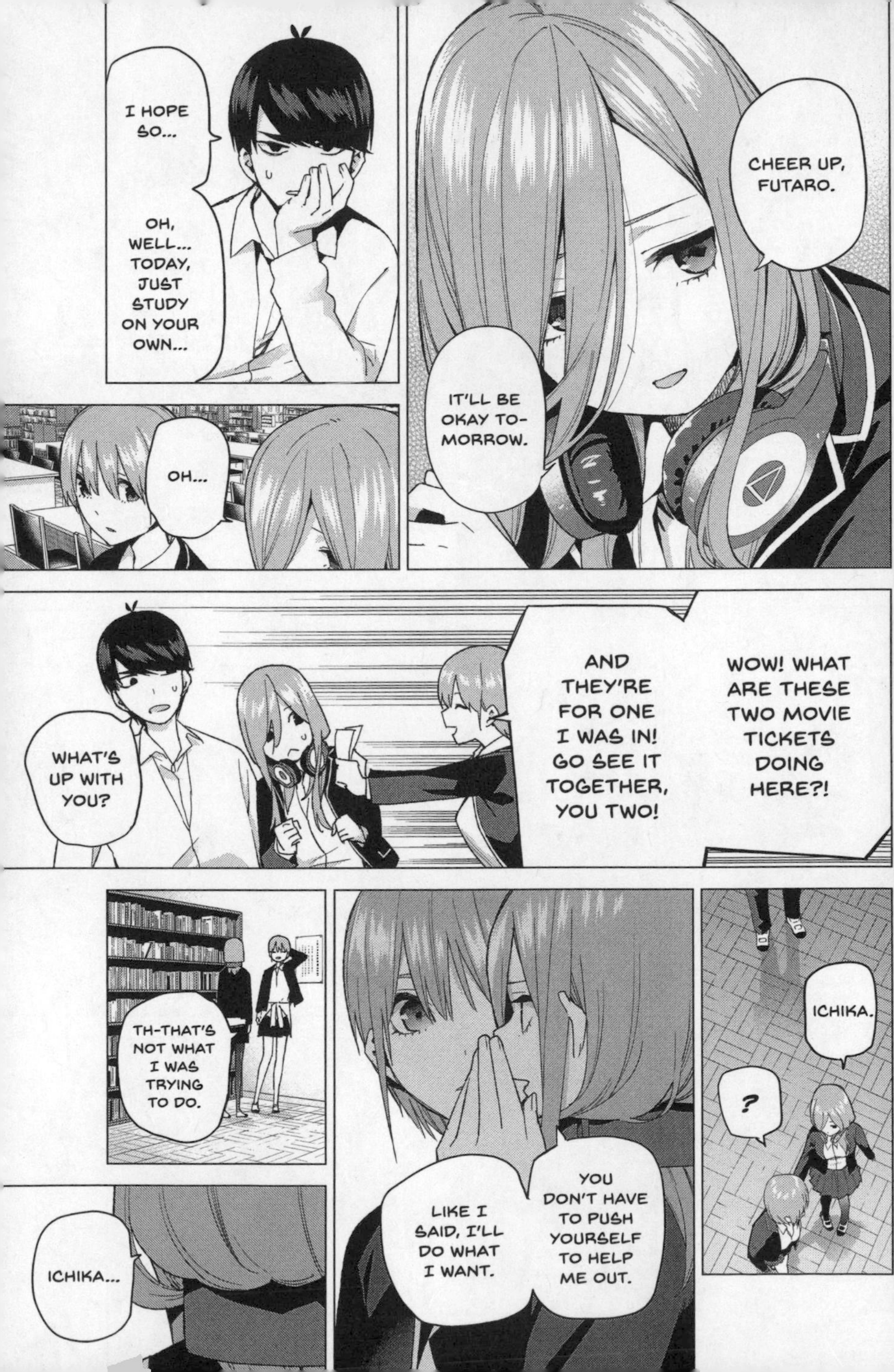
CHEER UP, FUTARO.
IT'LL BE OKAY TO-MORROW.
I HOPE SO...
OH, WELL... TODAY, JUST STUDY ON YOUR OWN...
OH...
WOW! WHAT ARE THESE TWO MOVIE TICKETS DOING HERE?!
AND THEY'RE FOR ONE I WAS IN! GO SEE IT TOGETHER, YOU TWO!
WHAT'S UP WITH YOU?
ICHIKA.
?
YOU DON'T HAVE TO PUSH YOURSELF TO HELP ME OUT.
LIKE I SAID, I'LL DO WHAT I WANT.
TH-THAT'S NOT WHAT I WAS TRYING TO DO.
ICHIKA...

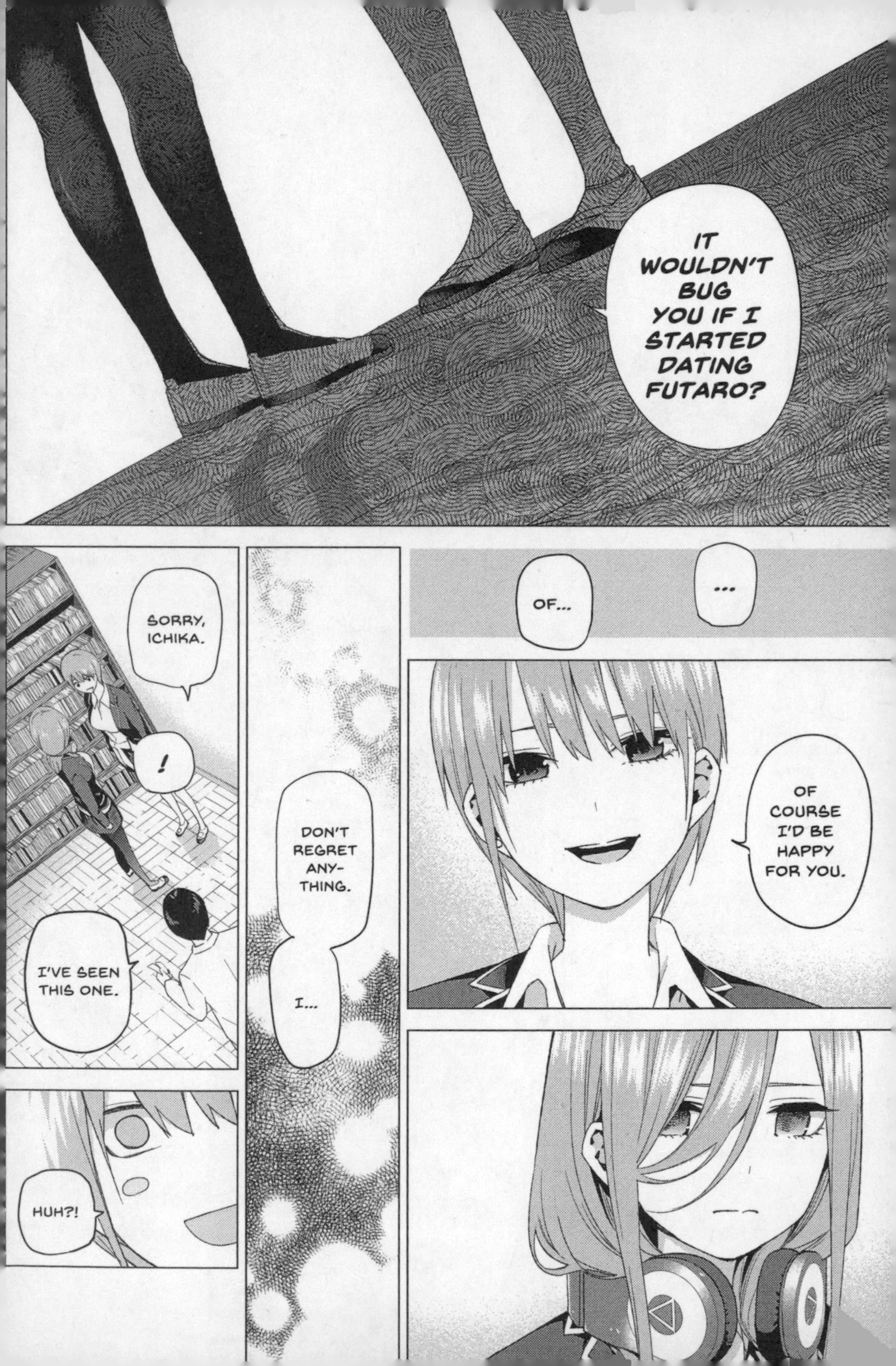
IT WOULDN'T BUG YOU IF I STARTED DATING FUTARO?
...
OF...
OF COURSE I'D BE HAPPY FOR YOU.
DON'T REGRET ANY-THING.
I...
SORRY, ICHIKA.
!
I'VE SEEN THIS ONE.
HUH?!

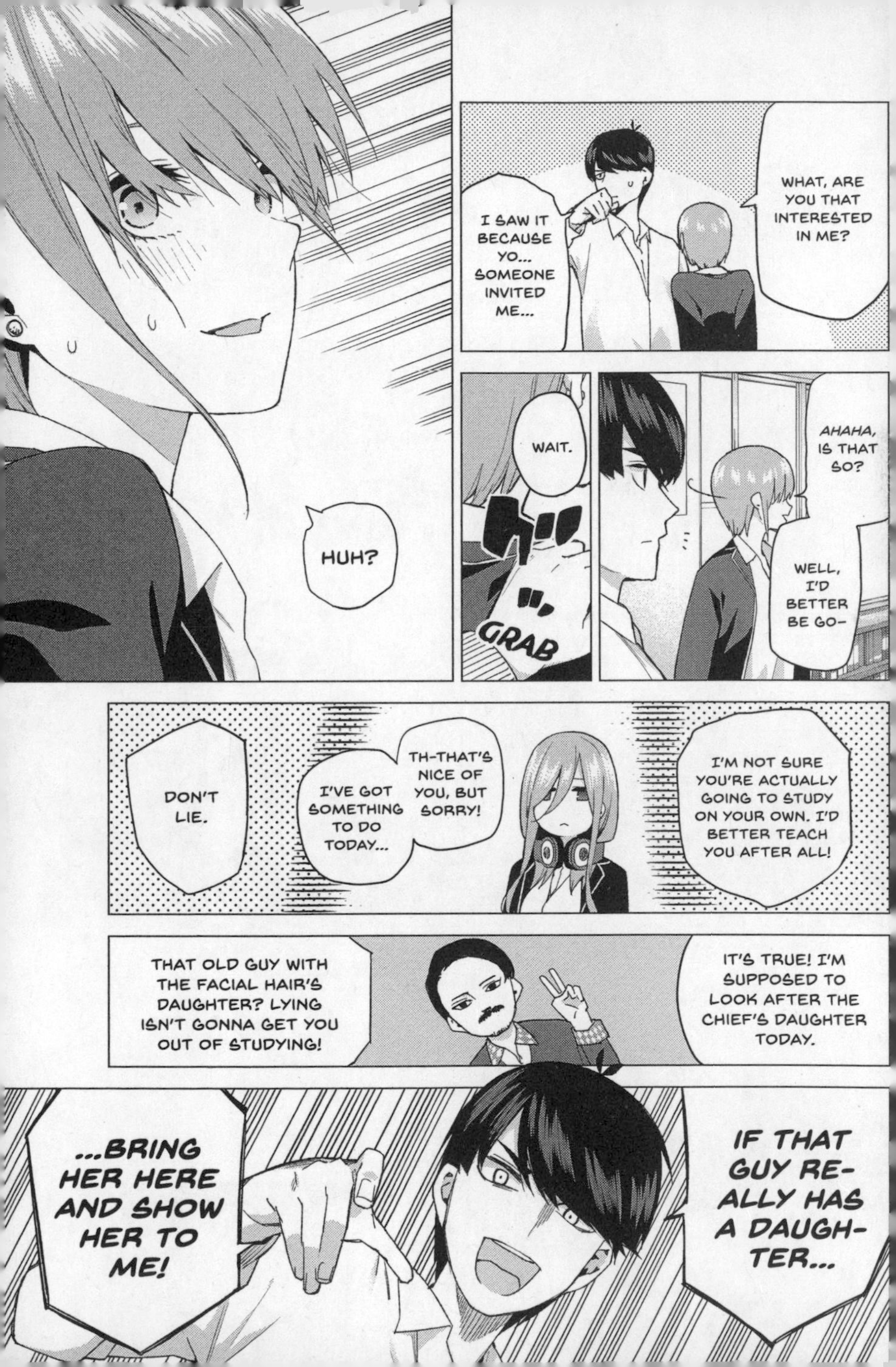
WHAT, ARE YOU THAT INTERESTED IN ME?
I SAW IT BECAUSE YO... SOMEONE INVITED ME...
AHAHA, IS THAT SO?
WELL, I'D BETTER BE GO-
WAIT.
GRAB
HUH?
I'M NOT SURE YOU'RE ACTUALLY GOING TO STUDY ON YOUR OWN. I'D BETTER TEACH YOU AFTER ALL!
TH-THAT'S NICE OF YOU, BUT SORRY!
I'VE GOT SOMETHING TO DO TODAY...
DON'T LIE.
IT'S TRUE! I'M SUPPOSED TO LOOK AFTER THE CHIEF'S DAUGHTER TODAY.
THAT OLD GUY WITH THE FACIAL HAIR'S DAUGHTER? LYING ISN'T GONNA GET YOU OUT OF STUDYING!
IF THAT GUY RE-ALLY HAS A DAUGH-TER...
...BRING HER HERE AND SHOW HER TO ME!

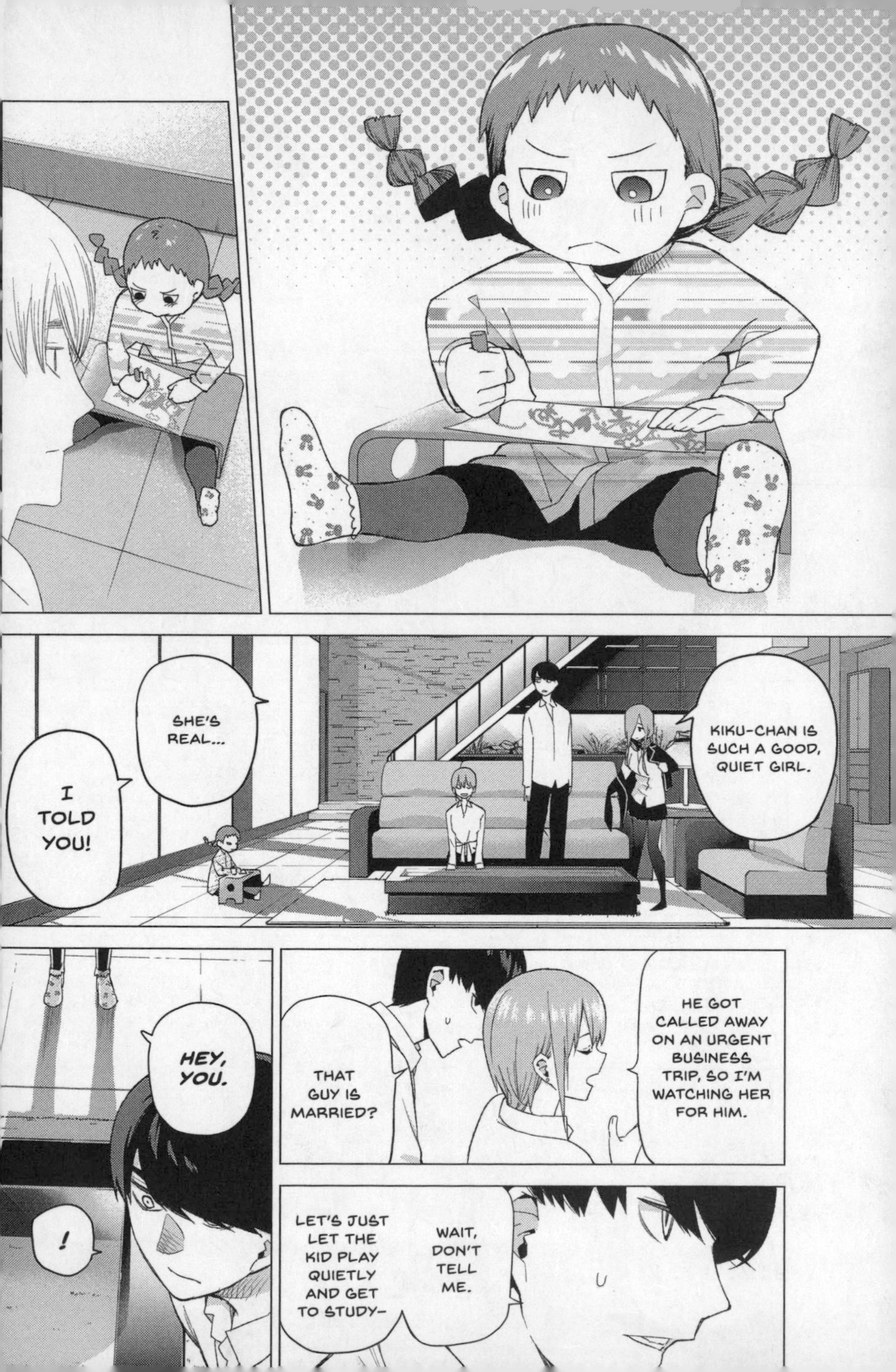
KIKU-CHAN IS SUCH A GOOD, QUIET GIRL.
SHE'S REAL...
I TOLD YOU!
HE GOT CALLED AWAY ON AN URGENT BUSINESS TRIP, SO I'M WATCHING HER FOR HIM.
THAT GUY IS MARRIED?
WAIT, DON'T TELL ME.
LET'S JUST LET THE KID PLAY QUIETLY AND GET TO STUDY–
HEY, YOU.
!

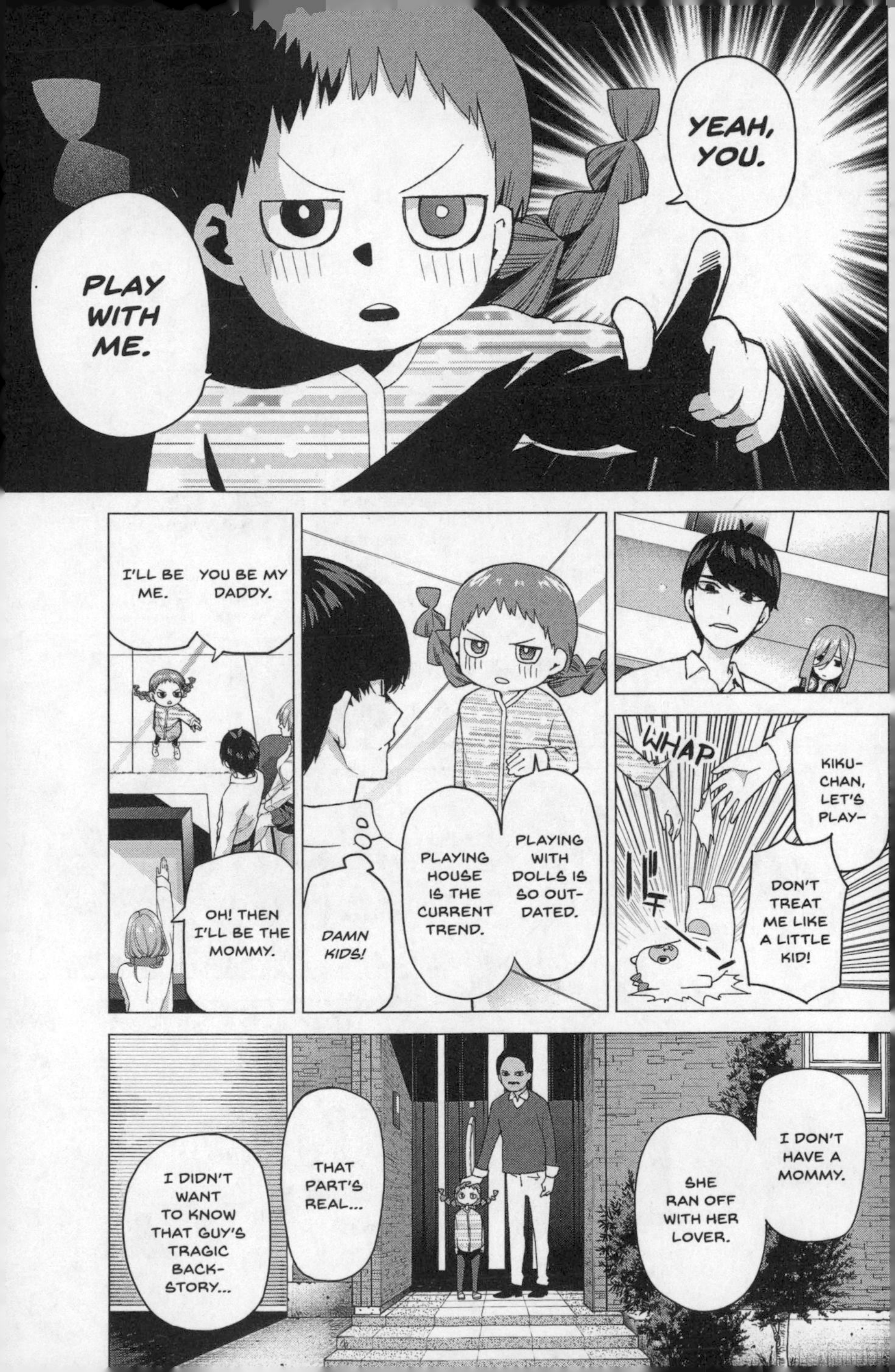
YEAH, YOU.
PLAY WITH ME.
KIKU-CHAN, LET'S PLAY—
WHAP
DON'T TREAT ME LIKE A LITTLE KID!
PLAYING WITH DOLLS IS SO OUT-DATED.
PLAYING HOUSE IS THE CURRENT TREND.
DAMN KIDS!
I'LL BE ME. YOU BE MY DADDY.
OH! THEN I'LL BE THE MOMMY.
I DON'T HAVE A MOMMY.
SHE RAN OFF WITH HER LOVER.
THAT PART'S REAL...
I DIDN'T WANT TO KNOW THAT GUY'S TRAGIC BACK-STORY...

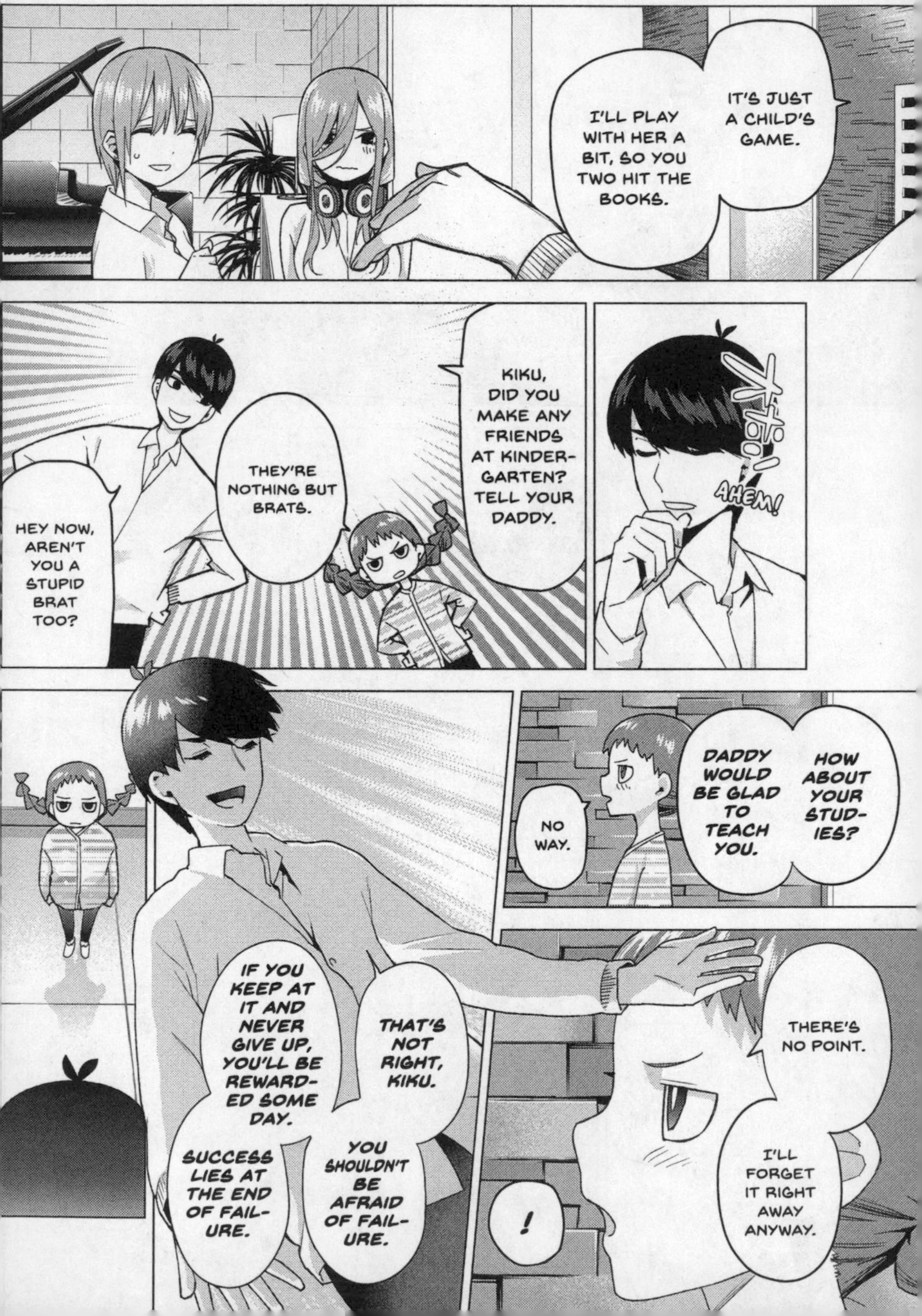
IT'S JUST A CHILD'S GAME.
I'LL PLAY WITH HER A BIT, SO YOU TWO HIT THE BOOKS.
AHEM!
KIKU, DID YOU MAKE ANY FRIENDS AT KINDER-GARTEN? TELL YOUR DADDY.
THEY'RE NOTHING BUT BRATS.
HEY NOW, AREN'T YOU A STUPID BRAT TOO?
HOW ABOUT YOUR STUD-IES?
DADDY WOULD BE GLAD TO TEACH YOU.
NO WAY.
THERE'S NO POINT.
I'LL FORGET IT RIGHT AWAY ANYWAY.
!
THAT'S NOT RIGHT, KIKU.
IF YOU KEEP AT IT AND NEVER GIVE UP, YOU'LL BE REWARD-ED SOME DAY.
YOU SHOULDN'T BE AFRAID OF FAIL-URE.
SUCCESS LIES AT THE END OF FAIL-URE.

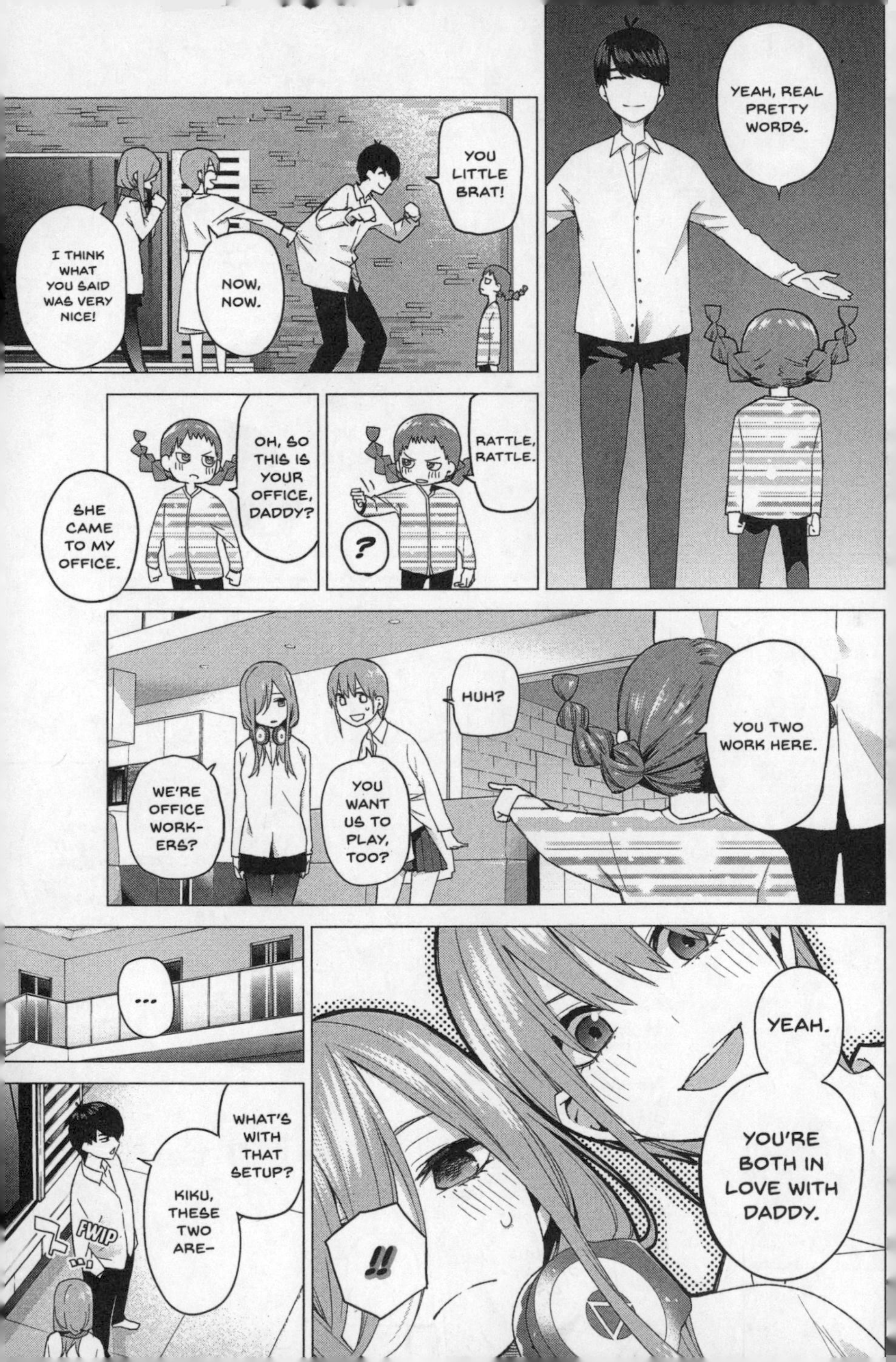
YEAH, REAL PRETTY WORDS.
YOU LITTLE BRAT!
NOW, NOW.
I THINK WHAT YOU SAID WAS VERY NICE!
RATTLE, RATTLE.
?
OH, SO THIS IS YOUR OFFICE, DADDY?
SHE CAME TO MY OFFICE.
YOU TWO WORK HERE.
HUH?
YOU WANT US TO PLAY, TOO?
WE'RE OFFICE WORKERS?
YEAH.
YOU'RE BOTH IN LOVE WITH DADDY.
!!
...
WHAT'S WITH THAT SETUP?
KIKU, THESE TWO ARE-
FWIP

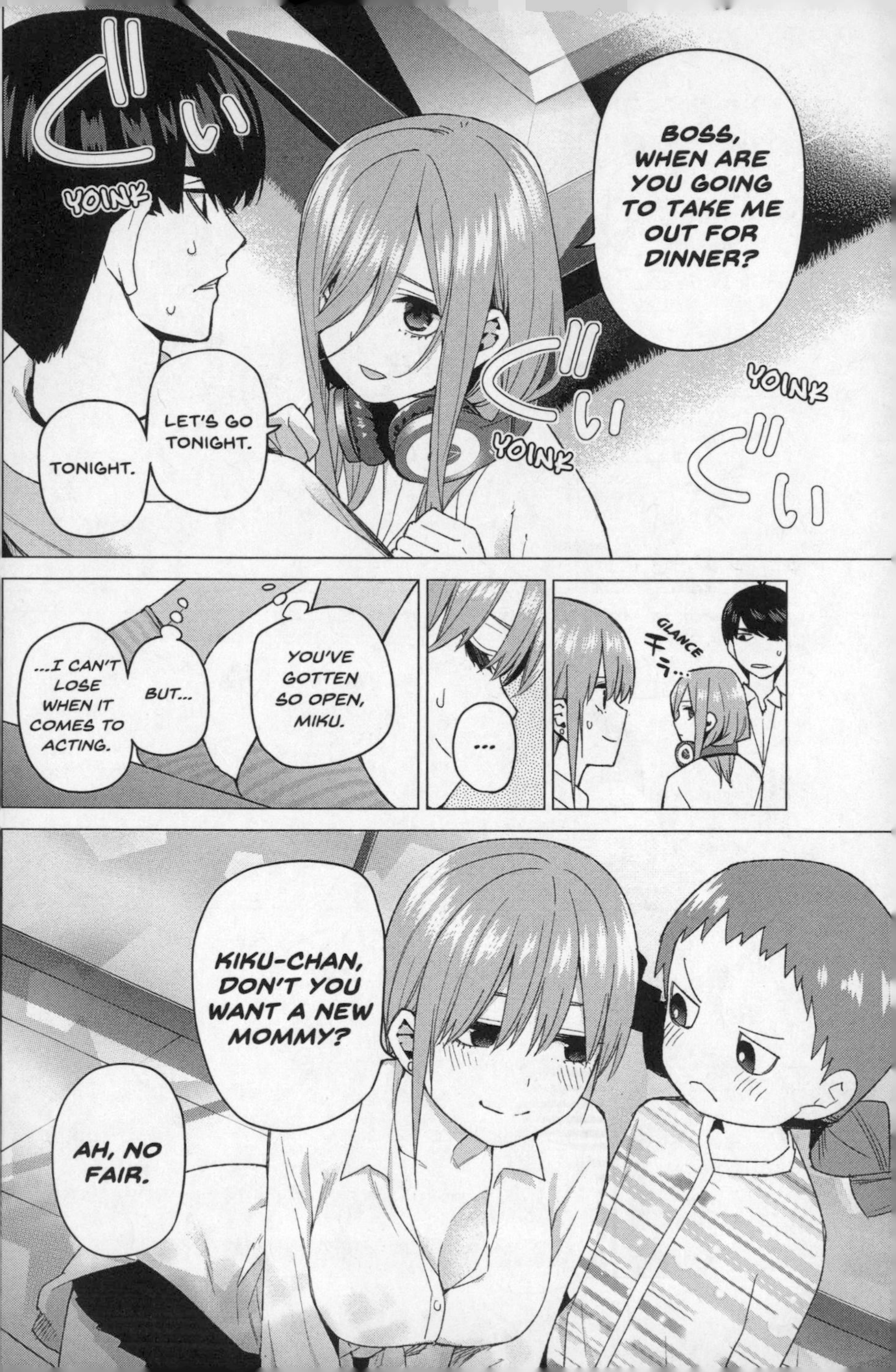
BOSS, WHEN ARE YOU GOING TO TAKE ME OUT FOR DINNER?
ぐい
YOINK
ぐい
YOINK
LET'S GO TONIGHT.
TONIGHT.
ぐい
YOINK
GLANCE
チラ...
...
YOU'VE GOTTEN SO OPEN, MIKU.
BUT...
...I CAN'T LOSE WHEN IT COMES TO ACTING.
KIKU-CHAN, DON'T YOU WANT A NEW MOMMY?
AH, NO FAIR.

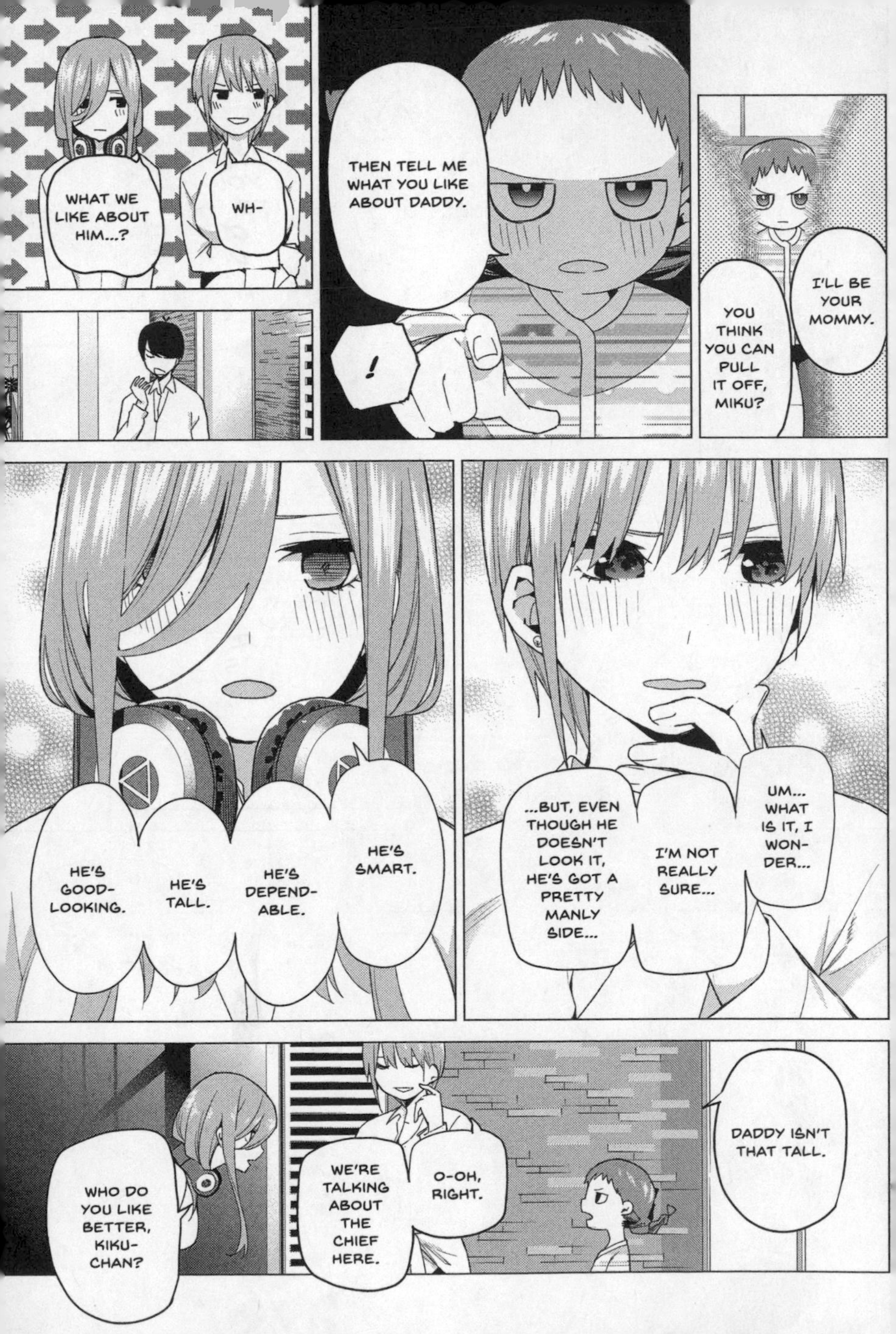
I'LL BE YOUR MOMMY.
YOU THINK YOU CAN PULL IT OFF, MIKU?
THEN TELL ME WHAT YOU LIKE ABOUT DADDY.
!
WH-
WHAT WE LIKE ABOUT HIM...?
UM... WHAT IS IT, I WONDER...
I'M NOT REALLY SURE...
...BUT, EVEN THOUGH HE DOESN'T LOOK IT, HE'S GOT A PRETTY MANLY SIDE...
HE'S SMART.
HE'S DEPENDABLE.
HE'S TALL.
HE'S GOOD-LOOKING.
DADDY ISN'T THAT TALL.
O-OH, RIGHT.
WE'RE TALKING ABOUT THE CHIEF HERE.
WHO DO YOU LIKE BETTER, KIKU-CHAN?

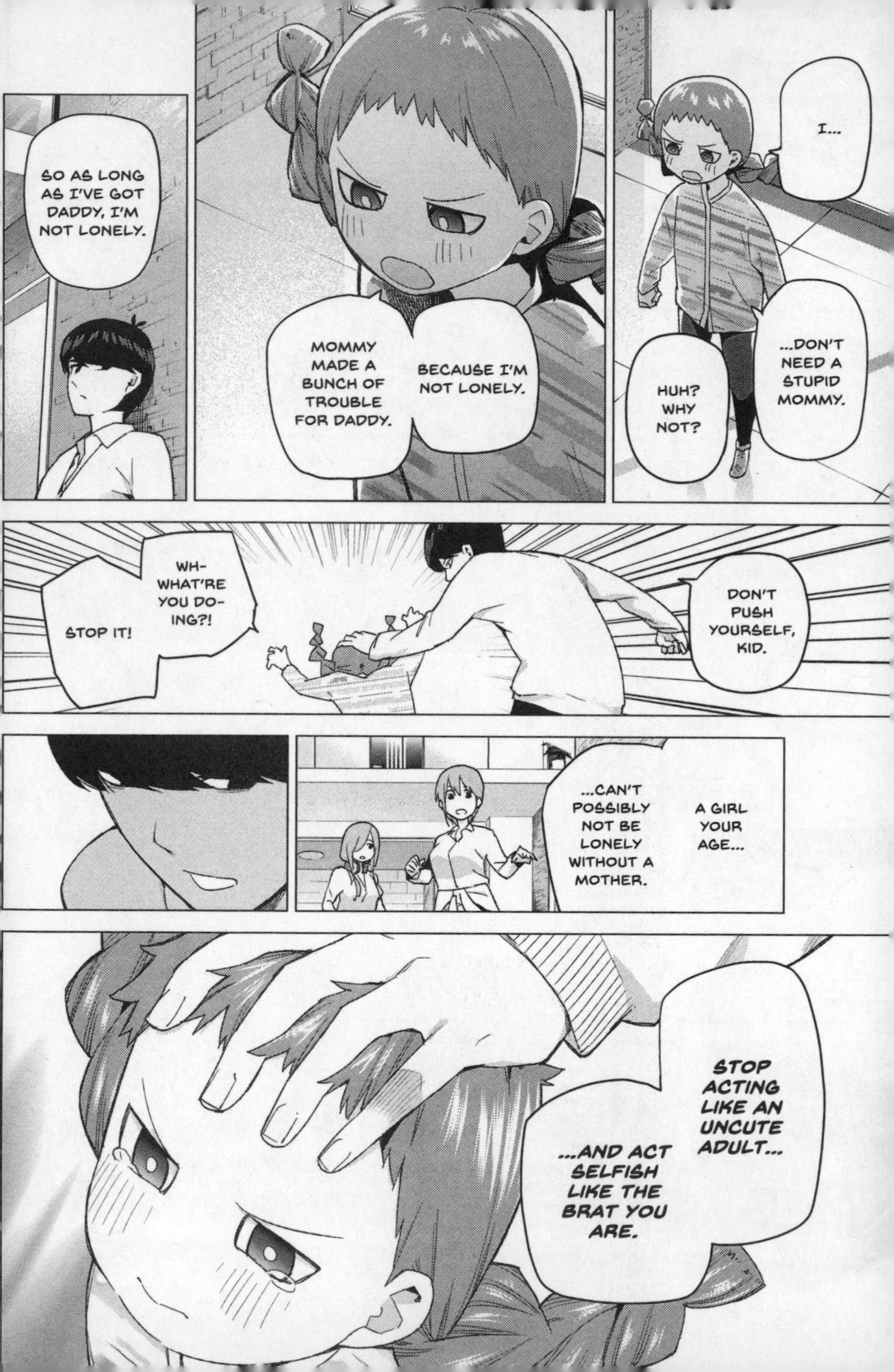
I...
...DON'T NEED A STUPID MOMMY.
HUH? WHY NOT?
BECAUSE I'M NOT LONELY.
MOMMY MADE A BUNCH OF TROUBLE FOR DADDY.
SO AS LONG AS I'VE GOT DADDY, I'M NOT LONELY.
DON'T PUSH YOURSELF, KID.
WH- WHAT'RE YOU DO- ING?!
STOP IT!
A GIRL YOUR AGE...
...CAN'T POSSIBLY NOT BE LONELY WITHOUT A MOTHER.
STOP ACTING LIKE AN UNCUTE ADULT...
...AND ACT SELFISH LIKE THE BRAT YOU ARE.

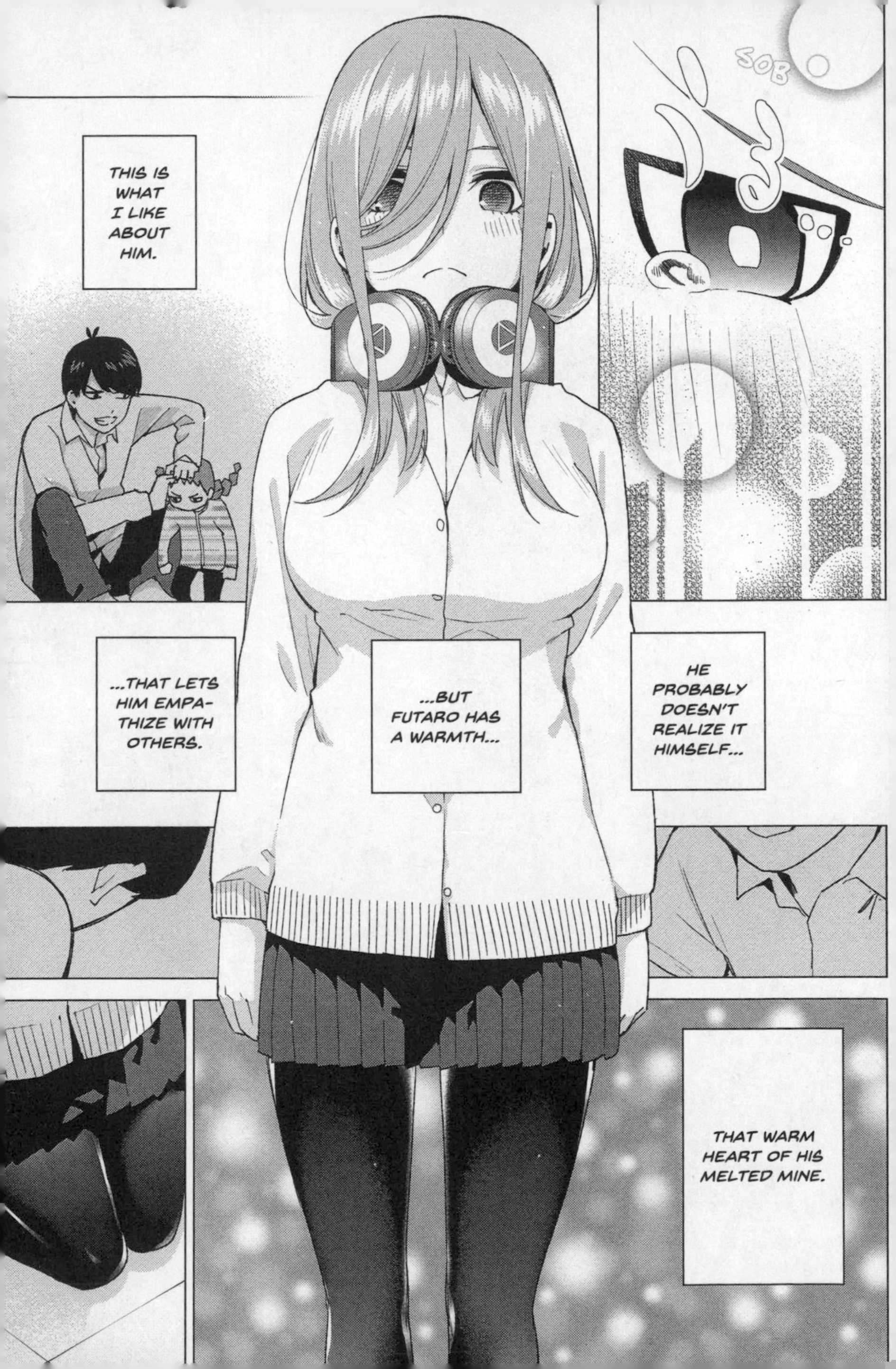
SOB
THIS IS WHAT I LIKE ABOUT HIM.
HE PROBABLY DOESN'T REALIZE IT HIMSELF...
...BUT FUTARO HAS A WARMTH...
...THAT LETS HIM EMPATHIZE WITH OTHERS.
THAT WARM HEART OF HIS MELTED MINE.

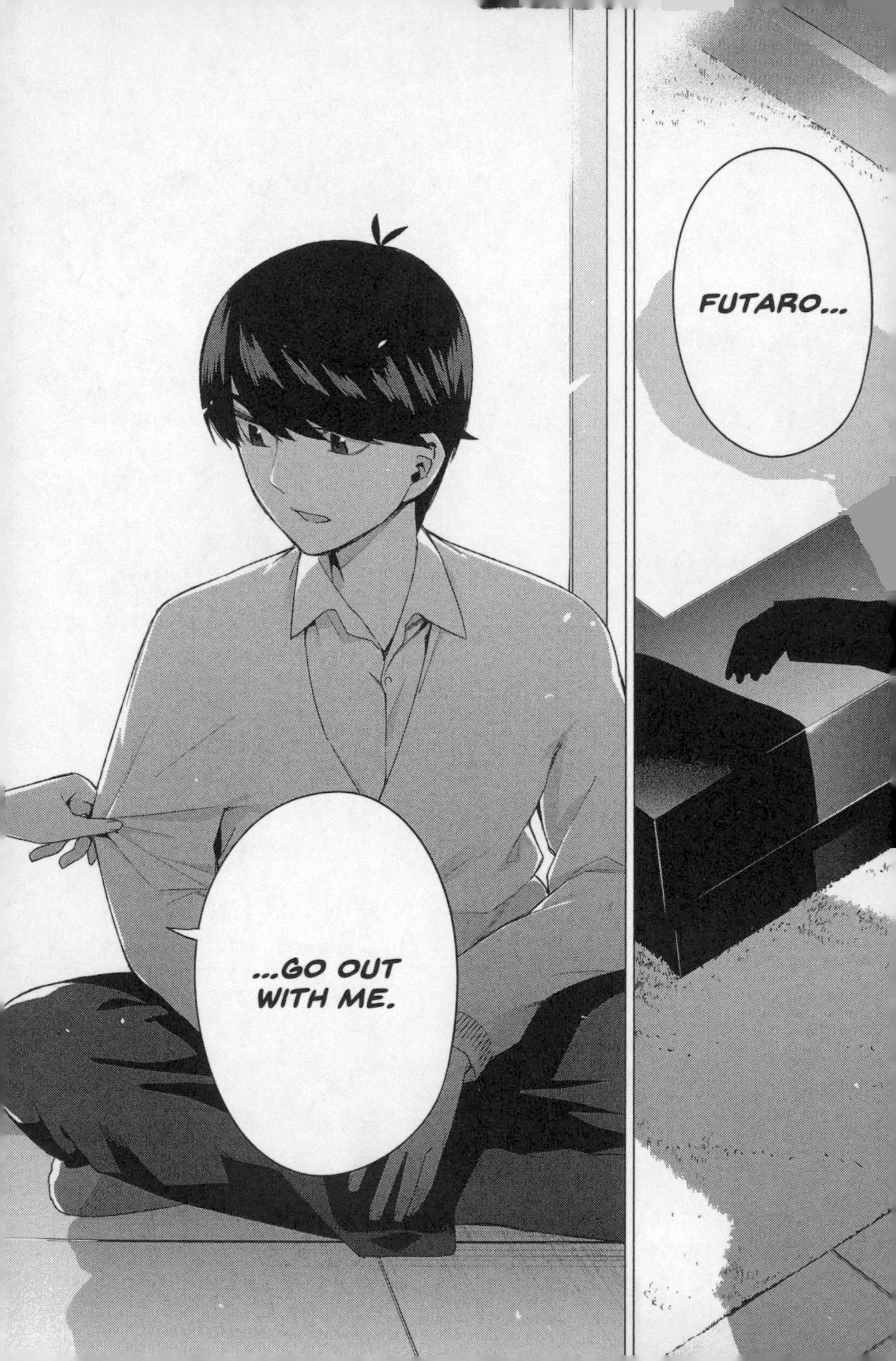
FUTARO...
...GO OUT WITH ME.

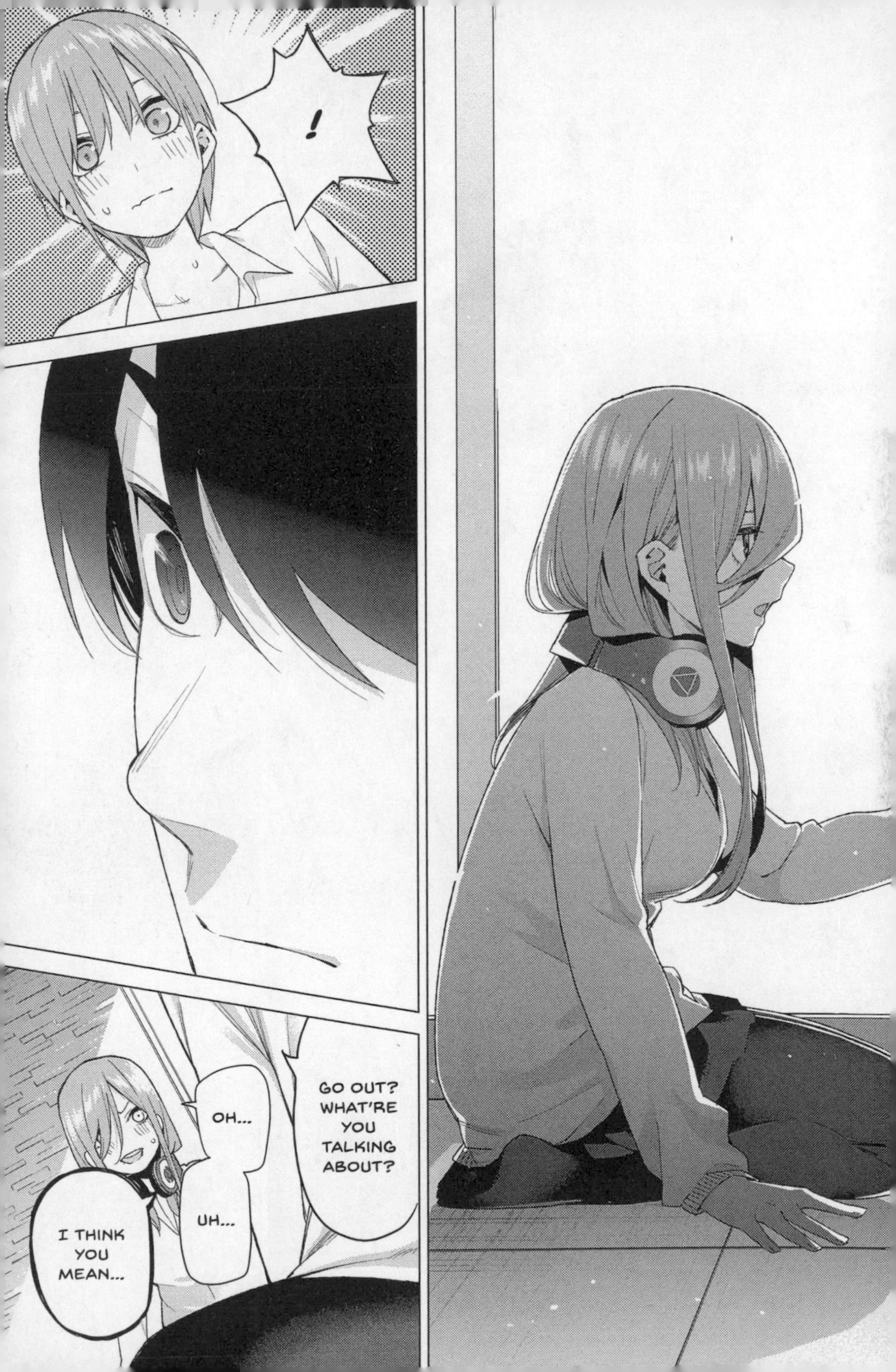
!
GO OUT? WHAT'RE YOU TALKING ABOUT?
OH...
UH...
I THINK YOU MEAN...

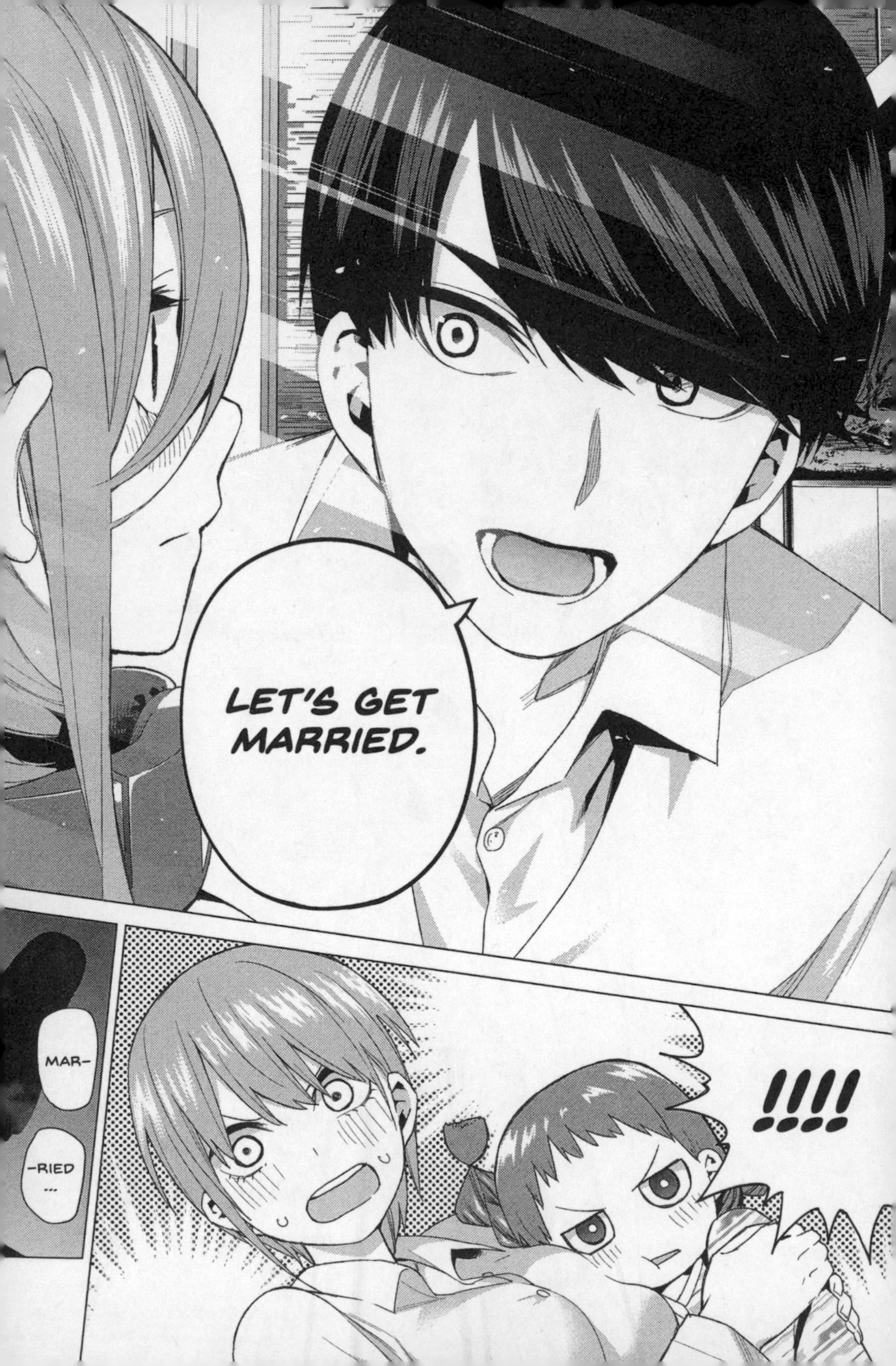
LET'S GET MARRIED.
!!!!
MAR–
–RIED ...

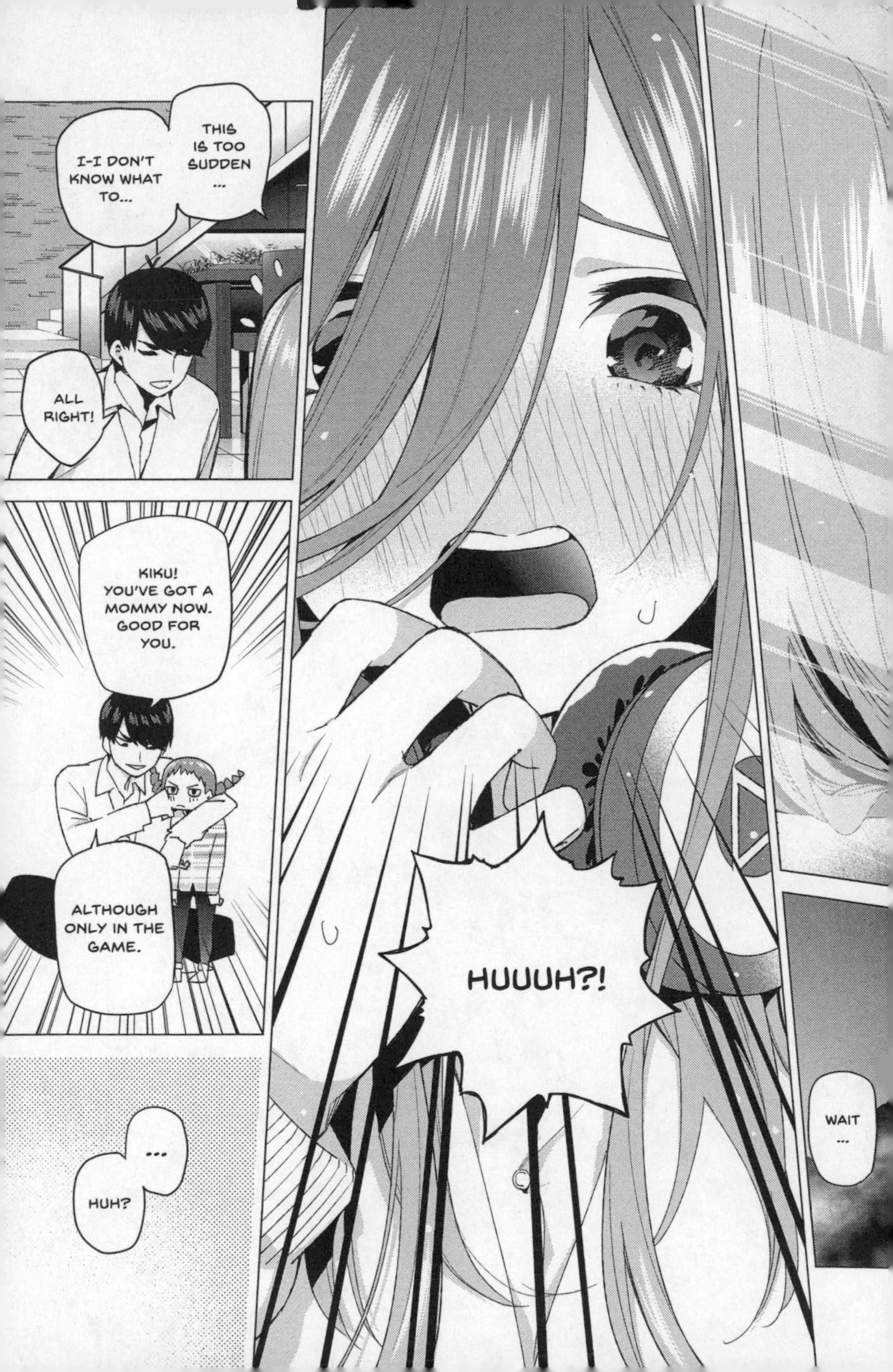
HUUUH?!
WAIT ...
THIS IS TOO SUDDEN ...
I-I DON'T KNOW WHAT TO...
ALL RIGHT!
KIKU! YOU'VE GOT A MOMMY NOW. GOOD FOR YOU.
ALTHOUGH ONLY IN THE GAME.
...
HUH?

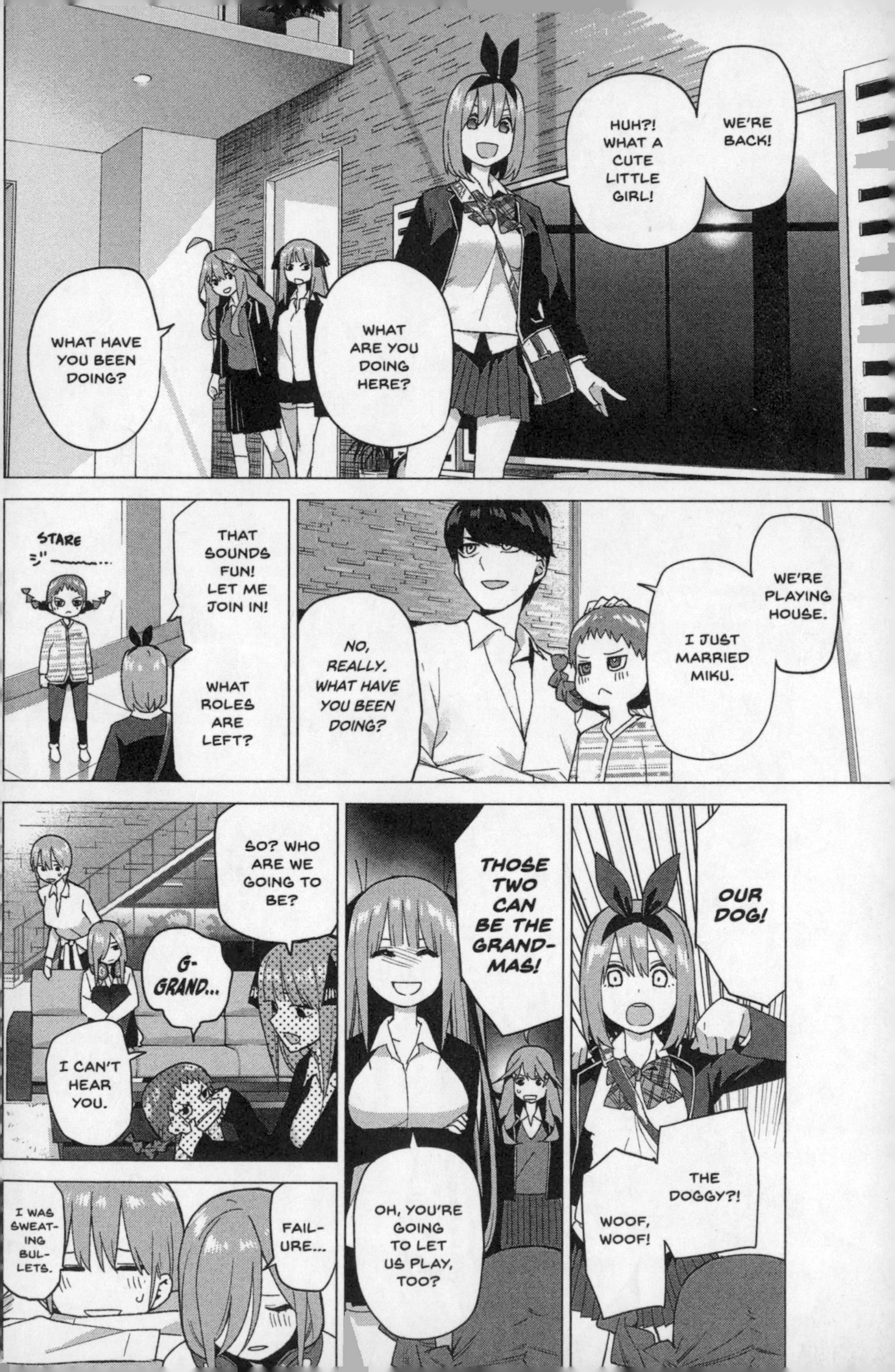
WE'RE BACK!
HUH?! WHAT A CUTE LITTLE GIRL!
WHAT ARE YOU DOING HERE?
WHAT HAVE YOU BEEN DOING?
WE'RE PLAYING HOUSE.
I JUST MARRIED MIKU.
NO, REALLY. WHAT HAVE YOU BEEN DOING?
THAT SOUNDS FUN! LET ME JOIN IN!
WHAT ROLES ARE LEFT?
STARE
OUR DOG!
THE DOGGY?!
WOOF, WOOF!
THOSE TWO CAN BE THE GRAND-MAS!
OH, YOU'RE GOING TO LET US PLAY, TOO?
SO? WHO ARE WE GOING TO BE?
G-GRAND...
I CAN'T HEAR YOU.
FAIL-URE...
I WAS SWEAT-ING BUL-LETS.

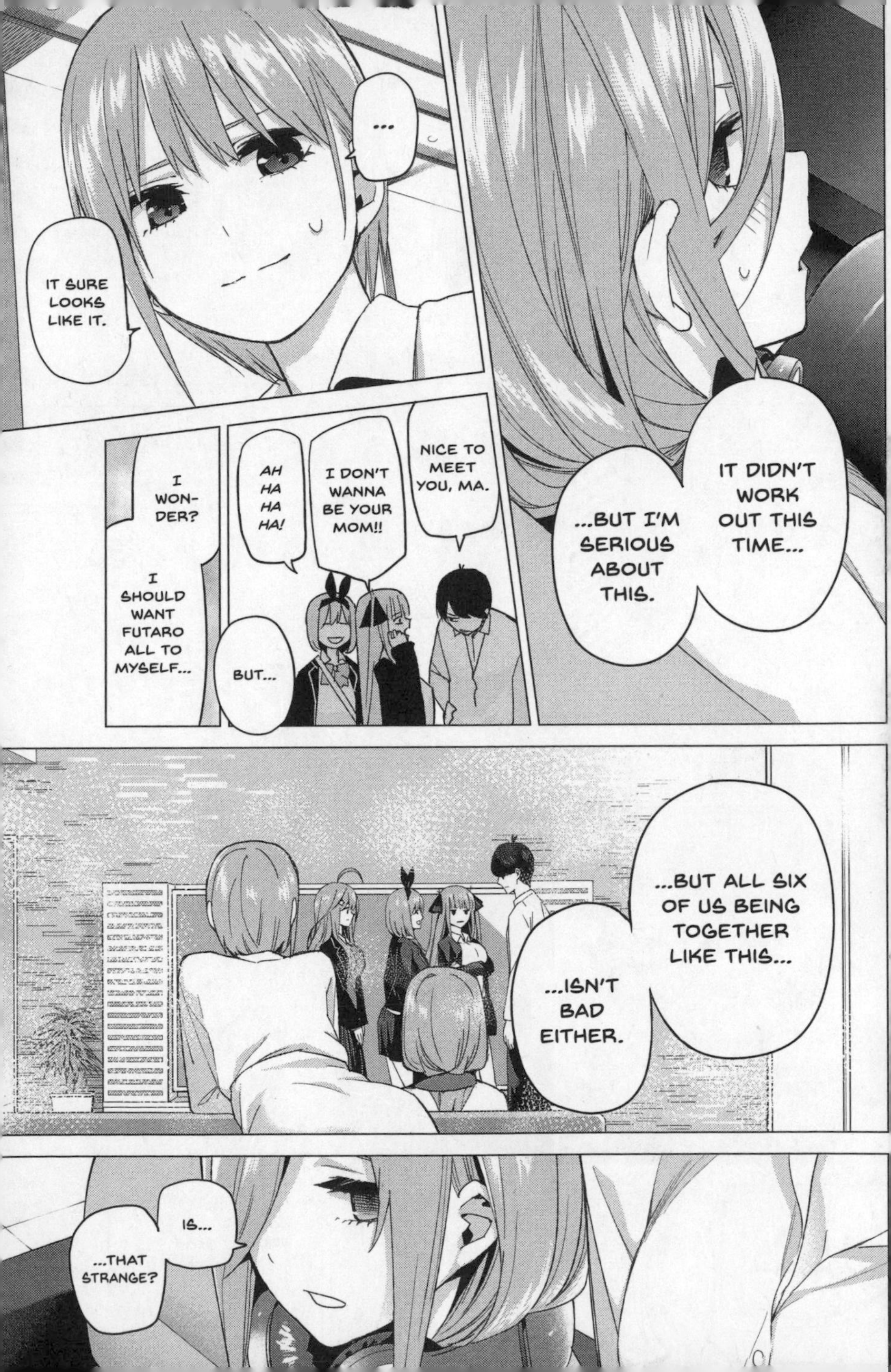
IT DIDN'T WORK OUT THIS TIME...
...BUT I'M SERIOUS ABOUT THIS.
...
IT SURE LOOKS LIKE IT.
NICE TO MEET YOU, MA.
I DON'T WANNA BE YOUR MOM!!
AH HA HA HA!
BUT...
I WONDER?
I SHOULD WANT FUTARO ALL TO MYSELF...
...BUT ALL SIX OF US BEING TOGETHER LIKE THIS...
...ISN'T BAD EITHER.
IS...
...THAT STRANGE?

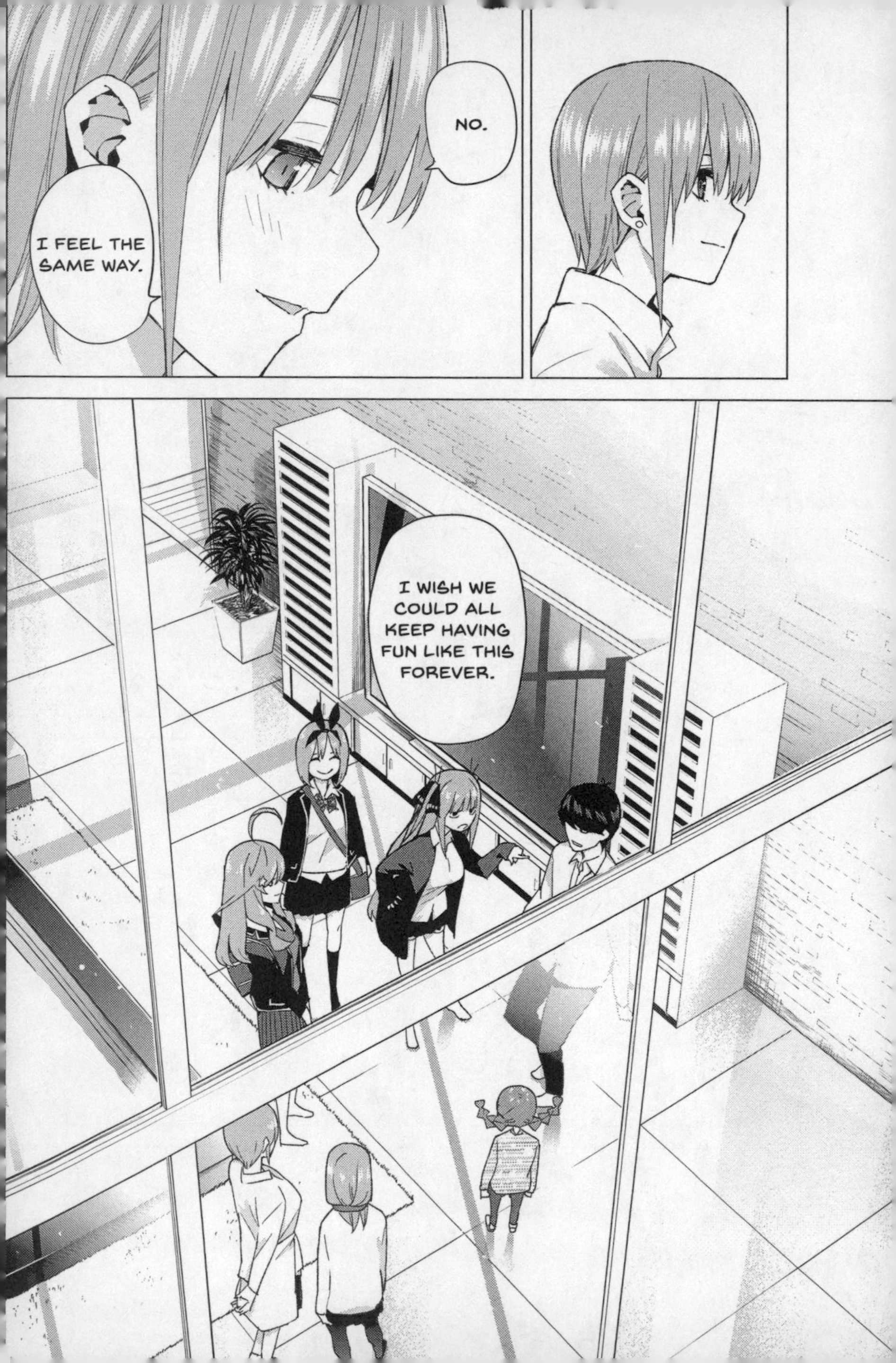
NO.
I FEEL THE SAME WAY.
I WISH WE COULD ALL KEEP HAVING FUN LIKE THIS FOREVER.

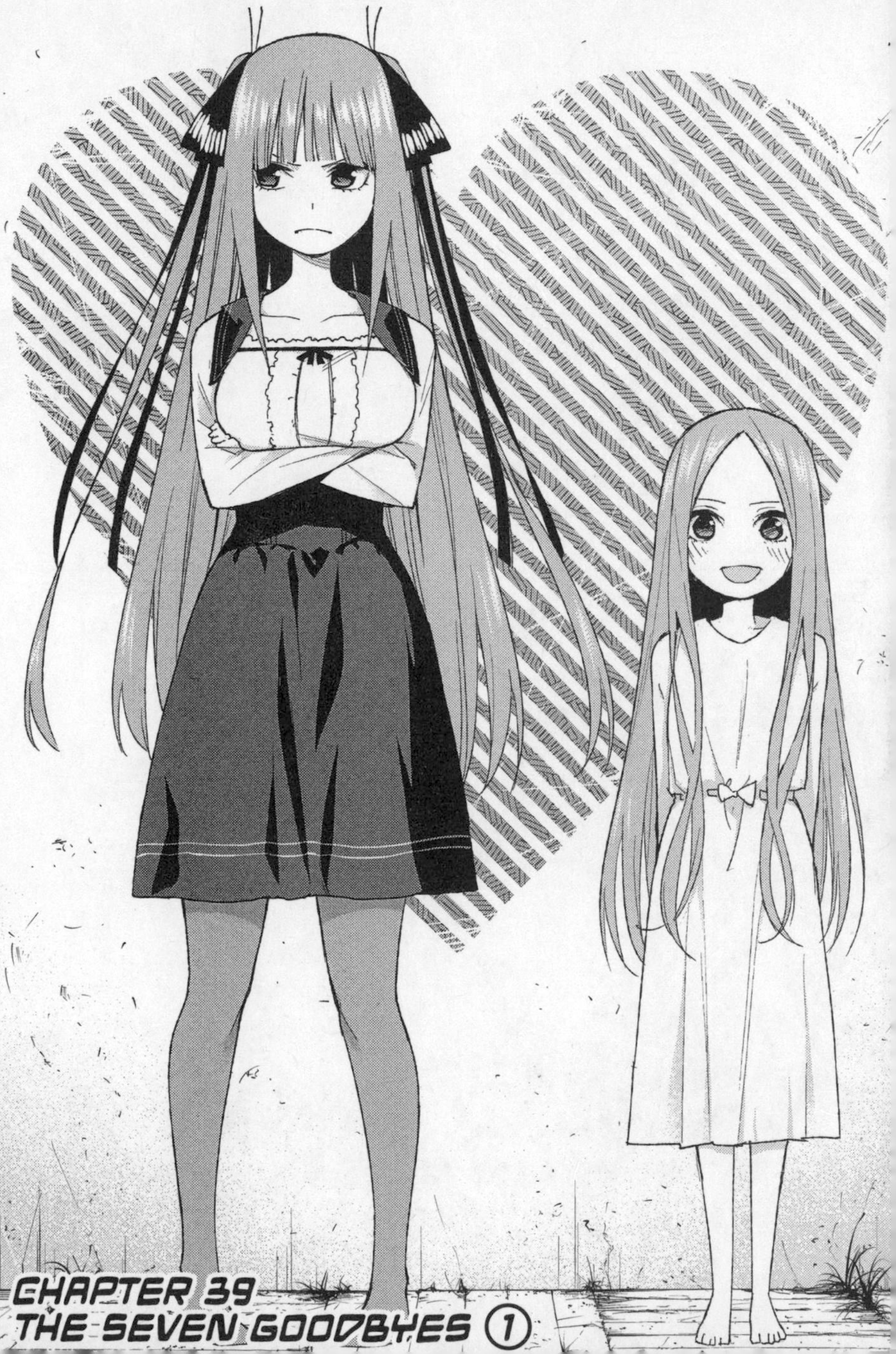
CHAPTER 39
THE SEVEN GOODBYES ①

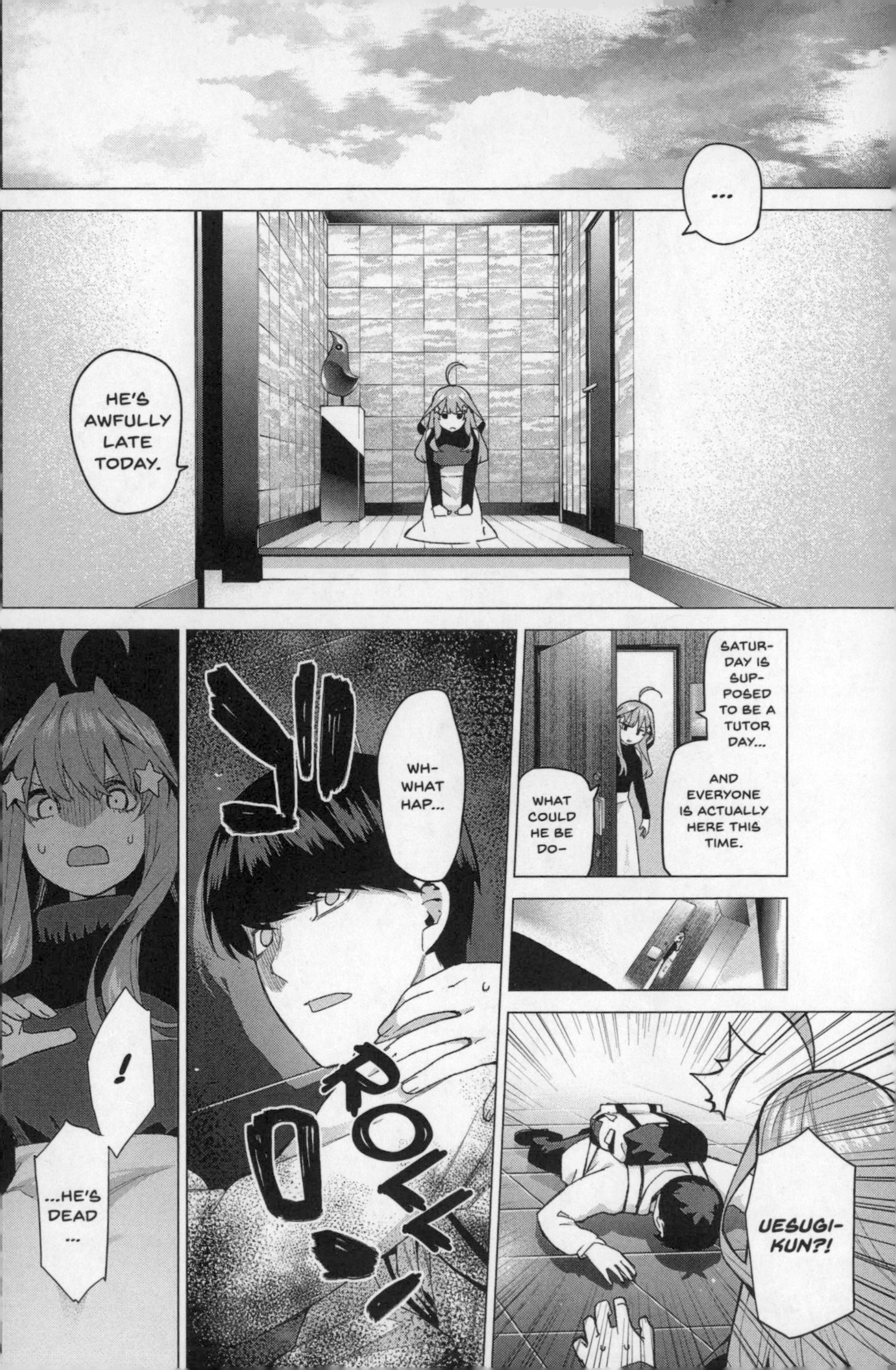
...
HE'S AWFULLY LATE TODAY.
SATUR-DAY IS SUP-POSED TO BE A TUTOR DAY...
AND EVERYONE IS ACTUALLY HERE THIS TIME.
WHAT COULD HE BE DO-
UESUGI-KUN?!
WH-WHAT HAP...
ROLL
!
...HE'S DEAD ...

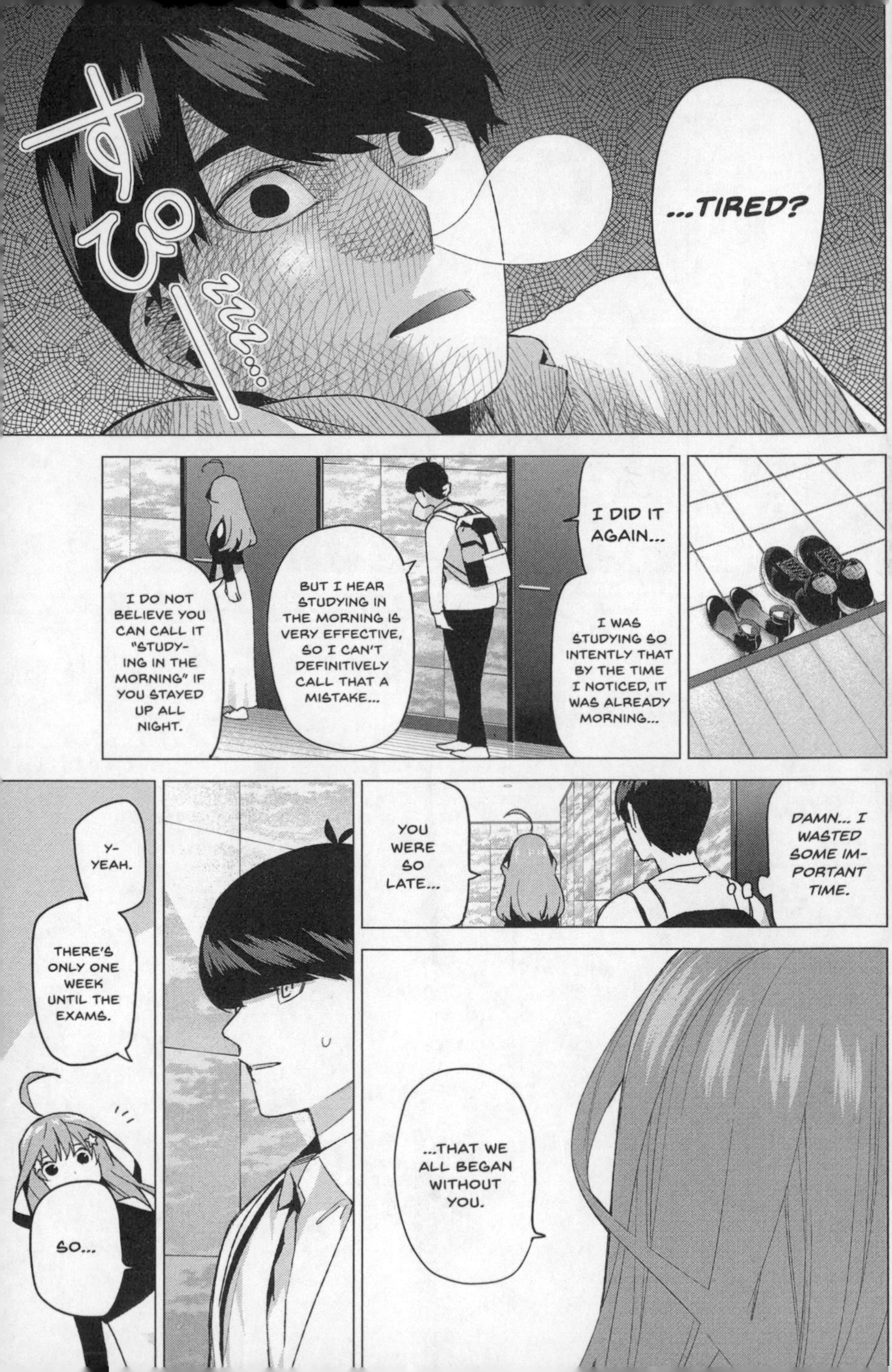
...TIRED?
すぴー
ZZZ...
I DID IT AGAIN...
I WAS STUDYING SO INTENTLY THAT BY THE TIME I NOTICED, IT WAS ALREADY MORNING...
BUT I HEAR STUDYING IN THE MORNING IS VERY EFFECTIVE, SO I CAN'T DEFINITIVELY CALL THAT A MISTAKE...
I DO NOT BELIEVE YOU CAN CALL IT "STUDYING IN THE MORNING" IF YOU STAYED UP ALL NIGHT.
DAMN... I WASTED SOME IMPORTANT TIME.
YOU WERE SO LATE...
Y-YEAH.
THERE'S ONLY ONE WEEK UNTIL THE EXAMS.
SO...
...THAT WE ALL BEGAN WITHOUT YOU.

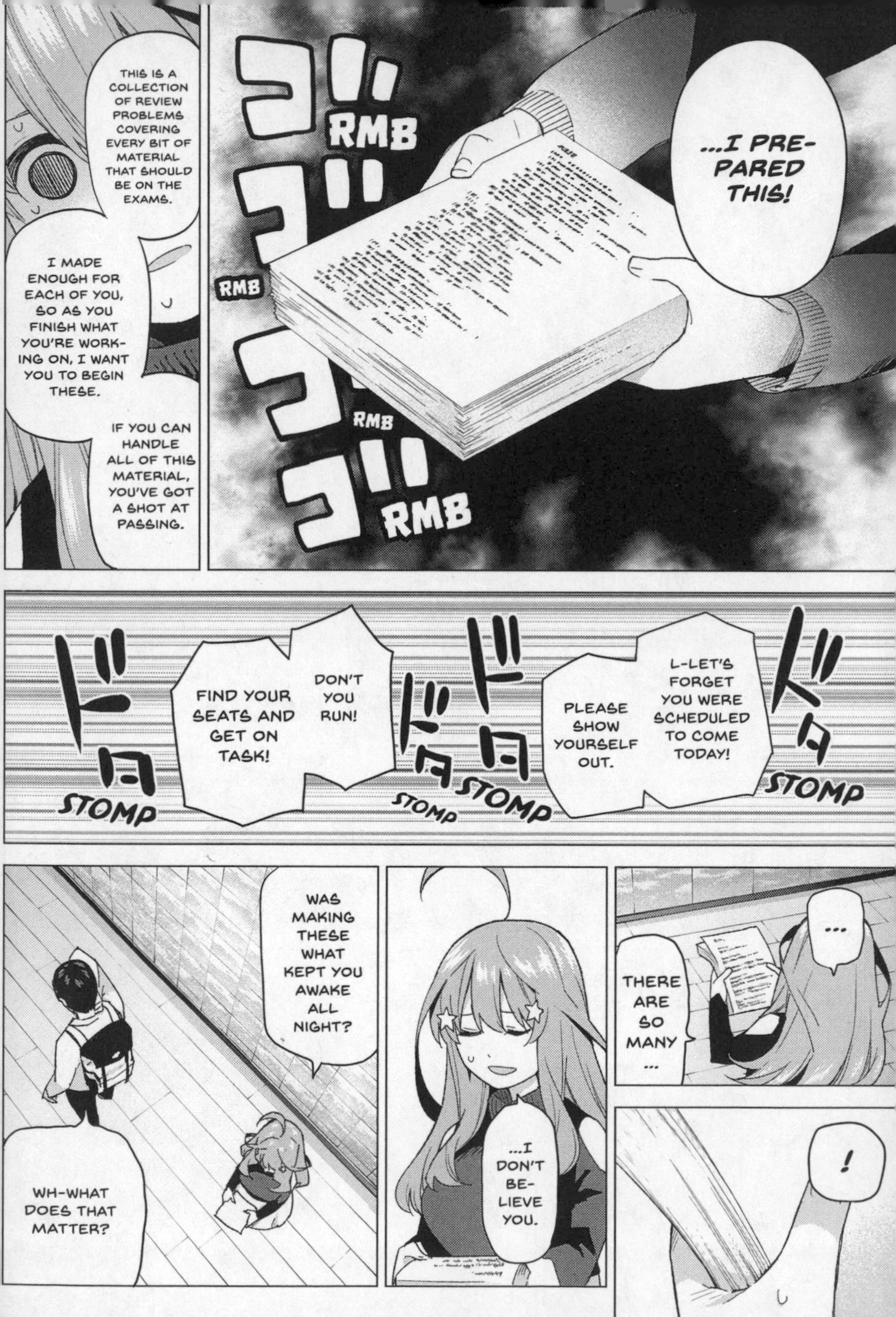
...I PRE-PARED THIS!
ゴ RMB
ゴ RMB
ゴ RMB
ゴ RMB
THIS IS A COLLECTION OF REVIEW PROBLEMS COVERING EVERY BIT OF MATERIAL THAT SHOULD BE ON THE EXAMS.
I MADE ENOUGH FOR EACH OF YOU, SO AS YOU FINISH WHAT YOU'RE WORK-ING ON, I WANT YOU TO BEGIN THESE.
IF YOU CAN HANDLE ALL OF THIS MATERIAL, YOU'VE GOT A SHOT AT PASSING.
ドタ STOMP
L-LET'S FORGET YOU WERE SCHEDULED TO COME TODAY!
PLEASE SHOW YOURSELF OUT.
ドタ STOMP
ドタ STOMP
DON'T YOU RUN!
FIND YOUR SEATS AND GET ON TASK!
ドタ STOMP
...
THERE ARE SO MANY ...
!
...I DON'T BE-LIEVE YOU.
WAS MAKING THESE WHAT KEPT YOU AWAKE ALL NIGHT?
WH-WHAT DOES THAT MATTER?

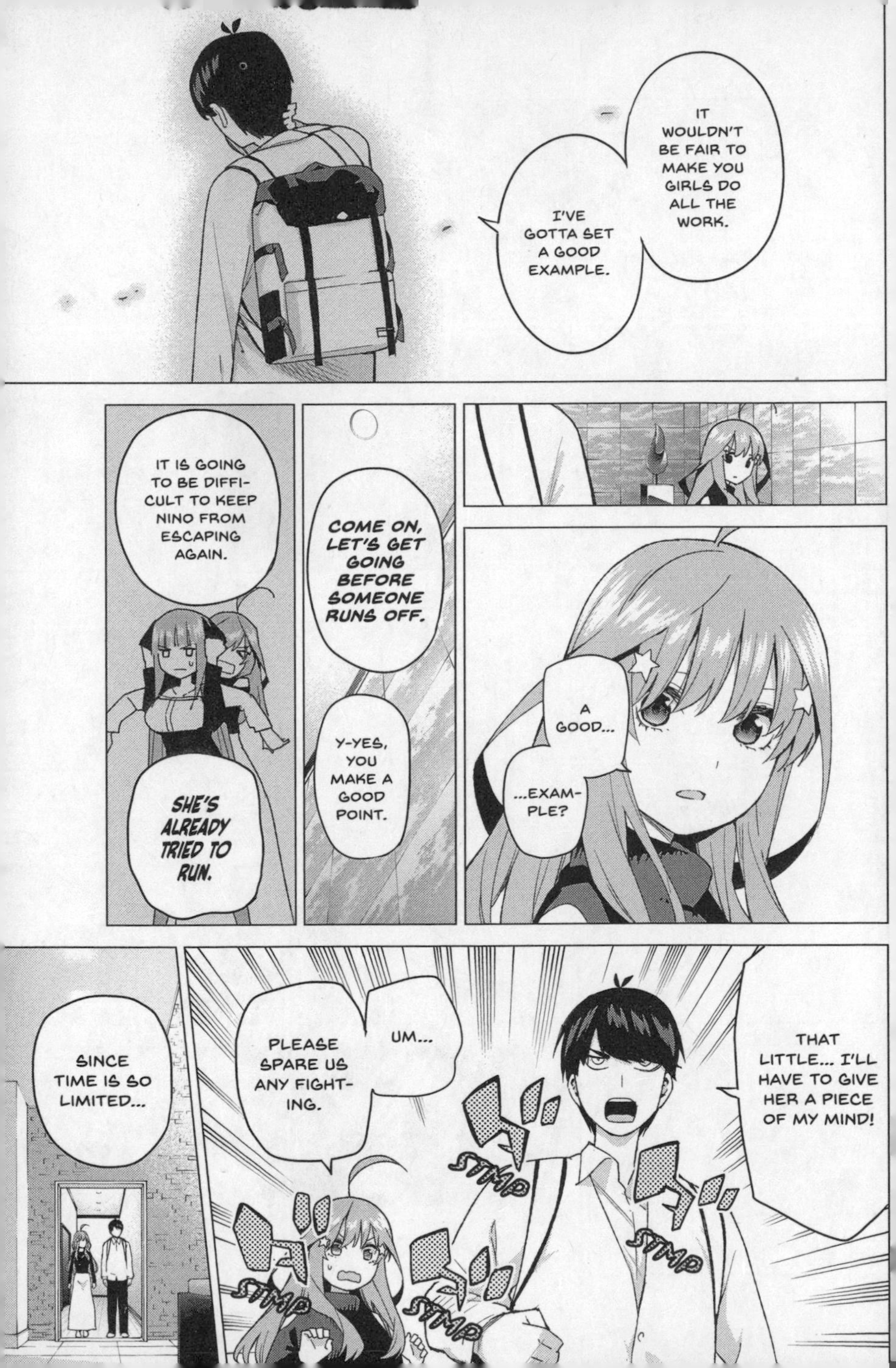
IT WOULDN'T BE FAIR TO MAKE YOU GIRLS DO ALL THE WORK.
I'VE GOTTA SET A GOOD EXAMPLE.
A GOOD...
...EXAMPLE?
COME ON, LET'S GET GOING BEFORE SOMEONE RUNS OFF.
Y-YES, YOU MAKE A GOOD POINT.
IT IS GOING TO BE DIFFICULT TO KEEP NINO FROM ESCAPING AGAIN.
SHE'S ALREADY TRIED TO RUN.
THAT LITTLE... I'LL HAVE TO GIVE HER A PIECE OF MY MIND!
STMP
STMP
UM...
PLEASE SPARE US ANY FIGHTING.
STMP
STMP
SINCE TIME IS SO LIMITED...

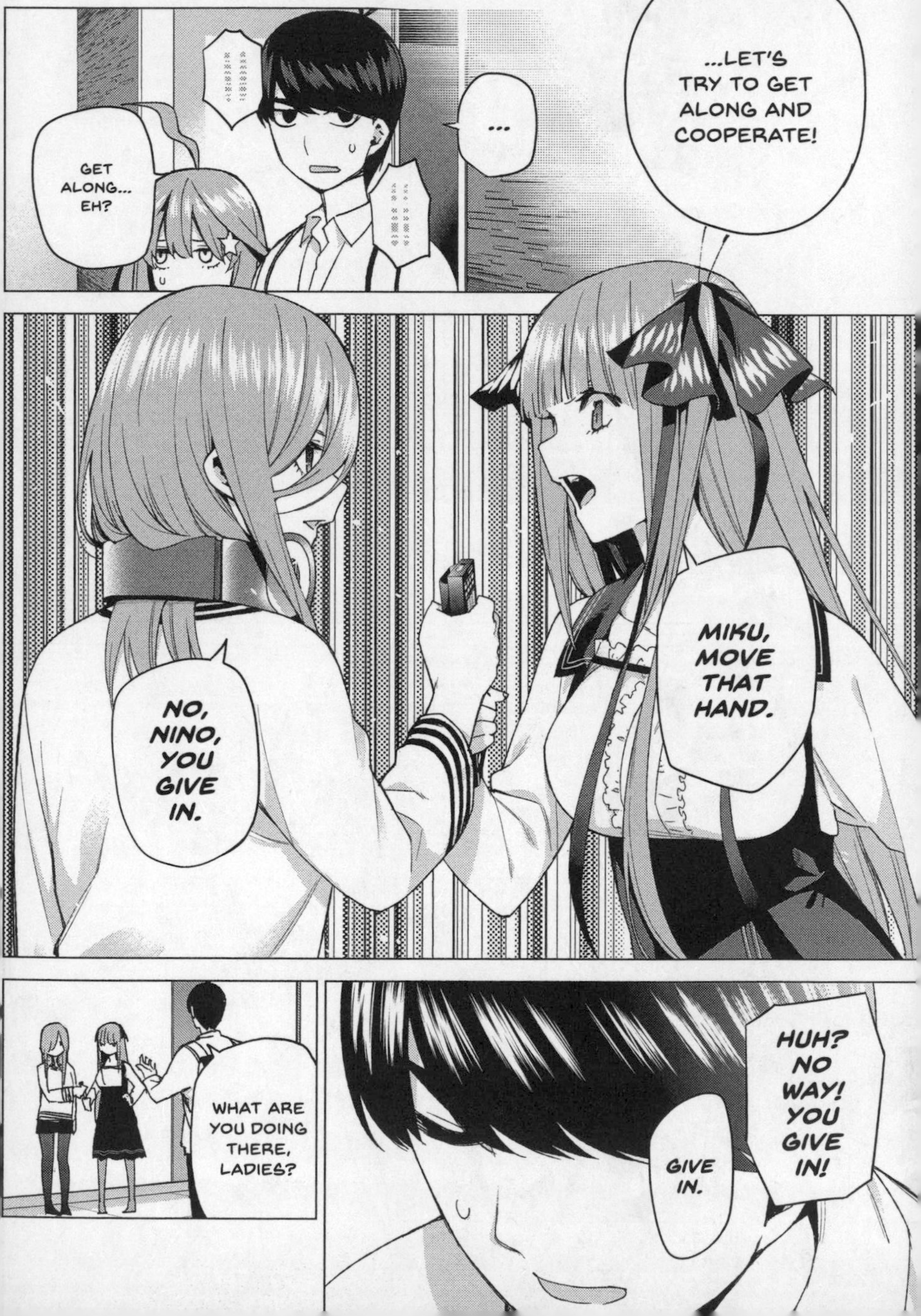
...LET'S TRY TO GET ALONG AND COOPERATE!
...
GET ALONG... EH?
MIKU, MOVE THAT HAND.
NO, NINO, YOU GIVE IN.
HUH? NO WAY! YOU GIVE IN!
GIVE IN.
WHAT ARE YOU DOING THERE, LADIES?

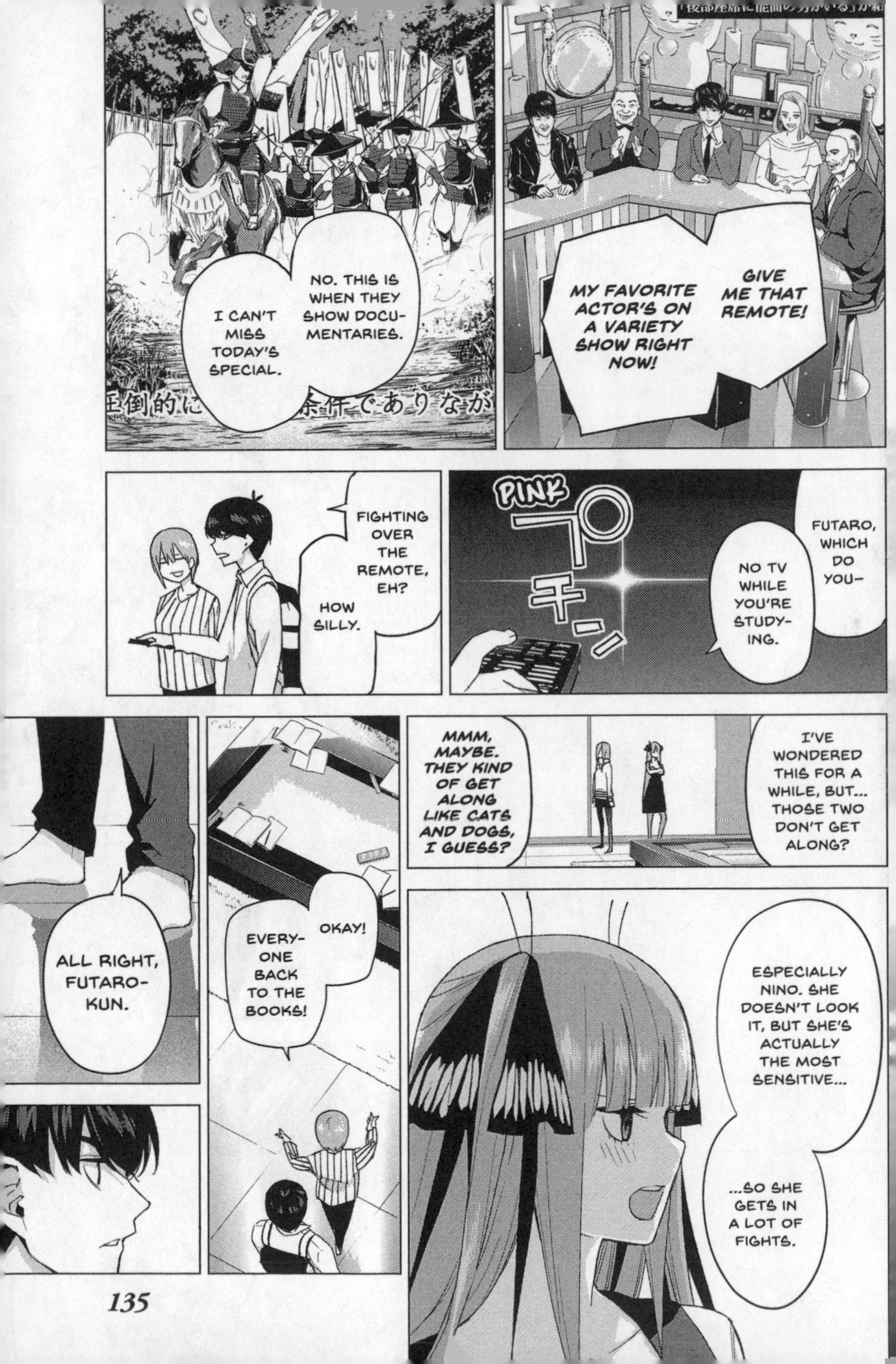
GIVE ME THAT REMOTE!
MY FAVORITE ACTOR'S ON A VARIETY SHOW RIGHT NOW!
NO. THIS IS WHEN THEY SHOW DOCUMENTARIES.
I CAN'T MISS TODAY'S SPECIAL.
FUTARO, WHICH DO YOU—
PINK
プチーン
NO TV WHILE YOU'RE STUDYING.
FIGHTING OVER THE REMOTE, EH?
HOW SILLY.
I'VE WONDERED THIS FOR A WHILE, BUT... THOSE TWO DON'T GET ALONG?
MMM, MAYBE. THEY KIND OF GET ALONG LIKE CATS AND DOGS, I GUESS?
ESPECIALLY NINO. SHE DOESN'T LOOK IT, BUT SHE'S ACTUALLY THE MOST SENSITIVE...
...SO SHE GETS IN A LOT OF FIGHTS.
OKAY!
EVERYONE BACK TO THE BOOKS!
ALL RIGHT, FUTARO-KUN.

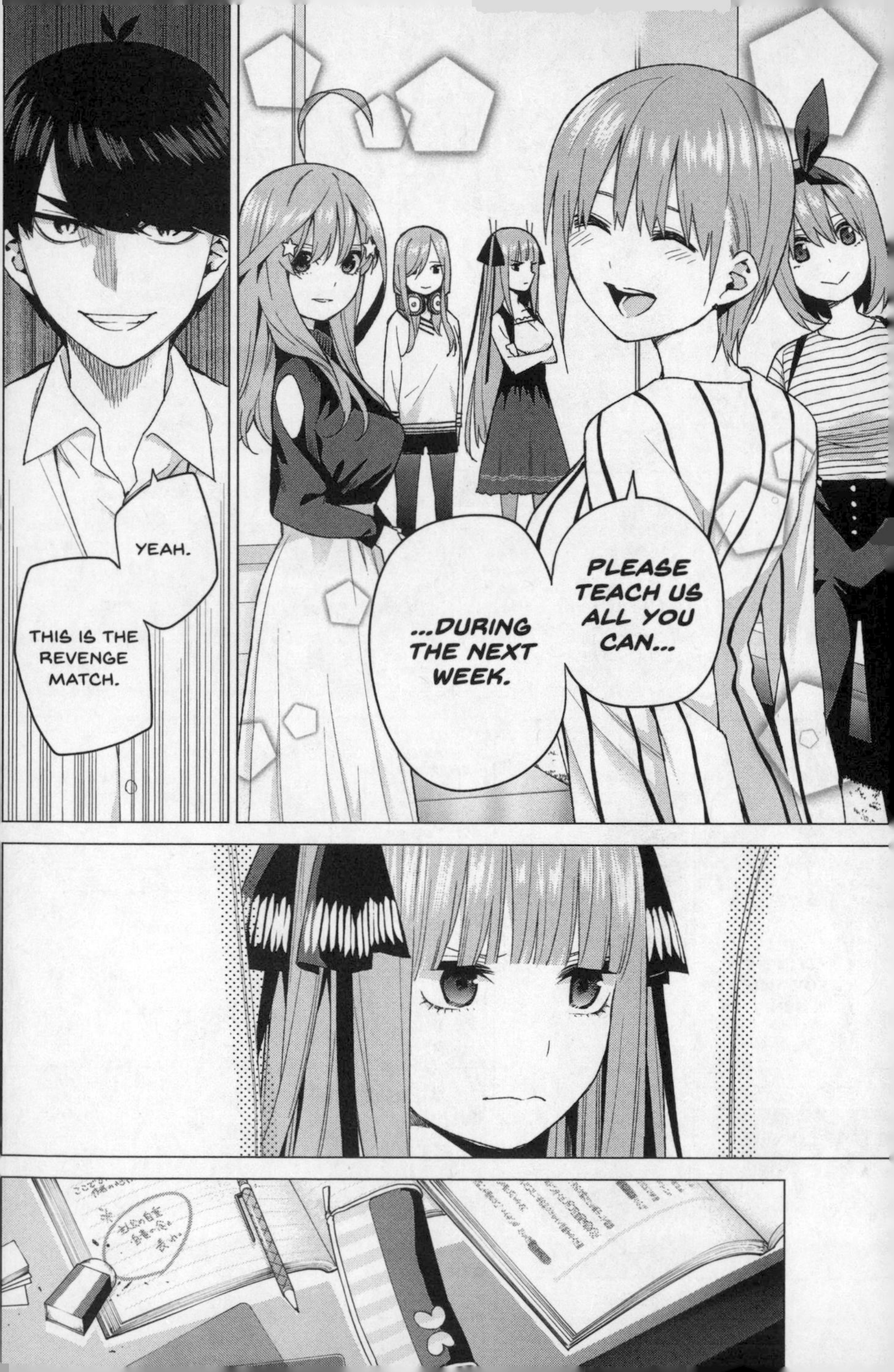
PLEASE TEACH US ALL YOU CAN...
...DURING THE NEXT WEEK.
YEAH.
THIS IS THE REVENGE MATCH.

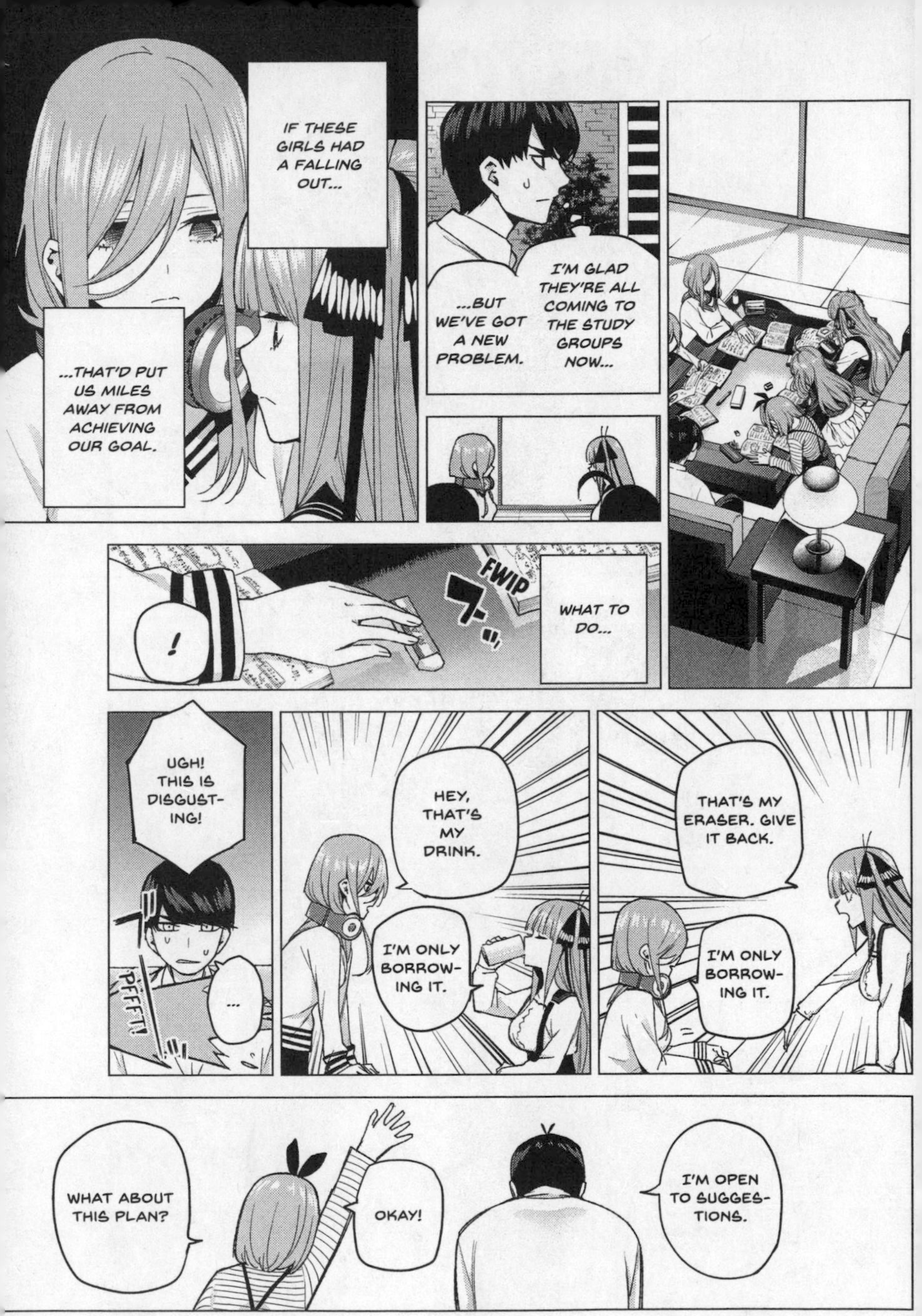
I'M GLAD THEY'RE ALL COMING TO THE STUDY GROUPS NOW...
...BUT WE'VE GOT A NEW PROBLEM.
IF THESE GIRLS HAD A FALLING OUT...
...THAT'D PUT US MILES AWAY FROM ACHIEVING OUR GOAL.
WHAT TO DO...
FWIP
!
THAT'S MY ERASER. GIVE IT BACK.
I'M ONLY BORROWING IT.
HEY, THAT'S MY DRINK.
I'M ONLY BORROWING IT.
UGH! THIS IS DISGUSTING!
PFFFT!
...
I'M OPEN TO SUGGESTIONS.
OKAY!
WHAT ABOUT THIS PLAN?

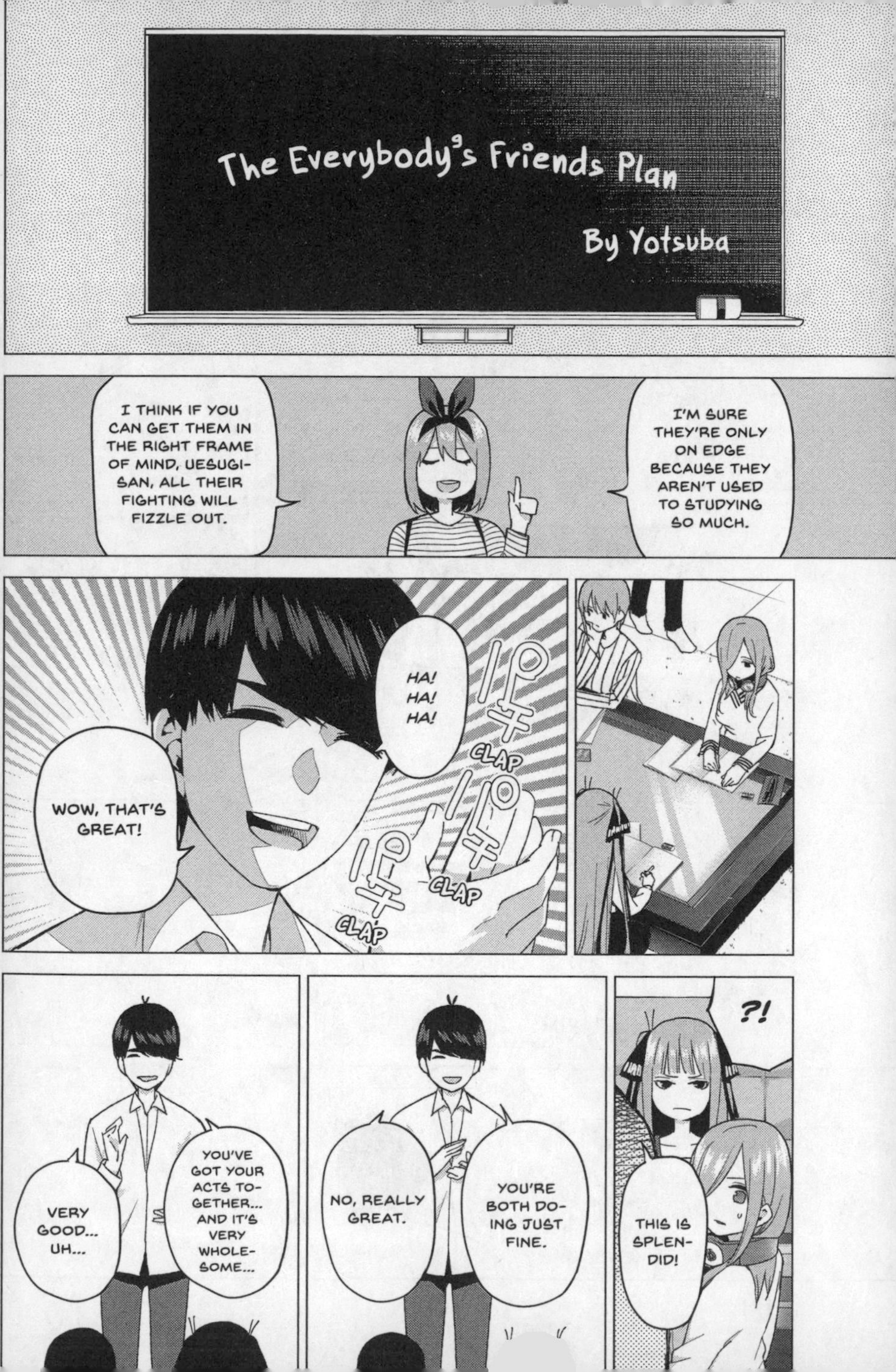

The Everybody's Friends Plan
By Yotsuba
I'M SURE THEY'RE ONLY ON EDGE BECAUSE THEY AREN'T USED TO STUDYING SO MUCH.
I THINK IF YOU CAN GET THEM IN THE RIGHT FRAME OF MIND, UESUGI-SAN, ALL THEIR FIGHTING WILL FIZZLE OUT.
HA! HA! HA!
CLAP
CLAP
CLAP
WOW, THAT'S GREAT!
?!
THIS IS SPLENDID!
YOU'RE BOTH DOING JUST FINE.
NO, REALLY GREAT.
YOU'VE GOT YOUR ACTS TOGETHER... AND IT'S VERY WHOLESOME...
VERY GOOD... UH...

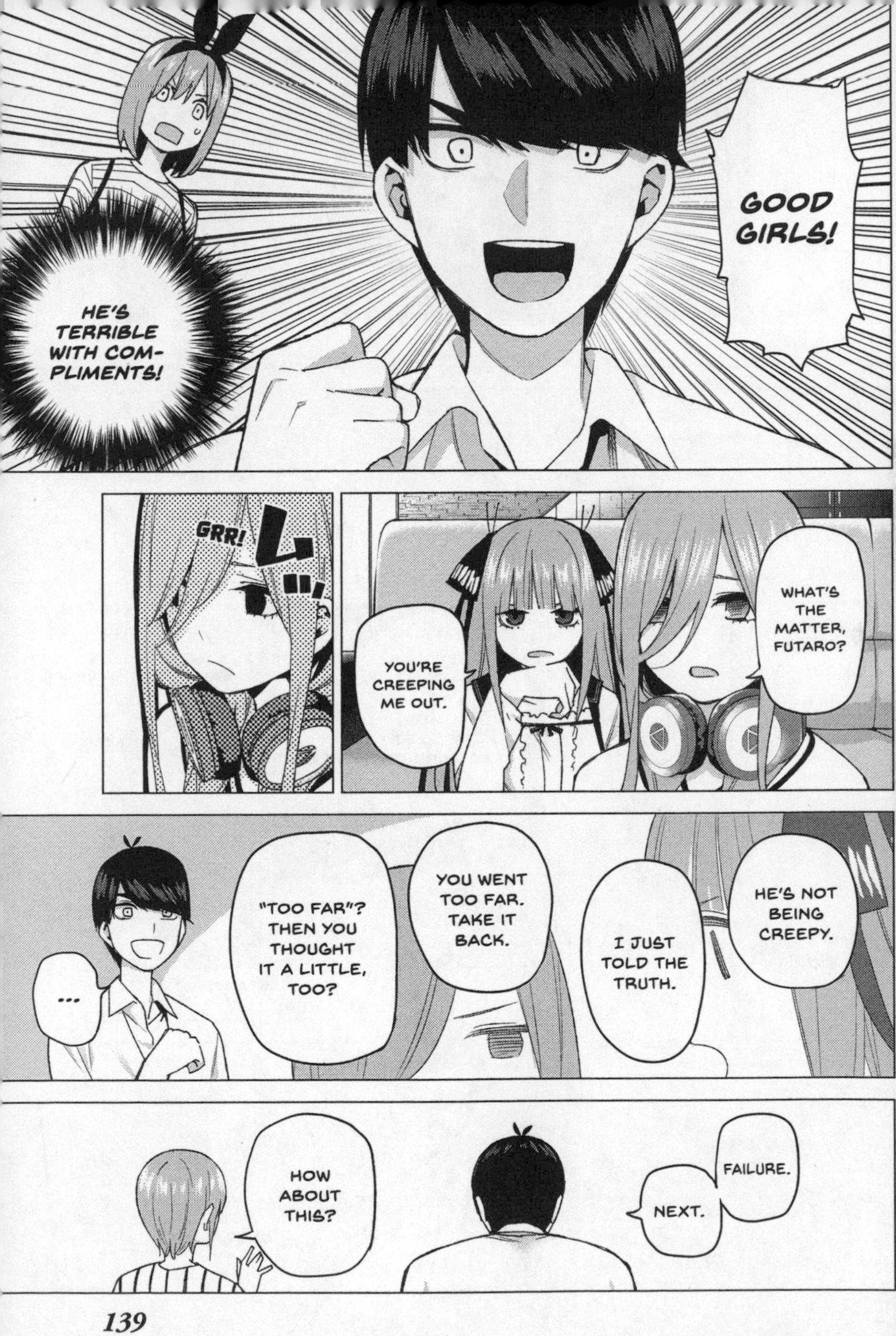
GOOD GIRLS!
HE'S TERRIBLE WITH COMPLIMENTS!
WHAT'S THE MATTER, FUTARO?
YOU'RE CREEPING ME OUT.
GRR!
HE'S NOT BEING CREEPY.
I JUST TOLD THE TRUTH.
YOU WENT TOO FAR. TAKE IT BACK.
"TOO FAR"? THEN YOU THOUGHT IT A LITTLE, TOO?
...
FAILURE.
NEXT.
HOW ABOUT THIS?

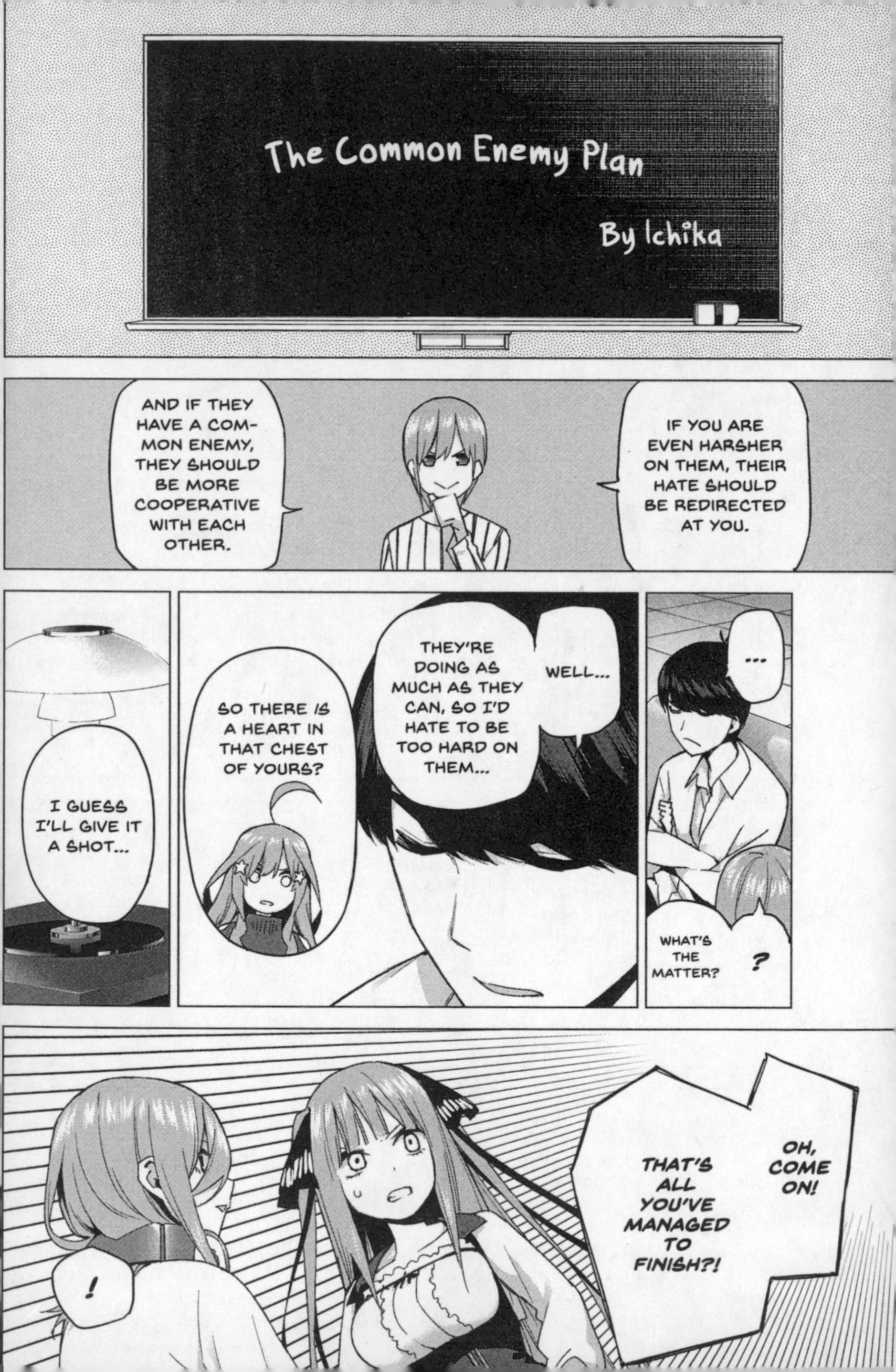
The Common Enemy Plan
By Ichika
IF YOU ARE EVEN HARSHER ON THEM, THEIR HATE SHOULD BE REDIRECTED AT YOU.
AND IF THEY HAVE A COMMON ENEMY, THEY SHOULD BE MORE COOPERATIVE WITH EACH OTHER.
...
WHAT'S THE MATTER?
?
WELL...
THEY'RE DOING AS MUCH AS THEY CAN, SO I'D HATE TO BE TOO HARD ON THEM...
SO THERE *IS* A HEART IN THAT CHEST OF YOURS?
I GUESS I'LL GIVE IT A SHOT...
OH, COME ON!
THAT'S ALL YOU'VE MANAGED TO FINISH?!
!

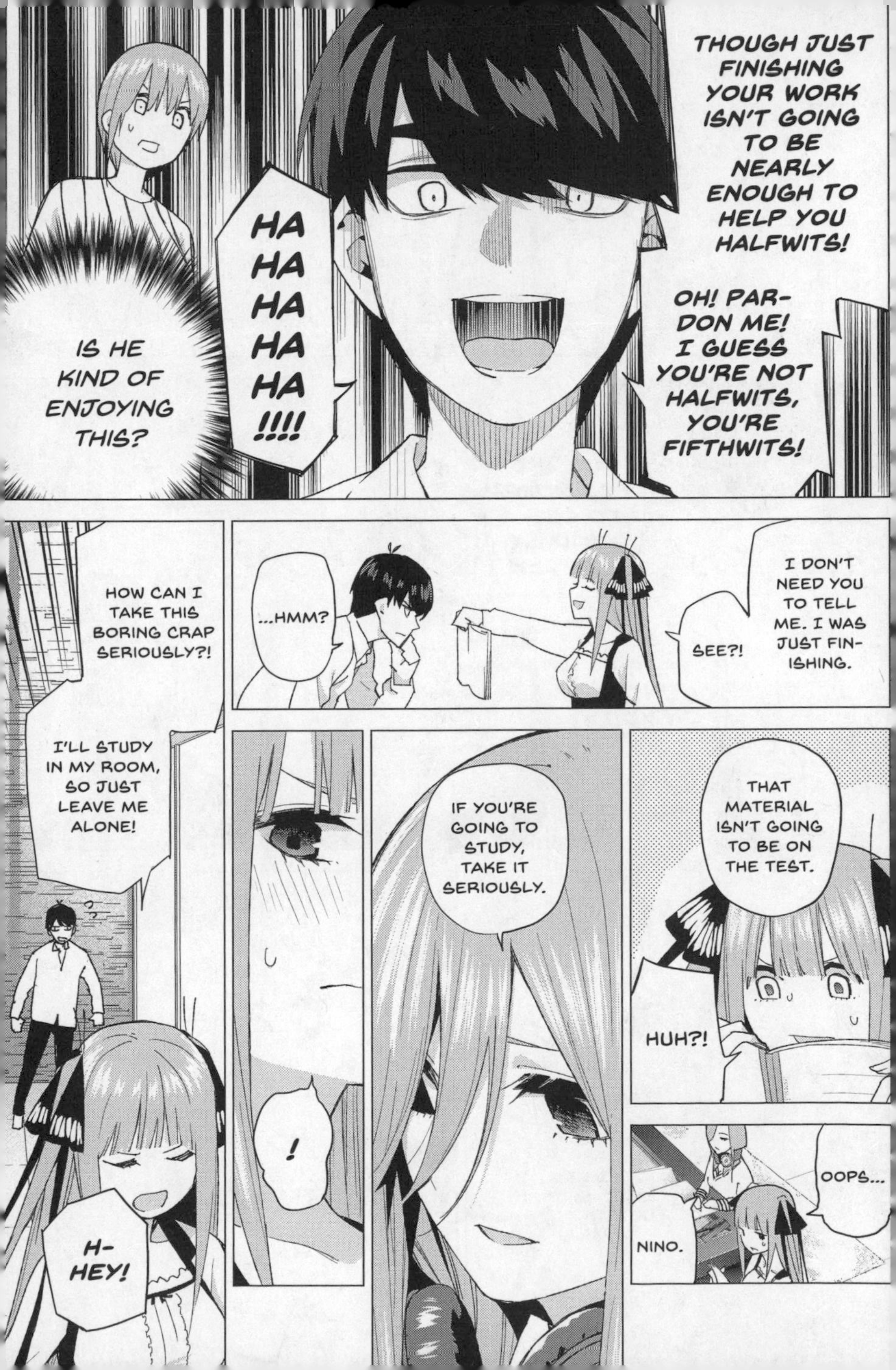

THOUGH JUST FINISHING YOUR WORK ISN'T GOING TO BE NEARLY ENOUGH TO HELP YOU HALFWITS!
OH! PAR-DON ME! I GUESS YOU'RE NOT HALFWITS, YOU'RE FIFTHWITS!
HA HA HA HA HA HA!!!!
IS HE KIND OF ENJOYING THIS?
I DON'T NEED YOU TO TELL ME. I WAS JUST FIN-ISHING.
SEE?!
...HMM?
THAT MATERIAL ISN'T GOING TO BE ON THE TEST.
HUH?!
OOPS...
NINO.
IF YOU'RE GOING TO STUDY, TAKE IT SERIOUSLY.
!
HOW CAN I TAKE THIS BORING CRAP SERIOUSLY?!
I'LL STUDY IN MY ROOM, SO JUST LEAVE ME ALONE!
H-HEY!

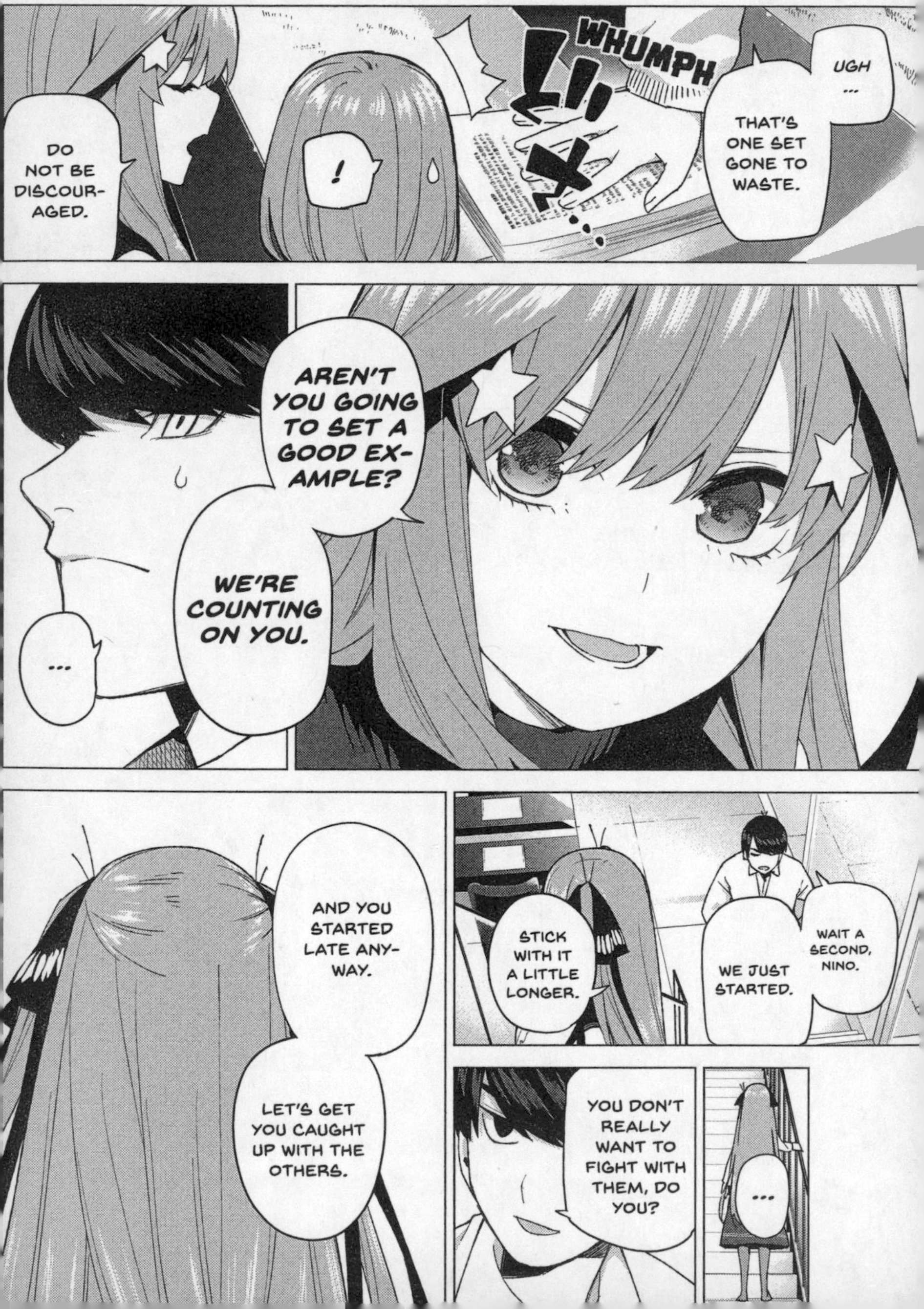
WHUMPH
UGH ...
THAT'S ONE SET GONE TO WASTE.
!
DO NOT BE DISCOURAGED.
AREN'T YOU GOING TO SET A GOOD EXAMPLE?
WE'RE COUNTING ON YOU.
...
WAIT A SECOND, NINO.
WE JUST STARTED.
STICK WITH IT A LITTLE LONGER.
...
YOU DON'T REALLY WANT TO FIGHT WITH THEM, DO YOU?
AND YOU STARTED LATE ANYWAY.
LET'S GET YOU CAUGHT UP WITH THE OTHERS.

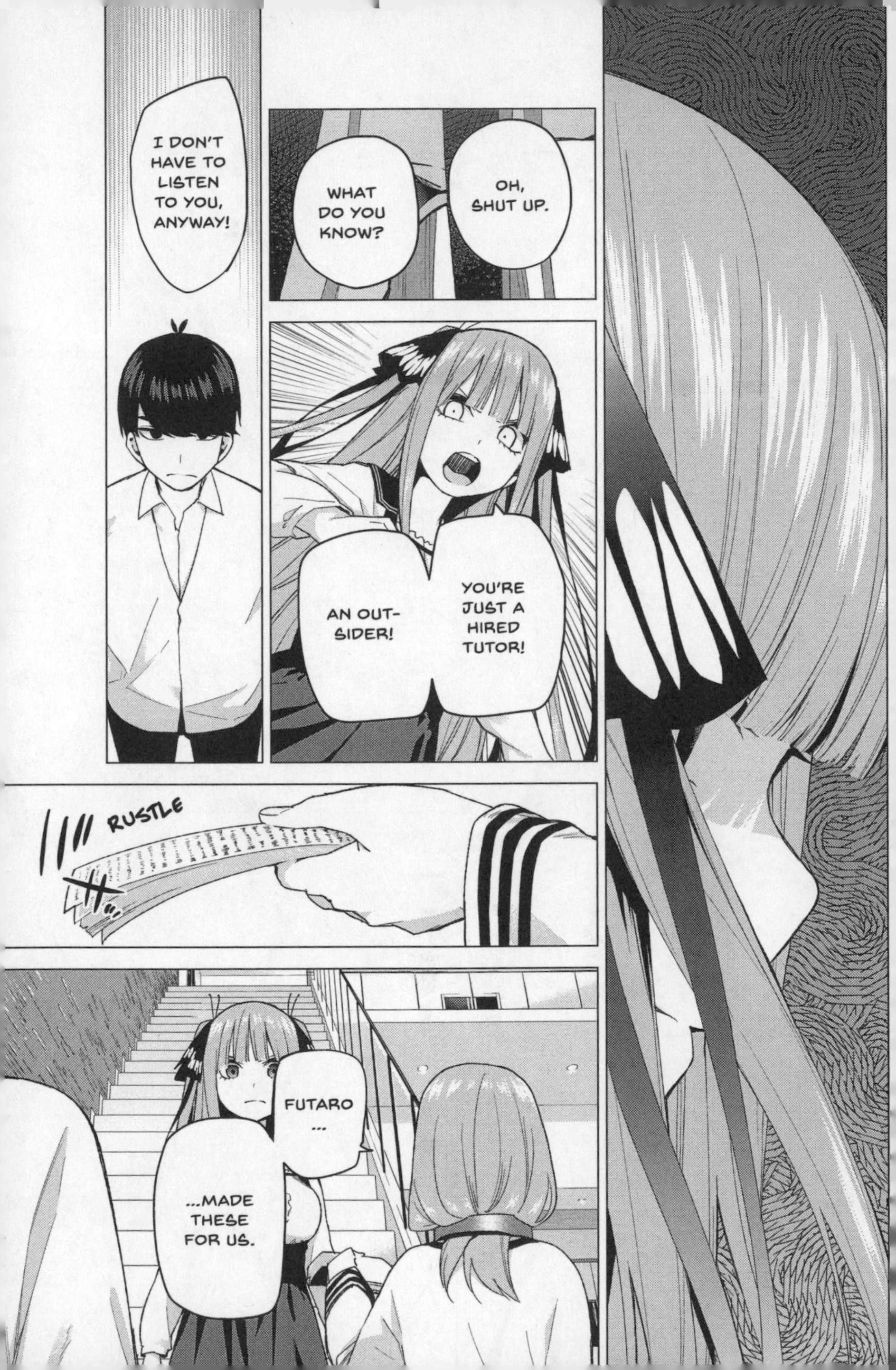
OH, SHUT UP.
WHAT DO YOU KNOW?
YOU'RE JUST A HIRED TUTOR!
AN OUT-SIDER!
I DON'T HAVE TO LISTEN TO YOU, ANYWAY!
RUSTLE
FUTARO ...
...MADE THESE FOR US.

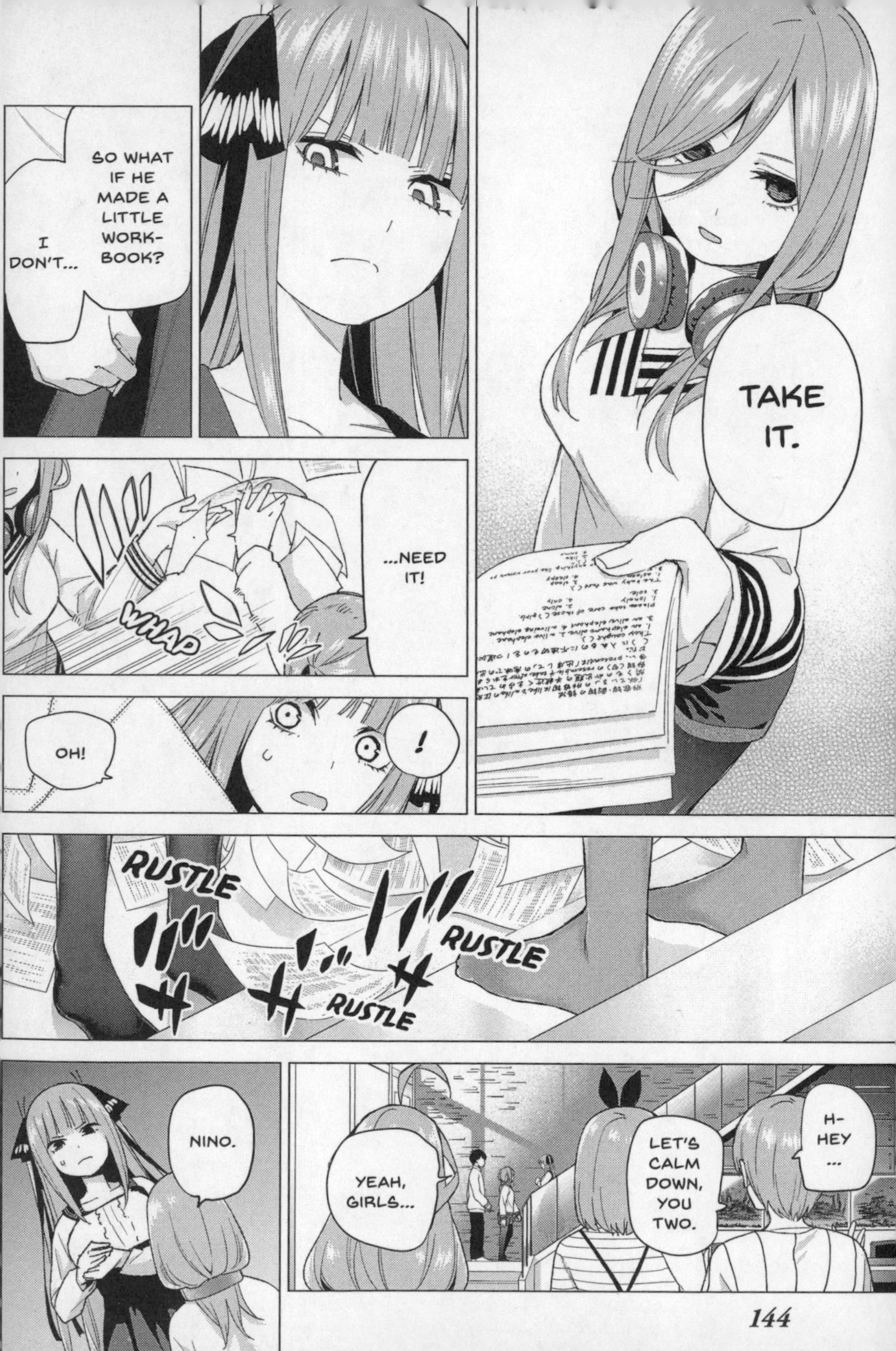
TAKE IT.
SO WHAT IF HE MADE A LITTLE WORK-BOOK?
I DON'T...
...NEED IT!
WHAP
!
OH!
RUSTLE
RUSTLE
RUSTLE
H-HEY...
LET'S CALM DOWN, YOU TWO.
YEAH, GIRLS...
NINO.

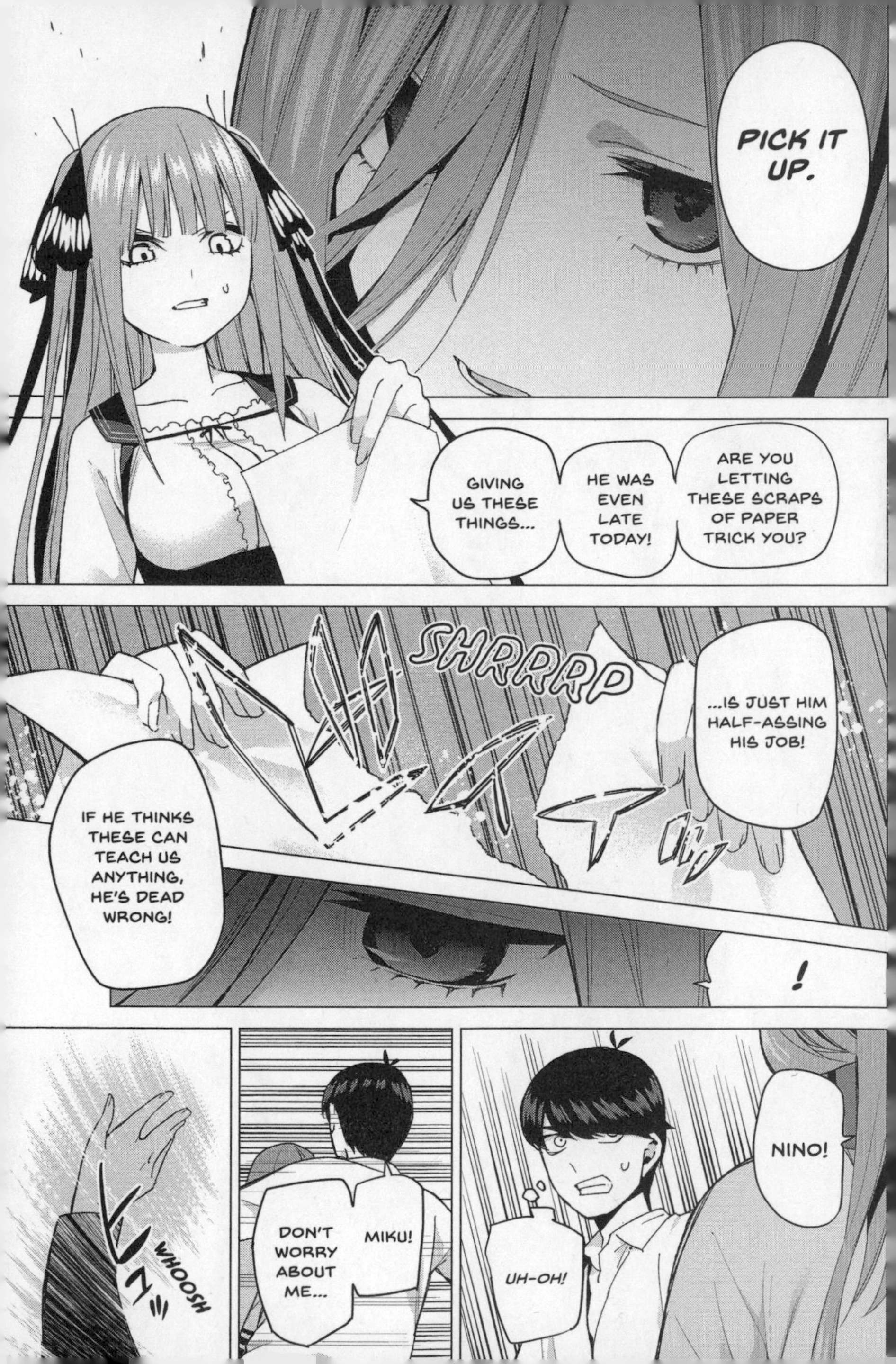
PICK IT UP.
ARE YOU LETTING THESE SCRAPS OF PAPER TRICK YOU?
HE WAS EVEN LATE TODAY!
GIVING US THESE THINGS...
SHRRRRP
...IS JUST HIM HALF-ASSING HIS JOB!
IF HE THINKS THESE CAN TEACH US ANYTHING, HE'S DEAD WRONG!
!
NINO!
UH-OH!
MIKU!
DON'T WORRY ABOUT ME...
WHOOSH

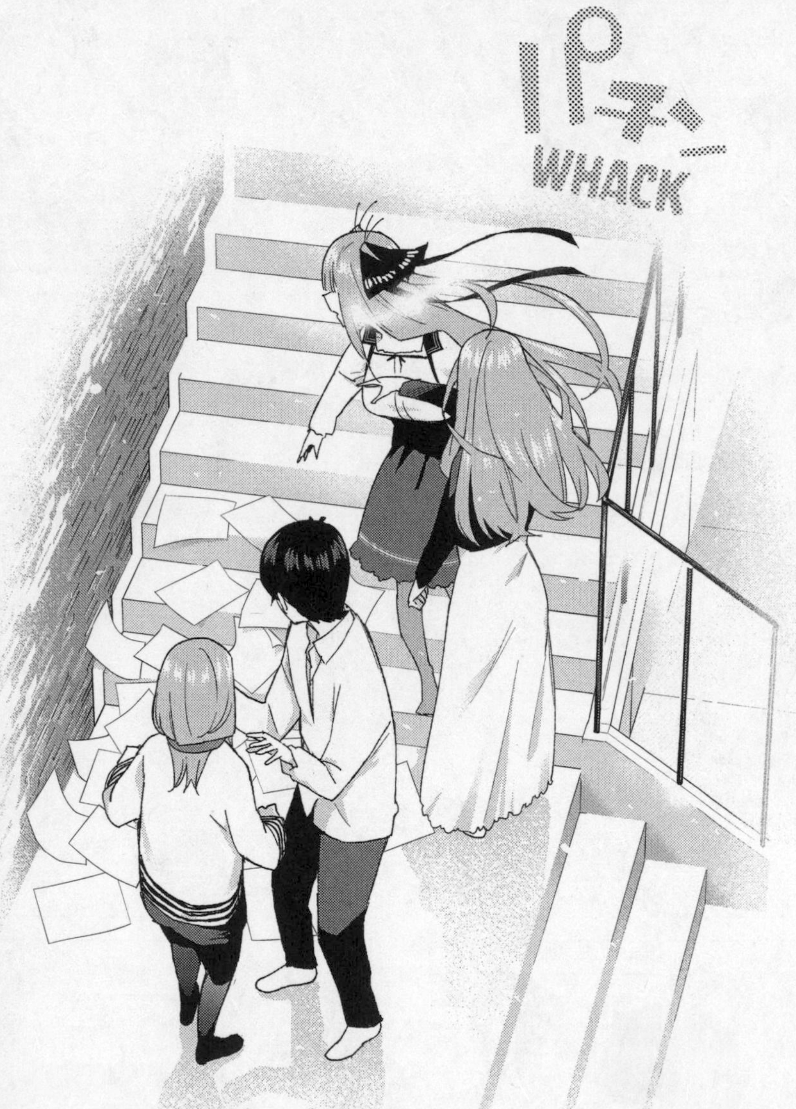
パチー
WHACK

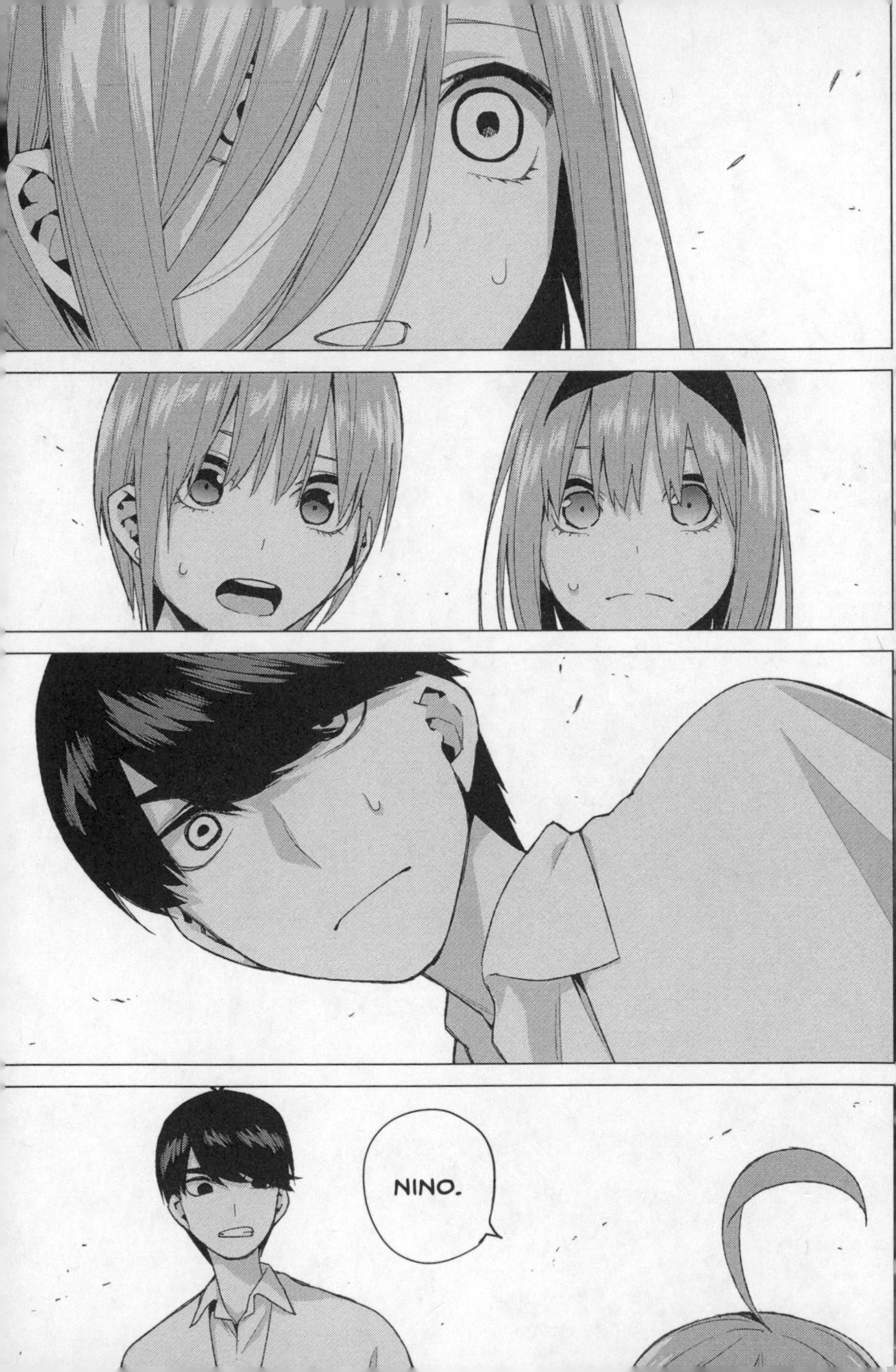
NINO.

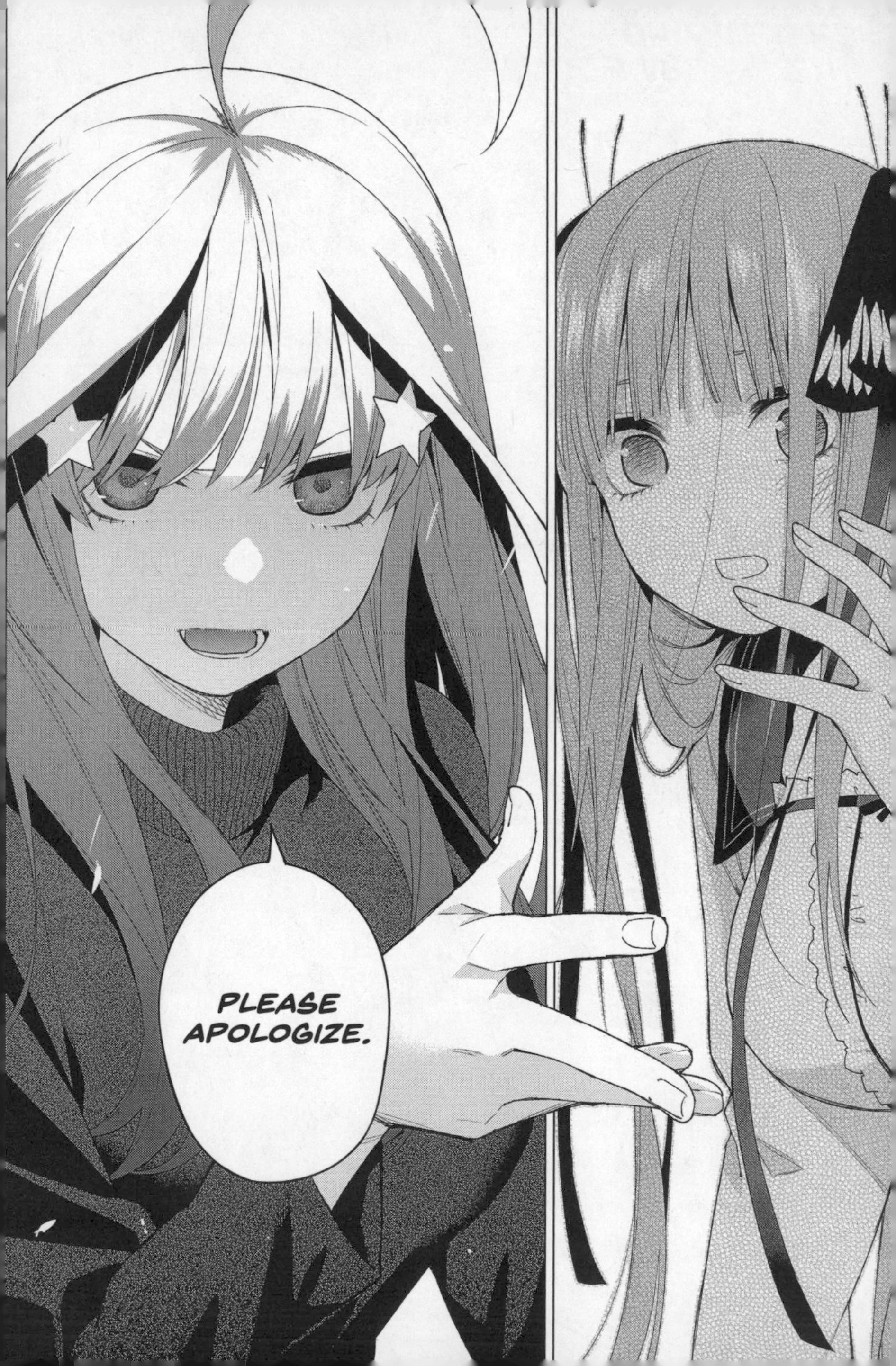
PLEASE APOLOGIZE.

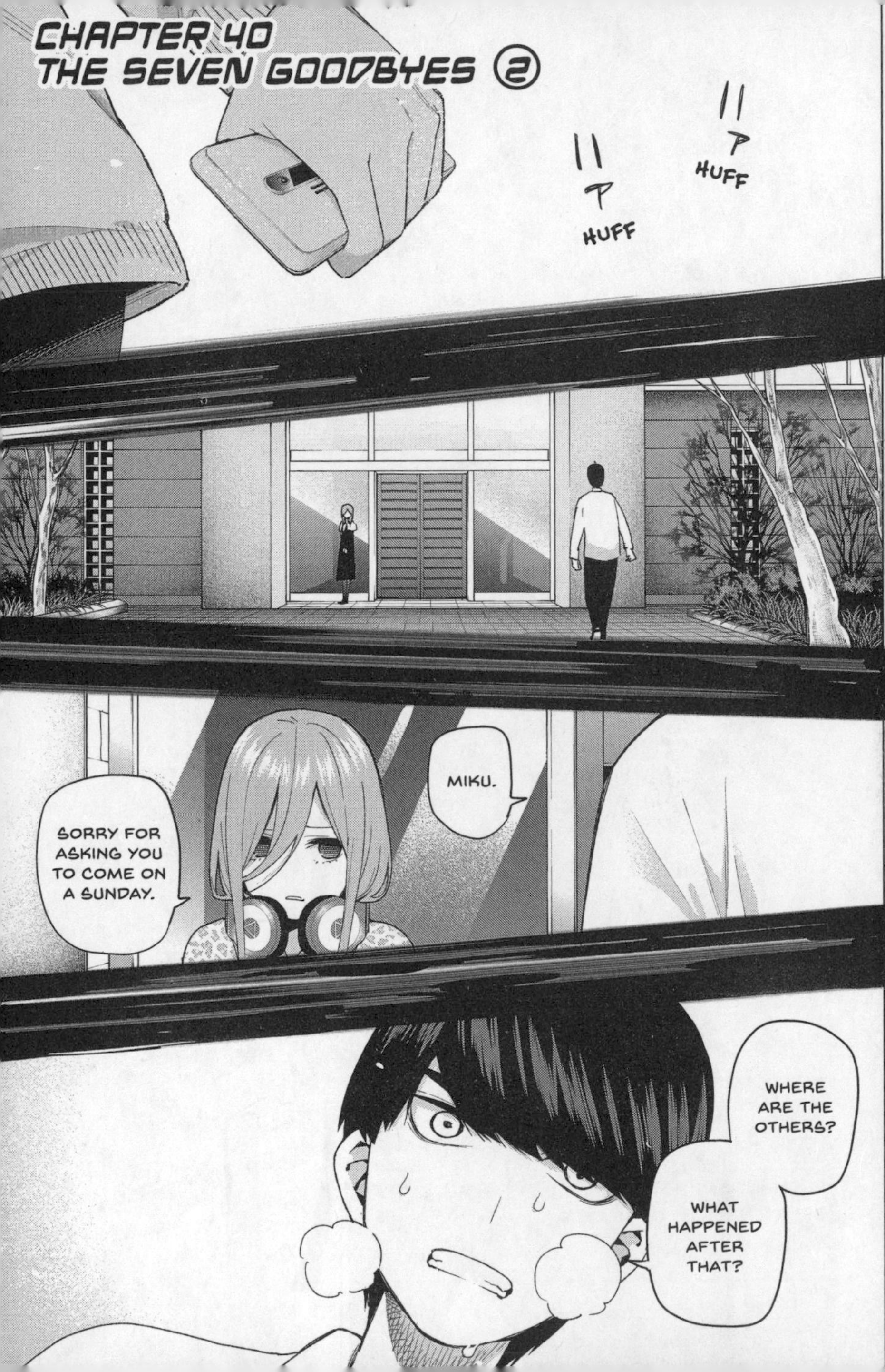
CHAPTER 40
THE SEVEN GOODBYES ②
HUFF
HUFF
MIKU.
SORRY FOR ASKING YOU TO COME ON A SUNDAY.
WHERE ARE THE OTHERS?
WHAT HAPPENED AFTER THAT?

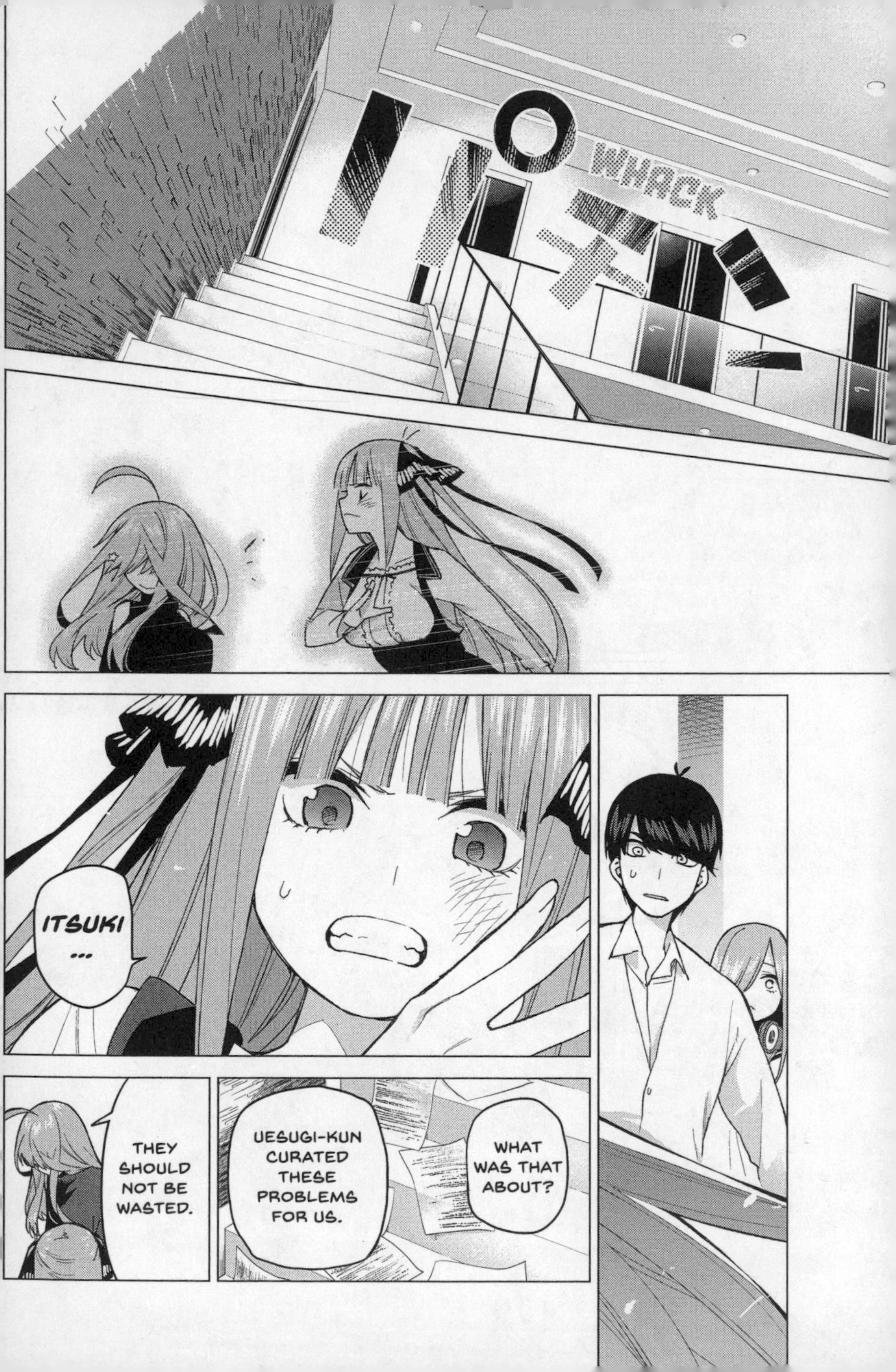
WHACK
ITSUKI...
WHAT WAS THAT ABOUT?
UESUGI-KUN CURATED THESE PROBLEMS FOR US.
THEY SHOULD NOT BE WASTED.

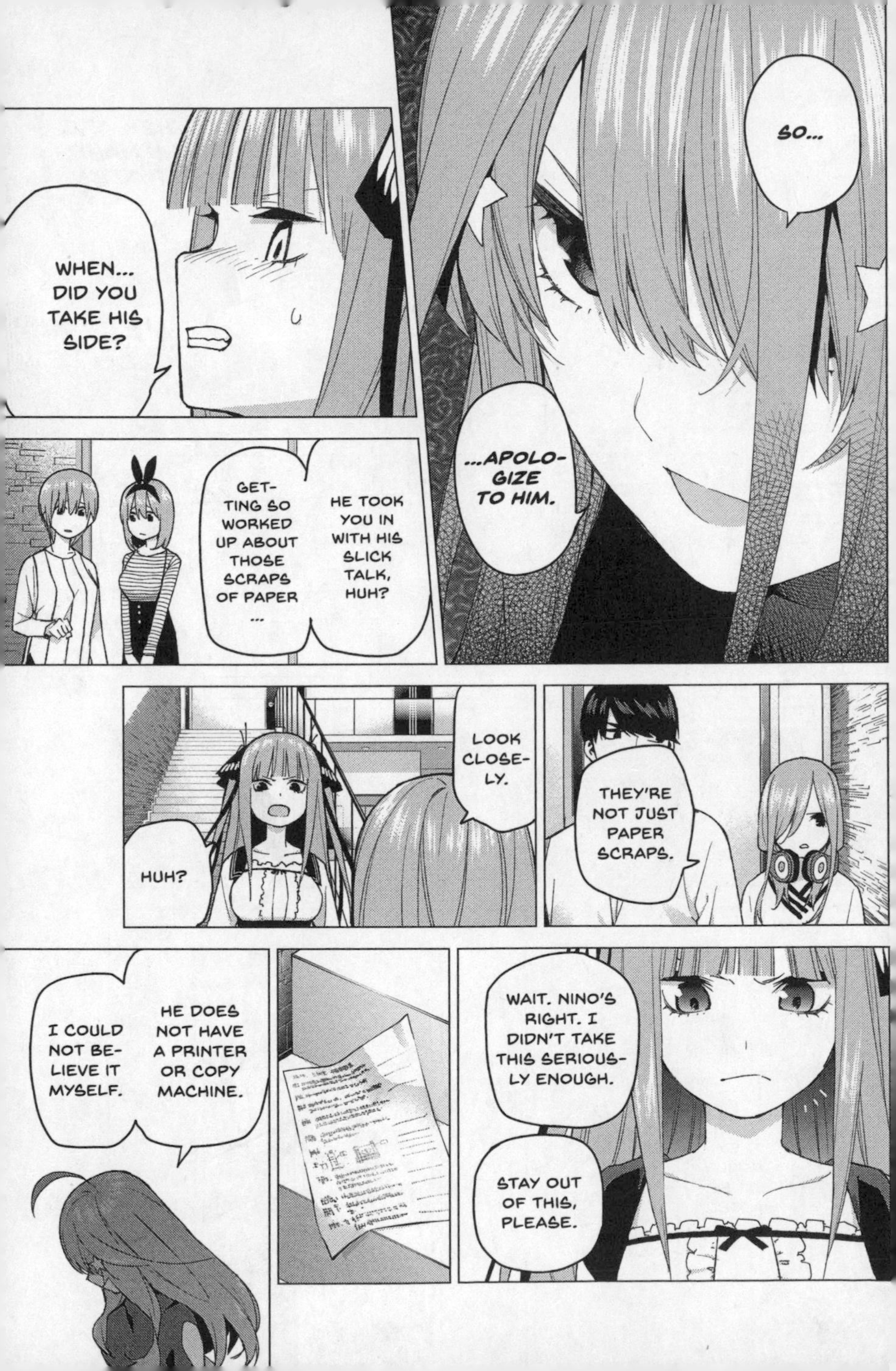
SO...
...APOLOGIZE TO HIM.
WHEN... DID YOU TAKE HIS SIDE?
HE TOOK YOU IN WITH HIS SLICK TALK, HUH?
GETTING SO WORKED UP ABOUT THOSE SCRAPS OF PAPER...
THEY'RE NOT JUST PAPER SCRAPS.
LOOK CLOSELY.
HUH?
WAIT. NINO'S RIGHT. I DIDN'T TAKE THIS SERIOUSLY ENOUGH.
STAY OUT OF THIS, PLEASE.
HE DOES NOT HAVE A PRINTER OR COPY MACHINE.
I COULD NOT BELIEVE IT MYSELF.

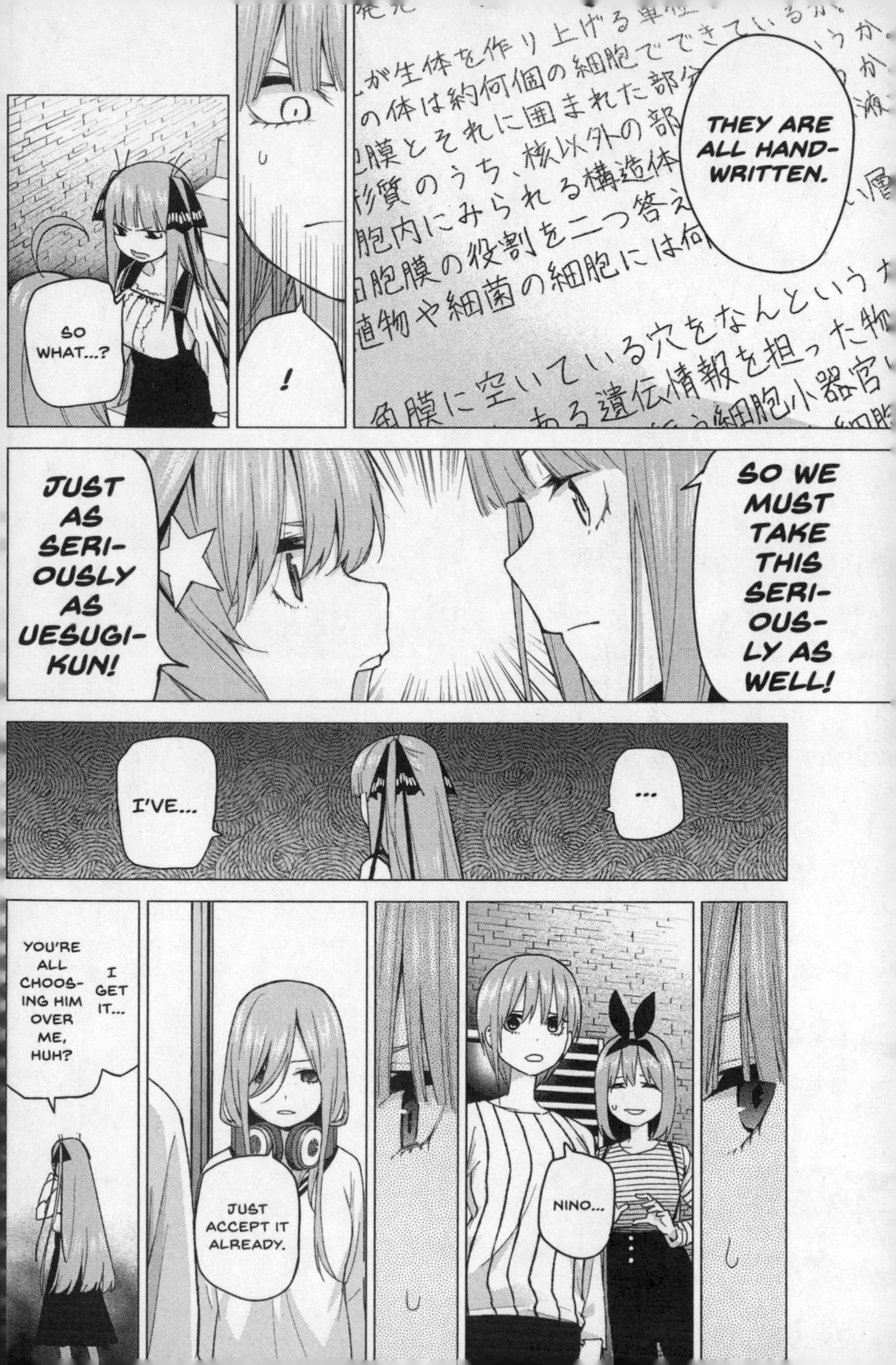
の体は約何個の細胞でできているか。
胞膜とそれに囲まれた部
形質のうち、核以外の部
胞内にみられる構造体
胞膜の役割を二つ答え
植物や細菌の細胞には
膜に空いている穴をなんという
ある遺伝情報を担った物
THEY ARE ALL HAND-WRITTEN.
!
SO WHAT...?
SO WE MUST TAKE THIS SERI-OUS-LY AS WELL!
JUST AS SERI-OUSLY AS UESUGI-KUN!
...
I'VE...
NINO...
JUST ACCEPT IT ALREADY.
I GET IT...
YOU'RE ALL CHOOS-ING HIM OVER ME, HUH?

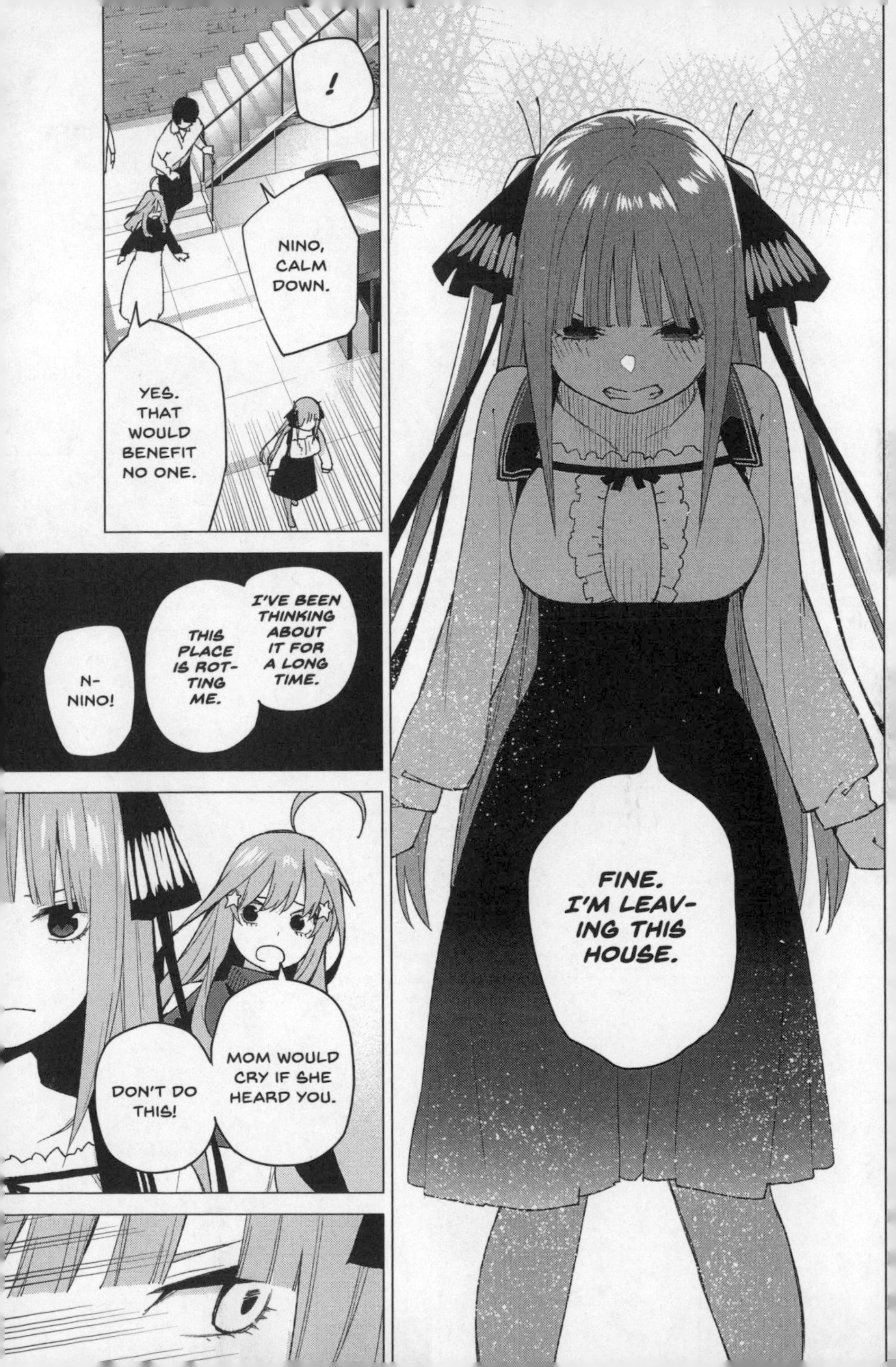
FINE. I'M LEAVING THIS HOUSE.
!
NINO, CALM DOWN.
YES. THAT WOULD BENEFIT NO ONE.
I'VE BEEN THINKING ABOUT IT FOR A LONG TIME.
THIS PLACE IS ROTTING ME.
N-NINO!
MOM WOULD CRY IF SHE HEARD YOU.
DON'T DO THIS!

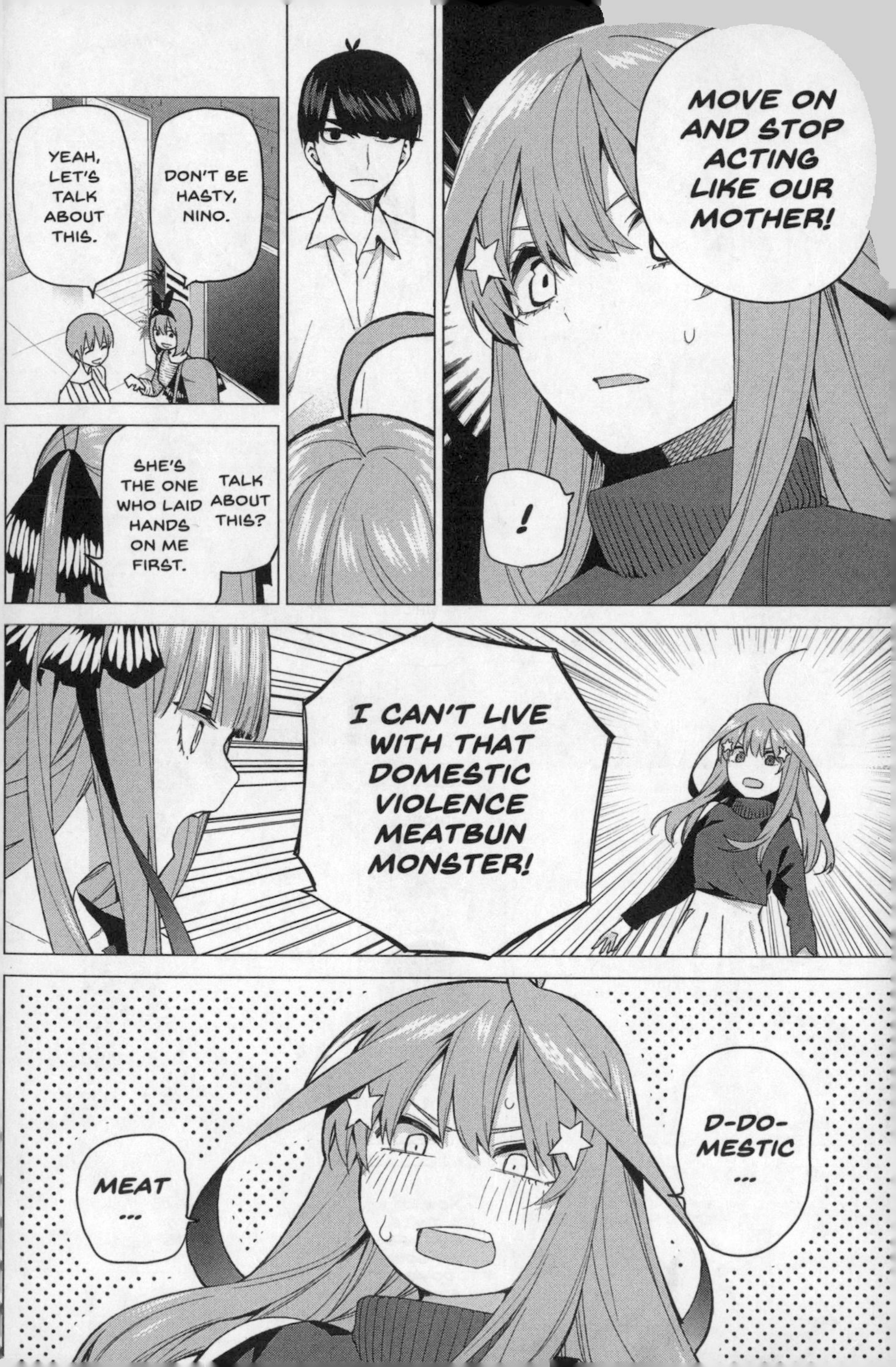
MOVE ON AND STOP ACTING LIKE OUR MOTHER!
!
DON'T BE HASTY, NINO.
YEAH, LET'S TALK ABOUT THIS.
TALK ABOUT THIS?
SHE'S THE ONE WHO LAID HANDS ON ME FIRST.
I CAN'T LIVE WITH THAT DOMESTIC VIOLENCE MEATBUN MONSTER!
D-DO-MESTIC ...
MEAT ...

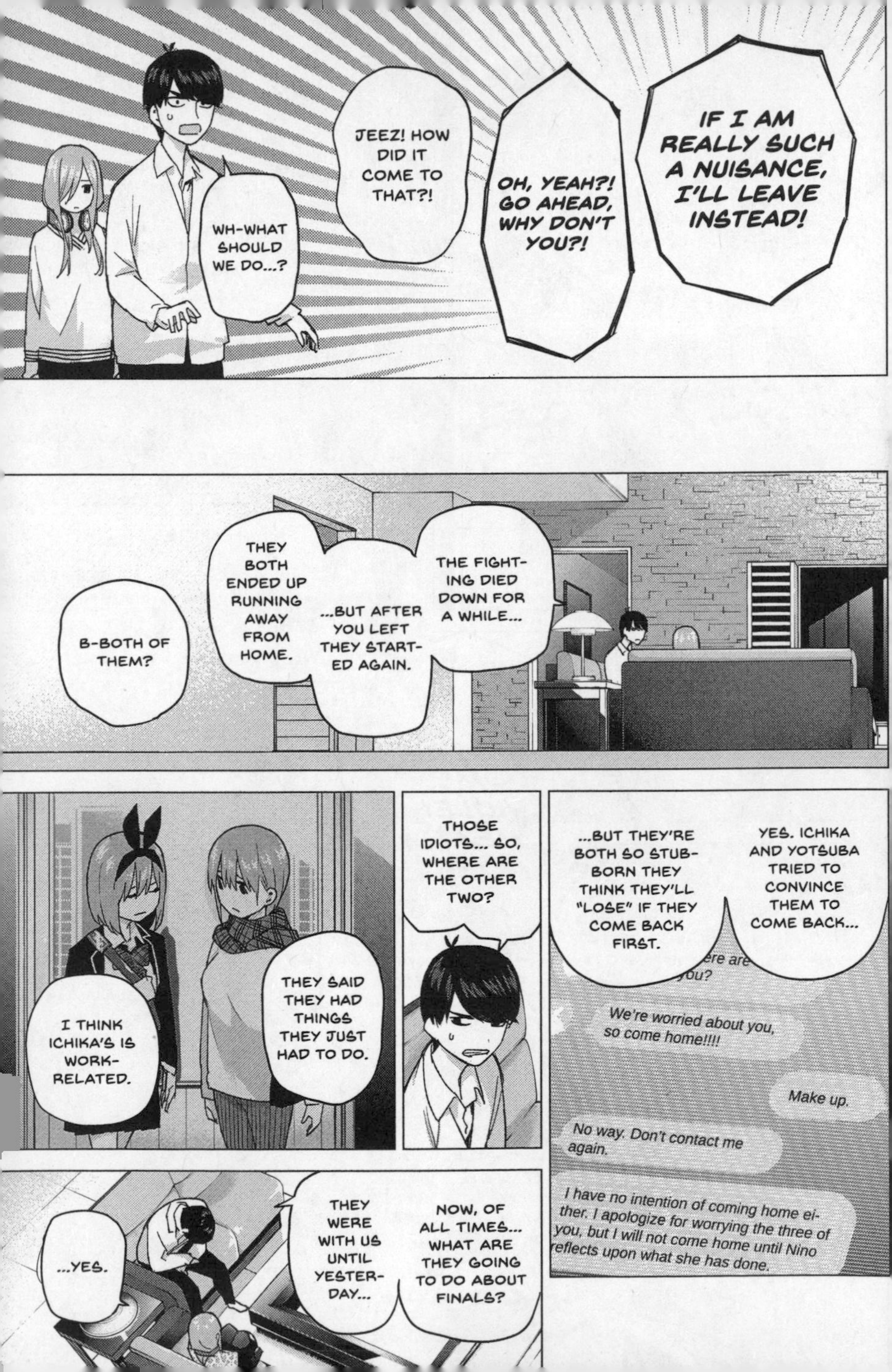
IF I AM REALLY SUCH A NUISANCE, I'LL LEAVE INSTEAD!
OH, YEAH?! GO AHEAD, WHY DON'T YOU?!
JEEZ! HOW DID IT COME TO THAT?!
WH-WHAT SHOULD WE DO...?
THE FIGHT-ING DIED DOWN FOR A WHILE...
...BUT AFTER YOU LEFT THEY START-ED AGAIN.
THEY BOTH ENDED UP RUNNING AWAY FROM HOME.
B-BOTH OF THEM?
YES. ICHIKA AND YOTSUBA TRIED TO CONVINCE THEM TO COME BACK...
...BUT THEY'RE BOTH SO STUB-BORN THEY THINK THEY'LL "LOSE" IF THEY COME BACK FIRST.
We're worried about you, so come home!!!!
Make up.
No way. Don't contact me again.
I have no intention of coming home ei-ther. I apologize for worrying the three of you, but I will not come home until Nino reflects upon what she has done.
THOSE IDIOTS... SO, WHERE ARE THE OTHER TWO?
THEY SAID THEY HAD THINGS THEY JUST HAD TO DO.
I THINK ICHIKA'S IS WORK-RELATED.
NOW, OF ALL TIMES... WHAT ARE THEY GOING TO DO ABOUT FINALS?
THEY WERE WITH US UNTIL YESTER-DAY...
...YES.

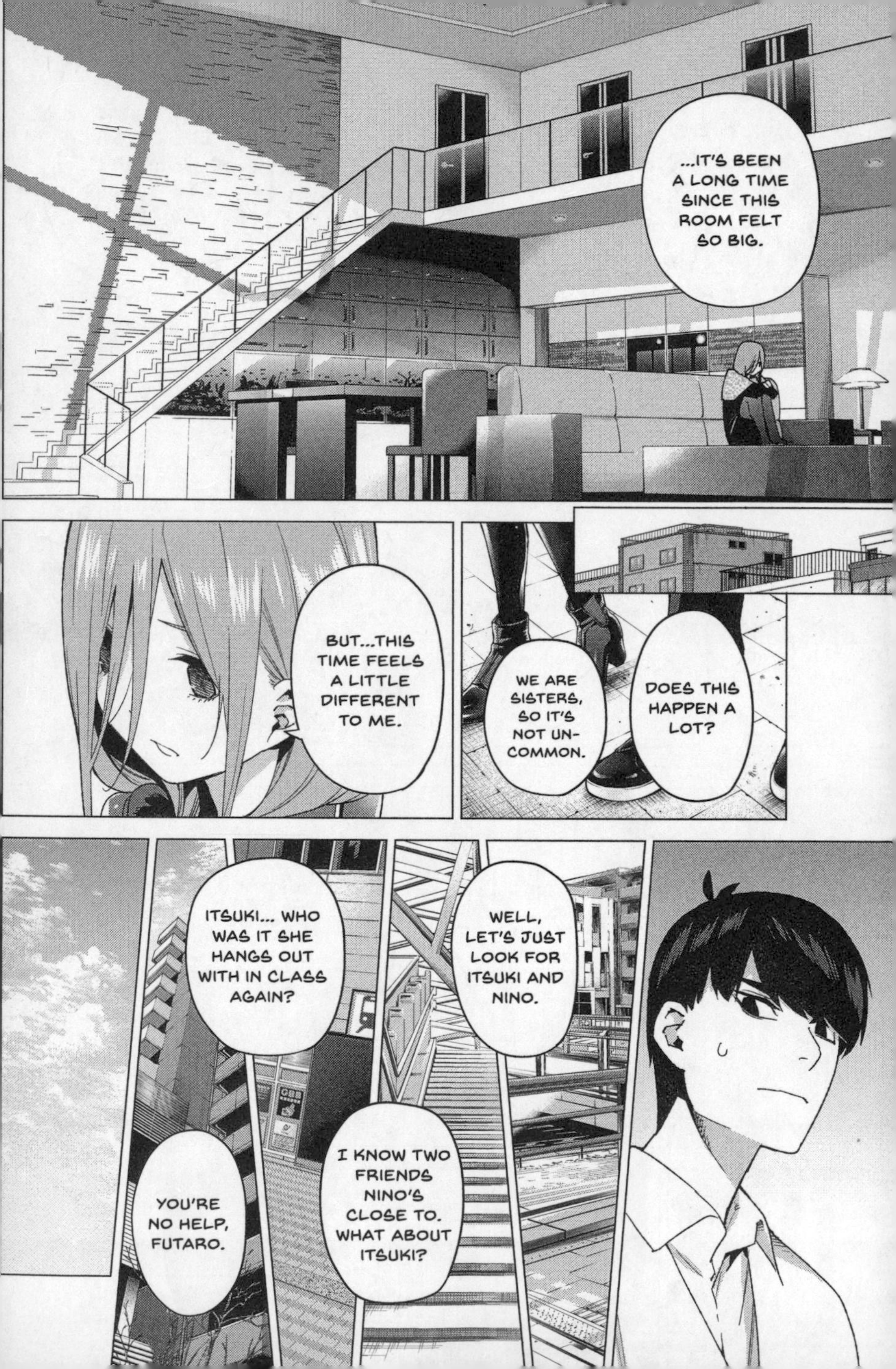
...IT'S BEEN A LONG TIME SINCE THIS ROOM FELT SO BIG.
DOES THIS HAPPEN A LOT?
WE ARE SISTERS, SO IT'S NOT UN-COMMON.
BUT...THIS TIME FEELS A LITTLE DIFFERENT TO ME.
WELL, LET'S JUST LOOK FOR ITSUKI AND NINO.
I KNOW TWO FRIENDS NINO'S CLOSE TO. WHAT ABOUT ITSUKI?
ITSUKI... WHO WAS IT SHE HANGS OUT WITH IN CLASS AGAIN?
YOU'RE NO HELP, FUTARO.

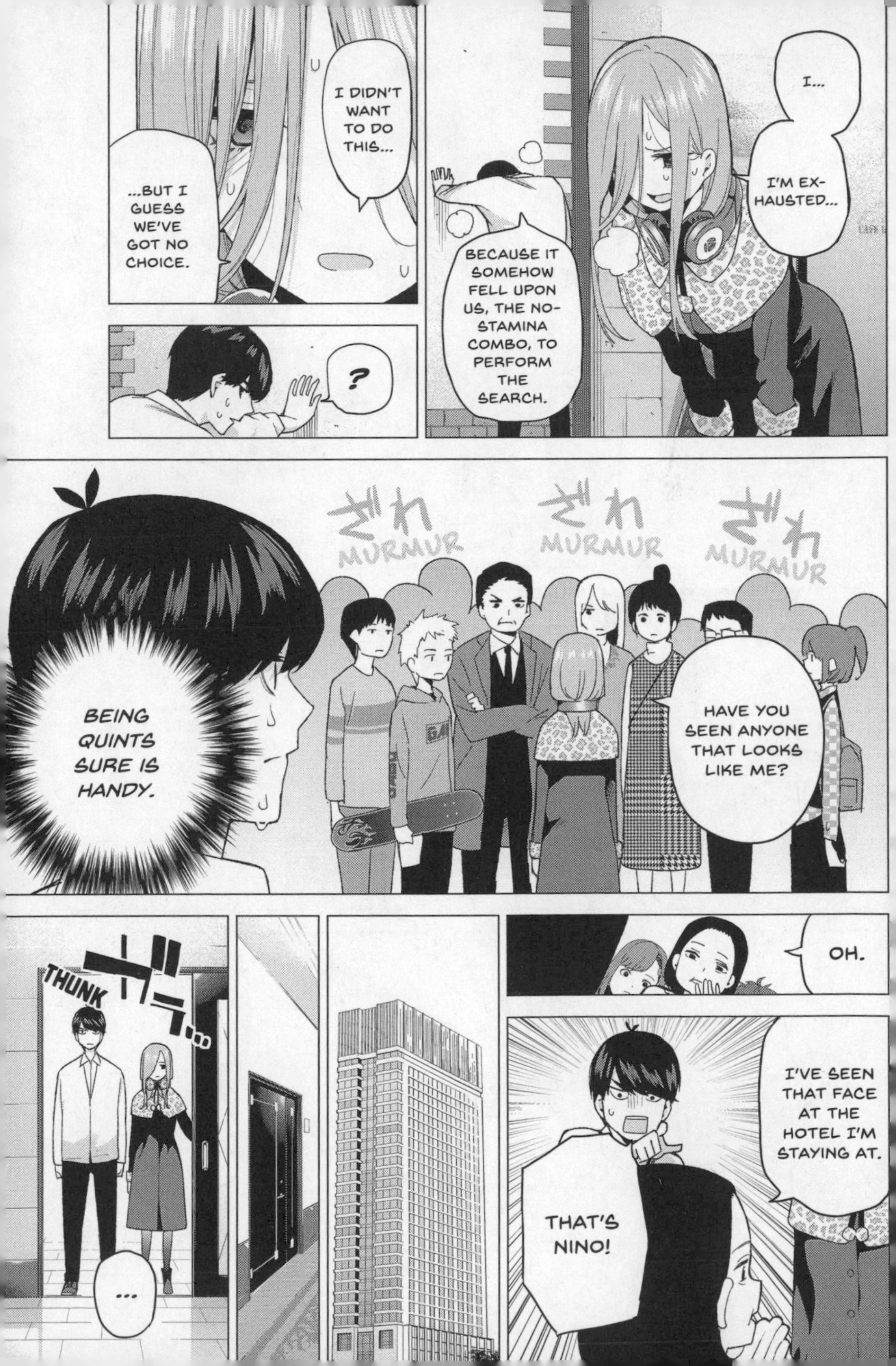

I...
I'M EX-HAUSTED...
BECAUSE IT SOMEHOW FELL UPON US, THE NO-STAMINA COMBO, TO PERFORM THE SEARCH.
I DIDN'T WANT TO DO THIS...
...BUT I GUESS WE'VE GOT NO CHOICE.
?
ざわ MURMUR
ざわ MURMUR
ざわ MURMUR
HAVE YOU SEEN ANYONE THAT LOOKS LIKE ME?
BEING QUINTS SURE IS HANDY.
OH.
I'VE SEEN THAT FACE AT THE HOTEL I'M STAYING AT.
THAT'S NINO!
ガラ... THUNK
...

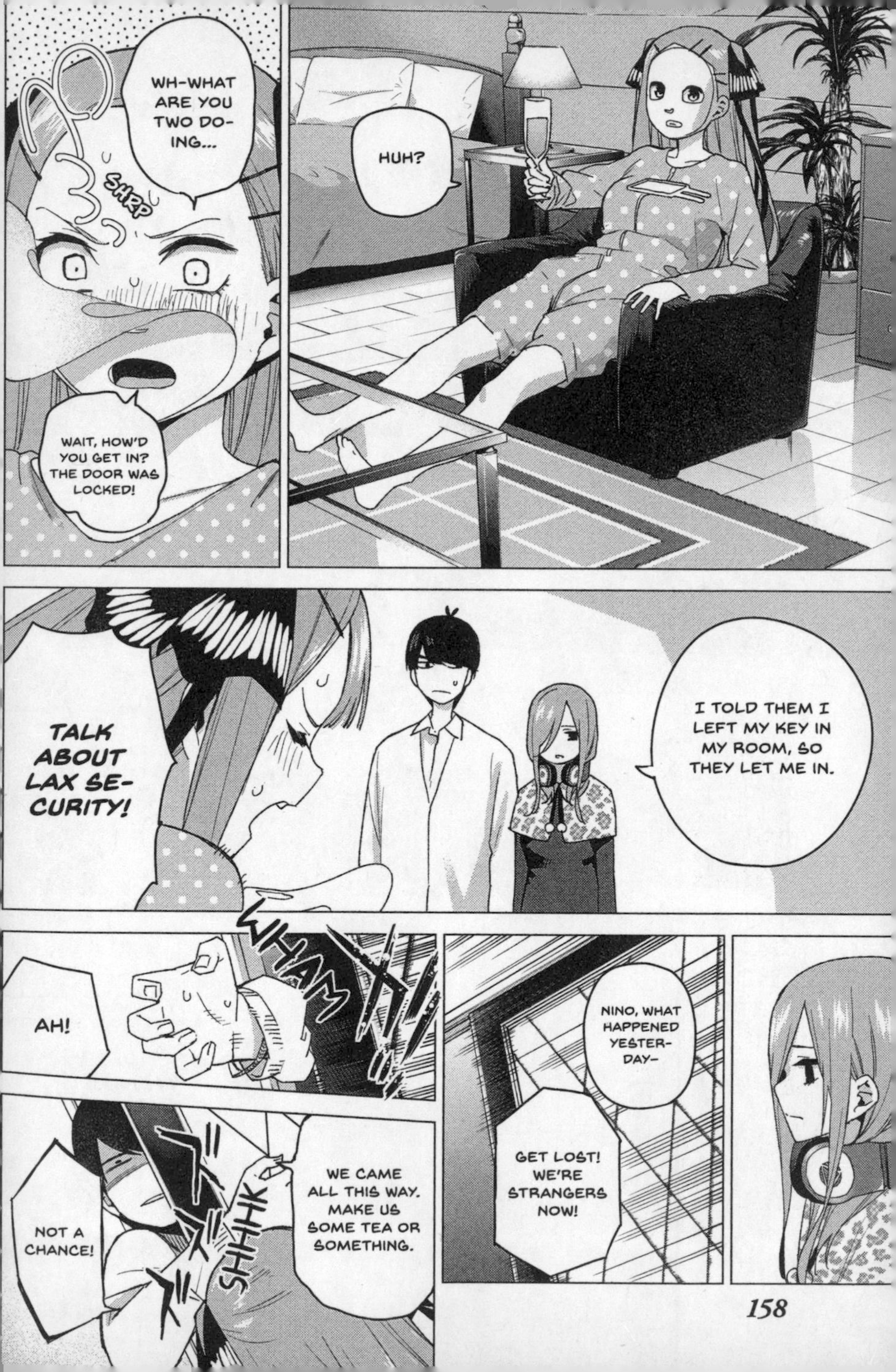
HUH?
WH-WHAT ARE YOU TWO DO-ING...
SHRP
WAIT, HOW'D YOU GET IN? THE DOOR WAS LOCKED!
I TOLD THEM I LEFT MY KEY IN MY ROOM, SO THEY LET ME IN.
TALK ABOUT LAX SE-CURITY!
NINO, WHAT HAPPENED YESTER-DAY-
GET LOST! WE'RE STRANGERS NOW!
WHAM
AH!
WE CAME ALL THIS WAY. MAKE US SOME TEA OR SOMETHING.
SHHHK
NOT A CHANCE!

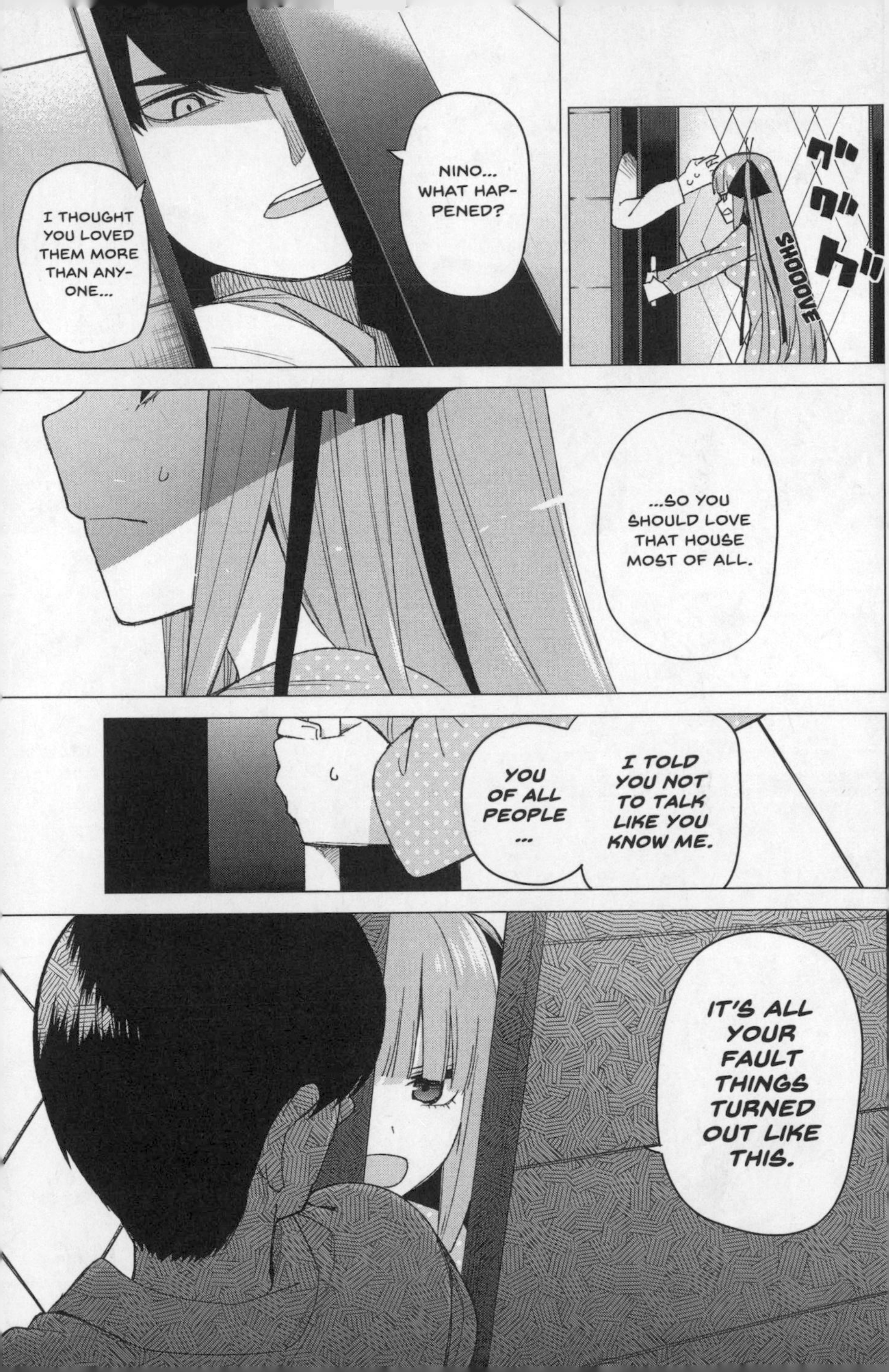
SHOOOVE
NINO... WHAT HAP-PENED?
I THOUGHT YOU LOVED THEM MORE THAN ANY-ONE...
...SO YOU SHOULD LOVE THAT HOUSE MOST OF ALL.
I TOLD YOU NOT TO TALK LIKE YOU KNOW ME.
YOU OF ALL PEOPLE ...
IT'S ALL YOUR FAULT THINGS TURNED OUT LIKE THIS.

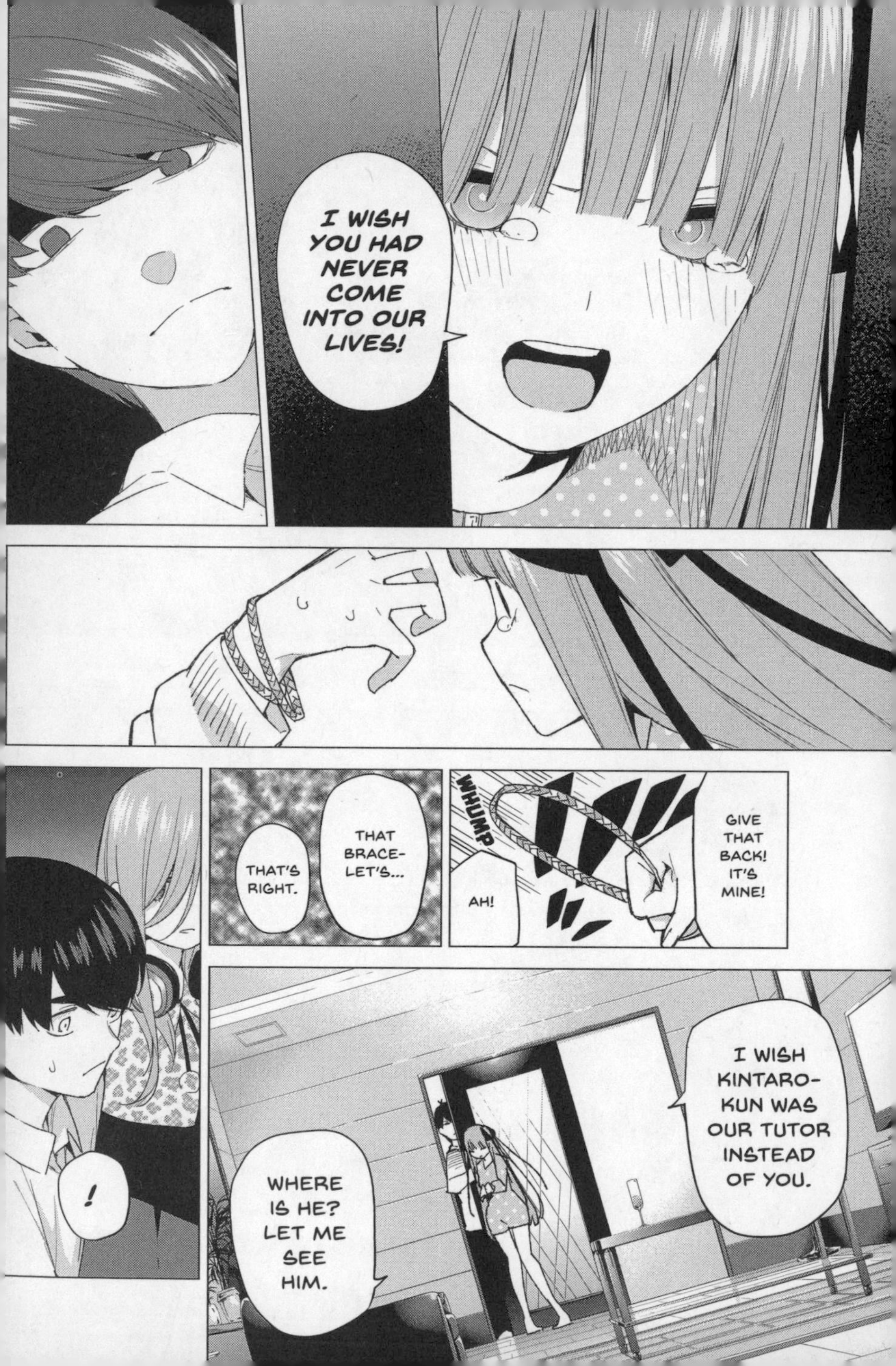
I WISH YOU HAD NEVER COME INTO OUR LIVES!
GIVE THAT BACK! IT'S MINE!
WHUMP
AH!
THAT BRACE-LET'S...
THAT'S RIGHT.
I WISH KINTARO-KUN WAS OUR TUTOR INSTEAD OF YOU.
WHERE IS HE? LET ME SEE HIM.
!

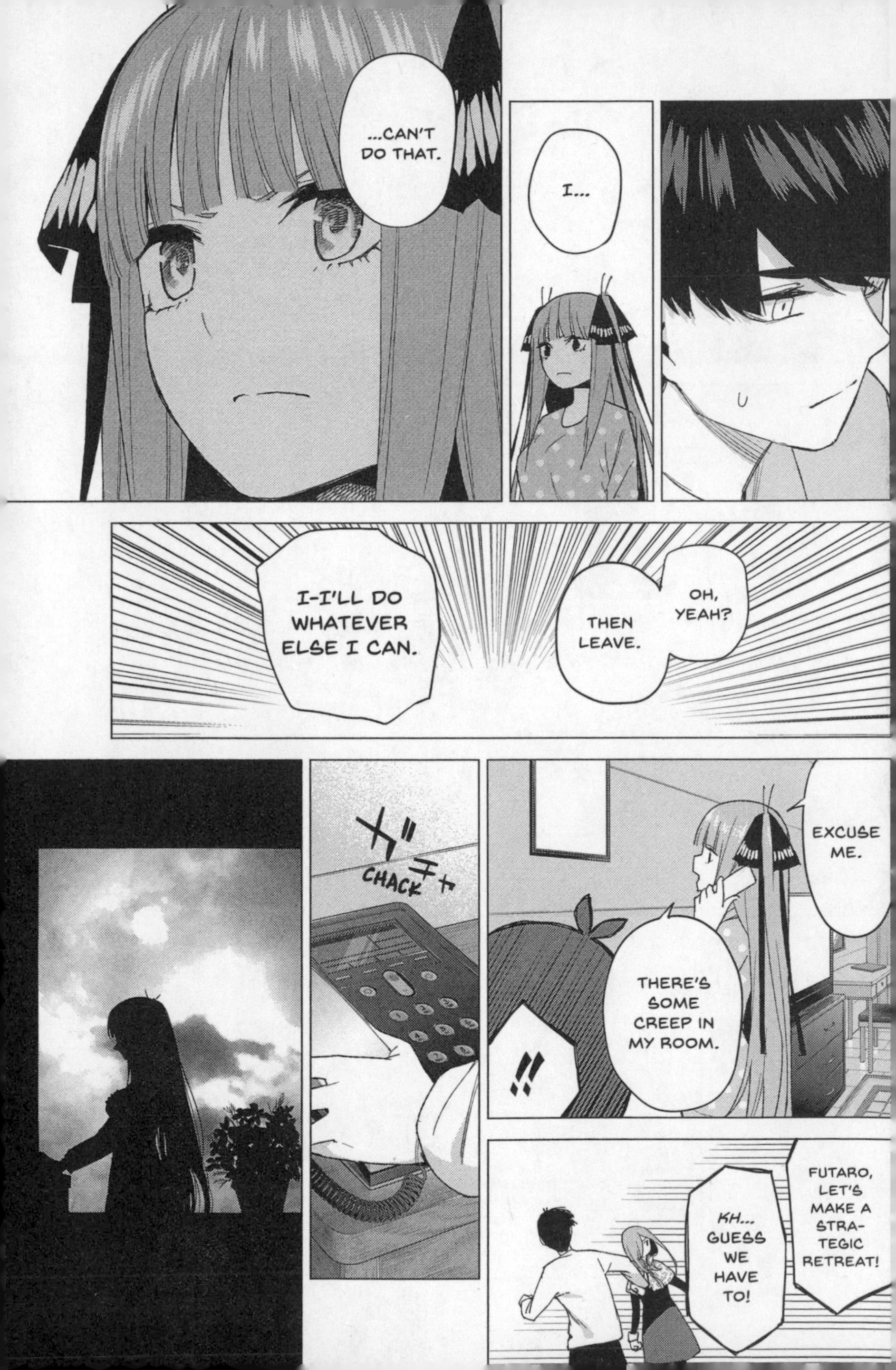
I...
...CAN'T DO THAT.
OH, YEAH? THEN LEAVE.
I-I'LL DO WHATEVER ELSE I CAN.
EXCUSE ME.
THERE'S SOME CREEP IN MY ROOM.
!!
FUTARO, LET'S MAKE A STRATEGIC RETREAT!
KH... GUESS WE HAVE TO!
ガチャ
CHACK

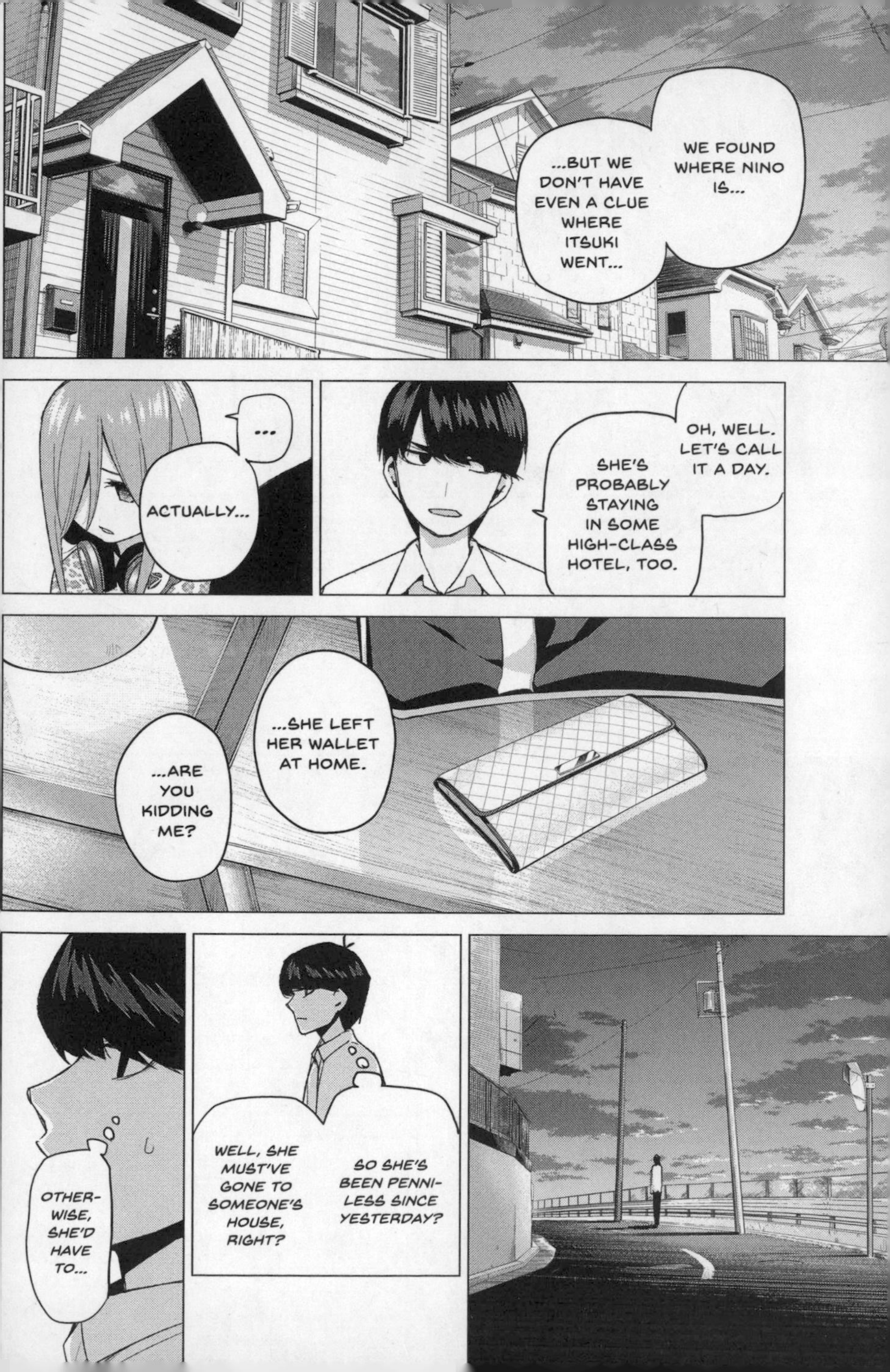
WE FOUND WHERE NINO IS...
...BUT WE DON'T HAVE EVEN A CLUE WHERE ITSUKI WENT...
OH, WELL. LET'S CALL IT A DAY.
SHE'S PROBABLY STAYING IN SOME HIGH-CLASS HOTEL, TOO.
...
ACTUALLY...
...SHE LEFT HER WALLET AT HOME.
...ARE YOU KIDDING ME?
SO SHE'S BEEN PENNILESS SINCE YESTERDAY?
WELL, SHE MUST'VE GONE TO SOMEONE'S HOUSE, RIGHT?
OTHERWISE, SHE'D HAVE TO...

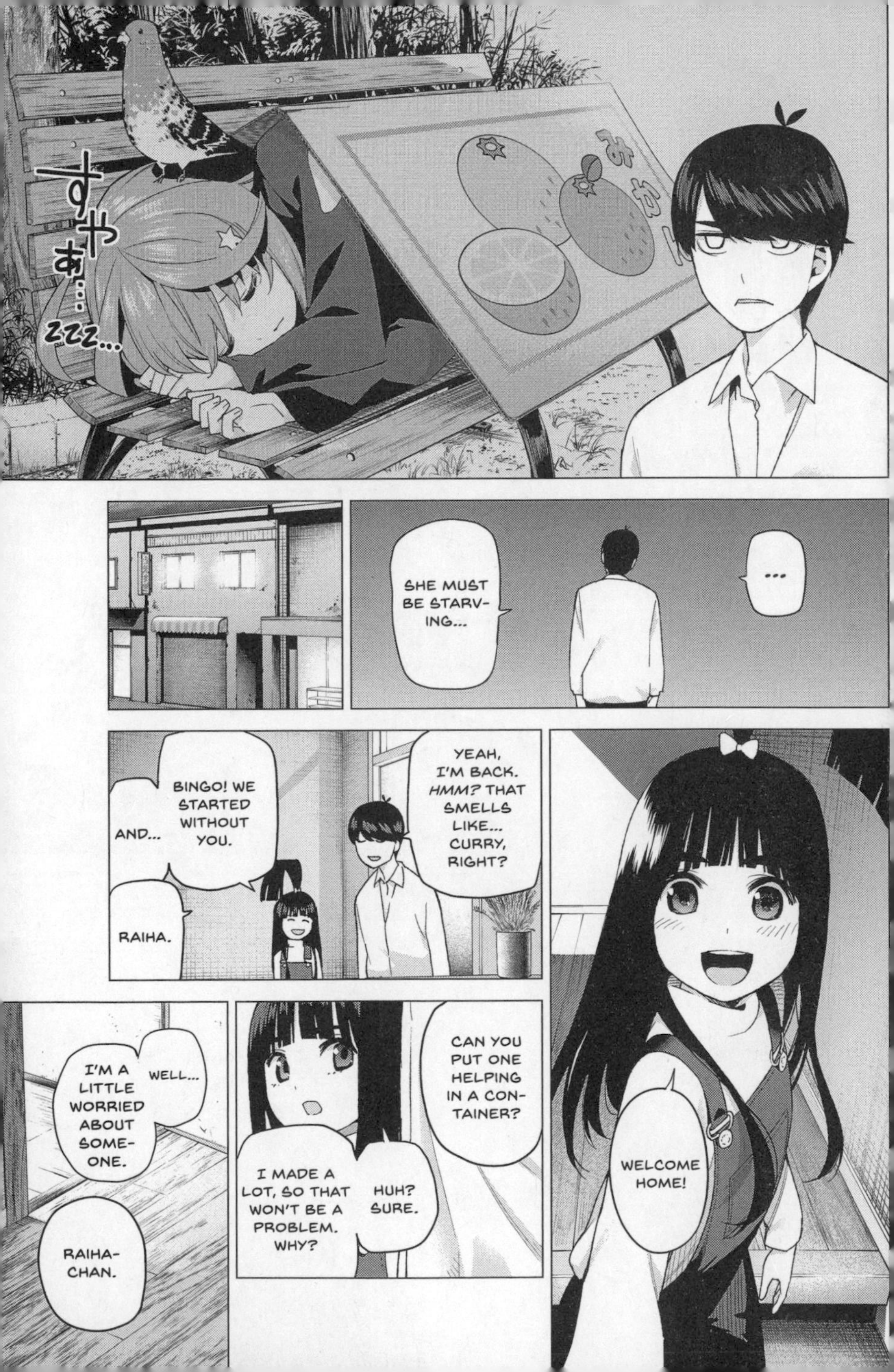
すやぁ…
ZZZ...
...
SHE MUST BE STARVING...
WELCOME HOME!
YEAH, I'M BACK. *HMM?* THAT SMELLS LIKE... CURRY, RIGHT?
BINGO! WE STARTED WITHOUT YOU.
AND...
RAIHA.
CAN YOU PUT ONE HELPING IN A CONTAINER?
HUH? SURE.
I MADE A LOT, SO THAT WON'T BE A PROBLEM. WHY?
WELL...
I'M A LITTLE WORRIED ABOUT SOMEONE.
RAIHA-CHAN.

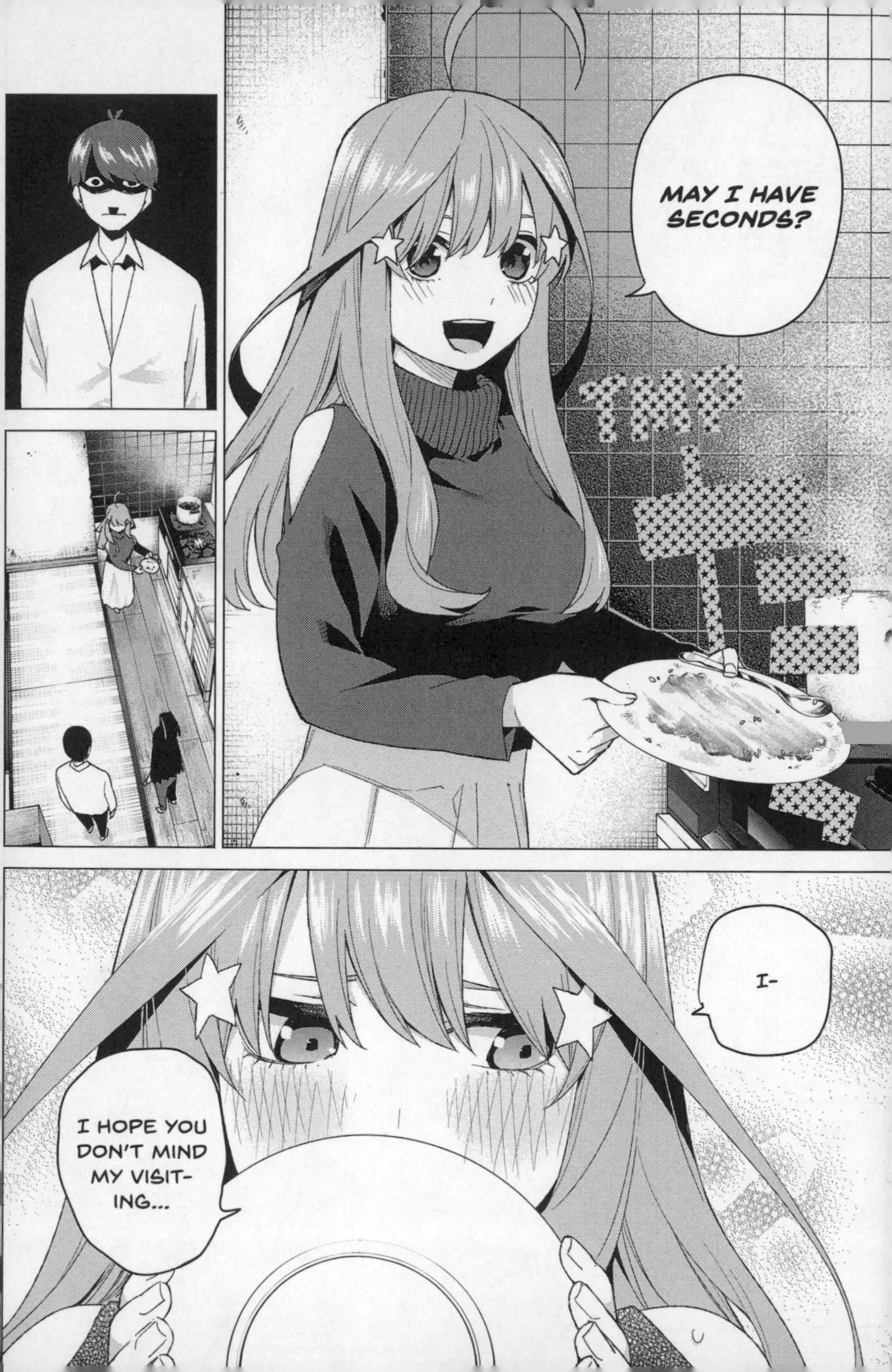
MAY I HAVE SECONDS?
I-
I HOPE YOU DON'T MIND MY VISIT-ING...

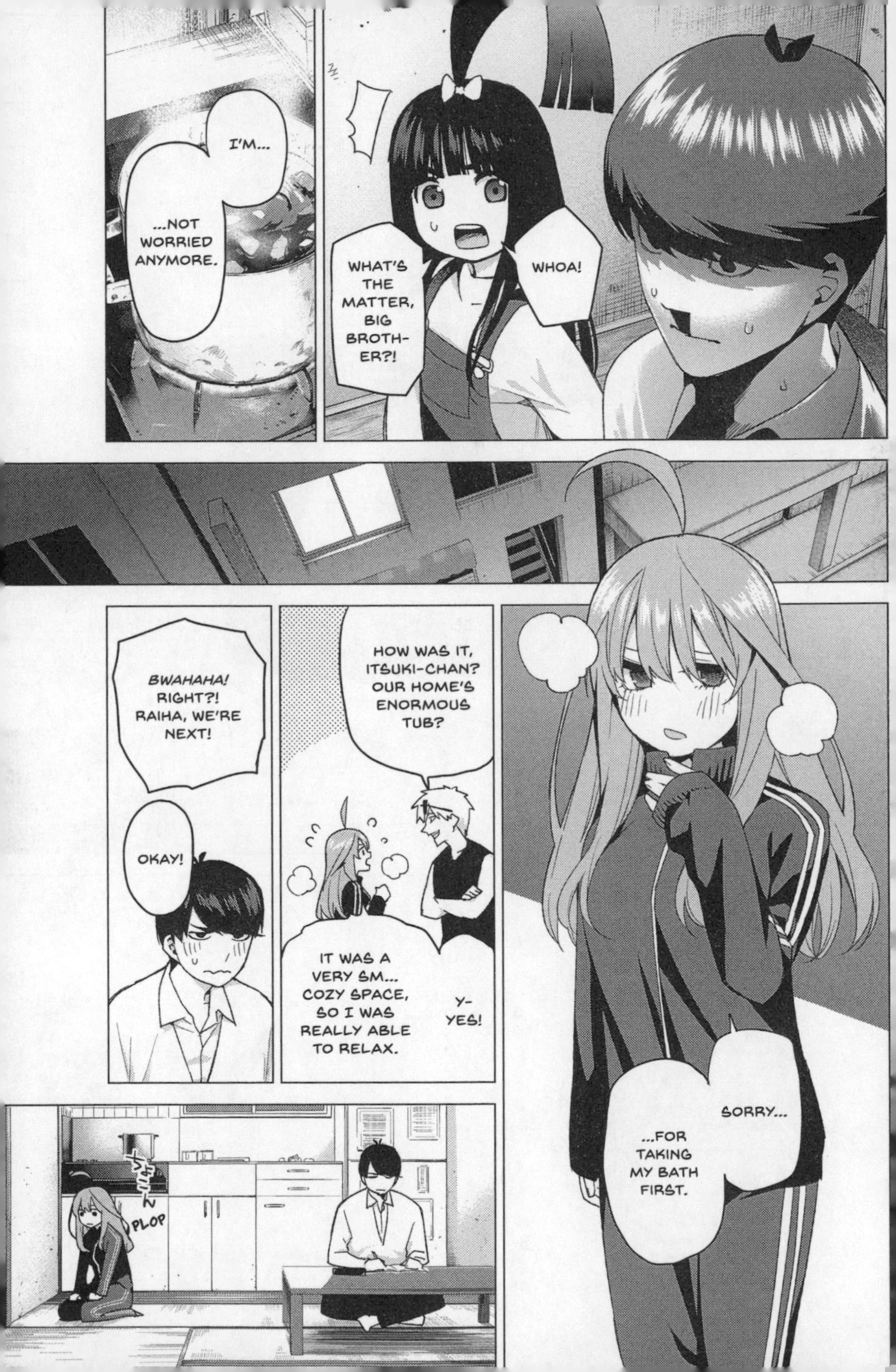
WHOA!
WHAT'S THE MATTER, BIG BROTHER?!
I'M...
...NOT WORRIED ANYMORE.
SORRY...
...FOR TAKING MY BATH FIRST.
HOW WAS IT, ITSUKI-CHAN? OUR HOME'S ENORMOUS TUB?
Y-YES!
IT WAS A VERY SM... COZY SPACE, SO I WAS REALLY ABLE TO RELAX.
*BWAHAHA!* RIGHT?! RAIHA, WE'RE NEXT!
OKAY!
PLOP

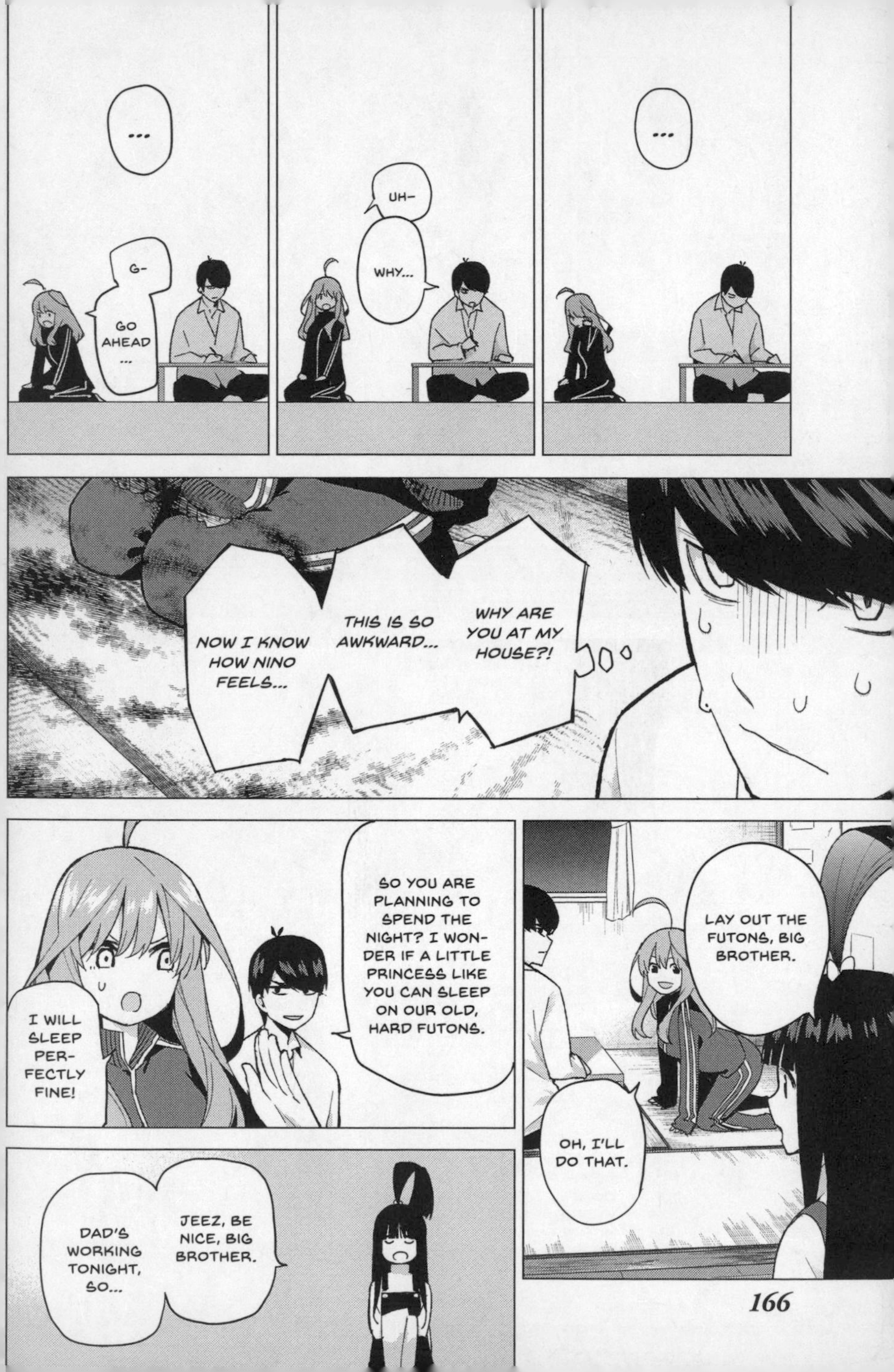
...
UH-
WHY...
G-
GO AHEAD ...
...
WHY ARE YOU AT MY HOUSE?!
THIS IS SO AWKWARD...
NOW I KNOW HOW NINO FEELS...
LAY OUT THE FUTONS, BIG BROTHER.
OH, I'LL DO THAT.
SO YOU ARE PLANNING TO SPEND THE NIGHT? I WONDER IF A LITTLE PRINCESS LIKE YOU CAN SLEEP ON OUR OLD, HARD FUTONS.
I WILL SLEEP PERFECTLY FINE!
JEEZ, BE NICE, BIG BROTHER.
DAD'S WORKING TONIGHT, SO...

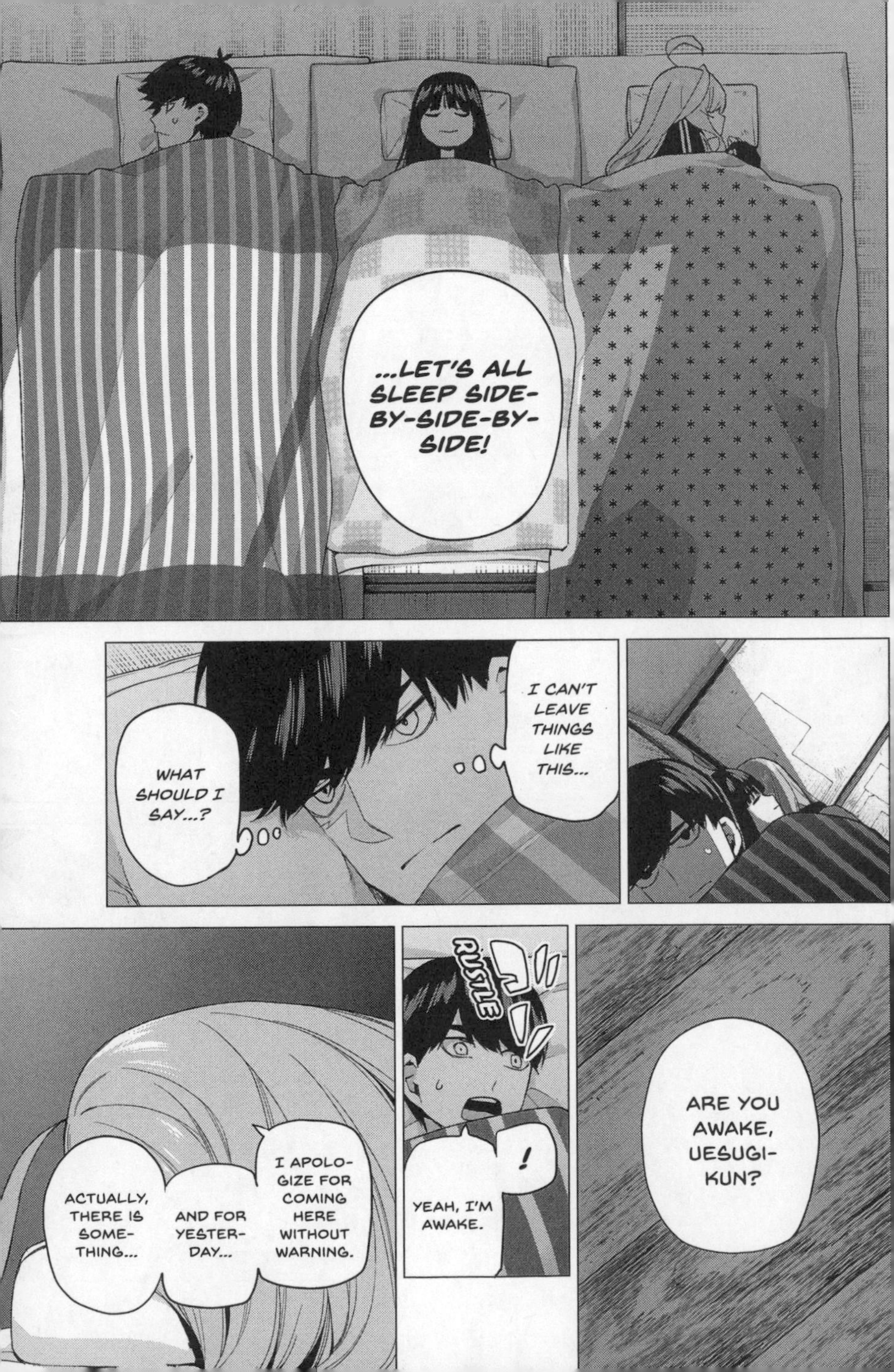
...LET'S ALL SLEEP SIDE-BY-SIDE-BY-SIDE!
I CAN'T LEAVE THINGS LIKE THIS...
WHAT SHOULD I SAY...?
ARE YOU AWAKE, UESUGI-KUN?
RUSTLE
!
YEAH, I'M AWAKE.
I APOLOGIZE FOR COMING HERE WITHOUT WARNING.
AND FOR YESTERDAY...
ACTUALLY, THERE IS SOMETHING...

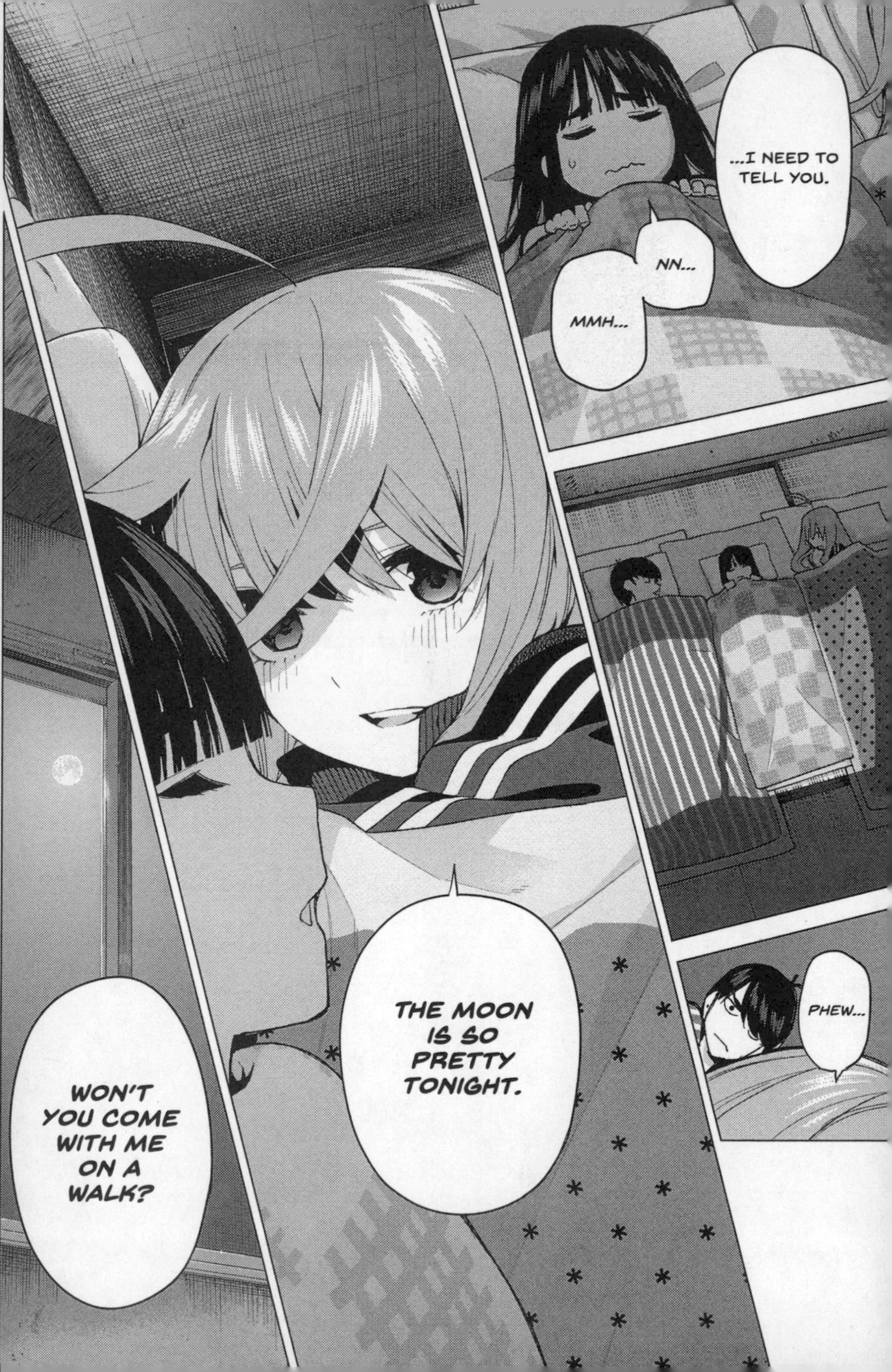
...I NEED TO TELL YOU.
NN...
MMH...
PHEW...
THE MOON IS SO PRETTY TONIGHT.
WON'T YOU COME WITH ME ON A WALK?

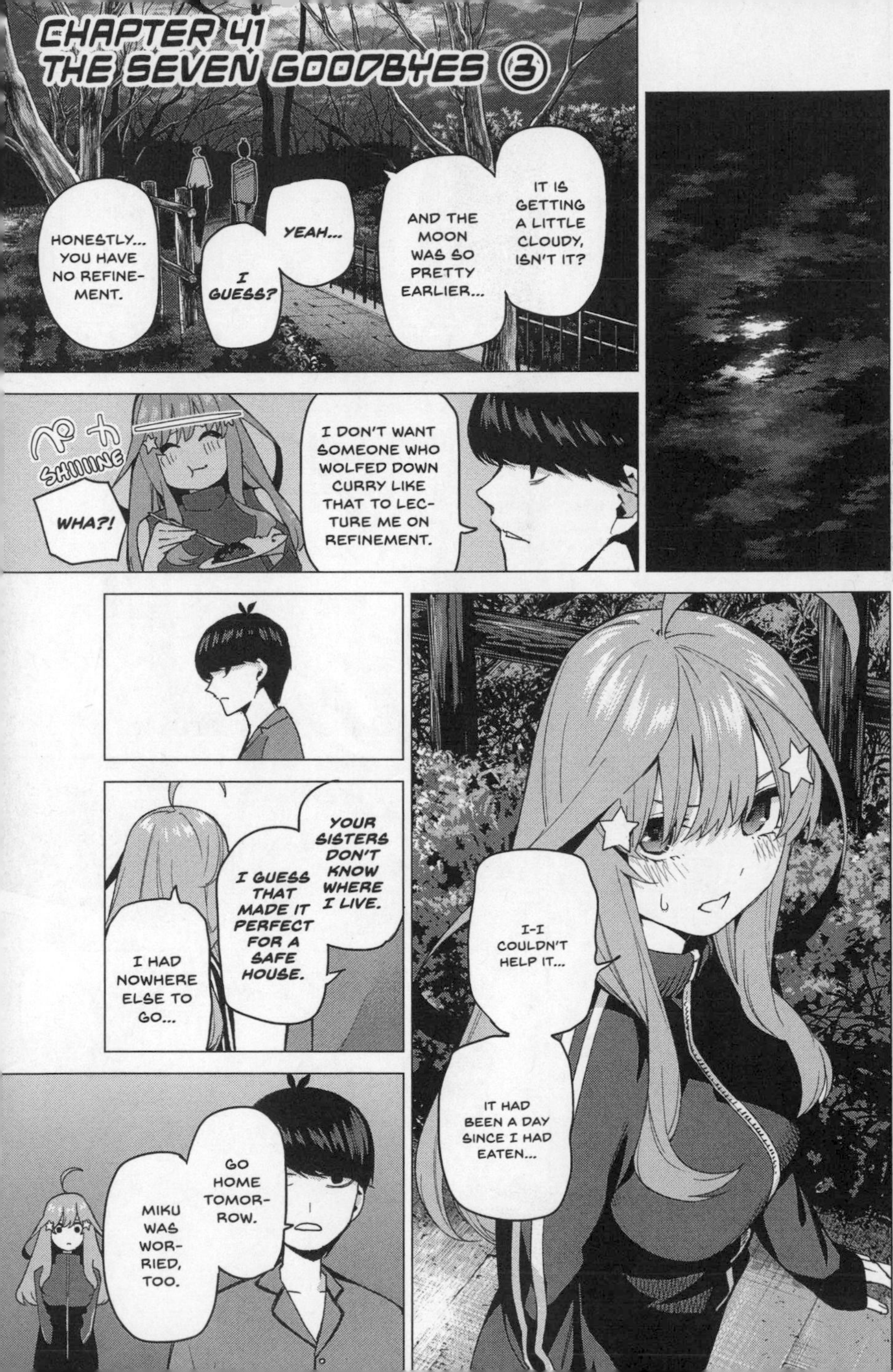
CHAPTER 41
THE SEVEN GOODBYES ③
IT IS GETTING A LITTLE CLOUDY, ISN'T IT?
AND THE MOON WAS SO PRETTY EARLIER...
YEAH...
I GUESS?
HONESTLY... YOU HAVE NO REFINEMENT.
I DON'T WANT SOMEONE WHO WOLFED DOWN CURRY LIKE THAT TO LECTURE ME ON REFINEMENT.
SHIIIINE
WHA?!
I-I COULDN'T HELP IT...
IT HAD BEEN A DAY SINCE I HAD EATEN...
YOUR SISTERS DON'T KNOW WHERE I LIVE.
I GUESS THAT MADE IT PERFECT FOR A SAFE HOUSE.
I HAD NOWHERE ELSE TO GO...
GO HOME TOMORROW.
MIKU WAS WORRIED, TOO.

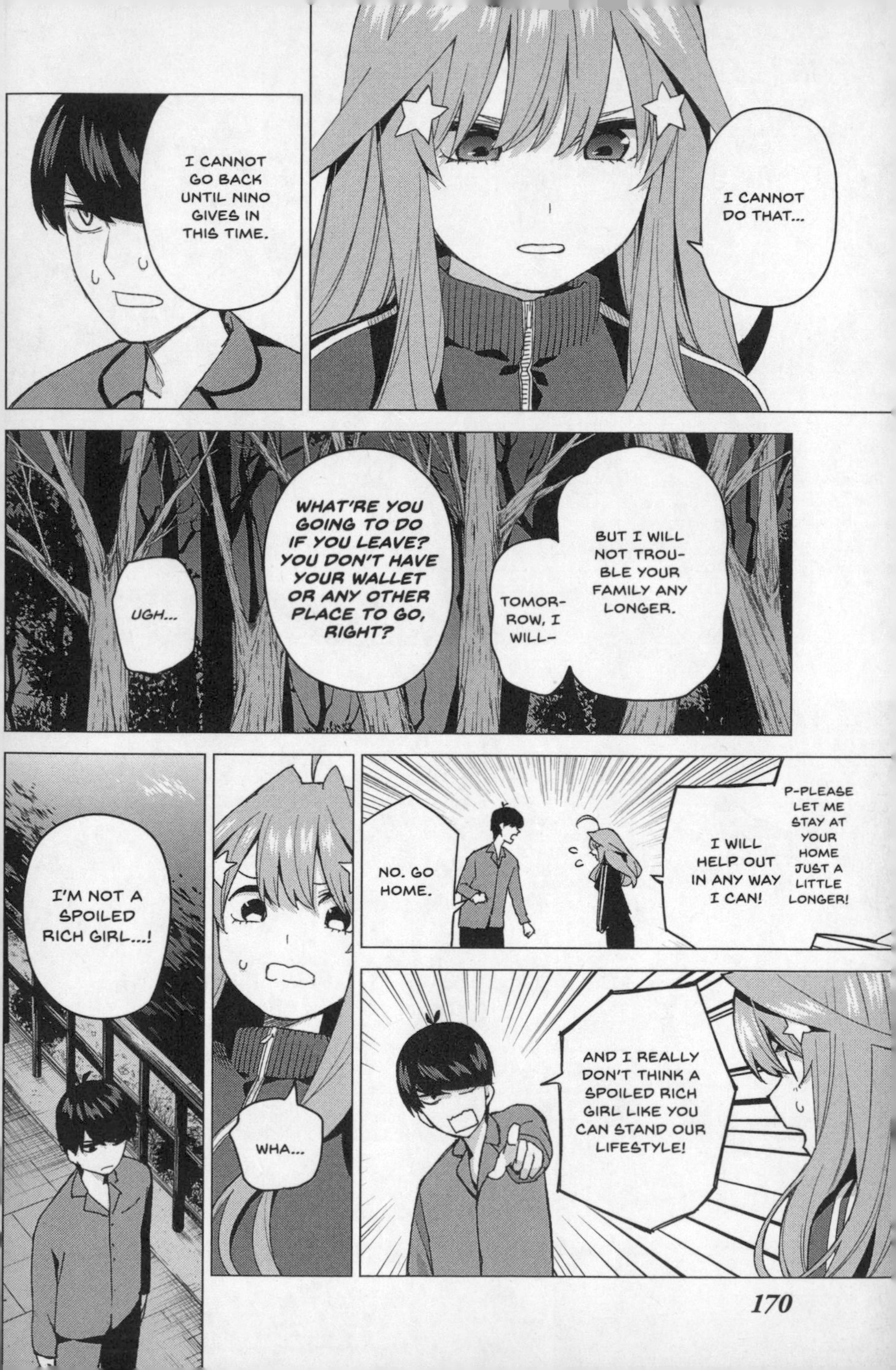
I CANNOT DO THAT...
I CANNOT GO BACK UNTIL NINO GIVES IN THIS TIME.
BUT I WILL NOT TROU-BLE YOUR FAMILY ANY LONGER.
TOMOR-ROW, I WILL-
WHAT'RE YOU GOING TO DO IF YOU LEAVE? YOU DON'T HAVE YOUR WALLET OR ANY OTHER PLACE TO GO, RIGHT?
UGH...
P-PLEASE LET ME STAY AT YOUR HOME JUST A LITTLE LONGER!
I WILL HELP OUT IN ANY WAY I CAN!
NO. GO HOME.
AND I REALLY DON'T THINK A SPOILED RICH GIRL LIKE YOU CAN STAND OUR LIFESTYLE!
WHA...
I'M NOT A SPOILED RICH GIRL...!

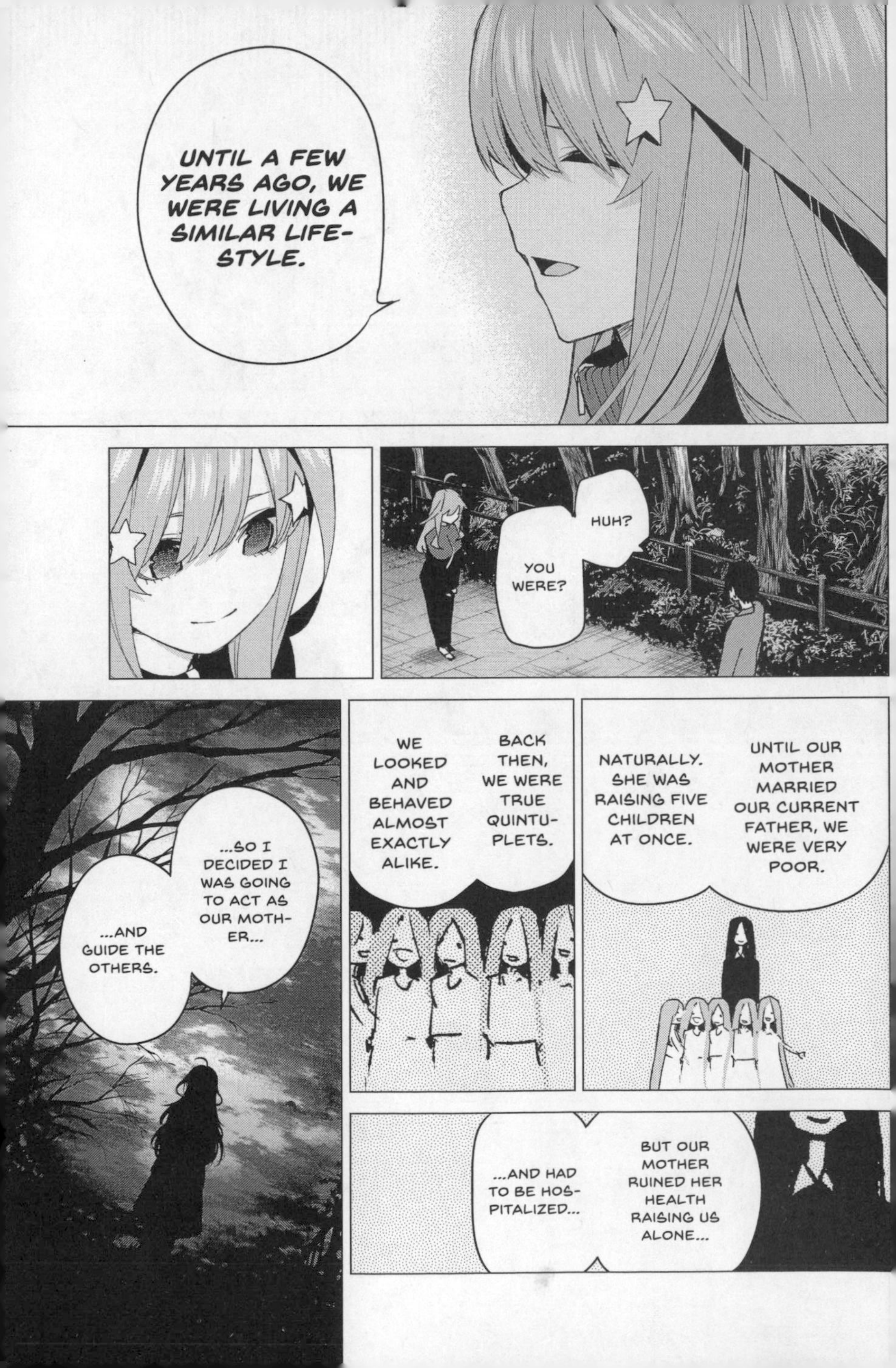
UNTIL A FEW YEARS AGO, WE WERE LIVING A SIMILAR LIFE-STYLE.
HUH?
YOU WERE?
UNTIL OUR MOTHER MARRIED OUR CURRENT FATHER, WE WERE VERY POOR.
NATURALLY. SHE WAS RAISING FIVE CHILDREN AT ONCE.
BACK THEN, WE WERE TRUE QUINTU-PLETS.
WE LOOKED AND BEHAVED ALMOST EXACTLY ALIKE.
BUT OUR MOTHER RUINED HER HEALTH RAISING US ALONE...
...AND HAD TO BE HOS-PITALIZED...
...SO I DECIDED I WAS GOING TO ACT AS OUR MOTH-ER...
...AND GUIDE THE OTHERS.

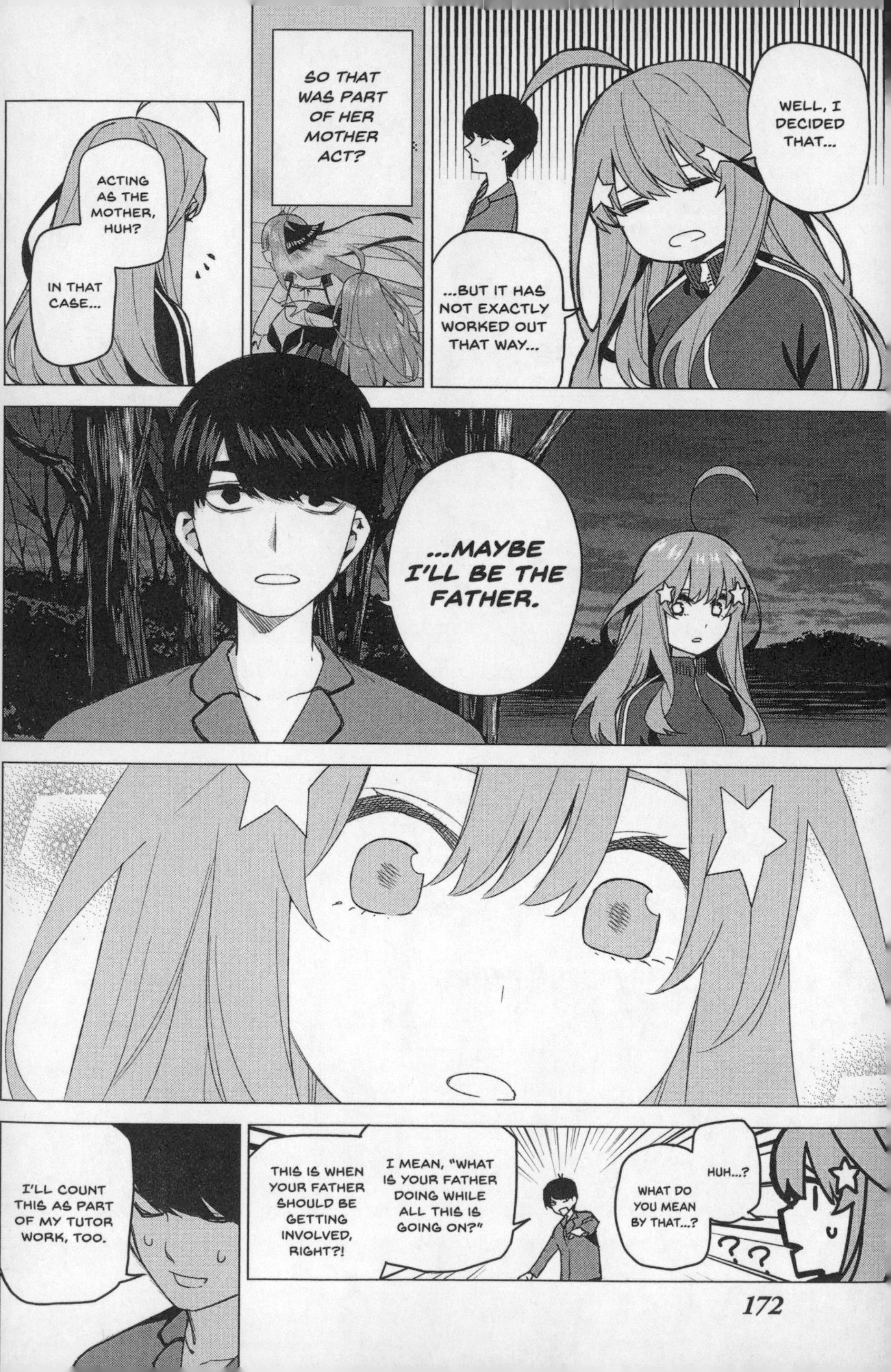
WELL, I DECIDED THAT...
...BUT IT HAS NOT EXACTLY WORKED OUT THAT WAY...
SO THAT WAS PART OF HER MOTHER ACT?
ACTING AS THE MOTHER, HUH?
IN THAT CASE...
...MAYBE I'LL BE THE FATHER.
HUH...?
WHAT DO YOU MEAN BY THAT...?
I MEAN, "WHAT IS YOUR FATHER DOING WHILE ALL THIS IS GOING ON?"
THIS IS WHEN YOUR FATHER SHOULD BE GETTING INVOLVED, RIGHT?!
I'LL COUNT THIS AS PART OF MY TUTOR WORK, TOO.

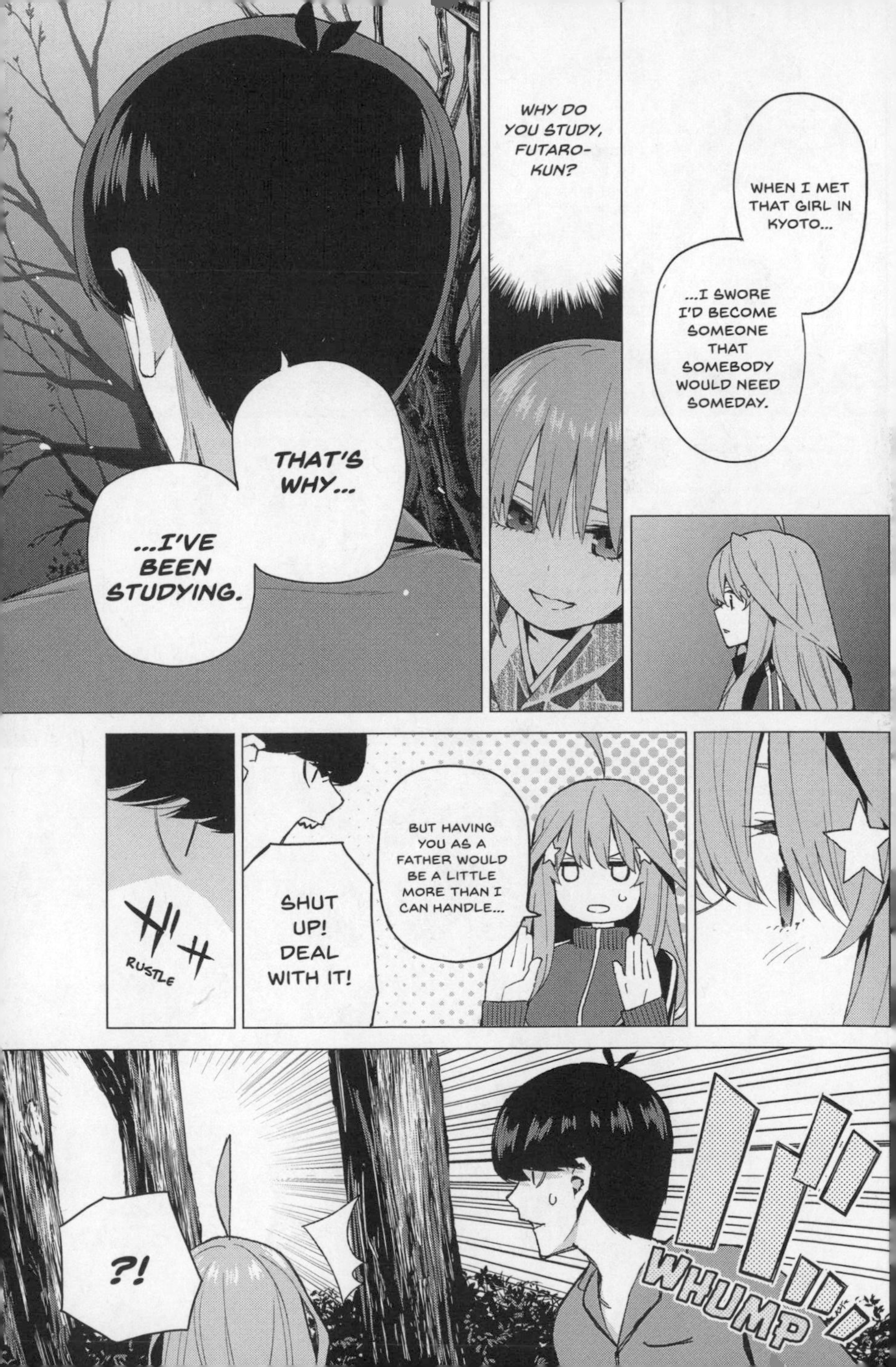
WHEN I MET THAT GIRL IN KYOTO...
...I SWORE I'D BECOME SOMEONE THAT SOMEBODY WOULD NEED SOMEDAY.
WHY DO YOU STUDY, FUTARO-KUN?
THAT'S WHY...
...I'VE BEEN STUDYING.
BUT HAVING YOU AS A FATHER WOULD BE A LITTLE MORE THAN I CAN HANDLE...
SHUT UP! DEAL WITH IT!
RUSTLE
WHUMP
?!

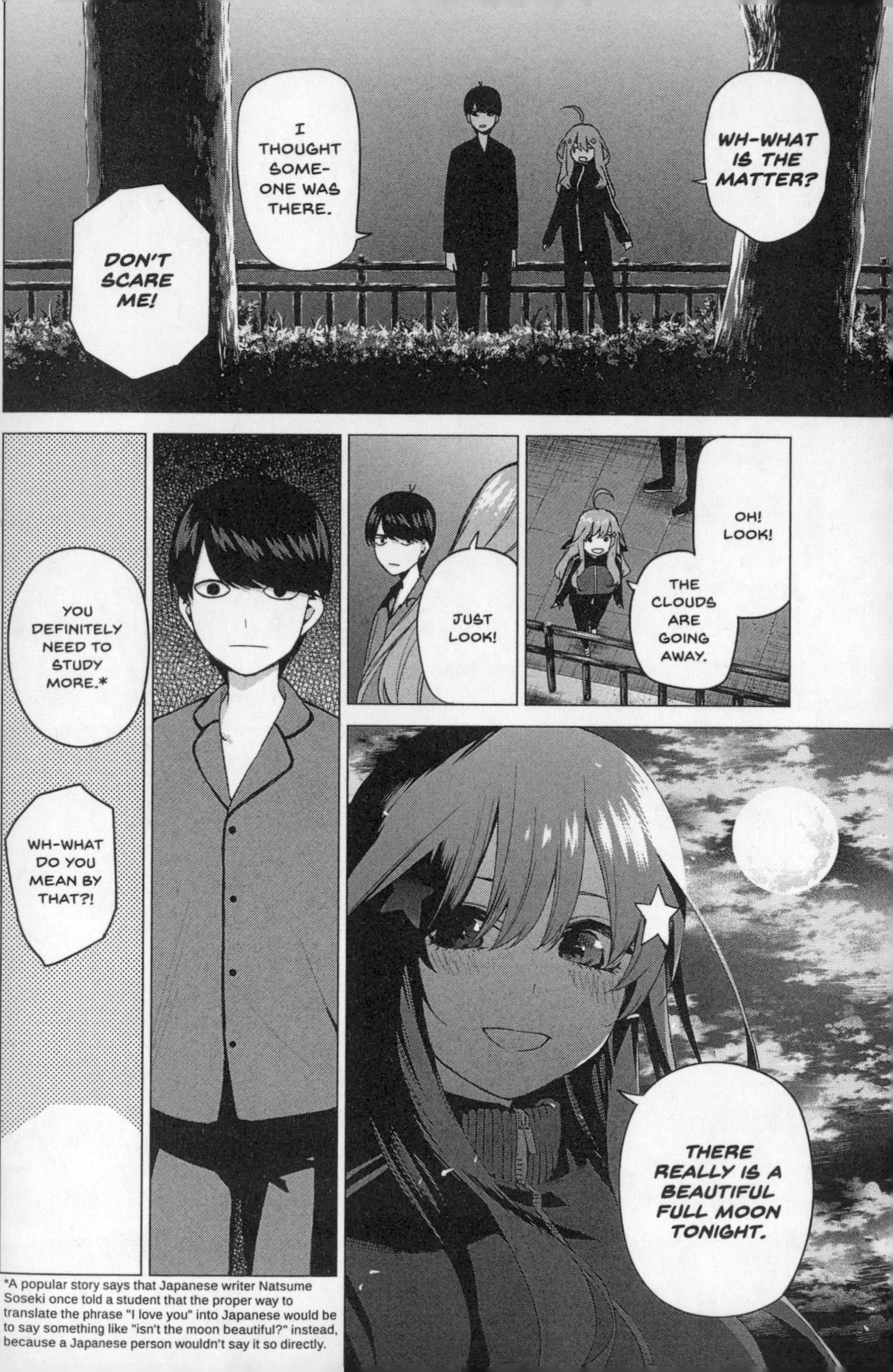
WH-WHAT IS THE MATTER?
I THOUGHT SOME-ONE WAS THERE.
DON'T SCARE ME!
OH! LOOK!
THE CLOUDS ARE GOING AWAY.
JUST LOOK!
THERE REALLY IS A BEAUTIFUL FULL MOON TONIGHT.
YOU DEFINITELY NEED TO STUDY MORE.*
WH-WHAT DO YOU MEAN BY THAT?!

*A popular story says that Japanese writer Natsume Soseki once told a student that the proper way to translate the phrase "I love you" into Japanese would be to say something like "isn't the moon beautiful?" instead, because a Japanese person wouldn't say it so directly.

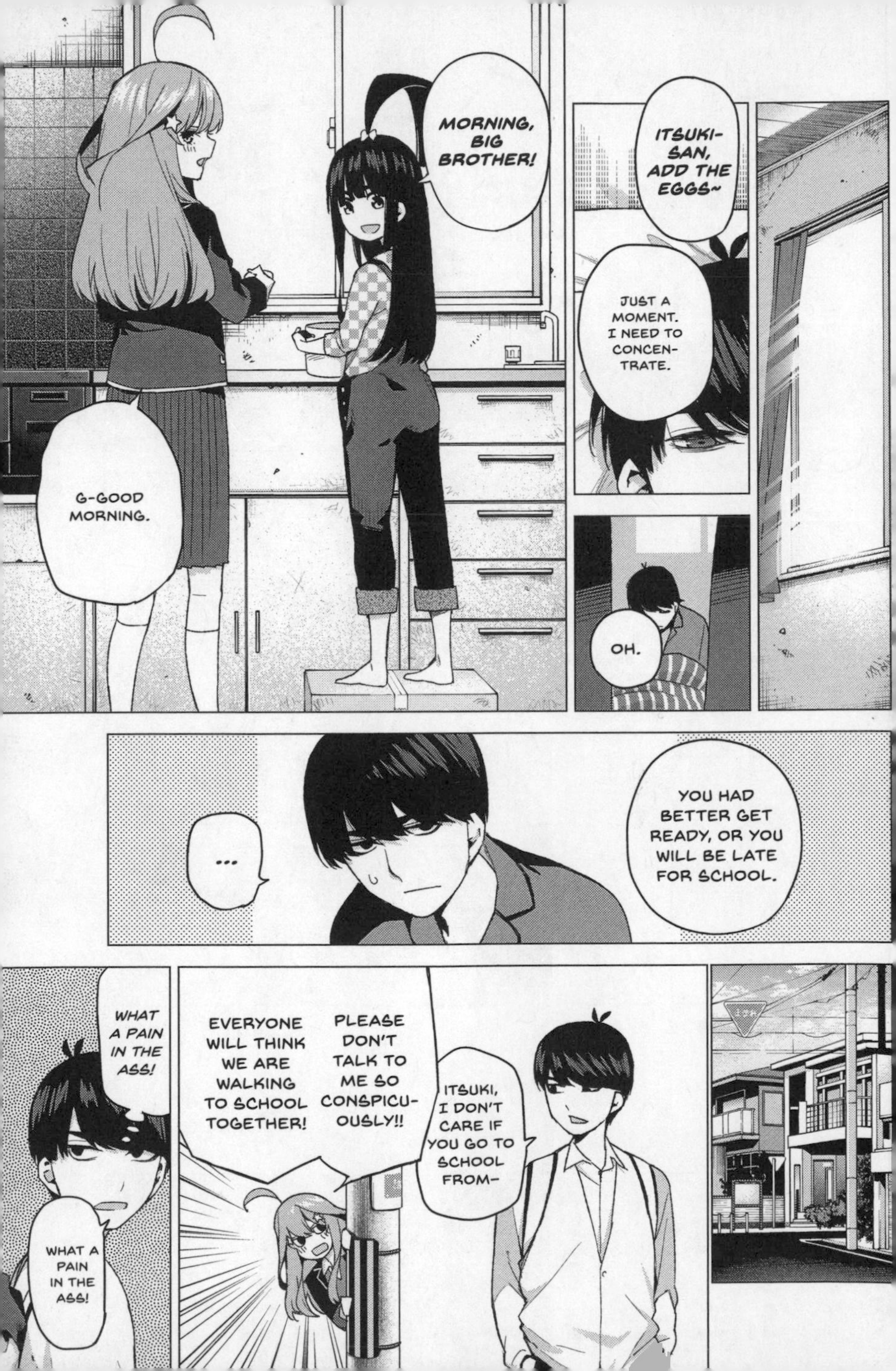
ITSUKI-SAN, ADD THE EGGS~
JUST A MOMENT. I NEED TO CONCENTRATE.
OH.
MORNING, BIG BROTHER!
G-GOOD MORNING.
YOU HAD BETTER GET READY, OR YOU WILL BE LATE FOR SCHOOL.
...
ITSUKI, I DON'T CARE IF YOU GO TO SCHOOL FROM-
PLEASE DON'T TALK TO ME SO CONSPICUOUSLY!!
EVERYONE WILL THINK WE ARE WALKING TO SCHOOL TOGETHER!
WHAT A PAIN IN THE ASS!
WHAT A PAIN IN THE ASS!

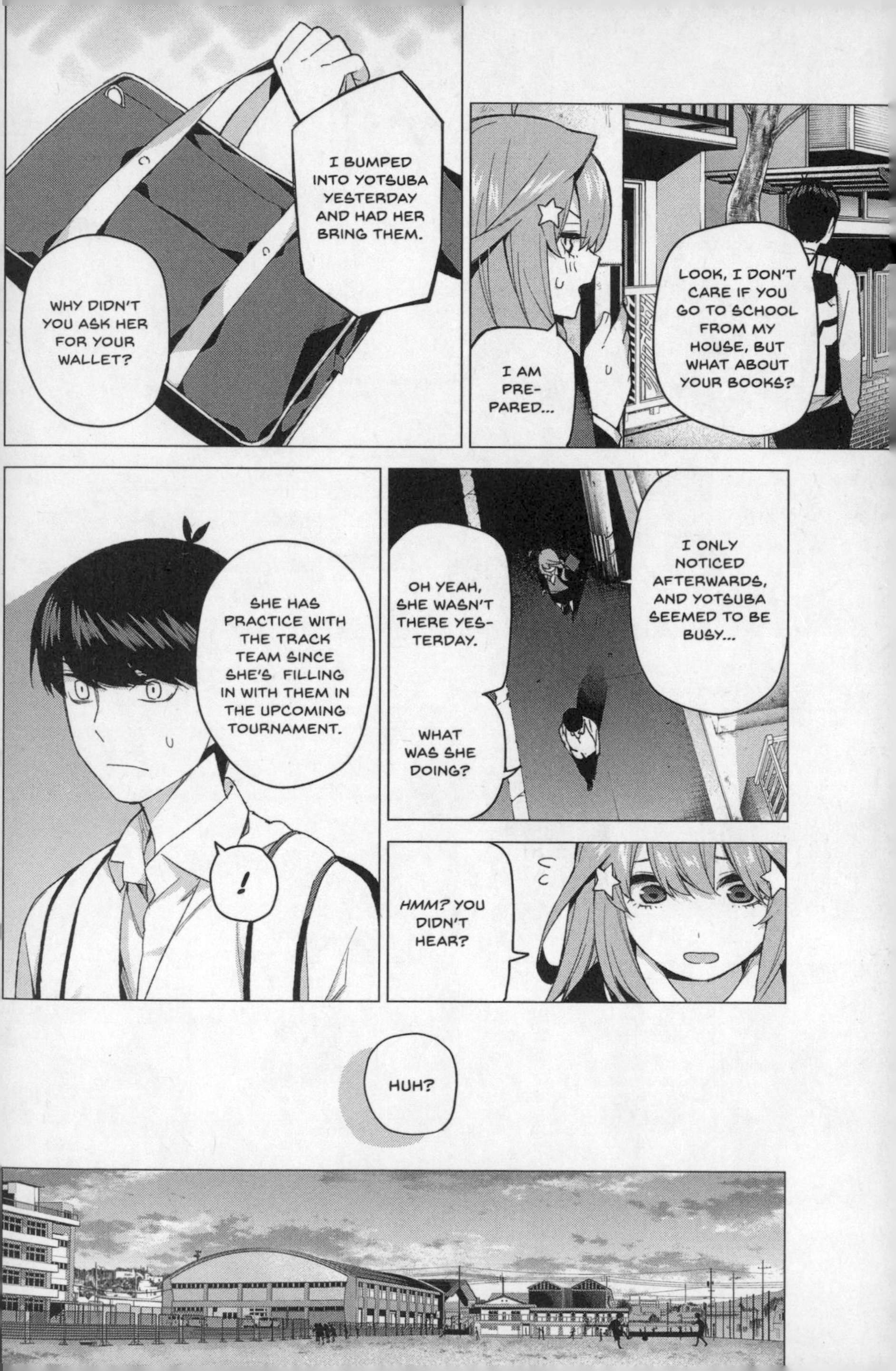
LOOK, I DON'T CARE IF YOU GO TO SCHOOL FROM MY HOUSE, BUT WHAT ABOUT YOUR BOOKS?
I AM PRE-PARED...
I BUMPED INTO YOTSUBA YESTERDAY AND HAD HER BRING THEM.
WHY DIDN'T YOU ASK HER FOR YOUR WALLET?
I ONLY NOTICED AFTERWARDS, AND YOTSUBA SEEMED TO BE BUSY...
OH YEAH, SHE WASN'T THERE YES-TERDAY.
WHAT WAS SHE DOING?
*HMM?* YOU DIDN'T HEAR?
SHE HAS PRACTICE WITH THE TRACK TEAM SINCE SHE'S FILLING IN WITH THEM IN THE UPCOMING TOURNAMENT.
!
HUH?

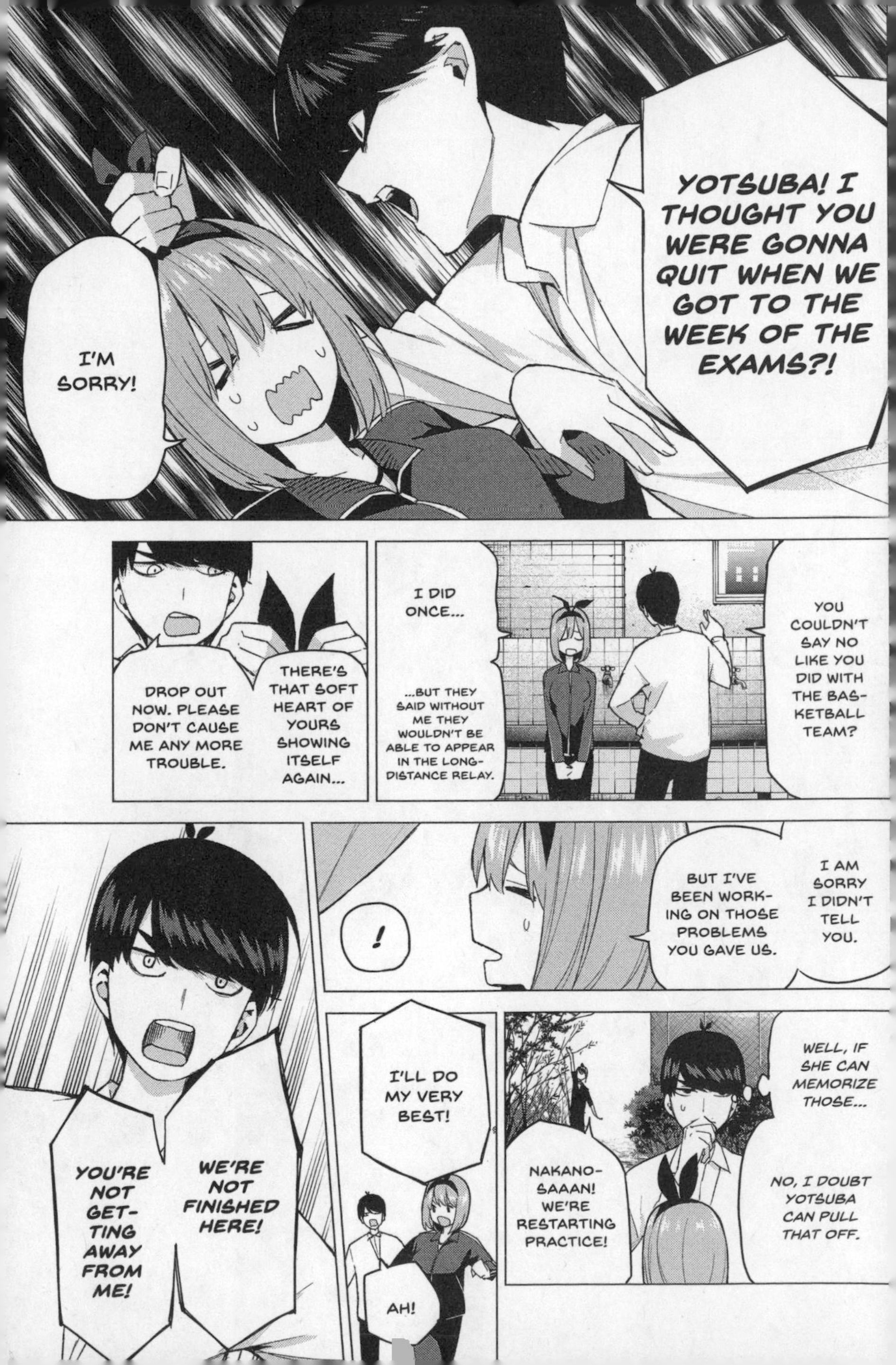
YOTSUBA! I THOUGHT YOU WERE GONNA QUIT WHEN WE GOT TO THE WEEK OF THE EXAMS?!
I'M SORRY!
YOU COULDN'T SAY NO LIKE YOU DID WITH THE BAS-KETBALL TEAM?
I DID ONCE...
...BUT THEY SAID WITHOUT ME THEY WOULDN'T BE ABLE TO APPEAR IN THE LONG-DISTANCE RELAY.
THERE'S THAT SOFT HEART OF YOURS SHOWING ITSELF AGAIN...
DROP OUT NOW. PLEASE DON'T CAUSE ME ANY MORE TROUBLE.
I AM SORRY I DIDN'T TELL YOU.
BUT I'VE BEEN WORK-ING ON THOSE PROBLEMS YOU GAVE US.
!
WELL, IF SHE CAN MEMORIZE THOSE...
NO, I DOUBT YOTSUBA CAN PULL THAT OFF.
NAKANO-SAAAN! WE'RE RESTARTING PRACTICE!
I'LL DO MY VERY BEST!
AH!
WE'RE NOT FINISHED HERE!
YOU'RE NOT GET-TING AWAY FROM ME!

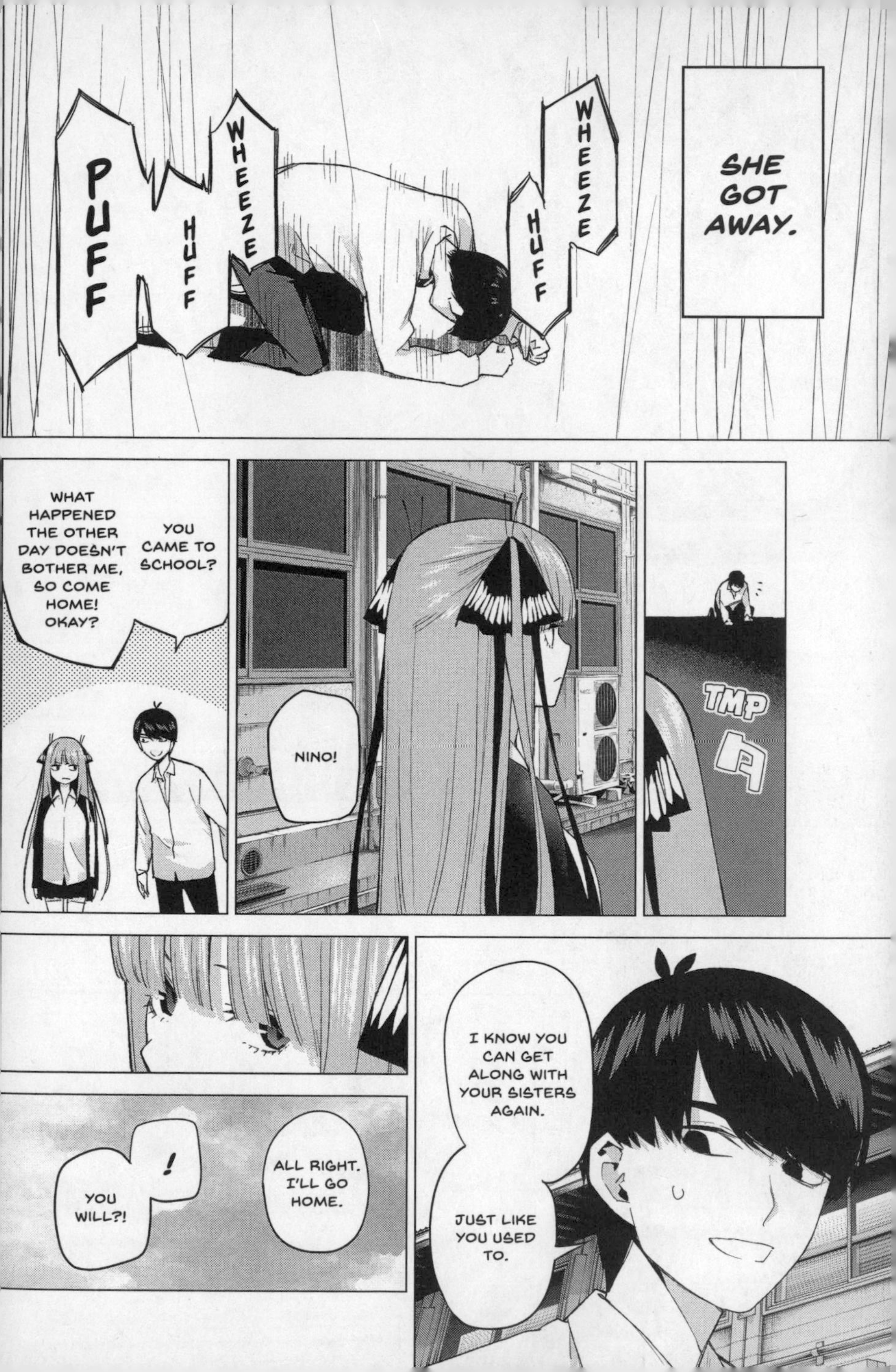
SHE GOT AWAY.
WHEEZE
HUFF
WHEEZE
HUFF
PUFF
TMP
NINO!
YOU CAME TO SCHOOL?
WHAT HAPPENED THE OTHER DAY DOESN'T BOTHER ME, SO COME HOME! OKAY?
I KNOW YOU CAN GET ALONG WITH YOUR SISTERS AGAIN.
JUST LIKE YOU USED TO.
ALL RIGHT. I'LL GO HOME.
!
YOU WILL?!

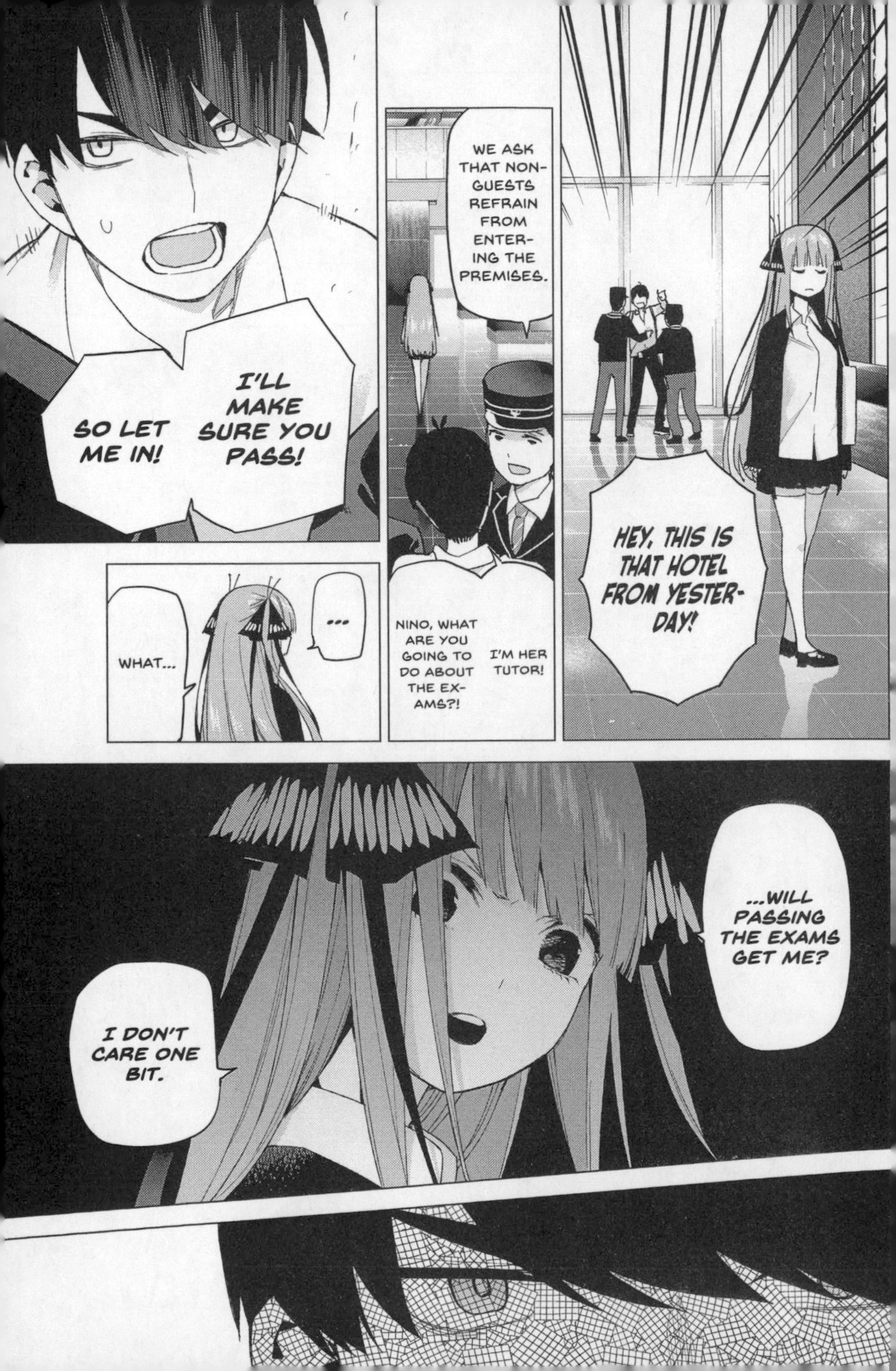
HEY, THIS IS THAT HOTEL FROM YESTERDAY!
WE ASK THAT NON-GUESTS REFRAIN FROM ENTERING THE PREMISES.
I'M HER TUTOR!
NINO, WHAT ARE YOU GOING TO DO ABOUT THE EXAMS?!
I'LL MAKE SURE YOU PASS!
SO LET ME IN!
...
WHAT...
...WILL PASSING THE EXAMS GET ME?
I DON'T CARE ONE BIT.

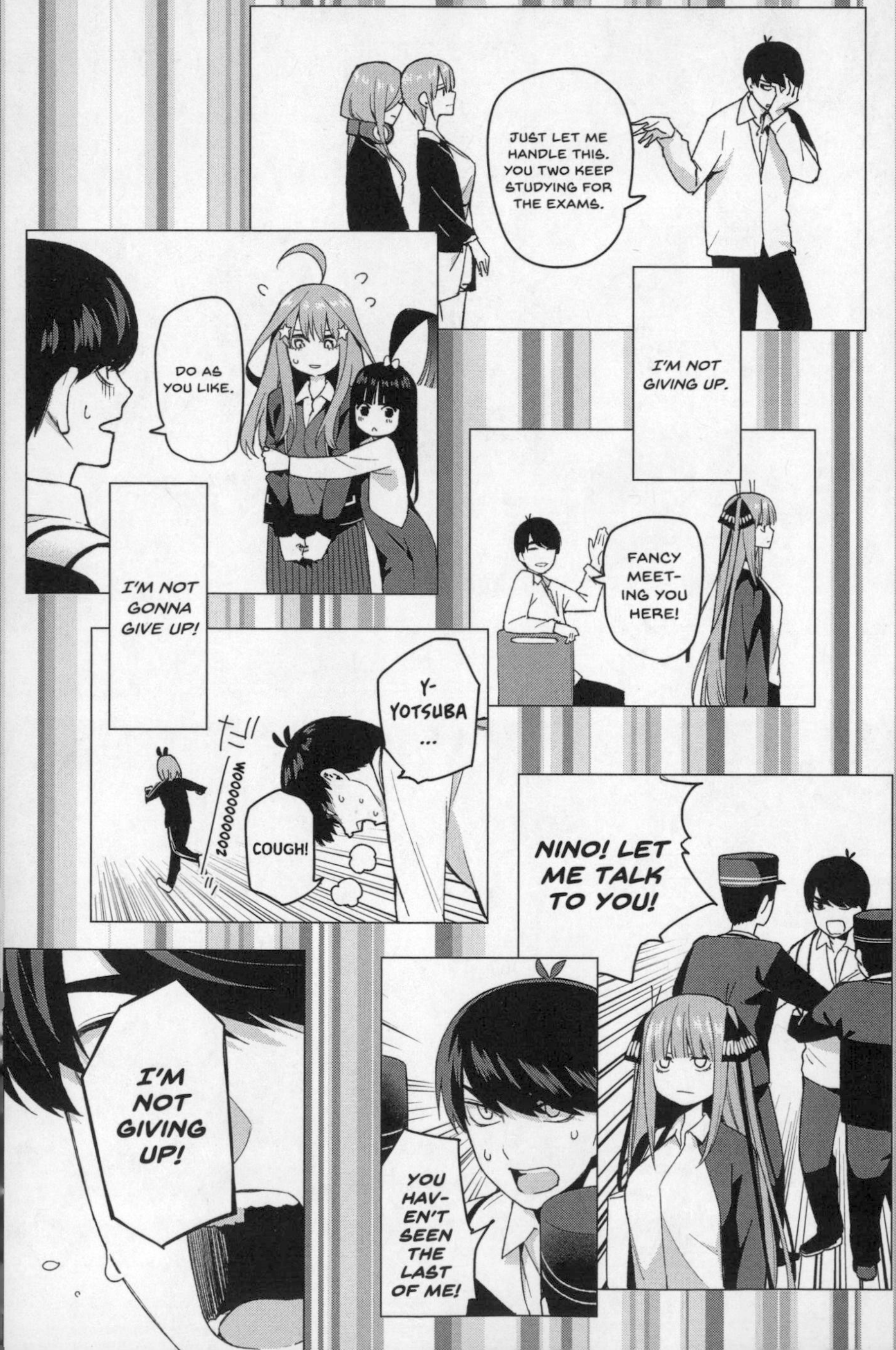
JUST LET ME HANDLE THIS. YOU TWO KEEP STUDYING FOR THE EXAMS.
I'M NOT GIVING UP.
DO AS YOU LIKE.
FANCY MEETING YOU HERE!
I'M NOT GONNA GIVE UP!
Y-YOTSUBA...
WOOOOOOOOOOZ
COUGH!
NINO! LET ME TALK TO YOU!
YOU HAVEN'T SEEN THE LAST OF ME!
I'M NOT GIVING UP!

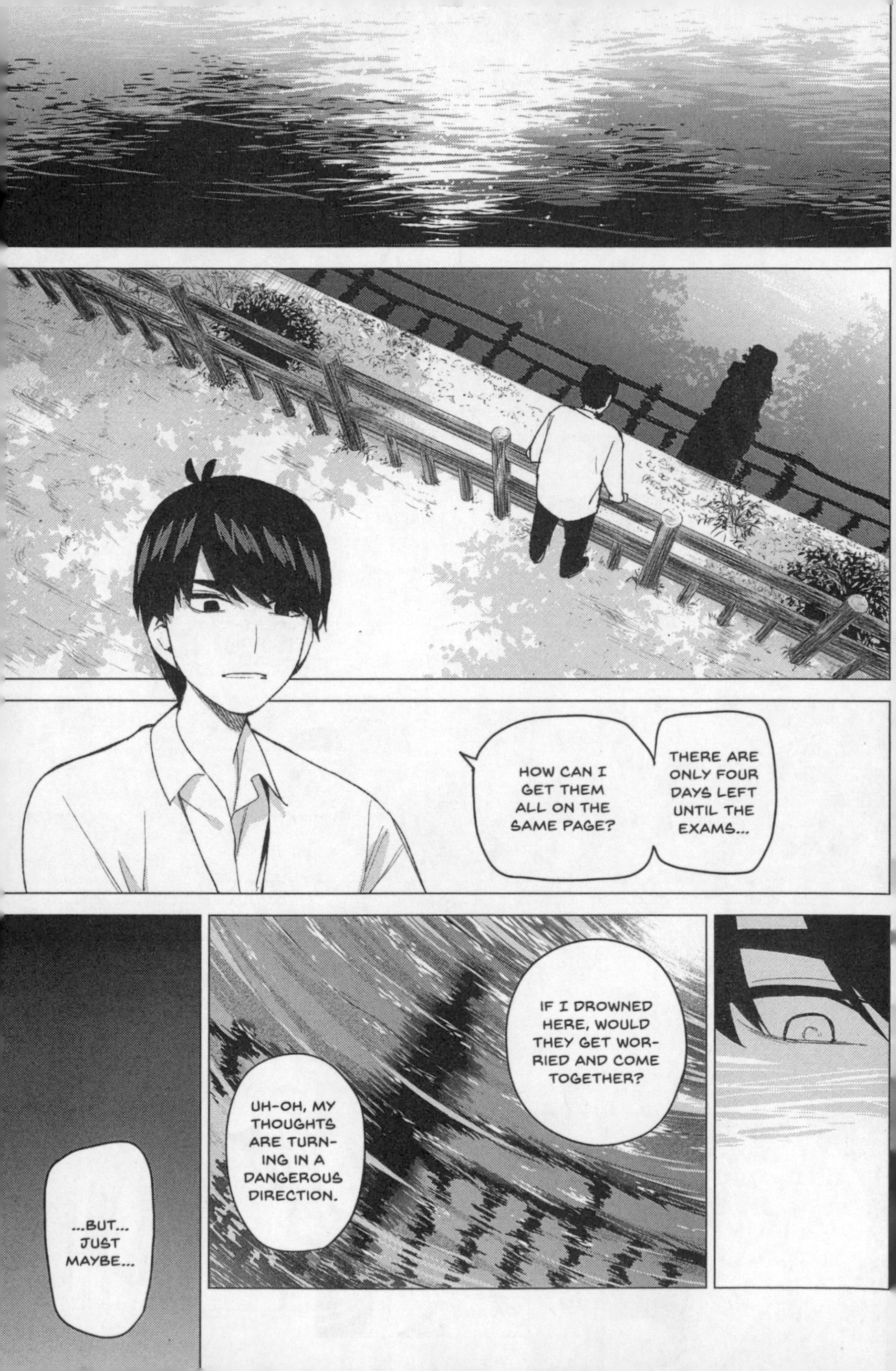
THERE ARE ONLY FOUR DAYS LEFT UNTIL THE EXAMS...
HOW CAN I GET THEM ALL ON THE SAME PAGE?
IF I DROWNED HERE, WOULD THEY GET WOR-RIED AND COME TOGETHER?
UH-OH, MY THOUGHTS ARE TURN-ING IN A DANGEROUS DIRECTION.
...BUT... JUST MAYBE...

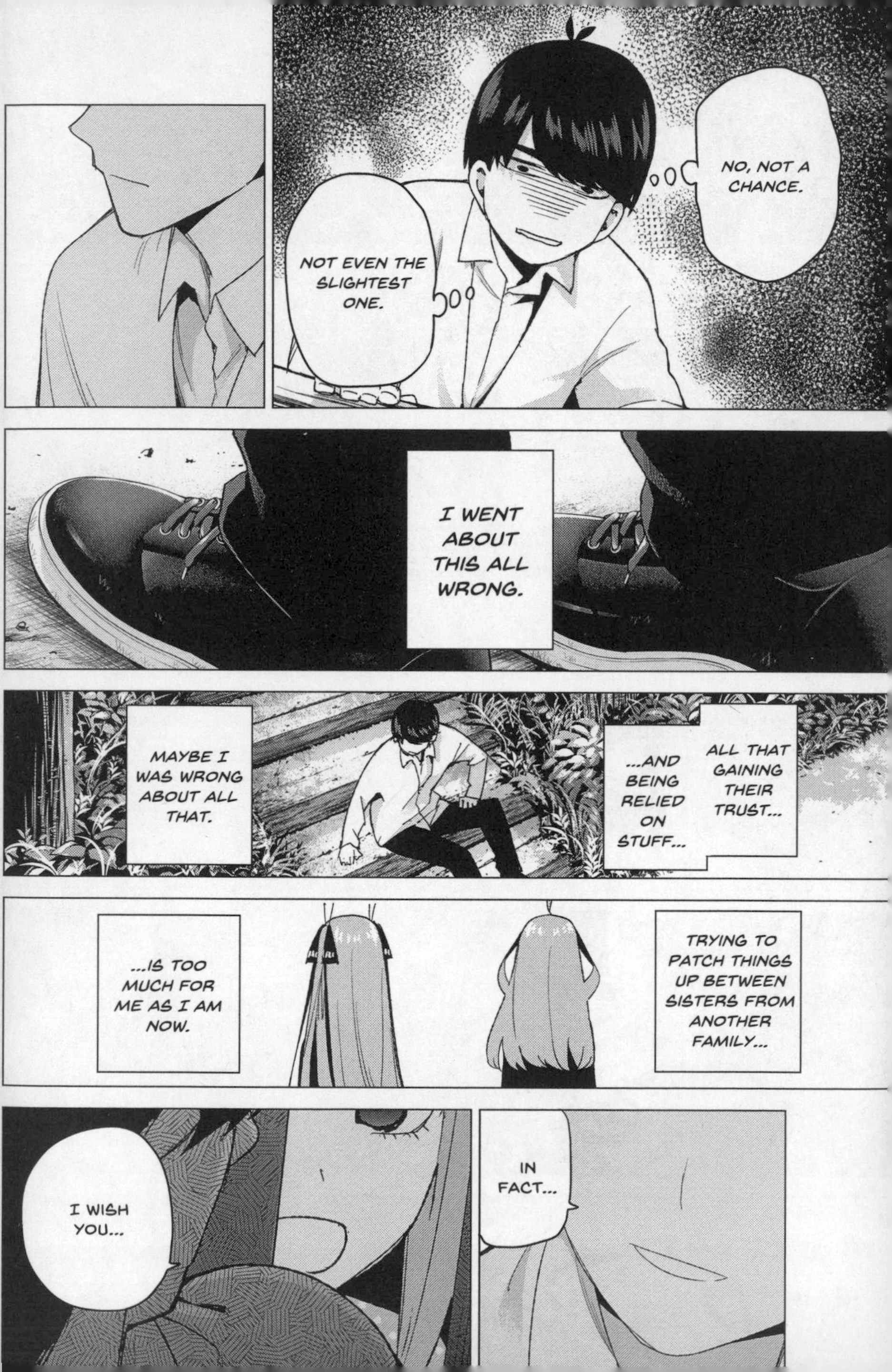
NO, NOT A CHANCE.
NOT EVEN THE SLIGHTEST ONE.
I WENT ABOUT THIS ALL WRONG.
ALL THAT GAINING THEIR TRUST...
...AND BEING RELIED ON STUFF...
MAYBE I WAS WRONG ABOUT ALL THAT.
TRYING TO PATCH THINGS UP BETWEEN SISTERS FROM ANOTHER FAMILY...
...IS TOO MUCH FOR ME AS I AM NOW.
IN FACT...
I WISH YOU...

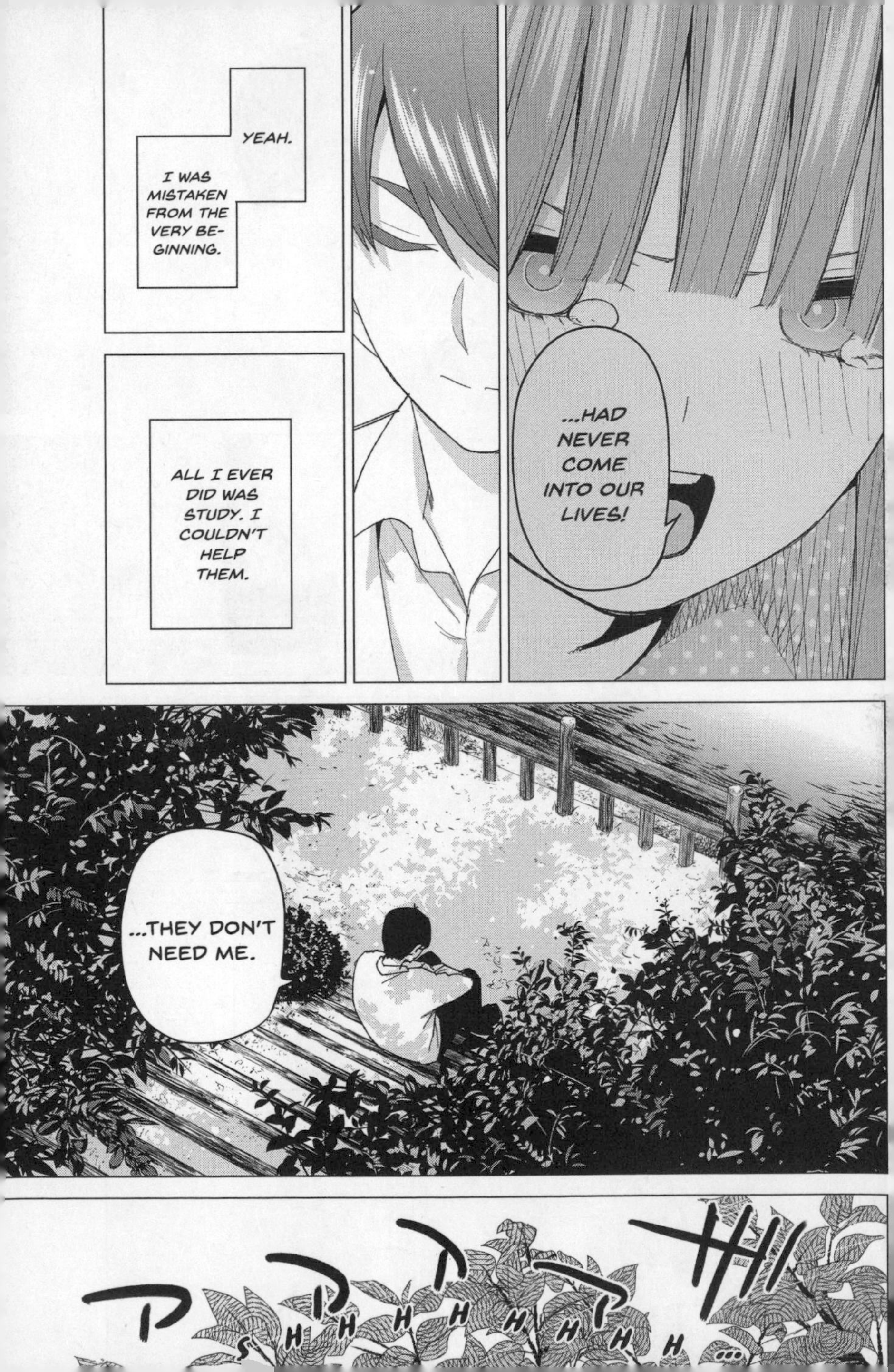
...HAD NEVER COME INTO OUR LIVES!
YEAH.
I WAS MISTAKEN FROM THE VERY BE- GINNING.
ALL I EVER DID WAS STUDY. I COULDN'T HELP THEM.
...THEY DON'T NEED ME.
SHHHHHHHH...

YOU'RE DEPRESSED AGAIN.

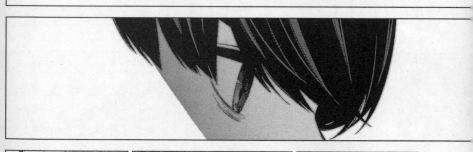

YOU JUST NEVER CHANGE, DO YOU?

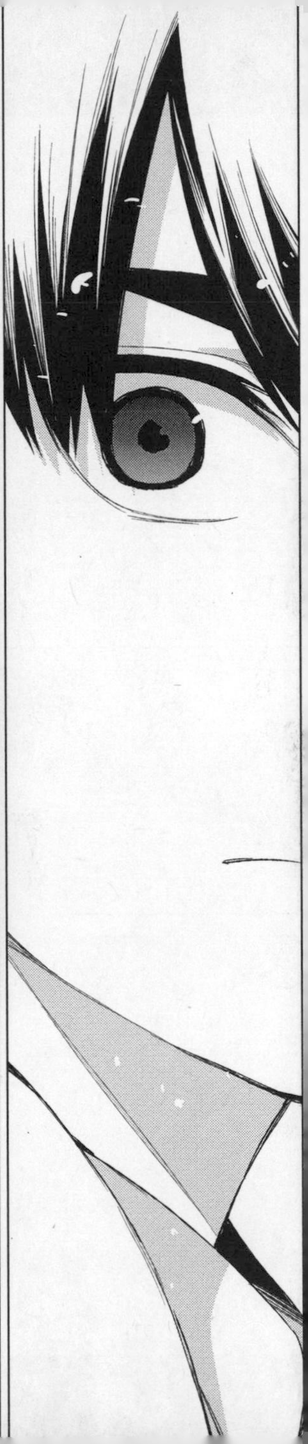
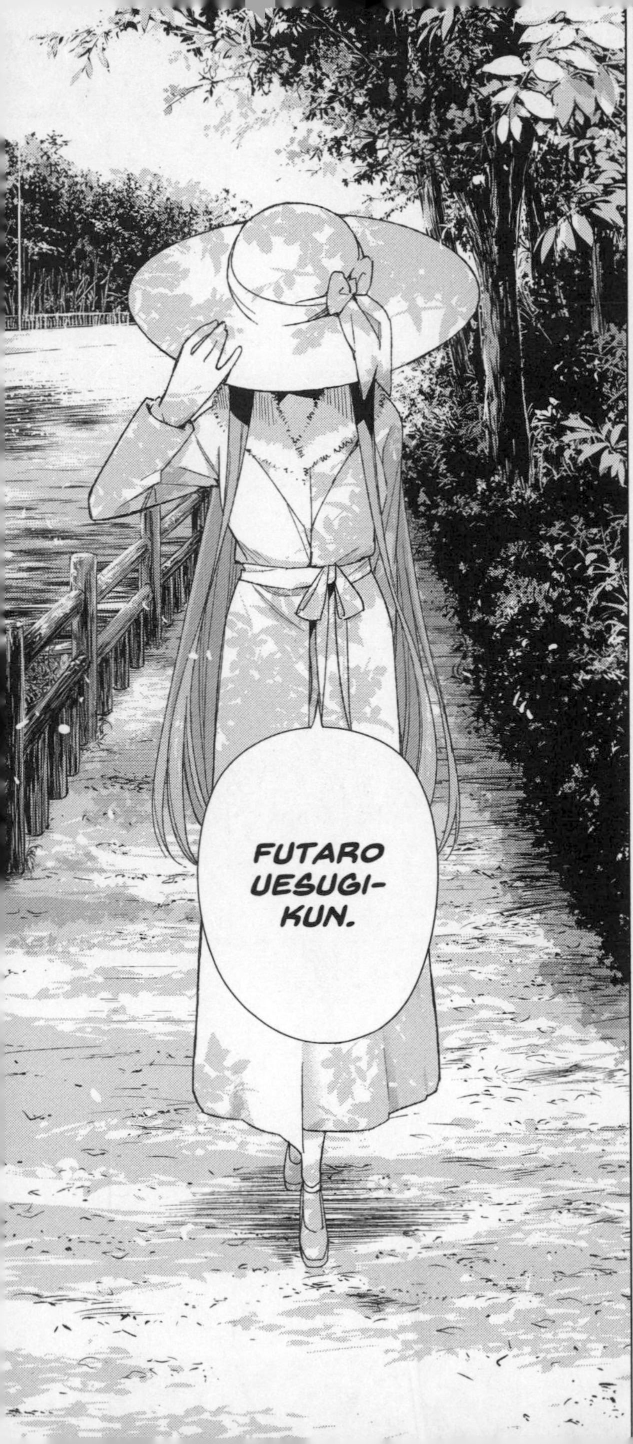
FUTARO UESUGI-KUN.

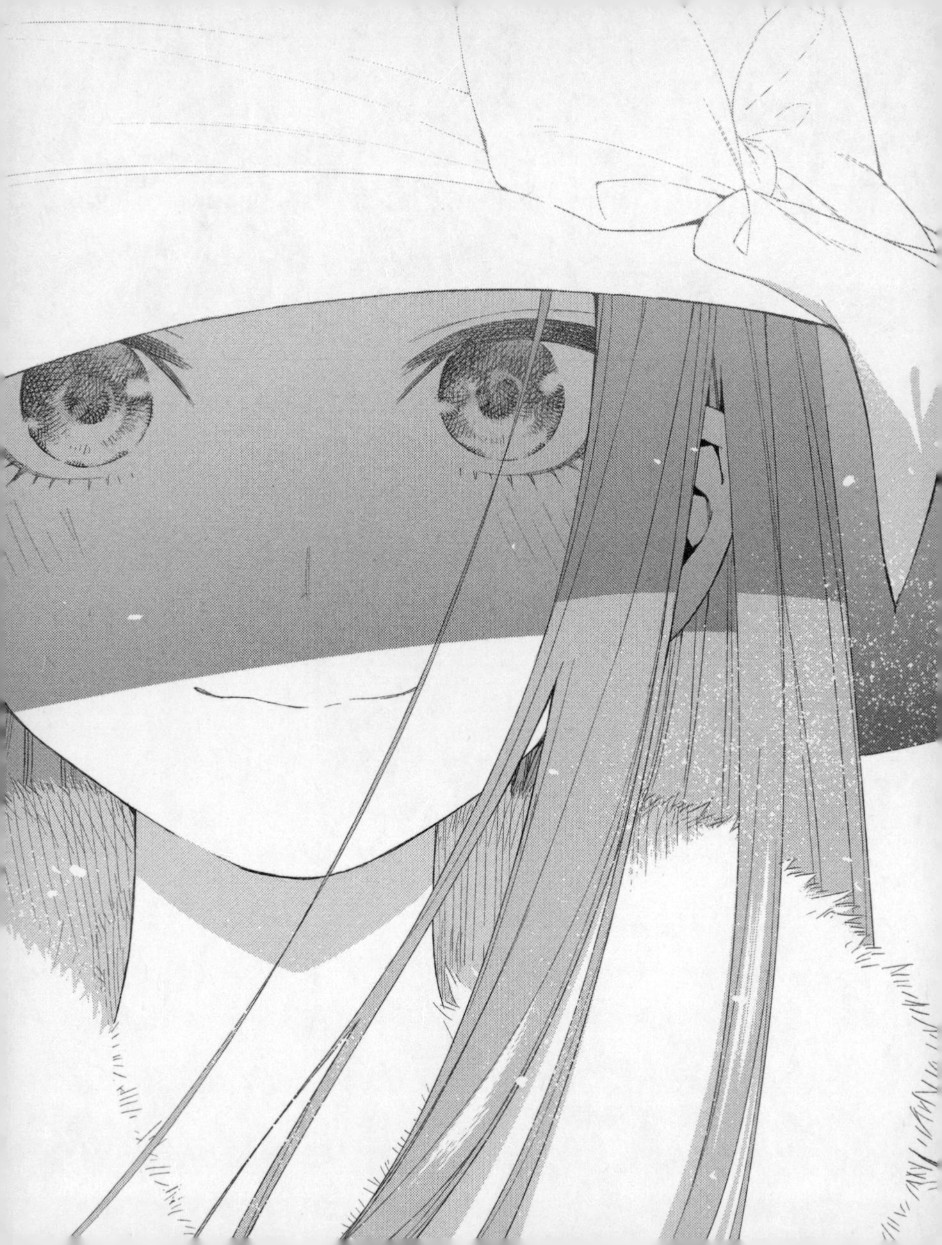

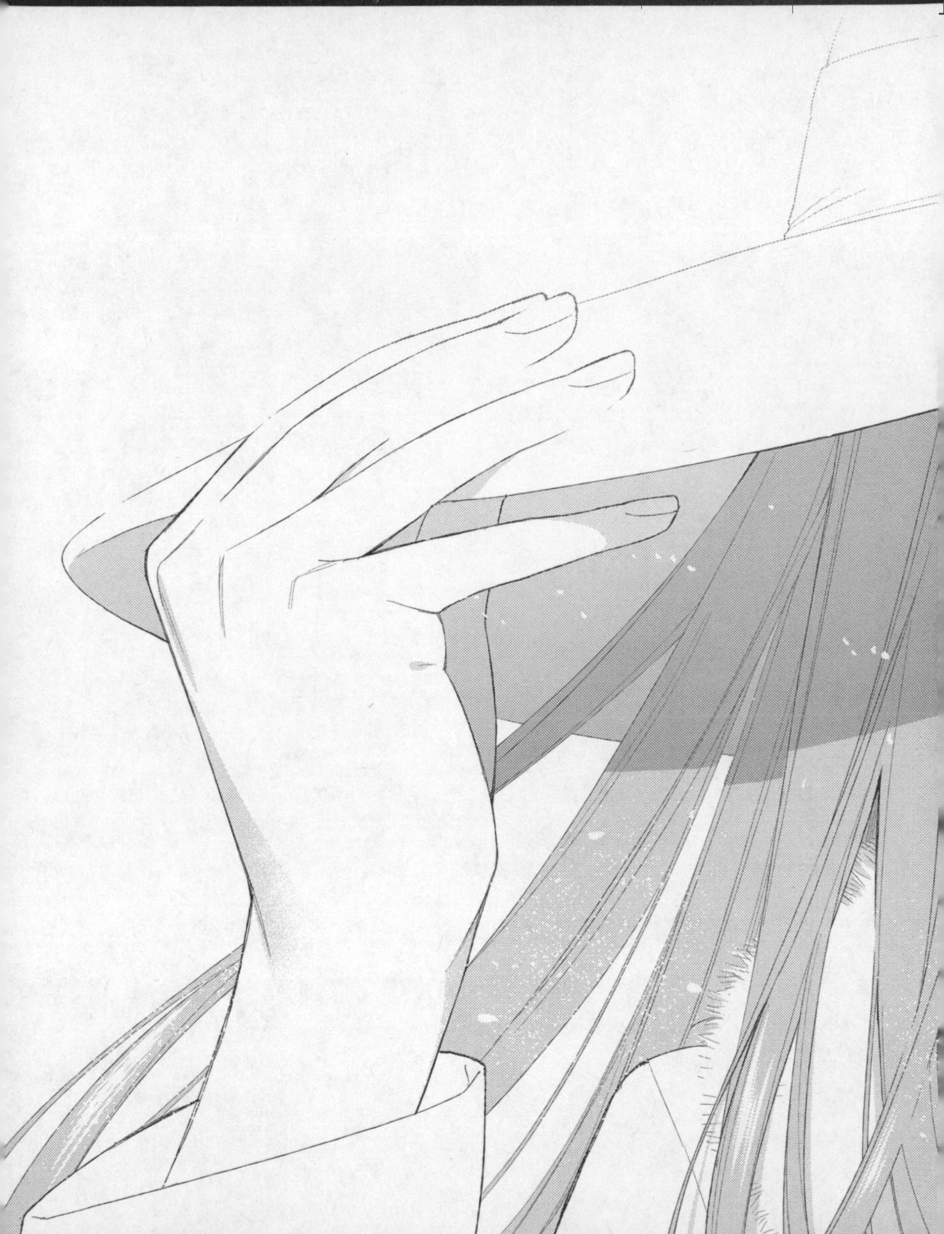

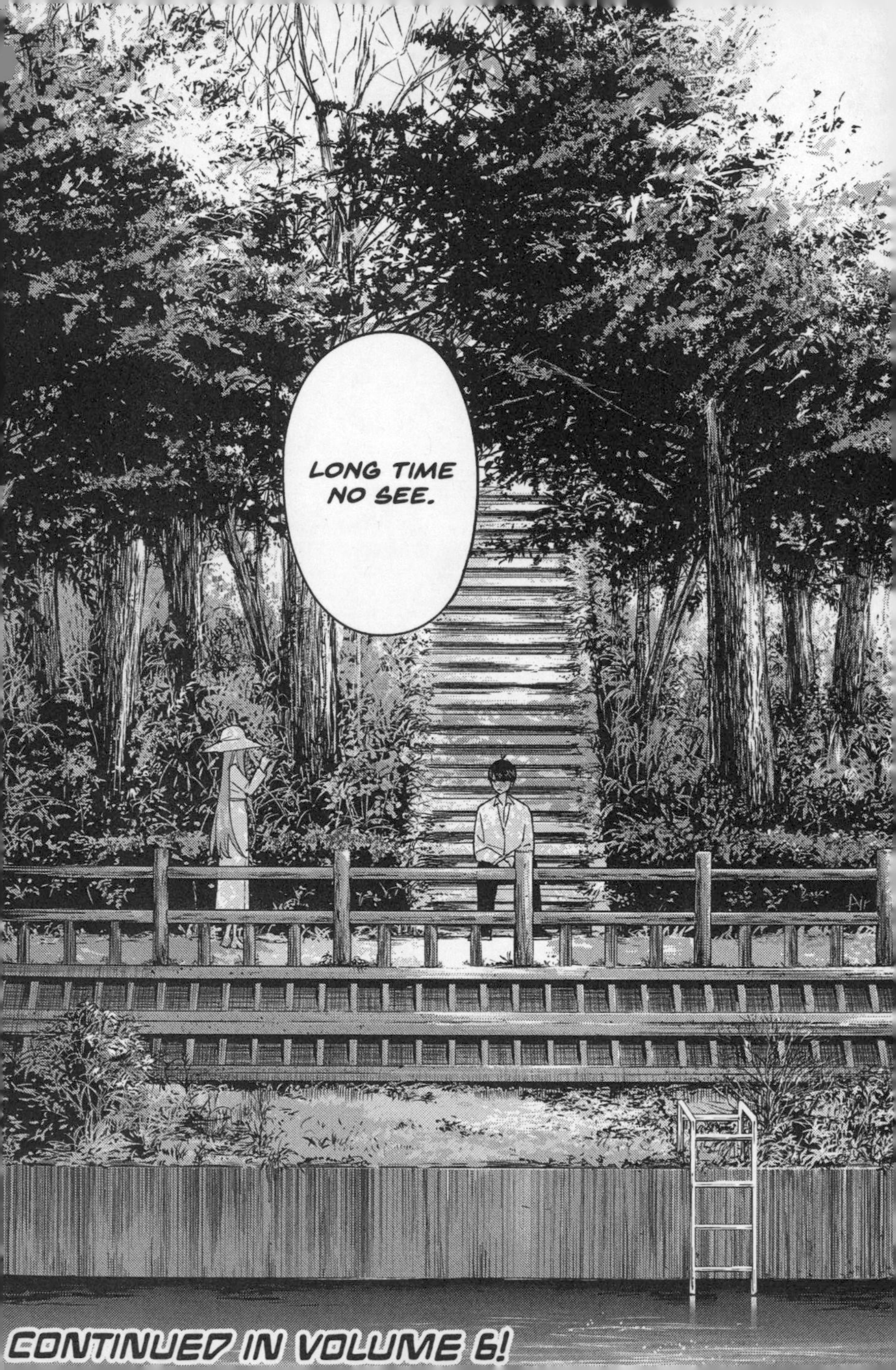
LONG TIME NO SEE.
CONTINUED IN VOLUME 6!

A Kodansha Comics Trade Paperback Original.

*The Quintessential Quintuplets* volume 5 copyright © 2018 Negi Haruba
English translation copyright © 2019 Negi Haruba

All rights reserved.

Published in the United States by Kodansha Comics,
an imprint of Kodansha USA Publishing, LLC, New York.

Publication rights for this English edition arranged through Kodansha Ltd., Tokyo.

First published in Japan in 2018 by Kodansha Ltd., Tokyo,
as *Gotoubun no Hanayome* volume 5.

Cover Design: Saya Takai (RedRooster)

ISBN 978-1-63236-854-6

Printed in the United States of America.

www.kodansha.us

9 8 7

Translation: Steven LeCroy
Lettering: Jan Lan Ivan Concepcion
Additional Layout: Belynda Ungurath
Editing: David Yoo, Thalia Sutton
Editorial Assistance: YKS Services LLC/SKY Japan, INC.
Kodansha Comics Edition Cover Design: Phil Balsman

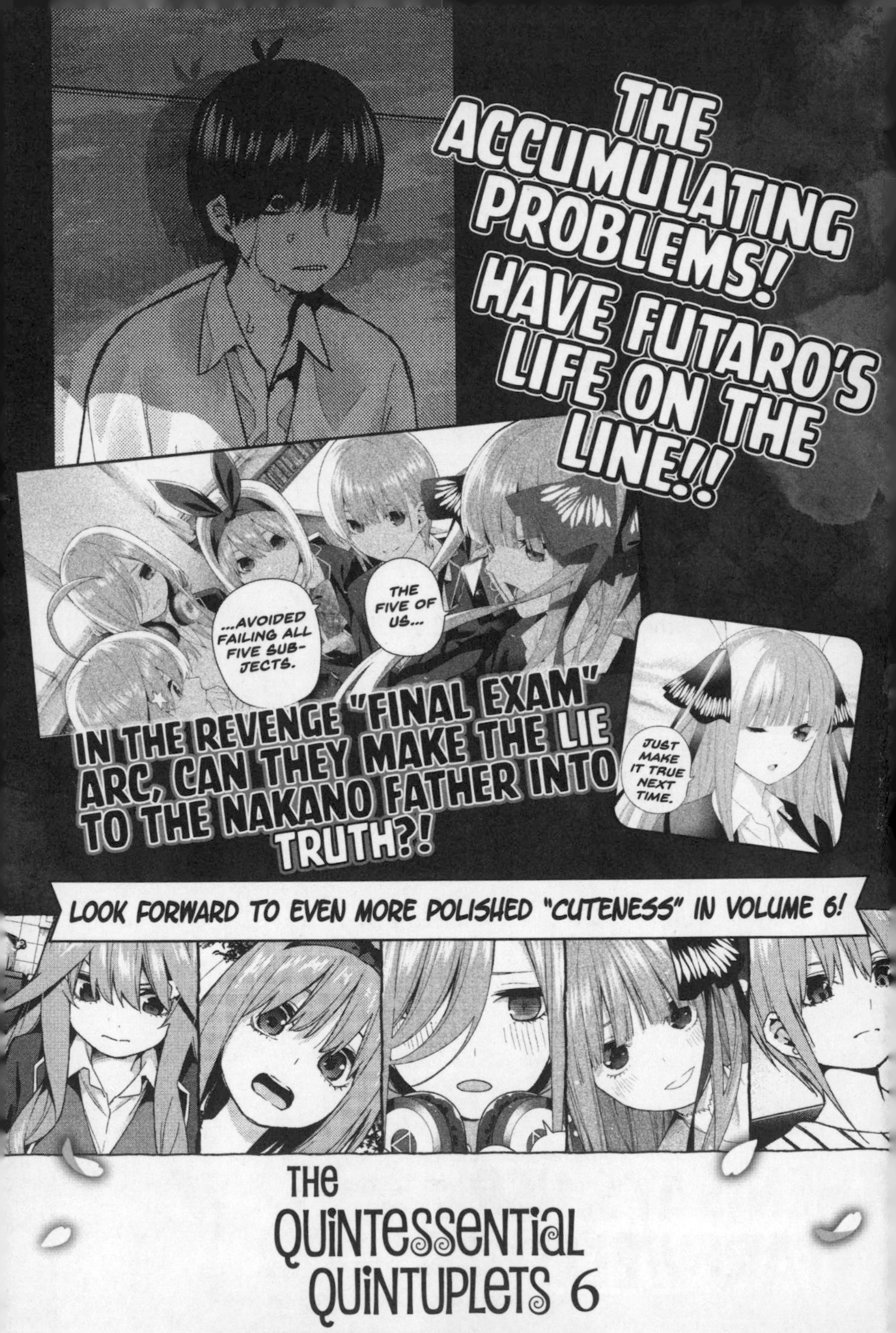
THE ACCUMULATING PROBLEMS! HAVE FUTARO'S LIFE ON THE LINE!!
THE FIVE OF US...
...AVOIDED FAILING ALL FIVE SUB-JECTS.
JUST MAKE IT TRUE NEXT TIME.
IN THE REVENGE "FINAL EXAM" ARC, CAN THEY MAKE THE LIE TO THE NAKANO FATHER INTO TRUTH?!
LOOK FORWARD TO EVEN MORE POLISHED "CUTENESS" IN VOLUME 6!

# THE QUINTESSENTIAL QUINTUPLETS 6

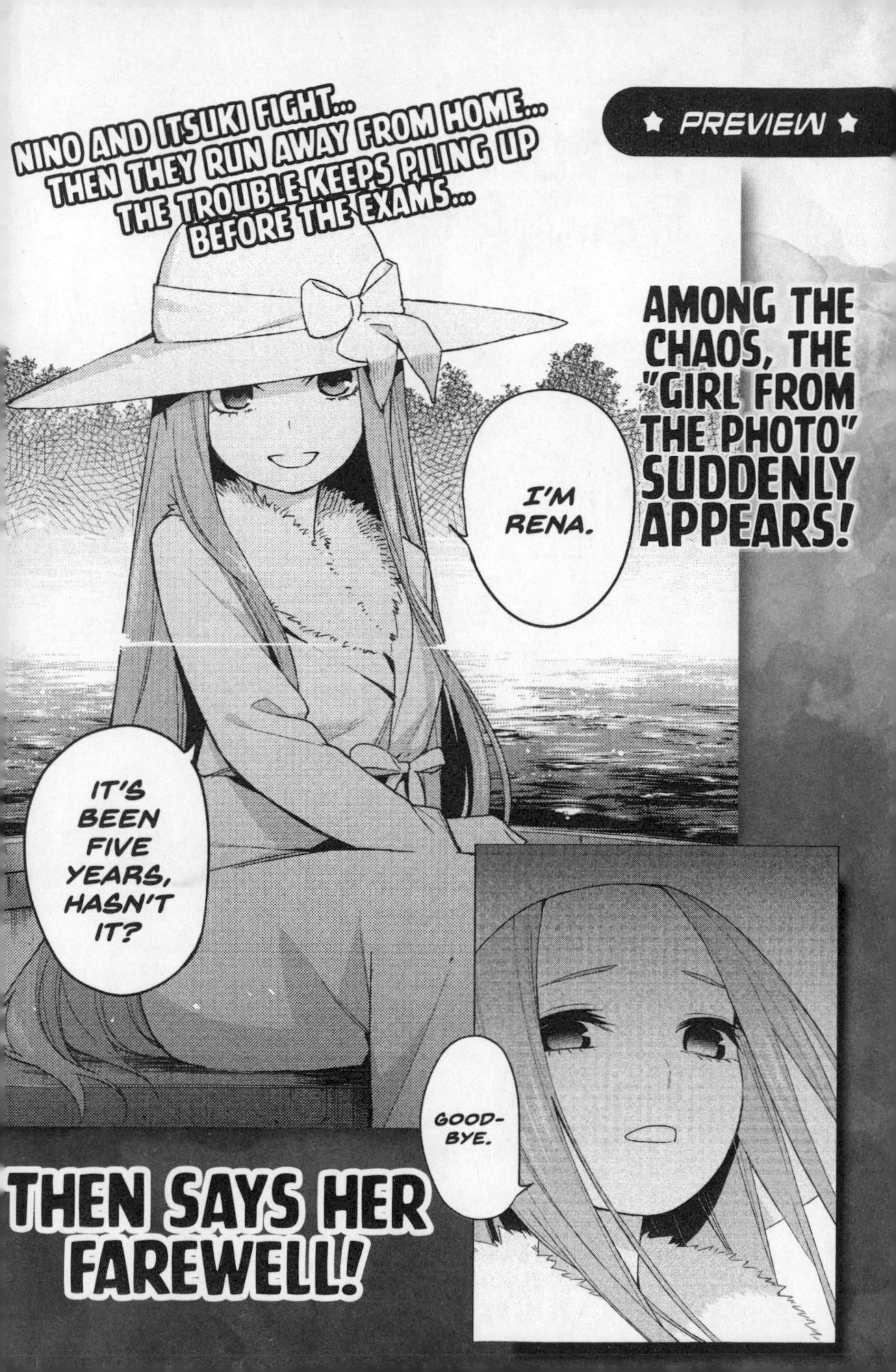
PREVIEW
NINO AND ITSUKI FIGHT... THEN THEY RUN AWAY FROM HOME... THE TROUBLE KEEPS PILING UP BEFORE THE EXAMS...
AMONG THE CHAOS, THE "GIRL FROM THE PHOTO" SUDDENLY APPEARS!
I'M RENA.
IT'S BEEN FIVE YEARS, HASN'T IT?
GOOD-BYE.
THEN SAYS HER FAREWELL!

# THE QUINTUPLETS CAN'T SHARE A GAME EVENLY

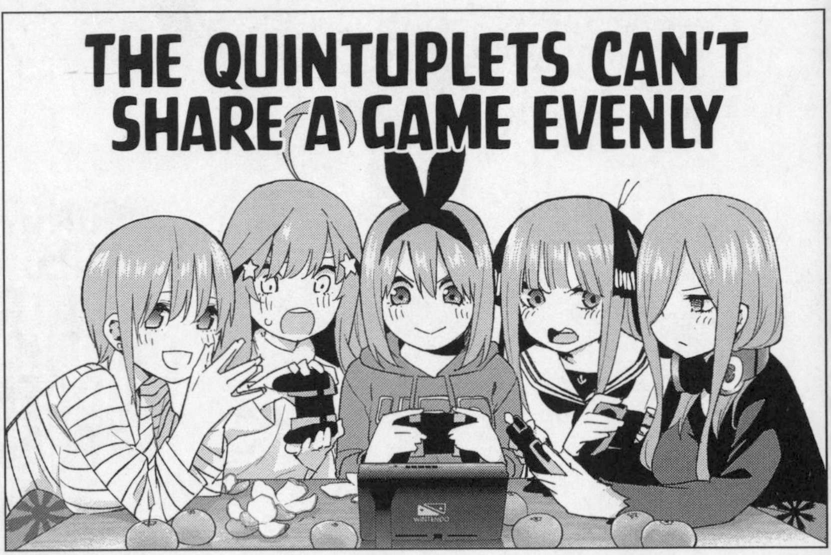

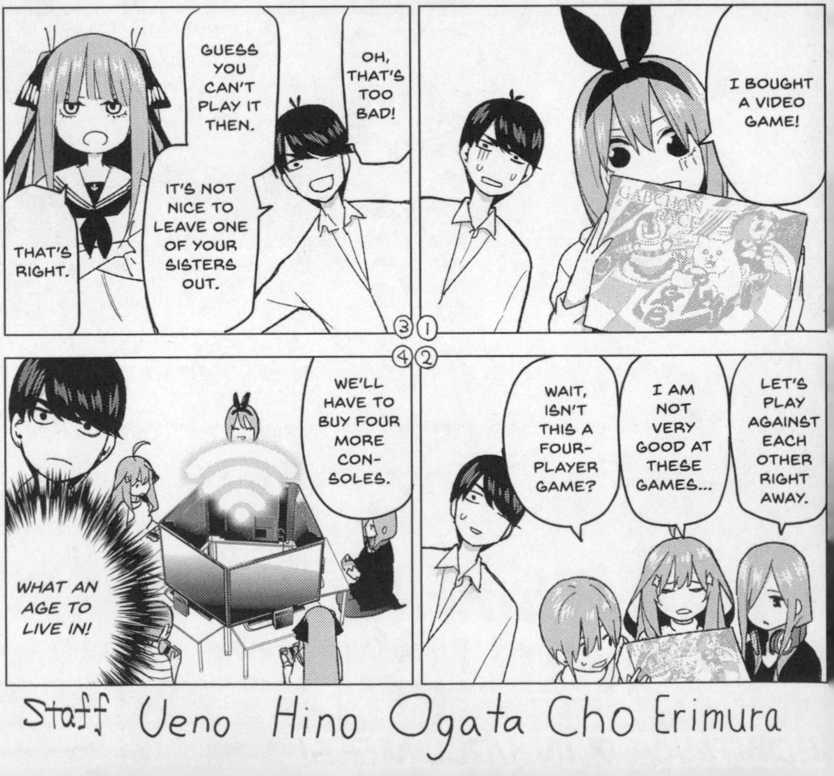
I BOUGHT A VIDEO GAME!
LET'S PLAY AGAINST EACH OTHER RIGHT AWAY.
I AM NOT VERY GOOD AT THESE GAMES...
WAIT, ISN'T THIS A FOUR-PLAYER GAME?
OH, THAT'S TOO BAD!
GUESS YOU CAN'T PLAY IT THEN.
IT'S NOT NICE TO LEAVE ONE OF YOUR SISTERS OUT.
THAT'S RIGHT.
WE'LL HAVE TO BUY FOUR MORE CON-SOLES.
WHAT AN AGE TO LIVE IN!

Staff Ueno Hino Ogata Cho Erimura